The Art and Design of
Contemporary Wine Labels

SANTA
MONICA
PRESS

Praise for . . .
The Art and Design of Contemporary Wine Labels

"Cynics would have you believe that every artistic, less-than-orthodox wine label is nothing more than a cheap marketing ploy, a trickery of sorts, attempting to distract the unwitting wine lover from what's truly important—the quality (or assumed lack thereof) of the wine itself. I have always thought about it rather differently. If the vigneron has gone about his task with great care and dedication and thus created something he is proud of, then he should give the wine the respect it deserves and present it with equal love and attention. Every creative chef carefully considers the plates on which he displays each dish. For every great painting, there is a perfect frame. Every jewel comes in a gorgeous jewel box. And so it should be with wine. The label and the bottle, the two of them combined, should invoke thought and give the wine lover a first sense of the woman or man who created this ethereal liquid. 'Art on the outside, craft on the inside' is what I used to say, but maybe it is the other way around. Tanya Scholes has put together the most comprehensive book on the subject of wine label art that I have ever seen. This beautiful new book illustrates what I am trying to say more eloquently. It will simultaneously stimulate your mind and taste buds."
—MANFRED KRANKL
Proprietor and Winemaker, Sine Qua Non

"I'm delighted with Tanya Scholes's fresh and thoughtful approach to the oft-overlooked art of wine labeling. Tanya brings the strength and value a label can add to a bottle of wine to life, and the label's ability to convey the history, future, character, and philosophy deep behind the paper. Her storyteller approach combines technical precision with colorful trivia, making this an absorbing and informative read for the designer, winemaker, or wine enthusiast. The reader will understand why creative efforts on labeling are never wasted. A good label engages a consumer before the wine is tasted; a great one seems at home on its chosen bottle and lingers in the mind long after the bottle is empty."   —MARTIN MALIVOIRE
Proprietor, Malivoire Wine Company

"The number of wineries and wine brands has utterly exploded in recent years, creating enormous pressure on wineries to essay to differentiate their products. As challenging as it has been for the wineries to weather this storm, it has been a boon year for label designers and aficionados of the wine label. The wine label provides the opportunity for the wine producer to provide a glimpse into his or her sensibility, and if well executed, can speak eloquently to the contents found within. Tanya Scholes has gathered together the most visually compelling labels and provided a great back-story to the semiotic treasure trove that is the universe of wine labels."   —RANDALL GRAHM
Founder and Winemaker, Bonny Doon Vineyard
and author of *Been Doon So Long: A Randall Grahm Vinthology*

"With verve, care, and humor, Tanya Scholes adeptly teases out the magic ghost that exists within a bottle of wine, and helps us understand how that spirit is manifested on the front in all its glory."
—KATHRYN BOREL JR.
author of *Corked*

"There is an artistry to winemaking that extends to its packaging. What I make, people consume; it's an act of intimacy, like music. How much closer can you get to someone? Contemporary winemakers must be able to convey that artistry and intimacy amid a massive sea of competition. Gone are the days of traditional, safe, labels. The wine labels showcased in Tanya Scholes's book are attractive to the current generation's way of communicating and are the essence of a wine language that people can relate to and actually understand."
—CHARLES SMITH
Owner and Winemaker, K Vintners and Charles Smith Wines

"To be a wine consumer today is very flattering indeed. It seems everywhere you turn, myriad wine labels beckon you to come hither like seagoing sirens. Confronted by literally thousands of choices, a simple grocery errand becomes an Odyssean quest. When, at their most beguiling, wines signal their distinctive personality through the label, with which one will you spend an intoxicating evening? The wine merchant's current inamorata, the impetuous South American upstart, the whimsical rapscallion, the pedigreed patrician . . . you can have them all, but which shall you take home tonight? Still the question remains: Is it art or is it science? Let author Tanya Scholes shed a little light on the arcane alchemy of wine label design in her book *The Art and Design of Contemporary Wine Labels*."
—JEFFREY CALDEWEY
Founder, Icon Design Group and co-author of *Icon: Art of the Wine Label*

"This is, without question, the most complete book on the 'story' of wine labels I have read. *The Art and Design of Contemporary Wine Labels* has qualities similar to those I find in good paintings. I believe a good painting must get your attention and pull you into it; it should seduce you. And then, when you take the time to 'read' it, you should be rewarded with new things. You should discover new pieces of information each time you approach the work. It requires that you keep coming back to the painting to continue the conversation. You are first captivated by the image from afar, and then held close by its substance. Tanya Scholes's book does this beautifully."
—BOB NUGENT
Curator of Collections, Benziger Family Winery and Imagery Estate Winery

"You can't judge a wine by its label, but you can deepen your sensory pleasure by looking more closely at it. This is just the book to help you do that. Beautifully illustrated with surprising insights, *The Art and Design of Contemporary Wine Labels* is its own work of art."
—NATALIE MACLEAN
author of *Red, White and Drunk All Over*
and publisher of the award-winning www.nataliemaclean.com

"The world of wine is an incredible melting pot of Mother Nature, people, history, geography, science, art, and design, and Tanya Scholes's *The Art and Design of Contemporary Wine Labels* captures it in all its glory. An absolute must."
—MATT SKINNER
Sommelier Consultant and author of *Heard It through the Grapevine*

To my Mom, who taught me anything is possible if you believe.
Believing is the means to my end.

Published by: Santa Monica Press LLC
P.O. Box 850
Solana Beach, CA 92075
1-800-784-9553
www.santamonicapress.com
books@santamonicapress.com

Printed in China

Santa Monica Press books are available at special quantity discounts when purchased in bulk by corporations, organizations, or groups.
Please call our Special Sales department at 1-800-784-9553.

ISBN-13 978-1-59580-046-6

Library of Congress Cataloging-in-Publication Data

Scholes, Tanya.
 The art and design of contemporary wine labels / by Tanya Scholes ; foreword by Michael Mondavi.
   p. cm.
 ISBN 978-1-59580-046-6
 1. Wine labels—History. 2. Wine labels—Pictorial works. 3. Commercial art. I. Title.
 TP548.5.L32S36 2010
 741.6–dc22
                        2010002729

Cover and interior design and production by Future Studio
Cover photography: © istockphoto.com/FMNG, jml5571, spiderstock

The Art and Design of
Contemporary Wine Labels

Tanya Scholes
Foreword by Michael Mondavi

Contents

10   Foreword by Michael Mondavi

13   A Brief History of Wine Labels

18   Wine Labels Today

The Labels

286 Acknowledgments

Foreword

by Michael Mondavi

"People buy with their eyes." The first time I heard this was in 1966. I was a young man just out of college and had only recently started the Robert Mondavi Winery with my father, Robert. In need of a label for our first Cabernet Sauvignon, we found ourselves at International Paper Company in San Francisco, where one of our business partners had connections. At International Paper, they had a dedicated wine room with a wall of label samples. All the big wine labels of the day were displayed: Paul Masson, Inglenook, Beaulieu, and Martin Ray, as well as many French and Italian labels. Although I grew up around wine, it was the first time I really looked at the labels objectively. We spent the next two hours with our partners talking about nothing but paper stock—should it be satin finish, gloss, or matte? The choices were overwhelming.

Then, there was a debate about whether or not my father's name should be on the label. Robert felt that people wanted a wine with a person standing behind it, not a company. He also wanted the logo, variety, and producer to be equally prominent—back then, the varietal was actually the brand on our label.

My father and I would buy great Bordeaux wines and put them next to California bottles. The Bordeaux bottles looked elegant and the California wines looked cheap. We wanted our wine to fit in among the great wines of the world. Robert felt the wine had to look proper on a credenza. To this day, I use a similar yardstick when evaluating labels for our wines: I will put the bottle on a shelf with its competitive set, take it home, and put it in the dining room. Does it grow or become tired?

The design we finally settled on, with my father's name and the iconic image of the winery's arch and tower, has since become a classic that is recognized globally.

Some years later, we were faced with another label challenge.

In 1980, we announced our partnership with Baron Philippe de Rothschild to create a single Bordeaux-style red wine. Again, we were faced with the arduous task of coming up with a name and label worthy of the wine's pedigree. The baron suggested the name, "Gemini," which is represented in the zodiac by the twins and would symbolize the past and present, east and west. Everyone liked the name until someone in the company found out that "Gemini" was also the name of a pornographic magazine in San Francisco. It was back to the proverbial drawing board.

The baron then came back to us with "Opus One," to signify the first masterwork of a great composer. With the name decided upon, the next step was the label design. A friend of mine created a label that had the outline of two profiles, my father and the baron, facing toward each other, forming the outline of wine goblet. I liked the design at first, but eventually we decided it was too cheesy. It just didn't convey the gravitas that Opus One called for.

We interviewed twenty design firms. Our top choice, Landor Associates, came up with more than eighty concepts and designs, yet we ended up rejecting all of them. None had the magic and energy, or iconic feeling that we were looking for. The quest continued.

We found a designer, Susan Pate, who tweaked the original profile concept. She combined my father's actual profile with that of the baron's and added their signatures, all in a royal blue hue. We knew we finally had our label; the final design was elegant, yet powerful, just like the wine itself.

Almost every wine has a story that is reflected in its label. *The Art and Design of Contemporary Wine Labels* is an enchanting exploration of those stories, some of which are based in history or, simply, whimsy. Through extensive interviews with winemakers and designers, Tanya Scholes has captured and recorded many inspiring, fascinating, and often educational tales behind well-known and obscure wine labels alike.

Since I started in this business, the wine landscape has changed greatly. Today, there are 127,000 approved labels in the U.S. alone. Creating a label that stands out on the shelf, and is also elegant, has become critical to the success of any wine. Of course, what's inside the bottle is what counts ultimately, but getting a consumer to pick your wine over another has become a delicate art if they don't know anything about either wine.

Not every label at Robert Mondavi was a runaway success. In the 1990s, we launched Robert Mondavi Coastal, a line of wines under fifteen dollars from California's Central Coast region. We developed a label that we thought was attractive and elegant with the emphasis on the name Robert Mondavi and the word "coastal" in a calligraphic font. Above the name was an artistic rendering of a flat coastal landscape. It wasn't until the wine was in the market that we realized it completely disappeared on the shelf among the other wines in its category. Although it passed our own shelf test, it failed aesthetically on the retail shelf.

The Coastal label was simply too generic. Also, we had used "Robert Mondavi" on the label, but not the image of the winery, which had become a visual icon among wine consumers by then. The wine was more successful with a redesigned label that featured an up-close rendering of the winery's famous Cliff May tower set among clouds, giving it a stronger visual impact and a familiar feeling for consumers.

Today, the average wine consumer also has changed. According to recent consumer research, "millennials" are the first generation in the U.S. to choose wine over beer and cocktails. Our industry, which has been long accustomed to catering to baby boomers, needs to appeal to much younger consum-

ers now. This younger generation is also more open to trying imported wines, which means the competitive field has widened even further.

At Folio Fine Wine Partners—the company I own today with my wife, Isabel, and our children, Rob and Dina—we represent more than one hundred wines. In addition to the wines that our family makes, Folio imports wines from family-owned wineries in Italy, Spain, Austria, Germany, New Zealand, and Argentina.

We are continually evaluating wines for our portfolio. After tasting the wine, we assess the package: Does the label pop? How can it be improved? Everyone on the team weighs in with an opinion—after all, we're also consumers. However, even getting ten people to agree on a label is tough. We look at target consumer, price point, where it will be sold, etcetera. Even with focus groups, finding a wine label that will resonate with a wide segment of consumers is hardly an exact science. At the end of the day, a wine label is a piece of art. Like any other art form, it will touch people in different ways.

It is interesting to see how other countries have ushered in wine label trends. For example, the Australians brought "critter labels" and bright colors to prominence, particularly for more inexpensive wines. Spanish wines often feature contemporary art on the label with modern graphics, or even black and white photography.

In 2008, I released my first signature wine, M by Michael Mondavi, a Cabernet Sauvignon made from grapes grown at our family's Animo Vineyard, which is located in Napa's Atlas Peak region. This small production wine has been a labor of love that I have shared with my family. My son Rob works closely with me in the vineyard and winery, and my daughter Dina, who has a background in art, played an integral role in the package design.

Dina wanted the label for M by Michael

Mondavi to express "terroir"—the wine's unique expression of the soil. She also wanted to create a label that was different, so we looked to designers outside of the wine industry.

We ended up collaborating with a designer named Karen Joyce, who has twenty years of branding experience in the luxury fashion industry working with brands such as Gucci, Burberry, and Ermenegildo Zegna.

We were presented with several designs, each captivating in their own way. I applied my shelf test and lived with the bottles side by side for a period of time. The one that stood out was a striking white-on-black silk-screened label, with a graphic representation of vine roots and soil underground.

As a winemaker, the final package should strike a chord with you personally. I am proud to have my name on M by Michael Mondavi. I believe the package we ended up with reflects the wine inside the bottle—deep, elegant, and rich.

Like many wine enthusiasts, I have collected labels over the years. I have a large scrapbook with vintage fruit crate labels and wine labels. It's amazing how wine labels have changed over the years. Wine labels of the past were more masculine, with nautical themes, for example. Although men still collect more wine than women, women have surpassed men in numbers when it comes to purchasing and consuming wine. Wineries are responding to this trend by creating labels that appeal more to women.

It will be interesting to see what the wine shelf will look like in another forty years, especially with the increasing proliferation of alternative packaging. I can remember not so long ago when consumers were reluctant to embrace screw caps, and now they are practically commonplace, even among higher-end wines.

With the growing acceptance of quality box wine, Tetra Pak wine, and even sparkling wine in aluminum cans, perhaps the hobby of collecting labels or creating corkboards will someday become a thing of the past.

Until then, there are plenty of wine labels out there to explore, admire and maybe even collect and *The Art and Design of Contemporary Wine* is the perfect source to begin that exploration.

I went into this business because I was intrigued by the wine-growing and winemaking side of it. After that day at International Paper Company in 1966, I became equally intrigued by the sales and marketing side of the wine business. Wine is an artistic process from the vine to the bottle, and it requires patience and passion.

After more than forty years in this business, I have learned that people do buy with their eyes. However, I have also learned that it is their palate that ultimately decides if a wine will truly stand the test of time.

Saluté!
MICHAEL MONDAVI

A Brief History of Wine Labels

The wine label is one of the smallest forms of visual communication, with its message fitting onto a 3.5″ × 3.5″ canvas, give or take. Despite its increased prevalence as a means of commercial communication, most obviously over the past half century, its historical progression has not been overly studied or documented. Since its advent, millions have been designed, printed, and displayed on wine bottles the world over, yet there still seems a scarcity of accounts documenting their birth, expedition across time and geography, as well as their aesthetic and functional evolution. In fact, until the very recent rise of wine labels being considered categorically as a piece of visual culture and a concerted effort to "up the ante" of their design, wine labels had rarely even been contemplated, much less celebrated, as a functional form of communicative art.

Perhaps this gap in the focus and commentary on wine labels as an authentic, creative, and communicative commercial art form is simply because there has been little evidence on which to base the commentary. Even though wine, the *raison d'être* of the label, does not have a definitively marked advent, there has been somewhat more of an ability to recount its chronicles based on the analysis of found ancient artifacts. These unearthed relics from ancient Mesopotamia have led to a logical presumption that man likely did not actually invent wine, but instead rested on the laurels of the natural self-fermentation of grapes found purely by accident. Consequently, these actual found artifacts have also enabled a better unfolding of wine's odyssey and staying power across time, over continents, and despite war, adverse politics, and debilitating disease.

On the other hand, only a brief snapshot of the short lifespan of the wine label and its progression through time is available, simply because very little wine label artifacts have actually been

discovered. From what has been collected, what can be confirmed is that these little pieces of paper that carry huge responsibilities (rivaled only by the postage stamp in size) have undergone some significant transformations. Once solely a functional system of identification, wine labels have increasingly become a purposeful communication vehicle, holding the obligation of being the "voice for the wine," while also moonlighting as art reflective of time and culture. Taking a step back in time, however, we can glimpse the wine label's speculative history, which provides a springboard for the fonder appreciation of its more evolved status today.

It is thought that the earliest wine labels yet to be discovered were those found in the tomb of King Tutankhamun. The Egyptians believed that to increase the likelihood of a smooth segue to a peaceful afterlife, wine should be entombed as an accompaniment to the deceased body. One can easily imagine that, being of the royal class, King Tut would have definitely had his fair share of the "nectar of the gods." In fact, of the three dozen dried-up wine containers decorated with simple hieroglyphics that were entombed with the young king (discovered in 1922 by the English Egyptologist Howard Carter), twenty-three of them had been labeled with enough information to actually meet the legalities of wine labeling criteria of some countries today. The labels are said to have included the name of the winemaker, the place where the grapes were sourced, and the year the wine was made. Given the gap between ancient times and our modern times, the similarities between the Egyptians' wine indication system and the labeling traditions practiced today are continued evidence of the Egyptians' progressive society.

Fast-forward a few thousand years from ancient Egyptian times, and there is documentation of wine's transformation in terms of production processes and consumption practices. While frequently considered a healthier option to contaminated drinking water, there also began a shift towards wine consumption being viewed as a "fruitful" commercial commodity. With colonization increasing the transfer of information to new cultures and down the chain of classes, wine was no longer an opulent pleasure limited only to the rich. But even with this increased cultural and secular progression, wine steadfastly connected to prevailing religious symbolism and ceremony. As a consequence, monasteries ended up perpetuating the wine industry in their own manner, as monks found solace in the growing and grooming of grapevines and the production of wine, while taking advantage of free sacrificial wine for "religious" ceremonial purposes.

Appropriately, considering monks' historical involvement with their production of wine, the oldest label found to date is said to have been scribed by Dom Pierre Perignon. Dom Perignon was a French Benedictine monk who was also the cellar master at Abbey of Hautvillers from 1668 until his death in 1715. Moët et Chandon, after purchasing the Hautvillers walls and vineyard in 1794, immortalized this skilled viticulturist and winemaker on their famed Champagne label in 1921. Dom Perignon is said to have improvised a makeshift classificatory labeling system simply by tying marked parchment paper "labels" to the necks of bottles, thus allowing the bottles being aged to be distinguished by vintage, varietal blend, origin, and quality. As such, one of the first-known labeling systems was born—intentionally or not.

Circa 1740, most wine was sold in bulk, whereby empty bottles were easily replenished at the local village store, leaving little requirement for the labeling of individual wine bottles. But, with many wines being stored in stackable jugs, there became a need for a cataloguing system, which was found in glazed ceramic pottery labels. Eventually, the benefits of leaving portions of the pottery labels unglazed to allow for the addition of, or change to, existing information was realized, thus allowing re-use with subsequent bulk wine bottlings.

During this period, hotels and restaurants also purchased barrels and bottled their own wine, serving wine from carafes adorned with what were known as "bottle tickets." Additionally, affluent families served their wines from glass decanters that also identified the contents in the same manner. These bottle tickets were most often crafted out of high quality silver or pewter and carried ornately engraved inscriptions of the contents. Too often, though, the names of the wines were misengraved with errors to the names of wines, such as "Clart" or "Clarrette," instead of Claret. Out of these costly errors, there seems to have then been a natural evolution, around the early nineteenth century, from metal identification plates to less expensive handwritten parchment labels—a step closer to the labels of today and back to those improvised years previously by Dom Perignon.

The first method for printing wine labels involved engraving the label's basic elements into a stone and replicating it onto parchment using an inked roller, stamping from the stone to a clean parchment surface. This changed significantly with the invention of lithography in what was then known as Bohemia, by the playwright Alois Senefelder. This process enabled mass flat surface print production using a chemical process that confined ink solely to the image area. The first paper labels to be printed lithographically are said to have been produced in Germany in the early nineteenth century using basic Gothic, Didot, or Bodoni typographic faces. These labels, though quite modern at the time, still offered negligible information on the wine, let alone offering any glimpse at its character or the its individuality as compared to today's standards.

The French Champagne houses of the early 1820s seem to have pioneered the more creative and imaginative aspect of wine labels that are closer in line with wine labels of today. Their labels, in true stylish and French *joie de vivre* form, extended beyond the standard black ink and simpler type styles customary of the times. Born out of a desire to promote festive events and celebrate popular local personalities, the Champagne house labels became the embodiment of pageantry, using gold, silver, bronze, and blue inks—definitely a novelty in those days. Eventually, competing to out-do each other's aesthetic efforts, the Champagne houses' labels evolved into flamboyant and artistic testaments of the times, displaying more than just the simple afterthoughts of what was housed inside the bottles. *Merci.*

Contemporaneous winemakers in Italy also elaborated the design of their labels to showcase coats of arms, captivating landscapes, family portraits, as well as often touting showy industry medals won by individual family estates.

Some might consider these imaginative nations the forefathers of modern day wine label design. Their precedents have paved the way for successive vintners and label designers alike. By demonstrating the communicative power of such miniature pieces of paper, they provided the first instance of expanding the purpose of the wine label to much more than what they were originally intended for.

With the continuous expansion of new wine varieties and the constant emergence of untapped markets, there arose a demand for the production and bottling of readily available wines for import, export, and distribution to the mass consumer. When the glass bottle industry arrived on the scene and with it, the invention of a glue strong enough to adhere paper to their surfaces, it was then possible to label the contents of every bottle with a paper label.

Published wine reviews became the norm and offered the historical, technical, financial, and aesthetic aspects of new wines. Thirsty consumers were thus armed with suitable information to influence their choices amongst an abundance of wines. Rivalry was healthy between the European winemakers and their New World protégés, and international wine competitions set the stage for the battle to win the highest industry accolades and, in turn, for the winners to boldly boast them in printed form on the bottle. There did exist a significant gap between the classification and labeling of Old versus New World wines, which became extremely prevalent in the twentieth century and still, to some extent, exists today.

France had long been pioneering the research and testing of grape cultivation and site selection before most other regions. In fact, an informal hierarchical system organically developed, which drove demand and pricing of wine based on the regions that were viewed and are still viewed as producing consistently the best quality of wine. Although not formally instituted until 1935, with the creation of the Institut National des Appellations d'Origine, the French dressed their bottles with the names and images of these well-known and trusted regions long before. This system, although not necessarily the first to be formally instituted internationally, became the benchmark for the rest of the world to follow, and many other countries have since created their own delineation classifications.

The use of classic imagery of the land and French châteaux became a commonly imitated theme for wine label design. At the beginning of the 1900s, New World winemakers had no point of reference or governing authority to designate or classify regions or their own châteaux to guide in the naming process. As a result, more often than not, the natural instinct was for winemakers to look to the descriptive color of the wines or the famous and trustworthy wine places in Europe that were often their ancestral homelands for naming and wine label design inspiration. As a result, renegade wine labels based on a style such as Bordeaux (Claret), Bourgogne (Burgundy), and Chianti (Chianti) cropped up, despite the wines not being produced in any vicinity of these regions. These broadly (and falsely) named wines paid little attention to the strict followings of the varietal requirements and production methods or techniques used by their famed and regulated Old World namesakes. Despite their misnomers, using these misappropriated wine names was the strongest labeling trend in the early twentieth century North American marketplace with little and slow change until the mid-1950s.

By 1919, the wine industry came to a drastic halt in the Americas as a result of Prohibition (1920–1933). It wasn't until post-World War II that soldiers, having grown accustomed to fine wines while in service throughout Europe, led the way to the resurrection of wine consumption and an all-new demand for it. Knowing that they could no longer pit their local wines (that simply emulated broad European wine regions with their names) against predominantly French imports that were heavily supported by the acclaim of their appellation credentials, nor could they rely on any officially approved geographic regions of their own, the American winemakers looked for something new and non-traditional to set them apart. They began to work at establishing their own unique characteristics through either varietal or proprietary labeling.

Distinguishing wines based on grape variety was not a new phenomenon, but it had little practice in the Americas until the 1950s when Frank Schoonmaker, an esteemed American wine writer and eventual importer and merchant, recommended the idea to his client, Almaden Vineyards. Mr. Schoonmaker seemed to have been inspired by wines of the French Alsace region that were not as restricted by France's stringent classification regulations and eagerly recommended marketing Almaden's new product as the varietal Grenache Rosé. This was a very big step in enabling the consumer to relate personally to wine. By using the varietal name, it became easier for consumers to associate a taste profile with a specific type of grape versus remembering the name of a region (or with New World producers, more likely a "borrowed" region) that showcased a diversity of varying flavors of a single producer—let alone the variance between different producers within an entire appellation or region. Thus, Almaden was able to effectively differentiate its wines in the marketplace, which in turn resulted in historical success for the vineyard. Robert Mondavi was one of the earliest adopters and advocates of the varietal labeling that paved the way for his contemporaries to follow suit.

With other vineyards catching on, the 1970s had varietal labeling tipping the scales and moving towards being the conventional method of labeling wines in the United States. By the 1980s, affordable Chardonnay, White Zinfandel, and Cabernet Sauvignon edged their way up on the less-intuitively labeled wines principally because consumers found the more minimal number of varietals uncomplicated, more accessible, and easier to remember than perhaps the thousands of vineyards that existed in numberous different appellations. Eventually, the New World Burgundy and Chablis had all but become extinct and varietal labeling established itself as the leader in identifying wine types across Australia, New Zealand, South Africa, Chile, Argentina, and most of the other New World wine producers.

Considering the functional progression of wine labels from a once-primitive classificatory system to a tool protecting the integrity and denoting controlled quality, then to a New World differentiation device and a means of connecting with the masses and, eventually, as an enabler of individual creative equity, little had changed from a visual standpoint until late in the twentieth century. Most often, wineries aspirationally adopted classic styles of labels that visually depicted scenes of nature or estates associated with the grape growing regions as initiated by the sage Old World wineries. More often than not, most stayed the course and rarely placed their own personalities into the brands that represented what they, in fact, had crafted and was, in essence, an extension of themselves.

However, with a shift away from generic wine labeling, there also began a concurrent shift in the visual direction of wine labels predominantly being led by graphic designers in North America and Australia. Today's iconic design names such as Jeffrey Caldewey, Chuck House, Susan Pate, Ralph Colonna, and John Farrell in the United States and Barry Tucker, Ian Kidd, and Ken Cato in Australia, began a movement away from taking design cues from the Old World and, instead, sought inspiration from other categories outside the wine industry to build New World individuality. These renegades broke the mold to tell the story of their wine, not only from a classification standpoint, but from a branding and visual storytelling perspective, as well. Some of these early visual innovators included Robert Mondavi Winery, Frog's Leap, and Imagery Estate Winery in the United States, Peter Lehmann of the Barossa in Australia and, though not in the New World, France's Château Mouton Rothschild's artist labels, which were certainly a monumental departure from the norm in France. These trailblazers were all at the forefront of the wine industry and used a visual language to represent the story of the wine vintage found in the bottle and made the connection from the people that produced the wine to the people that consumed it.

Today, more and more wineries are pushing the boundaries of wine label design and opting to use their own unique creative quotient to brand their wines. From die-cutting labels, to the use of out-of-the-box printing and photographic techniques on distinct substrates, innovative design is certainly taking the helm. At the intersection of art and business, wine labels are able to tell stories visually through creative design and, in doing so, offer implied and memorable information about the wines, not only connecting with the customer by attempting to cut through the retail clutter, but also as a token of historical, cultural, or personal homage.

This significant change in landscape arrived at the end of the twentieth century after winemakers realized two key consumer insights: the fact that many consumers found wine labels confusing and difficult to understand, as well as the common feeling that traditionally styled labels were intimidating and unidentifiable with the average consumer. It seems that overnight, the next phase of wines to blaze unabashedly onto the aisles and to initiate a movement in the wine retail market substantially were the likes of Fat Bastard from France and Yellow Tail from Australia. Although there had been wine that "marched to the beat of its own drummer" artistically previously, nowhere had there been such an impactful and mass shift from the traditional châteaux or estate landscapes.

With the influx of every animal under the sun hoping to follow in the footsteps of those unpretentious overnight success stories, change was inevitable. Although the animal trend seems to have run its course, its influx has profoundly effected change in the broad and creative manner which wineries are telling their stories visually and how they are expanding their relationship with the consumer by expounding upon the details of who and what are behind what's in the bottle. In today's changing and ultra-competitive marketplace, there is much more to it than "if you make it, they will come!"

Wine Labels Today

The legacy of wine labeling has certainly evolved regardless of whether the bottled wine is appellationally, varietally, or proprietary-blend driven. No matter what wine style lineage, more and more winemakers today are using every wine shop as a gallery and every wine label as a canvas. These small canvases offer the consumer extended information on the people, places, traditions, culture, history, geography, personal messages, and vintage anecdotes that are relevant to what's inside the bottle. Although wine labels are only legally required to provide the practical information outlined by individual countries and regions, the role of the wine label has become eclectic.

Initially, wine labels represent the product. They then act as an extension of and personify the characteristics, values, and pride of the people and places behind the wine. From a marketing perspective, the label functions as an opening dialogue of interaction with the consumer and, in turn, a lasting impression of the brand. Additionally, wine labels today demystify what has long held a reputation of being a pretentious and intimidating social pursuit. As wine brings people together in human connection, the wine label also performs an important part in the overall consumption experience: captivating labels are conversation starters.

People gravitate towards labels that reflect a sense of their own style and personality. The more the consumer associates with the story being told on the outside, the more they will desire exploring and building a relationship with what's on the inside. Further, people enjoy being part of the winemaking process and are curious to know more about the people who have so passionately crafted what they are consuming. The wine label's visual representation provides more intimate details on where the wine comes from more than simply a geographic perspective and, thus, allows a more inclusive feeling of participation in the overall experience. All

of these traits certainly get people talking about myriad subjects that just might coninue until the close of the evening . . . when the bottles are empty.

Given the multiplicity of their efforts, many wine labels have often undergone as diligent a creative process on the outside of the bottle as the wine has undergone on the inside. Besides the actual taste of the wine, the wine label is the most important variable in the success of a wine as it provides an upfront sensory stimulus prior to its actual enjoyment. Under normal circumstances, wine consumers do not have the opportunity to taste test each and every wine prior to purchase. The label, however, is accessible prior to the bottle being opened and tasted, and therefore needs to intrigue and impress enough to instigate a closer look. If the front label has done its job and captured the attention of the passerby, reliance is then on the canny effort of the back label to stir the senses of the consumer. Often, the back label delves deeper into the character of the wine, communicates the vision of the viticulturist, and tells the tale (be it true or tall!) behind the wine. In many instances, it is the story or information, with its more approachable appeal, together with the interesting visual statement that will fascinate and connect the consumer initially to the bottle.

The wine label persuades the purchaser by using compelling words and bold images that speak to consumers already affected by their own set of unique internal and external influences. Culture, social class, age, occupation, lifestyle, personality, beliefs, attitudes, and experiences influence the individual choices made from one person to the next. It is a highly individual decision process and purchase.

This is never to say that the label has become more important than the wine itself by any means. Most novice wine drinkers, however, do not have enough in-depth knowledge to allow intricate discrimination from one wine to the next. Or, if they do, despite comparing the grape variety, origin, and price, the consumer is most often still left with hundreds of different wines to choose from. Without distinctive labels, wine drinkers would be left to their own devices to work their way through a massive undertaking. Although extremely enjoyable, not only would this involve enormous amounts of time and money, given the saturated wine marketplace today, but would also leave little to aid in the differentiation and memorability from one bottle to the next. The label definitely works both ways. If the wine doesn't meet the expectations set by the wine label, the label will certainly be remembered likewise, and no matter how creative the label is or how endearing the story behind the wine is, the purchase of that wine will remain at the first initial bottle.

Although wine label design falls into a category that has allowed greater creative leniency, designers cannot be given absolute *carte blanche* to concoct whatever comes to the imagination due to individual legal restrictions legislated at the place of production, as well as the reality sizing constraints. Each country and/or state has separate legislations in place to safeguard both the vintner and the consumer alike. Depending on the wine, the respective label may be required to include a very long list of prerequisite information, often including: name of the wine, size of the bottle, vintage year, alcohol content, use of preservatives, vintner's name and address, bottler's name and address, shipper's name and address, importer's name, quality level of the wine, place where wine was bottled, country of origin, type of wine, region and appellation, and grape variety. Individual wineries will often want to include when the wine should optimally be drunk, at what temperature it is best to be kept, and food pairings that will allow ultimate consumption pleasure.

The checklist of legally required and supplementary information, although extremely important to the overall promotion and success of the wine, is daunting for such a small space. Talented designers and brand strategists, however, have the skillful ability to envision awe-inspiring layouts, while navigating the content limitations imposed on the design area. Imaginatively, they use novel stories inspired by the wineries and their committed teams to create visual interest through compelling graphics, fine art, photography, and typography to adorn their unique faces. Upfront, the label is the loudest and most prolific voice the product has. They provide the opportunity to translate uncolorful industry terms into something that is more commonly relatable, engaging, intriguing, and worthy of conversation.

The fine wine fanatic might say that anything besides the meat of the wine's classification is just gravy. But after observing reactions to labels, there should be a tendency to disagree.

Wine has a consuming effect of bringing people together. In the company of wine, people connect; prolific and memorable stories are created and life just happens. Ultimately, wine labels are the social lubricant's publicity agent that, as a creative conversation piece, salute what's in the bottle, the people behind it, and the places that the wine enables us to taste on our palates. The graphic messages on the labels reflect the heart and soul of the winery and their joint fruitful labor. They tell beautiful stories behind the wine while concurrently adding another layer to each unique quipping and quaffing experience.

Given the sheer volume of labels internationally, *The Art and Design of Contemporary Wine Labels* celebrates only a limited survey of the admirably creative wine labels that have been conceived. Each of the labels within is valued for its unique ability to stand out in a crowd and capture its own well-deserved audience. Be it through bold graphics, interesting illustrations, beautiful typography, cutting-edge photography, or the power of words, these labels provide a moment of entertainment and most often a conversation starting point prior to even taking that first sip of delicious juice. They are funny, elegant, artistic, eclectic, subtle, amusing, adventurous, inspiring, courageous, educational, thought-provoking, cheeky, and charming, amongst so many other things.

It is said that there are over ten thousand documented *vitis vinifera* grape varietals. With at least 1,200 wineries in the state of California alone, it is impossible to estimate how many different producers there are worldwide, and likewise, to approximate how many different brands of wine there are—which translate into perhaps millions of wine labels and of course, countless intimate stories that link that wine with the label.

The purpose of this book was to provide an expansive, but definitely unexhausted, survey of wine label art and the often-unknown story that has resulted in the visual representation of the showcased wines. It by no means is a fully realized depiction of the countless wine label works of art and design that exist internationally. However, it is my sincere hope that this book has provided a starting source of inspiration for every individual to personally attempt to uncover the hidden stories behind the miniature masterpieces that each and every wine label is and, in turn, to add another layer to every wine consuming experience by sharing with friends and family.

I know I most certainly continue to do so.

The Labels

In the absence of human intervention, the label becomes the single most important window to a wine's story. It speaks of tradition or modernity, conformity or irreverence, and accessibility or stately reservation, setting up a potential consumer's expectations and, ultimately, their perception of quality.　—JOHN SZABO
Editor, *Wine Access* First-in-Line Report
and Vice President, The Wine Writers' Circle of Canada

ALPHA BOX & DICE

[WESTERN AUSTRALIA/SOUTH AUSTRALIA ✎ AUSTRALIA]

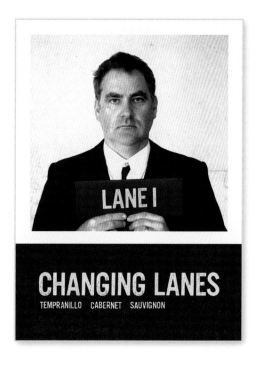
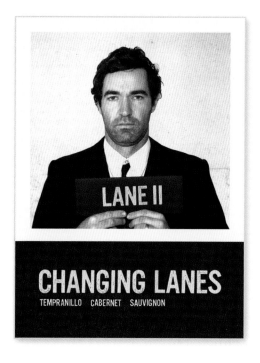

When acclaimed (and slightly eccentric) young Australian winemaker Justin Lane visited U.S. importer Ronnie Sanders, the first thing Ronnie said was, "You must know Mark Lane from Margaret River."

Now, Australia is a pretty big country with approximately 1,700 miles between Adelaide and Perth, but to Ronnie, it seemed to be quite impossible that these two winemakers, who shared not only the same nationality but also the same last name, had never met. Ronnie enthusiastically quipped that a meeting should take place and had a full project crafted out in his mind's eye.

As the night wore on and the wines washed down well, Justin and Ronnie laughed about the two coincidentally same-named winemakers on opposite sides of the country—the "right Lane," the "wrong Lane," the "fast Lane," the "slow Lane," the "left Lane," and "changing Lanes." The lips were loose and the jokes were flying. Though they were just having a laugh, some of the best ideas are born over a shared bottle and this project certainly was. It survived the often-critical night's sleep to the morning after, and again emerged not simply as the recollection of a trivial night of revelry, but instead as a solid possibility. And, in turn, an introduction between the Lanes took place.

The next thing Justin knew, he was en route to Western Australia to meet Mark, with whom he shared more than a surname. The two hit it off and began to workshop a concept wine, blending the Lanes together. In other words, using the best varietals from each of the Lane's respective regions to make a cracking great wine. From this master blending session arrived a two-Lane masterpiece blend. The Alpha Box and Dice Changing Lanes label ingeniously uses lenticular art that allows those crazy Lanes to morph from one into another, creating a wine label that literally "changes Lanes" seamlessly right before your eyes.

> The art of winemaking should not be limited to the contents of the bottle. That is why we spend a lot of time on the wine label in particular.
> We have a lot of fun discussing the wine's traditional color and palate, but also its personality, its story, and what it has to tell us about itself.
> —EMMA LANE
> General Manager, Alpha Box & Dice

ALPHA BOX & DICE

Appellation:	**Margaret River/McLaren Vale**
State:	**Western Australia/South Australia**
Country of Origin:	**Australia**
Type of Wine:	**Tempranillo and Cabernet Sauvignon Blend**
Web Site:	**www.alphaboxdice.com.au**
Design:	**Mash**
Designer's Web Site:	**www.mashdesign.com.au**

Andrew Murray Vineyards
[California ❦ United States]

As a child, Andrew Murray had the fortune of traveling to Europe with his family on fact-finding missions to benefit his parent's restaurant business. One of these trips found Andrew, a student of the French language, acting as the family's bona fide translator while they journeyed through France eating and drinking well—all in the sake of "research." Privy to the European lifestyle, where tasting wine doesn't begin at middle age, Andrew garnered quite an admiration and appreciation for Rhône varietals and returned to the United States decidedly armed with an abundance of French wine-related vernacular and knowledge, only to set off again. This time, though, it was in the opposite direction to the land down under.

Here, Andrew learnt a different perspective on his beloved Syrah—that of the famed Australian Shiraz. Upon his homecoming, this wine-infused wanderlust prompted Andrew to earn a degree in viticulture and oenology, which led to a subsequent career in the wine business. During his career, he focused on crafting wines with exceptionally low yields exclusively from those Rhône vine varietals, while using progressive viticulture methods.

Andrew's Days Off wines are a reflection of his *amour* for vines of all kinds—not just the classic Rhône varietals. This wine range was inspired by the incessant questioning about whether or not he was "cheating" on his first love, the Rhône. The wine labels are reminiscent of all of his family's fabulous vacations together, and reflective of a time during the '50s and '60s when life was simpler and days off weren't an anomaly, but rather sacred time ritually spent together making memories and enjoying life. With its fun-loving labels, the Days Off series is Andrew's gentle reminder to himself, as well as for those who enjoy the wines, that life in this big and beautiful world moves fast—make sure to take time to slow down and make your own days off a priority.

> **Conventional wisdom tells one to follow the "swirl, sniff, sip" ritual in order to truly appreciate the beauty of a fine wine. I would argue that the real appreciation starts long before that final moment of opening the bottle. It begins when one is convinced to actually pick the bottle up in the first place.**
>
> —Andrew Murray
> Owner and Winemaker,
> Andrew Murray Vineyards

ANDREW MURRAY VINEYARDS

Appellation:	**Santa Ynez Valley**
State:	**California**
Country of Origin:	**United States**
Type of Wine:	**Sauvignon Blanc, Riesling, and Viognier Blend**
Web Site:	**www.andrewmurrayvineyards.com**
Design:	**Monte Gifford Design**
Designer's Web Site:	**www.montegdesign.com**

ANTHEM

Anthem is more than a wine; it is a philosophy where the only things that are said to be predictable are change, quality, and diversity. With a vision of a wine destination that would co-exist within a village, offering a true sense of place and including a future bakery, chocolatier, restaurant, hotel, spa, and their own products, Anthem was born.

An anthem is defined as a traditionally patriotic song sung by a group of individuals in unison to form one common voice of shared belief. It is also, however, the title of Ayn Rand's 1938 dystopian science fiction novel, which Anthem wines have drawn inspiration from. The book reflected a strong statement of the era, pre-Russian Revolution, where there were conflicts between valuing the common good, and communal thought versus the qualities and celebration of individuality. The juxtaposing views of individuality and collectivism are both very much part of Anthem wine—the uniqueness or "individuality" of the Anthem concept invites people to free themselves from the status quo and share the belief that absolutely anything is possible with a optimistically fresh outlook. Importantly, Anthem inspires people to buck convention and to think differently by questioning the status quo.

Each of Anthem's wine labels evokes the theme of and is also motivated by the fictitious images inspired by Rand's words. The imagery tells the story of individuals, community, and a strong sense of place. While Anthem is meant to stand alone in its singularity, it is built on a common and collaborated dogma of quality, diversity, inspiration, and change that, together, ultimately makes Anthem possible.

The biggest thing for me is working with incredibly passionate and talented people. They all want to make the best wine ever, but they are all very different, which is reflected both in the wine and the visual imagery we create.

—HELEN MILNER
Brand Strategist and Creative Director,
Tardis Design and Advertising

	ANTHEM
Appellation:	**Central Otago**
Region:	**Otago**
Country of Origin:	**New Zealand**
Type of Wine:	**Pinot Noir**
Web Site:	**www.anthem.co.nz**
Design:	**Tardis Design and Advertising**
Designer's Web Site:	**www.tardis.co.nz**

	ANTHEM
Appellation:	**Central Otago**
Region:	**Otago**
Country of Origin:	**New Zealand**
Type of Wine:	**Riesling**
Web Site:	**www.anthem.co.nz**
Design:	**Tardis Design and Advertising**
Designer's Web Site:	**www.tardis.co.nz**

ANTICA TERRA

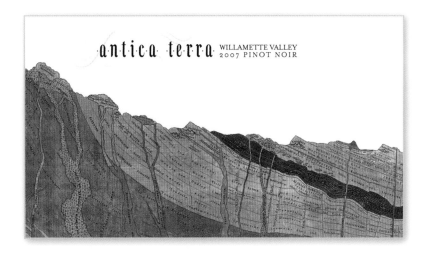

When winemaker Maggie Harrison and her partners, Scott Adelson, John Mavredakis, and Michael Kramer, purchased the Antica Terra vineyard, they were skeptical of keeping its given name. The name just sounded more foreign than fitting to them. However, once they began uncovering the property's history amidst the layers of soil, it became very clear that the most appropriate name for the estate could be nothing other than Antica Terra, literally meaning "ancient earth."

Unbeknownst to them, soil analysis revealed that buried under the surface there were astonishing samples of forty-million-year-old calcified fossils. After some research, they found out that their newly purchased vineyard sat on land that was very unusual and had quite a history, demonstrated through its layers upon layers of sediment and volcanic rock and silt.

Inspired by a fondness of antique maps and wanting to express the pedigree and ancientness of the soils, the hunt for something appropriate to express the age of the soils began. When a seventeenth-century copper etching of very old soil profiles was found, they knew that this aged artifact would provide the continuity needed for what existed long before them or their wines, and what would certainly exist long afterwards. Simply put: Antica Terra.

When designing for others, I make every effort to keep my own ego in check. The package design must ultimately be a distillation of the client's own vision for their project and my role is to act as guide, interpreter, and medium in the process.
— MICHAEL KIRTS
Owner and Designer, Heroist

Likewise, they also wanted to also depict what grew above the earth on these ancient lands and as such, the Botanica label was created for another of their portfolio wines. Using the support of authentic, antique botanical prints, the label also reflects what the soils of these ancient lands enable to continually flourish.

ANTICA TERRA	
Appellation:	**Willamette Valley**
State:	**Oregon**
Country of Origin:	**United States**
Type of Wine:	**Pinot Noir**
Web Site:	**www.anticaterra.com**
Design:	**Heroist**
Designer's Web Site:	**www.heroist.com**

ANTICA TERRA	
Appellation:	**Eola-Amity Hills**
State:	**Oregon**
Country of Origin:	**United States**
Type of Wine:	**Pinot Noir**
Web Site:	**www.anticaterra.com**
Design:	**Heroist**
Designer's Web Site:	**www.heroist.com**

In Mapudungun, the native language of the Chilean Mapuche people, the word *kuyen* means "moon." The Antiyal winery in Maipo Valley thought that it was an extremely fitting representation of its second wine and a perfect partner to stand along its flagship brand, Antiyal, or "son of the sun."

Very much in line with the beliefs of the Mapuche people who are closely linked to land and the natural elements, winemaker Alvaro Espinoza and his wife Marina's objective when making Kuyen wine is "to honor the ancient traditions and cosmic vision of the people of the earth." In doing so, they are not only dedicated to producing environmentally responsible wines, but also adopting biodynamic practices.

Biodynamic viticulture methods are said to have enhanced the overall well-being of the vineyards in the areas of biodiversity, soil fertility, crop nutrition, and pest, weed, and disease management, as well as to have further developed the flavor profile of wines. Much of the emphasis in biodynamic viticulture focuses on the preparation, which can include burying manure or ground quartz in cow horns beneath the soil, fermenting yarrow flowers in a deer's bladder and applying it to the compost, and applying horsetail tea to the vines, amongst many other seemingly far-out practices.

In some regards, these practices seem almost "shaman-like," which has been coincidentally reflected in the image on the Kuyen wine label to acknowledge an important link to the belief system of the Mapuche people. Though not intended to draw a parallel, the two practices seem to have some similar objectives, such as the warding off of evil in different forms, summoning the rains, curing diseases, and practicing wellness through the use of a variety of Chilean medicinal herbs.

While Espinoza would never liken the care for their crops and environment to that of the spiritual and medicinal leadership of the shaman, at the end of the day, it seems that both Espinoza, with his biodynamic ways, and the enlightened shaman play similar yet different roles as advocates for a good and prosperous earth.

ANTIYAL

Appellation:	**Maipo Valley**
Region:	**Santiago**
Country of Origin:	**Chile**
Type of Wine:	**Syrah, Cabernet Sauvignon, and Carménère Blend**
Web Site:	**www.antiyal.com**
Design:	**Internal**

Artisan Wine Co.

[British Columbia ✺ Canada]

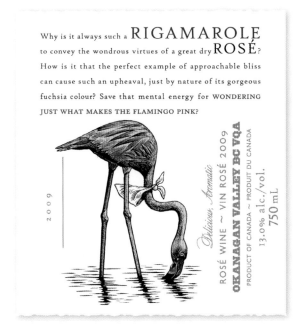

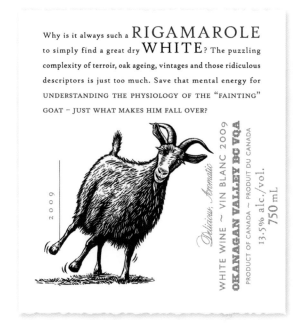

Drinking wine should be easy, accessible, and fun, not intimidating, daunting, or confusing—after all, we aren't solving life's problems with a glass (though historically speaking, many glasses of wine have been involved in deal-making in the past), or saving lives by fermenting grapes, or uncovering the unthinkable by being well-versed in varietals.

So what's all the rigamarole about? Why is buying wine perceived, more so than not, as such an affair to be reckoned with? Why not consider channeling the energy spent on figuring wine out to figuring out some of life's interesting and unresolved mysteries instead?

For instance, have you ever wondered why flamingos are pink? And why are Caribbean flamingos blessed with the brightest of crimson hues, while the poor Chilean flamingo is the palest? Or what about the goat that is said to faint (what reason would a goat have to faint)?

The solutions to these questions will definitely be more awe-inspiring than the hours of trepidation spent on choosing the right wine. The good news is, with wine, there is rarely a wrong answer. While perhaps the perfect pairing mightn't be made for your palate every time, the fun is in the practice, and help is really just a question away. When all else fails, if the wine you've chosen is really not making any magic whatsoever, you can always take some of the focus off the wine by asking if anyone knows why dolphins blush or perhaps you can reenact the startling of a goat into fainting, which is always much more amusing than stressing about wine. After all, it's only grape juice and as Artisan Wine Company's labels suggest, forget the rigamarole and just have fun.

ARTISAN WINE CO.	
Appellation:	**Okanagan Valley**
Province:	**British Columbia**
Country of Origin:	**Canada**
Type of Wine:	**Rosé**
Web Site:	**www.artisanwineco.ca**

ARTISAN WINE CO.	
Appellation:	**Okanagan Valley**
Province:	**British Columbia**
Country of Origin:	**Canada**
Type of Wine:	**White Blend**
Web Site:	**www.artisanwineco.ca**

ASTROLABE WINES

[MARLBOROUGH ❧ NEW ZEALAND]

While making wine might seem like a maze of peaks and valleys, and twists and turns, Astrolabe's second label is not, in fact, a visual metaphor for the tenuous (but fruitful) experience at vintage and throughout the year from bud to harvest. Rather, this meandering entanglement of greenery actually reflects Astrolabe winemaker and owner Simon Waghorn's foundational academic passion that has nonetheless overlapped with an unusual professional segue.

Prior to embarking on a life amidst vines, Simon lived a life amidst lower-lying greenery while studying towards a master's in natural resources. It was during this period that he was drawn to "vines of another kind," namely *durvillaea* seaweed, which is known to incessantly cling to the rocks of New Zealand's Marlborough Coast when exposed at low tide. To the locals, these living sea-vines are known as bull kelp. Having a strong connection to the ocean, Simon had originally planned to professionally farm this seaweed, but soon became enticed by grapes when he became a member of the university wine club. After seeing a brochure for a post-graduate course in winemaking through Roseworthy Agricultural College in South Australia (now Roseworthy Campus at the University of Adelaide), he felt compelled to change his professional course of direction from one green to another.

The Astrolabe Durvillea wine label recognizes Simon's commitment to nature and the wine industry. As an extension of this commitment, he and his wife, Jane Forrest, have endeavored to develop a product that is environmentally sensitive and combines elements of recycled materials, as well as grapes sourced from sustainable vineyards to produce a wine with a low carbon footprint. Further, the Durvillea label celebrates the island nation of New Zealand that is tied intimately to the sea, whose inhabitants recognize that their climate is moderated by this natural element, which in turn is reflected in the unique flavors of their wines.

The wine label is our book cover. It is the invitation to discover our story and the visual presentation of our wine. —JANE FORREST WAGHORN
Owner and Director, Astrolabe Wines

Although the foundation of the name of New Zealand's characteristic *durvillaea* seaweed has yet to be confirmed, there is an uncanny resemblance to the name of the explorer Jules Sébastien César Dumont d'Urville, who commanded the magnificent ship *L'Astrolabe* and landed on Marlborough's coast in the early 1800s. Waghorne's primary wine label commemorates the *L'Astrolabe* vessel, which circumvented the globe multiple times while d'Urville recorded and illustrated over 243 natural specimens, landscapes, and populations. This intimacy with New Zealand nature is shared in the making of Astrolabe's true New Zealand wines.

ASTROLABE WINES

Appellation:	**Marlborough**
Region:	**Marlborough**
Country of Origin:	**New Zealand**
Type of Wine:	**Sauvignon Blanc**
Web Site:	**www.durvilleawines.co.nz**
Design:	**Neogine Communication Design**
Designer's Web Site:	**www.neogine.co.nz**

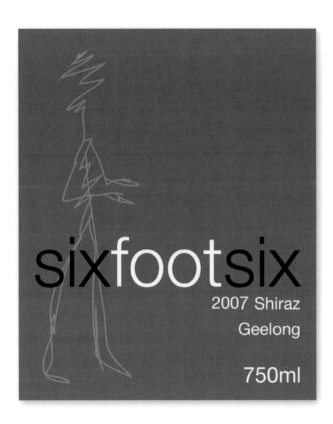

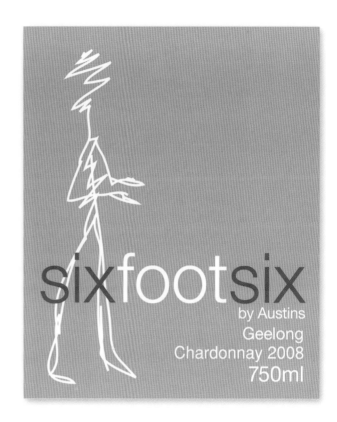

It is doubtful that William Buckley would have ever predicted that his escape from prison would go down in Australian history. It's even more unlikely that he would have ever envisioned himself being called a hero. But heroes come in all shapes and sizes, and this one—a towering 6 feet, 6 inches tall—comes with one of the greatest stories of survival and onset of social change in Australian history.

Buckley, an English convict deported to Australia, fled custody from the first official settlement of Port Phillip Bay, Victoria, in 1803. Against the odds, he led a nomadic and simple life amidst the Wathaurong, an indigenous Australian tribe, who truly believed him to be the spirit of an honored, deceased chieftain. Three decades later, this "wild white man" reemerged into English colonial society, barefoot and wearing animal pelts. In order to prevent bloodshed between the white colonists and Australia's indigenous natives, the escaped convict courageously surrendered himself to the land's prospectors. Despite his imposing stature, Buckley demonstrated a benevolent disposition promoting reconciliation and, ultimately, a shifting attitude towards the coexistence of the two diverse groups.

To celebrate Buckley's bicentennial, Austins Wines first created this big, full-bodied Shiraz, aptly named "sixfootsix." Today, the unruly, bold, and beguiling illustration that saluted the anniversary of this courageous Australian giant now graces each of the varietal labels that have followed suit.

AUSTINS WINES	
Appellation:	**Geelong**
State:	**Victoria**
Country of Origin:	**Australia**
Type of Wine:	**Shiraz**
Web Site:	**www.austinswines.com.au**
Design:	**Rachel O'Brien**

AUSTINS WINES	
Appellation:	**Geelong**
State:	**Victoria**
Country of Origin:	**Australia**
Type of Wine:	**Chardonnay**
Web Site:	**www.austinswines.com.au**
Design:	**Rachel O'Brien**

Bacio Divino Cellars

[California ❧ United States]

Adrifter. A traveler. A nomad. The word "vagabond" is one that immediately conjures up images of carefree, itinerant living. And as a citizen of the world, with a passport to prove it, it's a term that Claus Janzen, owner and winemaker at Bacio Divino Cellars, can certainly associate with. From his birth in Berlin to growing up in Canada, then living in Europe between college degrees to following his heart to Napa, and traveling extensively to just about all corners of the earth, you could say that many of the traits of an adventurous vagabond run parallel with Claus—especially his sheer zest for life!

The wine label gives us insight into the winemaker's soul. It is the visual and tactile expression not only of his character, but also of his vision of the wine.
—Claus Janzen
Proprietor and Winemaker,
Bacio Divino Cellars

The Vagabond wine is one that brings Claus Janzen full circle in his journey to create unique and stunning proprietary red wine blends. His first wine, Bacio Divino ("divine kiss"), was inspired by an atypical marriage of Syrah and Cabernet Sauvignon that he first discovered in some of the wines made by Eloi Durrbach of Domaine de Trevallon, found near Les Baux-de-Provence, France. Roused by a certain *je ne sais quoi* found in the winery's pioneer blending, Janzen was led to his own initial interpretation for Bacio Divino, born out of Cabernet Sauvignon, Sangiovese, and Petite Sirah grapes. Years later and still motivated by the alluring French blend, Claus Janzen and "co-conspiring master blender" (as Claus calls him) Kirk Venge went to work again and reinterpreted the blend, this time using the original pair of varietals to make a proprietary blend guided by its own unique compass.

This eclectic red has aptly been called Vagabond due to its singular blend of the familiar with the exotic. Drinking this wine is said to embody a true vagabond spirit that takes joy in the exploration and discovery of anything and everything unknown.

BACIO DIVINO CELLARS	
Appellation:	**Napa Valley**
State:	**California**
Country of Origin:	**United States**
Type of Wine:	**Syrah and Cabernet Sauvignon Blend**
Web Site:	**www.baciodivino.com**
Design:	**CF Napa Brand Design**
Designer's Web Site:	**www.cfnapa.com**

BARKAN WINERY

The decorative weathervane is internationally recognized as an instrument that easily and visually indicates the temperamental direction of the wind. Traditionally, these instruments have featured a cockerel and direction letters indicative of the points of the compass. Historically speaking, the Tower of the Winds in Athens, Greece, is said to have displayed a bronzed instrument including the god Triton holding an outstretched rod that rotated as the wind changed course of direction. The structure was also adorned with eight statuesque wine deities, sundials, and a water clock, and is said to have dated back to around 50 BC. The weathervane's Triton was eventually replaced with a clock as the Roman Empire emerged and converted to Christianity, and it has been said that the clock, in bygone eras, represented a need for watchfulness and humility.

Being watchful and using the weathervane to determine intricate wind direction changes can be a helpful resource when considered in conjunction with other conditions to make short-range forecasts and farming decisions.

Barkan Winery's vineyard sites span the breadth of growing regions in Israel—from the Lebanese border in the Galil and the Golan in the north, to the Jerusalem Mountains and coastal plains in central Israel and then to the Negev Mountains in the south. Drawing on the French word *domaine*, meaning "site" or "area," each wine is a distinct representation of the specific region from which it hails— each indicative of a very unique and diverse terroir. The symbolic weathervane that graces each of the dOmaine labels provides proud direction on the story of each of the wine's regional characteristics and emphasis on the diversity of regions spread throughout the vast country that is Israel.

I've been selling and marketing wine all my life. Throughout the years, wines and wine labels were always aimed at the elite and the elitists. The dOmaine series labels were born with a smile. Aimed at the young and urbane, they "educate" about the winery and its vineyards without intimidation and without people noticing they are being educated. —CARMI LEBENSTEIN
Marketing Director, Barkan Winery

BARKAN WINERY

Appellation:	**Tabor**
District:	**Northern District**
Country of Origin:	**Israel**
Type of Wine:	**Cabernet Sauvignon**
Web Site:	**www.barkan-winery.com**
Design:	**Ruti Kantor Studio**
Designer's Web Site:	**www.rutikantor.com**

BARKAN WINERY

Appellation:	**Samson**
District:	**Southern District**
Country of Origin:	**Israel**
Type of Wine:	**Petite Sirah**
Web Site:	**www.barkan-winery.com**
Design:	**Ruti Kantor Studio**
Designer's Web Site:	**www.rutikantor.com**

Baron Philippe de Rothschild
[Aquitaine ❧ France]

The Baroness Philippine de Rothschild has been noted as saying, "While history and wine are a wonderful pair, art and wine go hand in hand."

In view of this comment and the treasured labels that have been inspired by the Château Mouton Rothschild Premier Cru wines, no book on the design of contemporary wine labels would be complete without the praise of Baron Philippe de Rothschild's brazen experiment with design that perhaps was the crux of change in wine label design.

Up until 1924, like every vineyard in Médoc, each Château Mouton Rothschild vintage was sold by barrel to the wine merchants who handled the aging, bottling, and labeling of the wine. The vintners had no ownership over the finished wine and therefore paid little interest to the labeling of the end product. Often enough, it was the wine merchants whose prominence was greater on the label rather than the actual producer. However, Baron Philippe de Rothschild

A work of art on the label adds to the pleasure of drinking. As the poet proclaimed: "A thing of beauty is a joy for ever."

—Baroness Philippine de Rothschild
Proprietor, Baron Philippe de Rothschild

BARON PHILIPPE DE ROTHSCHILD	
Appellation:	**Pauillac (Bordeaux)**
Region:	**Aquitaine**
Country of Origin:	**France**
Type of Wine:	**Red Blend**
Web Site:	**www.bpdr.com**
Art:	**Henry Moore**
Artist's Web Site:	**www.henry-moore-fdn.co.uk**

BARON PHILIPPE DE ROTHSCHILD	
Appellation:	**Pauillac (Bordeaux)**
Region:	**Aquitaine**
Country of Origin:	**France**
Type of Wine:	**Red Blend**
Web Site:	**www.bpdr.com**
Art:	**John Huston**

BARON PHILIPPE DE ROTHSCHILD	
Appellation:	**Pauillac (Bordeaux)**
Region:	**Aquitaine**
Country of Origin:	**France**
Type of Wine:	**Red Blend**
Web Site:	**www.bpdr.com**
Art:	**Keith Haring**
Artist's Web Site:	**www.haring.com**

BARON PHILIPPE DE ROTHSCHILD	
Appellation:	**Pauillac (Bordeaux)**
Region:	**Aquitaine**
Country of Origin:	**France**
Type of Wine:	**Red Blend**
Web Site:	**www.bpdr.com**
Art:	**Lucian Freud**
Artist's Web Site:	**www.lucianfreud.info**

made a bold move to bottle and label the entire Château Mouton Rothschild harvest at the estate in 1924, an indication of taking greater responsibility of the wine. Again, well ahead of his time, the baron commissioned Jean Carlu to design the label for the 1924 vintage. Though a superb example of Cubist influence on commercial art, the label concept was too premature and as such lived in isolation for many years.

At the end of the war in 1945, however, the baron, inspired by a return to peaceful times and the victory sign that Churchill had iconically made throughout the war, commissioned a young Philippe Jullian to produce a graphic symbol of the "V" sign to embody *l'année de la victoire* ("victory year"). Since then, customary to each vintage, a new contemporary artist has been commissioned to create an irreplaceable work of art for the Château Mouton Rothschild labels. There have only been four exceptions to this tradition: the 1953 vintage, which celebrated the centenary of Baron Nathaniel de Rothschild's purchase of Mouton; the 1977 vintage, which celebrated the visit of Queen Elizabeth and the Queen Mother to Médoc; the 2000 vintage, which celebrated the new millennium; and the 2003 vintage, which paid tribute to the 150th anniversary of Mouton Rothschild.

The appreciation of fine wine and art truly go hand in hand. They both involve great study and subjective interpretation of complex layers to achieve a deeper understanding and appreciation of the nuances and subtleties of handmade craftsmanship. With the passing of the late Baron de Rothschild, his daughter Baroness Philippine has continued her exceptional commitment to the fine arts, as well as the art of winemaking. The relationship between the artist and the estate is one based on a mutual friendship and trust, with each artist at liberty to interpret themes of vines, pleasures taken from wine consumption, and/ or the Rothschilds' characteristic ram. Each label exposes an interpretation as artistically and individual as what's inside the bottle and has created a collection unlike that of any other in the world.

BELLBRAE ESTATE

[VICTORIA ❧ AUSTRALIA]

When it comes to sun, sand, and surf, Torquay on Australia's Victoria coast with famed Bells Beach is undoubtedly the surfing capital of the nation and a definitive destination for surfers around the world. The region is certainly steeped in history and full of regional character, which provides an unmatched uniqueness experienced only through the beach-based culture of the Great Ocean Road coastline.

Historically, the region was originally home to the Mon Mart clan of the Wathaurong tribe of indigenous Australians—often referred to as "the people of the rivers." Farmers and travelers from Geelong's nearby port were the first whites to begin to expand into the area as picnickers, campers, and fishermen made more frequent excursions to the coast.

In 1878, James Follet built a boarding house, a bathing house on the beach, and a wagonette transit service between Geelong and the region that had become a growing resort area. The renowned Bells Beach is a long and generous surf break and the coveted waves have long attracted some of the greatest names in surfing, including such pioneers of the '30s, '40s, and '50s as Rex "China" Gilbert, Dick Garrard, Joe Sweeney, and Peter Troy, amongst others.

These are the individuals that winemaker Matthew di Sciascio of Bellbrae Estate grew up around, learning to surf alongside their children. Through watching and being inspired by their epitomized coastal living and the culture that they shaped in the area, he developed a deep passion for life on the beach.

Through authentic vintage photographs—including one of Dick Garrard and wife Joan tandem surfing *(seen above)*—the Longboard wine labels tell the story of the unique region where Bellbrae Estate sits in Torquay, home to this

In simple terms, I believe terroir is the pure expression of the soil, climate, and local culture in a wine. The dominant colors of the label— deep blue and silver—represent the ocean and horizon under a gray cloudy sky, and classic "glassy" (no wind) surf conditions. Our Longboard label design is a visual way of showing the source terroir that is expressed in our wine.

—MATTHEW DI SCIASCIO
Winemaker, Bellbrae Estate

great surf history that continues to attract the hottest surfers in the world.

There are two very prominent lifestyles in this region that go hand in hand swimmingly: all natural, relaxed living with an enormous respect and appreciation for nature, and a glass of wine in one hand and your board in the other. What else is there?

BELLBRAE ESTATE	
Appellation:	**Geelong**
State:	**Victoria**
Country of Origin:	**Australia**
Type of Wine:	**Sauvignon Blanc and Sémillon Blend**
Web Site:	**www.bellbraeestate.com.au**
Art:	**Vintage Photograph (circa 1947)**

Venture capitalist and well-known art collector Dennis Scholl met master sommelier and wine director Richard Betts while casually dining at Little Nell in Aspen, Colorado. The two men became fast friends over their mutual love of fine food, wine, and art. Scholl enjoyed speaking about and further cultivating Betts's appreciation of contemporary art, while Scholl says that Betts was a "profound wine educator," even informally as friends. On one of these relaxed occasions, when the two were out picking seasonal mushrooms to be included in the evening's shared fare, Richard casually mentioned a winemaking project that he felt passionate about pursuing—making Grenache in Australia. Dennis, knowing the nature of his friend, was certain that he would be a fabulous partner because of his zest for life and his truly extraordinary rock-star quality with wine. Just as fast as the two became friends, the two became partners.

The emotion of a wine ought to be reflected in its label. For us, it's an organic extension of our vinous enthusiasm, so we let contemporary artist friends pop the cork and riff on wherever it takes them!

—RICHARD BETTS
Master Sommelier, Co-Founder,
and Partner, Betts & Scholl

When it came time to label their first wine, the partners looked at thousands of wine label designs, but decided that instead of briefing someone to design their label, they agreed that the creative process, beginning with the winemaking, should be taken a step further to allow an artist to create an organic extension of the wine based solely on their artistic interpretation after tasting it.

Enter Anna Gaskell. The young contemporary artist tasted the wine and couldn't have translated the Grenache inside the bottle, or the philosophy of the Betts and Scholl company, in a more artistically insightful manner—the wine knocked her socks off, and so she provided a de facto visual descriptor that sums up how both Richard Betts and Dennis Scholl are truly head over heels about everything they do in life.

The wine knocked her socks off, and so she provided a de facto visual descriptor that sums up just how both Richard Betts and Dennis Scholl approach their wines, art, and everything they do in life—head over heels.

BETTS & SCHOLL	
Appellation:	**Barossa Valley**
State:	**South Australia**
Country of Origin:	**Australia**
Type of Wine:	**Grenache**
Web Site:	**www.bettsandscholl.com**
Art:	**Anna Gaskell**
Artist's Web Site:	**www.yvon-lambert.com**

BIG HOUSE WINES

[CALIFORNIA ❧ UNITED STATES]

In the case of Big House Wines, the only "big house" being referred to is the Château di Soledad State Correctional Facility. Nestled amongst the vineyards, it was originally Bonny Doon's Randall Grahm who facetiously brought attention to an Old World-style wine with his rebellious New World ways. Not only did he take chances with his winemaking, but clearly with his labeling as well. Given the vineyard's proximity to the prison, putting the image of a correctional facility on the label was an accurate acknowledgment of exactly where the wines came from—the backyard of their yardbird neighbors. Designed originally by Chuck House, the labels provided an irreverent illustrative approach by referencing the vineyard's proximity to the penitentiary, thus very precisely pinpointing their terroir.

In 2002, when Big House Wines was purchased by Underdog Wine Merchants, the cleverly calculated label representation of the wines continued with new offenders—all being guilty of the same convictional ties to their roots. The Slammer tells the story of the "criminally rich" Syrah; The Lineup introduces us to three usual suspects: "Tiny" Grenache, Syrah (a.k.a. Shiraz), and "Mickey" Mourvèdre, who are always destined to be guilty as charged when banded together; The Prodigal Son plays off the supposed scorn by the Old World of a Petite Sirah, which they claimed had maturation issues, but was accepted with open arms by adoptive parents in the New World; The Birdman pays homage to the Birdman of Alcatraz (Robert Stroud), who was likely the most famous inmate to ever reside on Alcatraz Island. An exceptionally violent man, Stroud took a keen interest in canaries while imprisoned and authored two books on the subject, as well as developed and marketed medicines for various bird ailments. Who knew?

Labels with such an extensive rap sheet? Obviously the wines they represent are so rebellious it would be criminal not to steal a sip or two of this "bug juice."

> My favorite thing about wine is that it's not just about the wine. Wine is about toasting accomplishments; it's about celebrating with your family; it's about enjoying great food and laughing uproariously with your friends. Labels should pluck a chord and an effective label can (and should) evoke these emotions, even in the grocery aisle. —MONTE GIFFORD
> Principal, Monte Gifford Design

**BIG HOUSE WINES
(UNDERDOG WINE MERCHANTS)**

Appellation:	**Central Coast**
State:	**California**
Country of Origin:	**United States**
Type of Wine:	**Red Blend**
Web Site:	**www.bighousewines.com**
Design:	**Chuck House (Icon Design Group) and Monte Gifford Design**
Designer's Web Site:	**www.icondesigngroup.net and www.montegdesign.com**

**BIG HOUSE WINES
(UNDERDOG WINE MERCHANTS)**

Appellation:	**Central Coast**
State:	**California**
Country of Origin:	**United States**
Type of Wine:	**Syrah**
Web Site:	**www.bighousewines.com**
Design:	**Monte Gifford Design**
Designer's Web Site:	**www.montegdesign.com**

**BIG HOUSE WINES
(UNDERDOG WINE MERCHANTS)**

Appellation:	**Central Coast**
State:	**California**
Country of Origin:	**United States**
Type of Wine:	**Grenache, Syrah, and Mourvèdre Blend**
Web Site:	**www.bighousewines.com**
Design:	**Monte Gifford Design**
Designer's Web Site:	**www.montegdesign.com**

**BIG HOUSE WINES
(UNDERDOG WINE MERCHANTS)**

Appellation:	**Paso Robles**
State:	**California**
Country of Origin:	**United States**
Type of Wine:	**Petite Sirah**
Web Site:	**www.bighousewines.com**
Design:	**Monte Gifford Design**
Designer's Web Site:	**www.montegdesign.com**

**BIG HOUSE WINES
(UNDERDOG WINE MERCHANTS)**

Appellation:	**Central Coast**
State:	**California**
Country of Origin:	**United States**
Type of Wine:	**Pinot Grigio**
Web Site:	**www.bighousewines.com**
Design:	**Monte Gifford Design**
Designer's Web Site:	**www.montegdesign.com**

BIG TABLE FARM

[CALIFORNIA ❧ UNITED STATES]

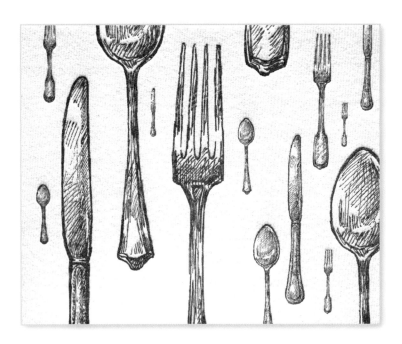

Brian Marcy began his winemaking career working for some of the most esteemed winemakers and wineries in Napa. It was while working for one of these acclaimed winemakers that Brian was given a vertical tasting of a very famous and coveted wine (that will remain unnamed) to take home with him to enjoy. His first reaction: call seventeen of his winemaking buddies to share this most rare but awesome wine experience together. Which is exactly what he did. Now that's a good mate.

Brian and his wife, Clare Carver, realized that coming together with such a large group of friends made the experience of sharing the legendary wine that much richer. As a result, their dinner club was born: a collection of twenty-two friends would come together, Brian and Clare would provide the groceries, everyone would bring wine, and at each gathering, a different appointed chef from the group would cook up a storm in the kitchen. Of course, you can't have a big dinner club without a bloody big table. As such, Brian and Clare built a giant 16-foot table to ensure that everyone would fit comfortably and memories would continue to be made.

In 2005, Brian and Clare left their lives in Napa behind to begin a new adventure in Oregon. Both having grown up on farms, Brian and Clare longed to get back to sustainable living and sought out property in the Willamette Valley to own their own farm and winery, and soon plant their own vineyard. It seemed only appropriate to name their homestead after their desire to provide a gracious and welcoming table covered with a cornucopia of handcrafted food and wine for friends and family. Thus, the farm became known as Big Table Farm.

Not having any estate grapes yet, an opportunity arose to purchase some premium Santa Barbara fruit and the couple took advantage of it. Of course, it wasn't without some trepidation. Not of the fruit, but of the financials that were tied to it for a couple who had just purchased 700 acres of land, some pigs, and some chickens—not your average family pets. However, Clare, an artist by trade, told her husband that every great artist needs the best paint and brushes for their art, and his tools just so happened to be those premium grapes. And so, in 2006, the inaugural Big Table Farm Syrah was artistically and lovingly crafted, and placed on the very big table for which it was named.

> **The wine labels that I find most inspiring are those that capture my mind and give me a sense of where the winemaker wants to take us. Dining is more than just a gustatory or organoleptic experience; it is visual, aural, and emotive. It is experiential art, and the bottles on the table are unquestionably part of that.** —BRIAN MARCY
> Winemaker and Owner, Big Table Farm

BIG TABLE FARM
Appellation: **Santa Barbara County (Non-Designated Appellation)**
State: **California**
Country of Origin: **United States**
Type of Wine: **Syrah**
Web Site: **www.bigtablefarm.com**
Design: **Bluelist Communications**
Designer's Web Site: **www.bluelist.net**

Big Table Farm

[Oregon ❧ United States]

laughing pig rosé

Clare Carver had a dream of producing a Rosé wine ever since she took a trip to Ireland and came face-to-face with some very exuberant local pigs. At the time, well before she and her husband had the idea of owning their own farm, having their own vineyard, or making their own wines was even conceived, Clare envisaged having a Rosé and calling it Laughing Pig to remember these affable animals. Upon their return home to Napa, she commemorated the affectionate pigs in a painting that eventually decorated the kitchen wall. Their kitchen then became known warmheartedly as the Laughing Pig kitchen. Now, no longer in the same kitchen, the wine label honoring those piglets has its own wine, just as Clare had the foresight to imagine it.

Each of the Big Table Farm wine labels is handprinted using a vintage letterpress and lovingly hand-glued individually by artisan printer Inge Bruggerman. Though the process is labor intensive, it not only produces less waste than other traditional printing methods, but is also more befitting to the contents inside the bottle as the Big Table Farm clan of creatures (such as Joleen the pig and Josephine the cow) represent where and who the wine comes from on the outside.

A great label is not only visually appealing, but truly reflects the wine's story. Our label is a reflection of our artistic collaboration in life and work and the care we put into everything we do. —CLARE CARVER
Designer and Owner, Big Table Farm

BIG TABLE FARM	
Appellation:	**Yamhill-Carlton District**
State:	**Oregon**
Country of Origin:	**United States**
Type of Wine:	**Pinot Noir**
Web Site:	**www.bigtablefarm.com**
Design:	**Bluelist Communications**
Designer's Web Site:	**www.bluelist.net**

BIG TABLE FARM	
Appellation:	**Eola-Amity Hills**
State:	**Oregon**
Country of Origin:	**United States**
Type of Wine:	**Rosé**
Web Site:	**www.bigtablefarm.com**
Design:	**Bluelist Communications**
Designer's Web Site:	**www.bluelist.net**

BLACKBIRD VINEYARDS

[CALIFORNIA ✺ UNITED STATES]

Perched in the heart of Napa's Oak Knoll region, which is most well known for its international caliber of Cabernet Sauvignon wines, there exists a little trailblazing piece of right-bank elegance in Blackbird Vineyards. With a terroir and rural and rustic character similar to that of Bordeaux's Pomerol, the less popular Merlot grape has been able to build its own little niche amongst the region's more traditional varietal.

Prior to 2003, Blackbird Vineyards was simply the provider of fruit to other premium wineries. Being a wine aficionado and having wanted to purchase a vineyard for upwards of ten years, businessman Michael Polenske realized that when he bought the house that just happened to come with 10 acres of prime vines, he had found the lifestyle and business he had been waiting for.

When it was revealed that in French patois, *merlot* actually means "little blackbird," he knew his dream of making world-class Pomerol-style boutique wines was coming true. As such, the little winged "merlots" that grace the Blackbird Vineyards wine labels are a perfect indicator of the vines that are nestled in amongst more right-bank-influenced plantings and are a reminder of the wines that Michael Polenske is obviously meant to be making.

A wine's label represents the brand promise. The imagery presented should strive for an iconic position so that when that customer returns to it for years to come, the imagery evokes an emotion from a previous savoring or a memorable experience that is unique only to that bottling.
—PAUL L. LEARY
President, Blackbird Vineyards

BLACKBIRD VINEYARDS
Appellation: **Oak Knoll District of Napa Valley**
State: **California**
Country of Origin: **United States**
Type of Wine: **Merlot, Cabernet Franc, and Cabernet Sauvignon Blend**
Web Site: **www.blackbirdvineyards.com**
Design: **Level**
Designer's Web Site: **www.levelinc.com**

BLACKBIRD VINEYARDS
Appellation: **Oak Knoll District of Napa Valley**
State: **California**
Country of Origin: **United States**
Type of Wine: **Rosé**
Web Site: **www.blackbirdvineyards.com**
Design: **Level**
Designer's Web Site: **www.levelinc.com**

BLACK SHEEP FINDS

[CALIFORNIA ✺ UNITED STATES]

She said:

Tired of the life of being another starving, blonde actress looking for her break on the big screen in Los Angeles, Amy Christine (the "she" of Black Sheep Finds) found time between waitressing shifts to drown the sorrows of her casting rejections in fine wine. So much so that she became certified through the Court of Master Sommeliers in 2001. Impressive.

Just before Christmas in 2004, Christine met Peter Hunken (the "he" of Black Sheep Finds) in Lompoc, California, during a wine tour of Stolpman Vineyards, where Peter was the assistant winemaker. After their brief initial encounter, Peter was off to Los Angeles to visit and an intercity romance quickly ensued.

But then, she dumped him, saying, "Ugh! Santa Barbara is so far away!"

He said:

After long exerting his creative inclinations as an artist, photographer and, in his own words, a "bohemian ne'er-do-well," the idea of a career in wine came a-knocking. At the beginning of his apprenticeship at Stolpman Vineyards in 2001, he knew he had found the calling of his craft. It was true love.

Just before Christmas in 2004, he says he got an early gift when he met Amy Christine, who was from Los Angeles. An intercity romance quickly ensued.

That was before she dumped him a few weeks later. Oh well, her loss.

She said:

Coming to her senses in late February 2005, "one cameraman and studio executive later," Amy Christine called Peter three times *and* left three messages (at 4:00 AM!) about what a mistake she'd made.

He said:

By 8:00 AM, Peter heard the frantic messages. He knew she'd come to her senses.

They said:

And, hocus-pocus, the two who found each other through the love of wine, were back together again.

Hocus Pocus is a project that just happened out of the blue. It allowed the couple (after those 4:00 AM phone calls) to collaborate on what brought them together through fate in the first place—wine. Meeting on common grounds to make this liquid magic bridged the geographical gap between Amy's home in the City of Angels and Peter's in Lompoc. Things worked well as they are now happily married (and living in the same city!). This label is all about the magic the couple continues to make together in life and wine.

BLACK SHEEP FINDS	
Appellation:	**Santa Ynez Valley**
State:	**California**
Country of Origin:	**United States**
Type of Wine:	**Syrah**
Web Site:	**www.blacksheepfinds.com**
Design:	**Heroist**
Designer's Web Site:	**www.heroist.com**

BLACK SHEEP FINDS
[TUSCANY ❧ ITALY]

Truth be told, Italy is nothing if not a wine and foodie delight. The food, the wine, the landscape, and the sense of community all come together to continue age-old gastronomical traditions. Having the privilege of knowing a native in this delicious land heightens the authenticity of the experience, enabling one to truly live like a local and to take a piece of Italian culture and the cuisine home with you in your heart and in your stomach.

Husband-and-wife winemaking duo Peter Hunken and Amy Christine say that this was their experience on a trip to Italy together in 2007. It all started in 2006 when Peter visited Tuscany and found himself walking through a friend's vineyard in the old village of Cerreto Guidi, just under 20 miles from Florence. Suddenly, without any real warning, all that is Italy took hold of him and he immediately made a $52 phone call to his wife, telling her frantically that they had to make wine together in Italy and that she must join him at once. As soon as Amy got over the shock of Peter's lunacy, and she had been successfully convinced, she found herself on a plane en route to Italy, the country that knows no limits when it comes to gastronomic delights. Again, the magic and romance that is Italy took over and there was no turning back. Anyone that knows Italy knows that she always seems to get her way.

In May 2007, Peter and Amy ventured back to Tuscany to settle on a blend and to taste the wine components they had left entrusted with a close friend to care for under "strict" Tuscan standards. Again, they overly enjoyed another authentic Italian experience filled with wine, food, friends, food, vineyards, food, food, food, and maybe a little more wine (how can you not?). The couple says that they added on a few pounds of Italian love and as a result were charged an excess baggage fee for their surplus weight (according to Amy, mostly carried in Peter's midsection).

We want our label images to be memorable and brand names to be a bit playful. Obviously, the quality of the wine is paramount, but without a distinctive name or an image to grasp on to, your wine can easily be forgotten.
—PETER HUNKEN
Owner, Black Sheep Finds

It was this purest form of pleasure that inspired the name of the Black Sheep Finds Chianti project: Dalla Pancia, which translates literally to "from the belly." Peter and Amy definitely agree, and after those telling trips of laughter, food, and wine, all good things certainly are. The Dalla Pancia wine label remembers these happy memories spent in the Italian village amongst friends, which they were able to bottle and now share with others back home.

BLACK SHEEP FINDS

Appellation:	**Chianti**
Region:	**Tuscany**
Country of Origin:	**Italy**
Type of Wine:	**Sangiovese and Merlot Blend**
Web Site:	**www.blacksheepfinds.com**
Design:	**Marcel Sarmiento**
Art:	**Julia Rothman**
Artist's Web Site:	**www.juliarothman.com**

BLACK SHEEP FINDS

When embarking on producing wine from the much-admired Bordeaux varietals, Peter Hunken and Amy Christine of Black Sheep Finds knew that they were treading a slippery slope with the shady history of Cabernet Sauvignon in the Santa Ynez Valley. Despite the gamble on the grape, they sourced their fruit from the eastern boundaries of the valley where in days gone by, Kentucky Derby champions were reared and raised in a field of green called Happy Canyon.

Today, densely planted along the slope, there is a vineyard committed to Cabernet Sauvignon, Merlot, and Petit Verdot. Though Cabernet has had the reputation of being risky, according to Hunken, this vineyard has shown the capacity to produce a subtler varietal, which is uncommon for Cabernets of Santa Barbara—a genuine coup.

Alongside this planted pocket of Bordeaux varietals runs a road named after a chestnut mare that won the 1980 Kentucky Derby—she was also the first filly to ever finish in the money at all three U.S. Triple Crown races. Her name, and the honorary name of the road to this day, was Genuine Risk. It seemed like just the right name for this precarious wine pursuit, which certainly was a genuine risk. The label pays tribute to this special parcel of land where the famed filly once grazed, now home to these risky vines that require a bit of a balancing act to harness.

Of note: Genuine Risk produced two fouls, Genuine Reward and Count-Our-Blessings. Further, she was inducted into the National Museum of Racing's Hall of Fame in 1986 and ranked in the top 100 racehorses of the twentieth century by *The Blood-Horse* magazine. If a namesake has anything to say about it, Genuine Risk is certainly destined to be a winner.

> **Clever, interesting labels don't always translate to relevant, high-quality wines. It's a bit like seeing a beautiful woman, taking her on a date, and realizing it's not all there. That said, a sexy blonde gets more dates than a disheveled rocket scientist, so it's good to cover all your bases. Make the wine good, make the label appropriate to the target demographic, and your chances of succeeding in a saturated wine market are greatly increased.**
>
> —AMY CHRISTINE
> Owner, Black Sheep Finds

BLACK SHEEP FINDS

Appellation:	**Santa Ynez Valley**
State:	**California**
Country of Origin:	**United States**
Type of Wine:	**Cabernet Sauvignon**
Web Site:	**www.blacksheepfinds.com**
Design:	**Heroist**
Designer's Web Site:	**www.heroist.com**

BLASTED CHURCH VINEYARDS
[BRITISH COLUMBIA ❧ CANADA]

Underneath the irreverence of these wine labels lies actual, legitimate "blast"-phemy.

The vineyard's name and wine labels are inspired by and tell the true story of a local church with an unusual past found in the winery region's history. As the story goes, in 1929, an aged church, well into its hundreds, sat abandoned in a neighboring mining camp. The locals, a pious bunch determined not to let it go to waste, decided that they would claim the deserted church as a place for their own worship. Now in those days, a few kilometers was quite a hike, so when these pioneers decided to bring the church home to Okanagan Falls, it would surely have been a large feat. The plan, initiated by Harley Hatfield, was to gently disassemble the church . . . with *dynamite*.

Blowing up a church? Sacrilege. But they didn't see it that way, and steadfastedly, they set off to accomplish their exploit. Using a controlled blast, they loosened the nails and spared the wood from damage that it would have actually undergone using a more "sacred" method. Except for losing the steeple, the plan was a success and the 108-year-old church now rests in its second home in Okanagan Falls.

Of course, when locals were asked whether or not they ever referred to it as the "blasted church," the answer was always a disapproving "no," and the young winery and vineyard in Okanagan Falls knew that it had its name. By naming its vines and wines "Blasted Church," and recounting the unforgettable story, Blasted Church Vineyards celebrates the crafty innovation of its creative local ancestors.

Each of the wine labels includes fun bits of the authentic local nostalgia that tell the story of the holy heist, as well as other factual local follies. For instance, The Dam Flood remembers the region's Campbell Meadows Dam that burst, sending waters 6–10 feet high crashing over the town, farms, and orchards in May 1936. (Harley Hatfield, of church-blasting fame, was part of the initial dam construction just a short time before.) The dam was reconstructed and completed in 1941, but wouldn't you know it, the damn thing burst again in June 1944.

BLASTED CHURCH VINEYARDS

Appellation:	**Okanagan Valley**
Province:	**British Columbia**
Country of Origin:	**Canada**
Type of Wine:	**Merlot and Cabernet Sauvignon Blend**
Web Site:	**www.blastedchurch.com**
Design:	**Brandever**
Designer's Web Site:	**www.brandever.com**
Art:	**Monika Melnychuk**
Artist's Web Site:	**www.drawsattention.com**

BLASTED CHURCH VINEYARDS

Appellation:	**Okanagan Valley**
Province:	**British Columbia**
Country of Origin:	**Canada**
Type of Wine:	**Pinot Noir**
Web Site:	**www.blastedchurch.com**
Design:	**Brandever**
Designer's Web Site:	**www.brandever.com**
Art:	**Monika Melnychuk**
Artist's Web Site:	**www.drawsattention.com**

BLASTED CHURCH VINEYARDS

Appellation:	**Okanagan Valley**
Province:	**British Columbia**
Country of Origin:	**Canada**
Type of Wine:	**White Blend**
Web Site:	**www.blastedchurch.com**
Design:	**Brandever**
Designer's Web Site:	**www.brandever.com**
Art:	**Monika Melnychuk**
Artist's Web Site:	**www.drawsattention.com**

BLASTED CHURCH VINEYARDS

Appellation:	**Okanagan Valley**
Province:	**British Columbia**
Country of Origin:	**Canada**
Type of Wine:	**Lemberger and Merlot Blend**
Web Site:	**www.blastedchurch.com**
Design:	**Brandever**
Designer's Web Site:	**www.brandever.com**
Art:	**Monika Melnychuk**
Artist's Web Site:	**www.drawsattention.com**

When it comes to the subject of wine, you can't help but hear the Mondavi name tossed around, at least once or twice. Few, however, know the story that really got the famed Mondavi family's ball rolling in the wine industry.

In 1906, Cesare Mondavi emigrated from the Marche region of Italy to the United States in search of a new life filled with opportunity. He found himself in Minnesota working in the iron mines while his wife, Rosa, ran a boarding house. When the ambitious young couple saved enough money, they opened a saloon. Prohibition, however, would stunt the growth of their business. Not allowing circumstance to get the better of him, Cesare looked for alternate opportunities, which he found with his local Italian club. Under Prohibition law, each family was authorized to make up to 200 gallons (or four barrels) of "fruit juice" each year. With that in mind, Cesare headed to California on behalf of the local families to investigate and purchase the grapes needed to keep their strong Italian tradition of home winemaking alive, despite unfortunate times. He chose the Lodi area because Zinfandel grapes were known to make good red wine, while also having the advantage of thick skins that allowed easier shipping across the country without spoilage. He chose the covert name "bocce" for the crates' labels after his favorite recreational game.

Eventually, Cesare Mondavi moved his family to the land he had admired for being plentiful and full of sunshine. When Prohibition laws were repealed, he bought a small winery in Napa Valley and started to produce bulk wines. It was here that the Mondavi wine empire began.

This label pays tribute to the Mondavi heritage by the third generation of thriving California Mondavi winemakers, Michael Mondavi, grandson of Cesare. The design of the Bocce wine label is a close replication of the labels used on the wooden grape crates that were instrumental in the family's journey into the wine industry.

BOCCE WINES
(FOLIO FINE WINE PARTNERS)

Appellation:	**Non-Designated Appellation**
State:	**California**
Country of Origin:	**United States**
Type of Wine:	**Pinot Grigio**
Web Site:	**www.boccewines.com**
Art:	**Vintage Label Art**

Bodega Del Río Elorza

[Río Negro ✥ Argentina]

verum

PATAGONIA

PINOT NOIR

ALTO VALLE DEL RIO NEGRO ARGENTINA

2 0 0 7

As the old adage goes, "in wine there's truth," or *in vinum illic est verum*.

In the high valley of Río Negro in Argentina, there are two truths: the region, also identified as the northern edge of Patagonia, is known for its idyllic grape-growing and winemaking setting due to its fertile soils, abundance of sunlight, availability of water, and wide thermal amplitude, and also for the reality of the effects of the liveliness of the region's signature winds.

Known as the "land of the living wind," Río Negro boasts such hyper-blustery airstreams that reality and sensibility are questioned when trees can be seen growing sideways and when birds can be seen flying backwards or surfing on the gusty waves of the wind. It is this visual of the birds in flight carried on the back of the wind that the Del Río Elorza winemaking family chose for its wine label, to express the truth of what's inside the Patagonian Verum—a certainty of the soils, sun, water, and the ever-ubiquitous and influential winds.

BODEGA DEL RÍO ELORZA

Appellation:	**Alto Valle del Río Negro**
Province:	**Río Negro**
Country of Origin:	**Argentina**
Type of Wine:	**Pinot Noir**
Web Site:	**www.delrioelorza.com**
Design:	**Boldrini & Ficcardi**
Designer's Web Site:	**www.bfweb.com.ar**

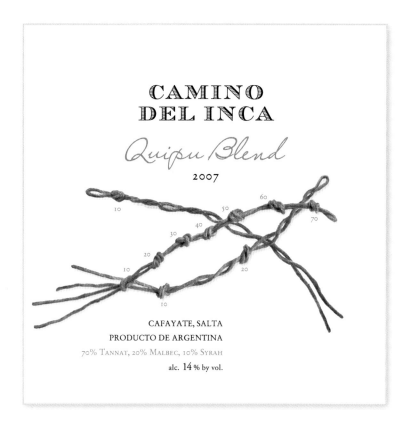

Cafayate, in northwestern Argentina, is considered to be the wine capital of the region. Given its high altitude (approximately 6,000 feet above sea level), arid conditions, close proximity to water sources, perpetual daily sunshine, and highly variable temperature fluctuation in the evening, it has optimal conditions for growing grapes, if nothing else.

The first grapes were planted by the Jesuits in the eighteenth century, but in pre-colonial times, the region was governed predominantly by a large Incan population from the twelfth century to beginning of the sixteenth century, until the conquistadors arrived. Though the region today has a strong Hispanic way of life, the indigenous descendants, such as the Quechua and Aymara peoples, have inherited an Incan influence to their culture and traditions.

One such Incan innovation that is still around today is the Inca *quipu*, otherwise known as "talking knots." True to their name, *quipus* were constructed out of llama or alpaca hair that had been spun into thread and tied into encoded knots. They ranged in number of threads from just a few to two thousand and were used as a recording system for tracking a variety of things that kept the community organized such as labor output, taxes, money exchange, and the calendar. Though it has been said that some of the threads may have been color-coded to offer another layer of recording capability, it is also noted that many of the Incan *quipucamayocs* (*quipu* readers) could read with closed eyes.

While only an estimated six hundred Incan *quipu* have survived, modern *quipu* are still often used for primitive operations or recordings within some of today's Andean communities. Bodegas El Porvenir, located in Cafayate, pays homage to its Incan ancestors and indigenous descendents by recording the varietals that make up its Camino del Inca Quipu red blend through the visual use of a *quipu* on the label.

BODEGAS EL PORVENIR DE LOS ANDES
Appellation:	**Cafayate**
Province:	**Salta**
Country of Origin:	**Argentina**
Type of Wine:	**Tanat, Malbec, and Syrah Blend**
Web Site:	**www.bodegaselporvenir.com**
Design:	**Boldrini & Ficcardi**
Designer's Web Site:	**www.bfweb.com.ar**

BODEGAS YSIOS

[LA RIOJA ❧ SPAIN]

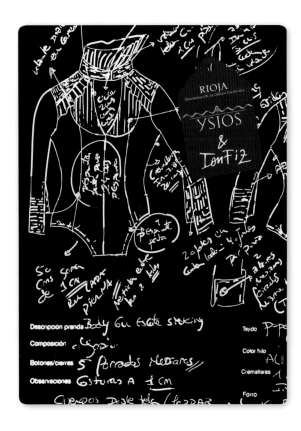

When the owners of Bodegas Ysios met Spanish fashion designer Ion Fiz at a Cook and Fashion event, the thought immediately crossed their minds to use fashion design as a support of the launch of an upcoming wine. Fittingly, the design of the label used a selection of Ion Fiz's sketches from a collection of bras, or *brassiere*, which comes from the French word *brasser*, or "support."

The bra has been documented as early on as the times of ancient Greece, however 1907 was the first mention of the word *brassiere* in an American copy of *Vogue*. Though many designers have tried to claim ownership of designing the first bra, the first patented bra was by Mary Phelps Jacobs in 1914.

For Ion Fiz, who is considered Spain's *enfant terrible de la mode*, "dressing a great wine is as much inspiration as dressing a great woman." On FashionfromSpain.com, it has been indicated that his "design and philosophy are very sophisticated. He wants women to look elegant, though not so much by an appearance of being modern, because you can be modern without having to wear modern clothes. Modernity is all about personality, about being elegant and having the right attitude to life." Likewise, the same can almost be said about wines. In wanting them to be elegant, they need to have the right attitude and be modern, but not so modern that they reject traditional winemaking conventions and style.

A good label shows the content of what it represents, it advances you what you will find when you taste the wine. It is the perfect complement to a good wine. —LUIS ZUDAIRE
Winemaker, Bodegas Ysios

The Bodegas Ysios wine label designed by Ion Fiz suggests that fashion is like winemaking in that it is the design details that count. It's the small particulars that, in fashion, maybe only the designer or seamstress are aware of. In winemaking, it is also often the small nuances that only the winemaker shares between the grapes and the wine while it is being designed that set it apart and make it more beguiling than another. That, and a fashionable wine label, of course.

**BODEGAS YSIOS
(DOMECQ BODEGAS)**
Appellation: **Rioja Alavesa**
Community: **La Rioja**
Country of Origin: **Spain**
Type of Wine: **Tempranillo**
Web Site: **www.bodegasysios.com**
Design: **Ion Fiz**
Designer's Web Site: **www.ionfiz.es**

BONNY DOON VINEYARD

[CALIFORNIA ❧ UNITED STATES]

When approaching anything on the subject of wine, most would say that Randall Grahm is unconventional, from the grapes that he chooses to plant right down to the manner in which he chooses to promote his wines through his very creative wine labels.

Take, for example, the Bonny Doon 2003 Ca' del Solo label, designed by renowned designer Chuck House. While many other winemakers might choose an image immediately associable with Italy in order to bridge the gap between the Old World grape varietal and the New World market, Grahm puts much deeper thought into his outer layer. This label is actually more suggestive of a historical aspect of the varietal, yet is delivered in a more quick-witted (but subtle) manner befitting today's wine drinkers.

At first glance, the Ca' del Solo Sangiovese label tells the story of a little girl creating havoc, reminiscent of well-known literary darlings such as Madeline and Eloise. Upon closer inspection, however, this illustrative situation might be better representative of a "fiasco," rather than just the tomfoolery of a little girl.

Here's the label's subtlety. Anyone who has enjoyed a Sangiovese in its natural habitat (Chianti, Italy), especially some years back, would *beve il fiasco* or "drink from the flask" no matter if one, two, or three bottles were consumed (usually a sign that a fiasco could ensue). Most notably, Chianti wines are housed in iconic round-bottomed bottles and bound by a basket, typically made out of raffia or seaweed dried by the sun. The basket—or, as it is genuinely called in Italian, *il fiasco*—protects the bottle during transportation and also provides a flat base to the bulbous bottles, which prove much easier to produce when hand-blowing the glass. Of course *il fiasco* is most beneficially able to easily keep a wine bottle upright on the table when all other fiascos can catastrophically bring everything else tumbling down.

While many think that labels are simply pretty pictures, Randall Grahm's Bonny Doon labels are obviously exceptionally intelligent, esoterically artful, and always the means of a good conversation.

BONNY DOON VINEYARD

Appellation:	**Monterey**
State:	**California**
Country of Origin:	**United States**
Type of Wine:	**Sangiovese**
Web Site:	**www.bonnydoonvineyard.com**
Design:	**Chuck House (Icon Design Group)**
Designer's Web Site:	**www.icondesigngroup.net**

BORRA VINEYARDS

Stephen Juvenal Borra is a third-generation Lodi winemaker and farmer with roots tracing back over a century to the small Italian village of Carrù in the region of Piedmont.

It was from this village that Giuseppe Manassero set out seeking a fresh life in the New World. Eventually, he found himself in Lodi, California, wanting to build a foundation that was reminiscent of his heritage—a vineyard founded on his homeland's traditions and vine cuttings—which would become the family business.

Soon after, Guiseppe's friend Giovenale Borra would journey toward the dream of a new life as well and settle in Redwood City, where he would open his own store, Joe's Barber Shop. Giovenale's son, however, would not follow in the barber's trade, as he grew to love farming, instead. While honing his love for agriculture, he also met and fell in love with Giuseppe's daughter, Lucille. The two married and soon settled on their own property, raising a family and farming their own vines. Stephen Juvenal Borra—their son, and the grandson of Giovenale Borra—is the current proprietor of Borra Vineyards, along with his wife, Beverly Bowman.

The Borra Vineyards Barbera Fiera del Bue Grasso wine label is a tribute to the Borra family's lineage back to Carrù. An image of the region's iconic Piedmontese bull adorns the label. Originally driven from an area in what today is Pakistan some 25,000 years ago and then left in the mountains, the bulls, through natural selection, became domesticated. In Carrù, the villagers knew that their cattle were something quite special and still take great pride in raising and celebrating them. So exalted are these bulls, that since 1910, on the Thursday before Christmas each year, the villagers still celebrate *Fiera del bue grasso*, or the "Fair of the Fat Bull."

Back in Lodi, the chosen farming for the Borra family was grapes rather than the exalted cattle livestock. Three generations later, the vines are still farmed with pride, devotion, and constant hard work. So much so that each day before dawn, at two thirty in the morning, you'll find Stephen Juvenal Borra out in his vineyards, tending to his prized grapes. Ask Mrs. Borra, she'll tell you—it's no bull.

BORRA VINEYARDS	
Appellation:	**Lodi**
State:	**California**
Country of Origin:	**United States**
Type of Wine:	**Barbera**
Web Site:	**www.borrawinery.com**
Design:	**Curtis Parker Illustration**
Designer's Web Site:	**www.curtisparker.com**

BORRA VINEYARDS	
Appellation:	**Lodi**
State:	**California**
Country of Origin:	**United States**
Type of Wine:	**Merlot**
Web Site:	**www.borrawinery.com**
Design:	**Curtis Parker Illustration**
Designer's Web Site:	**www.curtisparker.com**

BOUTINOT

[LANGUEDOC-ROUSSILLON ❧ FRANCE]

The term "bin" comes from the Old English word *binn* dating back to pre-twelfth century. Defined as "a box, frame, crib, or enclosed place used for storage," the term has come to most commonly be associated with the word "garbage"—a "garbage bin" being a receptacle of rubbish.

In the wine industry, particularly in Australia, however, the term "bin" has become widely used in relation to storing wines in a cellar, with each successive harvest having the same style of wine allocated to the same numbered bin year after year. After time, the systematic consistency of wine storage often saw specific styles of wines being called by their associated bin storage number. Further, wineries have often branded their wines by the bin number, which has led to consumers also recognizing a style of wine by its number.

In the United Kingdom, the term is most commonly associated with the former usage, however they also mark their bins, though with a household number and more so to indicate ownership of the trash receptacle and to curtail having to consistently replace it. Playing on this household habit, Boutinot decided to create cheeky and urban landscapes that played on the juxtaposition of both while sending the not-so-secret message that it thinks that its classic French wines are so damn good that any other Shiraz or Merlot seems really just rubbish by comparison.

To be memorable; to reflect the spirit of the wine; to reassure. These are the elements that a label should bring to the wine. —PAUL BOUTINOT
Owner, Boutinot

BOUTINOT	
Appellation:	**Languedoc-Roussillon**
Region:	**Languedoc-Roussillon**
Country of Origin:	**France**
Type of Wine:	**Shiraz**
Web Site:	**www.boutinot.com**
Design:	**Dare!**
Designer's Web Site:	**www.dare.uk.net**

BOUTINOT	
Appellation:	**Languedoc-Roussillon**
Region:	**Languedoc-Roussillon**
Country of Origin:	**France**
Type of Wine:	**Merlot**
Web Site:	**www.boutinot.com**
Design:	**Dare!**
Designer's Web Site:	**www.dare.uk.net**

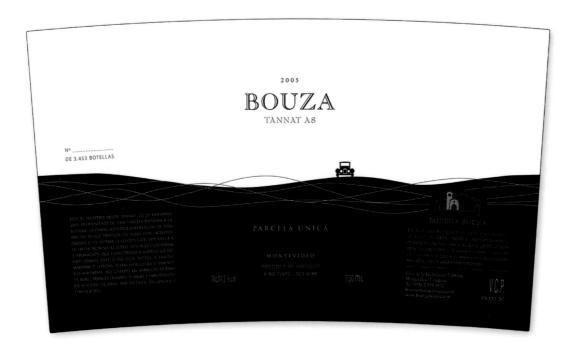

The Bouza family is nostalgic, which is said to be a characteristic demonstrated by many Uruguayans. In fact, in Montevideo (and even in some of the rural interiors), an annual event that is called *Noche de la nostalgia* (or "Nostalgia Night") is celebrated every August 24 on the eve before Uruguay's Independence Day. Particularly with the Bouza family, their nostalgia is more a true sense of tradition and the desire to honor and protect it, especially when it comes to the family's shared passions. Both of their undisputed passions are intertwined together, and stem from a deep respect of things born from nature, as well as things engineered by man. Namely, making wine from the family's vineyards and restoring classic cars of days gone by, respectively.

The objective with both is to maintain that which is original. This means providing the grapes with an adequate enough environment to develop and maintain the characteristics of the vintage and the flavors of their specific terroir. And with the cars, it means restoring the vehicles in a classic sense so they not only appear as they once did, but can be enjoyed through their smooth ride as well.

The wine label and its wine must be in such balance that the label must seduce, while the wine inside should surprise, delight, and conquer.

—ELISA TRABAL DE BOUZA
Owner, Bouza Bodega Boutique

When it comes to wine and classic cars, everyone has their own individual tastes. Just as every palate is different, so are the cars a person gravitates towards. Elisa Trabal de Bouza says that while her personal favorite of the family's restored cars is a 1960s Alfa Romeo Spider, which she feels is a sexy and feminine car and likens it to a Chardonnay or a Merlot, her husband is more partial to his Model Ts, especially the 1936, as they are more masculine and almost bullish like a Tannat wine.

No matter what their individual preferences are, however, the same care and respect goes into making each of their wines, as well as restoring all of their classic cars. The Parcela Unica wine label, with its 1926 Model T (the first car that was restored on the Bouza estate), represents this value of the land, fruit and classic cars of yesteryear. All of the Bouza family's twenty vintage cars run, and visitors to the Uruguayan hills are privy to nostalgic drives through the vineyard, taking a glimpse back to times that were simpler, while making new memories with the Bouza family over a glass of delicious wine.

BOUZA BODEGA BOUTIQUE	
Appellation:	**Melilla**
Department:	**Montevideo**
Country of Origin:	**Uruguay**
Type of Wine:	**Tannat**
Web Site:	**www.bodegabouza.com**
Design:	**Zemma & Ruiz Moreno**
Designer's Web Site:	**www.zrm.com.ar**

Brazin Cellars

In 2006, when the winemaking team at Delicato Family Vineyards tasted the Zinfandel made from the fruit of the Cusamano vineyard, they knew that they had tasted something very special. In fact, it was said to be unlike any of the Zins they'd ever made before.

While the winemaking team was taken aback by this big, bold, and spicy flavor profile, the wines weren't surprised with themselves at all. They say that with age comes wisdom, and the vines of Cusamano vineyard (with all due respect) do have a few years on them. At this age, vines know what they are doing and what to do to achieve it, if the farmers and winemakers work together with them, that is. At Cusamano, the farmers come from a European background and are used to head-trained vines, whereas elsewhere they may not like to let vines grow so freely. If grapevines had a choice, they would rather grow without restraint, without any poking, prodding, or having a steel stake forced upon them. Sounds quite reasonable, doesn't it? There aren't many of us that would actually like a steel rod stuck up where the sun don't shine.

This head-training method lets the vines be who they want to be without any manipulation, and makes them happy, happy, happy. You can tell just how happy they are by their characteristic look.

And happy vines make good wines.

This particular Zinfandel was so happy, the DFV winemaking team said it was dangerously good. That it was defiant. That it was different. In fact it was brazen—or, more appropriately, bra*zin*.

These bush vines are gnarly and old, but "bra*zin*ly" beautiful at the same time. For once, people are urged to judge a vine by its cover.

**BRAZIN CELLARS
(DFV WINES)**

Appellation:	**Lodi**
State:	**California**
Country of Origin:	**United States**
Type of Wine:	**Zinfandel**
Web Site:	**www.brazinwine.com**
Design:	**CF Napa**
Designer's Web Site:	**www.cfnapa.com**

BRIDESMAID WINES

[CALIFORNIA ❧ UNITED STATES]

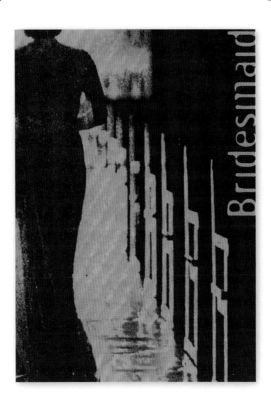

Everyone knows the old idiom, "always a bridesmaid, never a bride," suggests that the role of bridesmaid is one of lowly status compared to that of a bride. In fact, it was a Listerine mouthwash ad that first suggested this scorned bridesmaid stereotype.

Good label design isn't just an ornament for the wine bottle, but should be infused with ritual and story, hinting at what is inside.
—KATHRYN HAVENS
Principal, Kathryn Havens Design

The reality may be, however, that the bridesmaid, though never the center of attention, is always of pinnacle importance in the orchestration of a bride's big day, second only to the maid of honor. Supportive, important, and usually oh-so-available for any task at hand, bridesmaids are a true blend of the multiple personalities required to pull off the intricate details of a successful wedding. Not to mention, they are always good fun.

For Pam Starr and Bridesmaid Wines partner Drew Neiman, this wine is a collection of the best Napa Valley bridesmaids—meant for bridesmaids and not necessarily brides—brought together in a Bordeaux-style blend and squeezed into a broody and mysterious bottle. The label is a reminder that, paired with (or without!) a satin dress never to be worn again, this bridesmaid's duties are done and all that is left is good fun—just what bridesmaids should always be about.

The wine label parallels designer fashion. The outfit draws attention and intrigue by combining color, style, and texture alluring the onlookers to want to know more.
—PAM STARR
Winemaker and Co-Owner,
Bridesmaid Wines

So forget about the Lambert Brothers' Listerine mouthwash ad of 1920s that shunned the bride's right-hand lady. As if! Who needs to be a bride when you can be the life of the party as a perpetual bridesmaid? Bridesmaid Wines certainly supports the cause. The only mouth-washing needed when being a bridesmaid is with a good glass of red or white.

BRIDESMAID WINES

Appellation:	**Napa Valley**
State:	**California**
Country of Origin:	**United States**
Type of Wine:	**Cabernet Sauvignon**
Web Site:	**www.bridesmaidwines.com**
Design:	**Kathryn Havens Design**

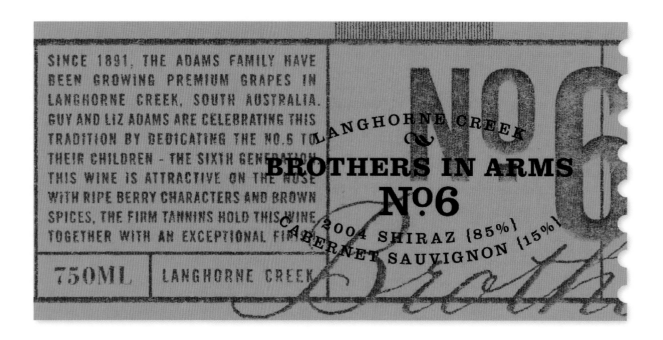

The phrase "brothers in arms" has traditionally referred to soldiers defending a cause by banding together. For the Adams family of Langhorne Creek in South Australia, it is the chosen name for its Metala Estate wines, reflecting 125 years of strength banded together on the property.

Originally, the traditional vines of Cabernet Sauvignon and Shiraz were planted in 1891 by the family's ancestors, meaning that grapes have been farmed at Metala for more than a hundred years. Of the original twenty-one rows of Shiraz planted, 3.9 acres are still growing strong, and of the fourteen rows of Cabernet planted, 2.0 acres are still at it. A further 5.4 acres of Shiraz was planted in 1894—all of which continue to produce high-quality fruit.

Predominantly focused on fruit farming, the Adamses' ancestors were also known to make their own wines. From 1890 until 1910, Arthur Formby, current owner Guy Adams's great-great-grandfather, produced his own wines. Records suggest that the 1903 vintage saw 9,000 gallons of wine produced, second only in the area of Frank Potts in Bleasdale. As of 1910, wine produced from Metala fruit was moved to Stonyfell until 1955. In the 1960s, Guy's father made wine for the family's own enjoyment, stating that he would have to live to 180 years in order to get through all of the wine he'd made simply as a hobby. This hobby was passed down to his son, and in 1998, Guy and Liz got serious with their pastime by releasing their first vintage of Brothers in Arms wines from vines as old as 117 years.

If the value you create is genuine and outstanding, customers will think they have always wanted your product, even if it never existed before. The personality the label conveys is fundamental to creating this value, thereby fulfilling this goal.
—JAMES HALL
General Manager, Sales and Marketing,
Brothers in Arms

The Adams family's Brothers in Arms label pays tribute to the generational band of brothers who have dedicated their lives to the land, the vines, the wines, and commitment to a common goal: the strength of the region. The No. 6 label celebrates Metala's six-generation strong legacy of growers and producers on the homestead.

BROTHERS IN ARMS	
Appellation:	**Langhorne Creek**
State:	**South Australia**
Country of Origin:	**Australia**
Type of Wine:	**Shiraz and Cabernet Sauvignon Blend**
Web Site:	**www.brothersinarms.com.au**
Design:	**Detour Design Studio**
Designer's Web Site:	**www.detourdesign.net.au**

THE BROWN KIDS
[VICTORIA ✤ AUSTRALIA]

Coming from a hundred-year lineage of Brown family winemaking naturally meant that the fourth generation, six young Brown cousins, grew up together amongst the vines in wine country. Charming images of impish and starry-eyed children scampering amongst the vines, dressed to the nines in fancy frocks, and chasing butterflies might come to mind. But for the youngest Brown girls, their adventures were more amusing. Wily tricks—maybe even a little wicked—were played on their solitary male cousin and they say there were definitely no dresses allowed for these vineyard mischief-makers.

There amongst the vines, these cousins grew up and as they did, their bonds as friends grew, too. They vowed that one day, they too would make wine that would represent this special time spent together.

The Brown kids, now kids no more, have made good on their childhood promises. With cousin Nick, now an esteemed winemaker himself, at the helm and the rest of the cousins pulling their weight with the blending and tasting, and blending and tasting (and tasting and tasting), they've let their imaginations run free with wines in their own style that tell the tales of their exceptional holidays spent together: wildly roller-skating in the winery, climbing on top of the tanks playing hide-and-seek, Mum squashing poor Squishy the duck, drunken Wilbur the pig, stealing the yabbies from a hidden bunyip, and Dad turning the smelly wombat white—not your average Little Golden Book tale of the times. And while these grown-up cousins sure clean up well, don't let them fool you with their style and grace. Wise Madame Winkle and Dashing Master Huntley, old friends of those Brown kids from way back, say they still can get up to their same old japes and capers. Now, it's just with a little wine instead of yabbies. 'Tis true, kid you not.

	THE BROWN KIDS
Appellation:	**Heathcote/King Valley**
State:	**Victoria**
Country of Origin:	**Australia**
Type of Wine:	**Tempranillo and Graciano Blend**
Web Site:	**www.kidyounot.com.au**
Design:	**The Hub Group**
Designer's Web Site:	**www.hubgroup.com.au**

	THE BROWN KIDS
Appellation:	**King Valley/Central Victoria**
State:	**Victoria**
Country of Origin:	**Australia**
Type of Wine:	**Rousanne and Viognier Blend**
Web Site:	**www.kidyounot.com.au**
Design:	**The Hub Group**
Designer's Web Site:	**www.hubgroup.com.au**

BULLY HILL VINEYARDS
[New York ❧ United States]

The saying "can't get my goat" has never been more appropriate than in the case of Walter Steven Taylor versus Taylor Wine Company.

The story begins with the Taylor Wine Company, founded by Walter's grandfather and still around today, but not what it once was. After surviving Prohibition, the prolific outfit expanded so rapidly that it required a move from its original site atop Bully Hill. The family sold the original winery and began operations at a new site.

Taylor Wine took a different approach to winemaking in that it used native, American grape varieties that were better known to make great jellies, jams, and juices and, some say, compromised wines. While he followed the patriarchal lineage as the fourth generation to be involved with grape growing and winemaking, Walter was not one to turn a blind eye on his own convictions. Staying true to his winemaking ideals, he publicly criticized—while employed by his family's company—the manner in which Taylor was making its wine. Obviously, this enraged the board of directors. Despite wanting to take immediate action and fire Walter, they weren't able because Walter's own father was the chairman of the board. That is, no action was taken until Walter's dad missed a meeting.

Not one to let adversity get the best of him, Walter proceeded to open his own winery right down the road. He called it Bully Hill, the name of where he lived and produced his wines, but also the name of the original Taylor estate. The first Bully Hill vintage was in 1967, and the label highlighted Walter S. Taylor as the proprietor and purposely threw in an acknowledgment that Bully Hill wine was produced at the original Taylor estate. To add insult to injury, the Taylor board of directors sued Walter for trademark infringement. Of course, Walter did everything but back down. He objected loudly, publicly, and at every opportunity he could, stating that everything on his label was true—after all, he was just using his given name. Were they going to try to take away that as well?

Sure enough, that's exactly what happened when Taylor Wine Company won the lawsuit and Walter was ordered to remove the name "Taylor" from all Bully Hill packaging. Instead of redesigning the labels, however, he merely took black markers and crossed out his surname. When it came time to reprint the labels, he stayed the course and continued to blank the Taylor name out. Of course, this just got him into more trouble, and Taylor Wine Company wasn't about to lose the battle. And lose it the company did not—Walter was forced to change his labels outright. He definitely won in the battle for publicity, though. He went on to stir things up when he personally designed the proprietary Love My Goat label with the conviction "They Got My Heritage, But They Couldn't Get My Goat" underneath and it is this modification of the label that is still around today.

BULLY HILL VINEYARDS

Appellation:	**Finger Lakes**
State:	**New York**
Country of Origin:	**United States**
Type of Wine:	**Red Blend**
Web Site:	**www.bullyhill.com**
Design:	**Walter S. Taylor**

Burnt Spur Martinborough
[Wellington ∾ New Zealand]

During the late nineteenth and early twentieth centuries, New Zealand was abound with "swaggers." The name "swagger" was coined for the nomadic workers who would carry their personal belongings in a bundle or "swag" as they moved around in search of work. Manual labor, such as the clearing of dense vegetal scrub in preparation for planting crops, was one of the most common and highly relied upon jobs for swaggers to pick up.

Of the most famous of these swaggers was a man named Russian Jack. Russian Jack is said to have made his way to New Zealand from Latvia by means of a career in the merchant marine. When the ship that he sailed upon, *The Star of Canada*, capsized off the Gisborne coast in 1912, it is said that he set off on foot towards Wellington to catch another ship. Somewhere along the way, however, the spirit of the land captivated him and his destiny was changed forever. Christened "Russian Jack" likely due to his strong accent, Barret Crumen or Barnis Krumen (as he was formally known) became a familiar swaggie traveling and working between Wairarapa, Manawatu, and Rangitikei, and staying at bivouacs along the way. He is said to have been a well-respected man for his honesty and hard work. Many people were known to stop the familiar figure along his travels to share a quick conversation with the local icon of unusual celebrity status. Although his was a meager existence, the contribution he and the other swaggers made to the cultivation of the land was indeed significant.

When asked why he took to the hard labor and a modest life on the roads of the North Island, Russian Jack is said to have claimed, "Man, oh man, I vos *free*! Free to have a beer, have a smoke—happy what you can call all the time, you know. They was free days." Freedom, it's a simple concept that we all look for and often take for granted after all.

Through the Russian Jack label, Burnt Spur Martinborough celebrates the swaggers of yesteryear, as well as the Russian Jacks of today that play such an important role in shaping the fertile lands. Through their arduous labor, people everywhere reap the fruitful rewards. A glass of good wine at the end of a day with good friends is always a liberating experience.

BURNT SPUR MARTINBOROUGH	
Appellation:	**Martinborough**
Region:	**Wellington**
Country of Origin:	**New Zealand**
Type of Wine:	**Pinot Noir**
Web Site:	**www.burntspur.co.nz**
Design:	**Bang**
Art:	**Scott Kennedy**

BUSH BIKE

[WESTERN AUSTRALIA ✤ AUSTRALIA]

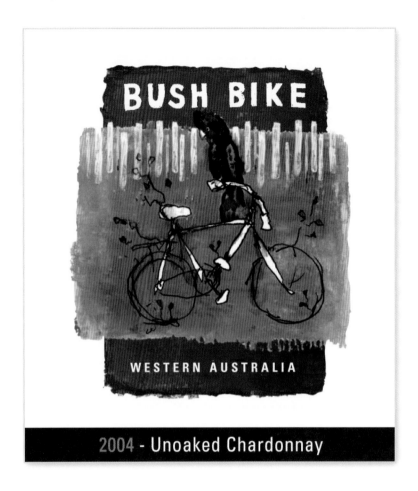

*M*unda biddi is a Noongar phrase that means "a path through a forest." The Munda Biddi Trail is just that, albeit a 560-mile path that passes through some of Australia's most remote and enchanted forests and bushland. Starting on the west coast at Mundaring, on the outskirts of Perth, the winding trail allows cyclists to travel amongst unspoiled nature all the way to the township of Albany on the southwestern coast.

Besides its awesome scenery, the trail is said to be famous for a few other things, one being the occasional sighting of the loud, but wildly exquisite and rare, red-tailed black cockatoo. More frequently seen would be the string of abandoned bikes that spent riders have left behind in their ultimate effort to ease the strain by literally ditching their bikes.

The grapes for Bush Bike wines have been sourced from vineyards close to the splendor of the Munda Biddi Trail. Conquest Beverage Group's Bush Bike wine label promotes enthusiasm for the outdoors and encourages people to get out and enjoy the surroundings we are blessed with—and maybe to try and catch a sight of the famed red-tailed black cockatoo at least once. If not, the trail of abandoned bikes amidst the splendor of the surroundings is certainly memorable, too.

BUSH BIKE	
(CONQUEST BEVERAGE GROUP)	
Appellation:	**Non-Designated Appellation**
State:	**Western Australia**
Country of Origin:	**Australia**
Type of Wine:	**Chardonnay**
Design:	**Braincells**
Designer's Web Site:	**www.braincells.com.au**

CAFÉ CULTURE

[WESTERN CAPE ❧ SOUTH AFRICA]

From the French word for coffeehouse, cafés have become part of an international vernacular understood worldwide. These coffee-serving establishments have been around since the fifteenth century and began as gentlemen's gathering places to drink coffee, listen to music, read, play chess, and listen to recitations of poetic or literary works. As times evolved, coffeehouses inseminated into all corners of the globe as social gathering spots, making their first appearances outside the Ottoman Empire in Europe during the seventeenth century, and continued to gain mass popularity far and wide.

From a cultural standpoint, coffeehouses became a congregational spot for idea, information, and philosophy exchange. (Café Procope in Paris was a popular gathering point for the French Enlightenment, was frequented by Voltaire, Rousseau, and Diderot, and is suggested to be the birthplace of the first modern encyclopedia, *Encyclopédie*.) They are also further identified as places of business, news exchange, performance, creative collaboration, and just plain chitchat.

Today's international café culture is an evolution of this historic café heritage, steeped in information exchange, the gathering of thinkers, leaders, free spirits, trendsetters, eccentrics, academics, artists, and those who often enjoy a little debate and banter in a socially spirited setting.

KWV's Café Culture wine celebrates the gathering together of vibrant people and is inspired particularly by the unique and intrinsic toasted mocha flavor profile of this distinct South African Pinotage. It is a wine of distinction that, in true café culture form, is guaranteed to get people talking. Soap box, please.

CAFÉ CULTURE (KWV)	
Appellation:	**Non-Designated Appellation**
Province:	**Western Cape**
County of Origin:	**South Africa**
Type of Wine:	**Pinotage**
Web Site:	**www.cafeculturewines.com**
Design:	**Herdbuoys éKapa**
Designer's Web Site:	**www.herdbuoys.com**

CANONBAH BRIDGE WINES
[NEW SOUTH WALES ❧ AUSTRALIA]

Long before there was a vineyard, there were sheep. And before there were sheep, there was a town that was deserted. And before there was a town that had been deserted, there was a town. And long before there was a town that became deserted that bordered a sheep station that now has a vineyard planted on it, there was a bend in a river. That was two thousand years ago, and this means that Canonbah Bridge Wines has effectively been two millennia in the making.

In the 1880s, Shane McLaughlin's great-grandfather arrived in the Warren district of New South Wales, Australia, from Ireland. Having a gut feeling that the land was special, he marked the property to grow wheat. As it turns out, the McLaughlins didn't end up being famous farmers of wheat as intended. Rather, it was the farming of their Australian Merino wool on a 30,000-acre sheep station in Merryanbone.

Shane's great-grandfather wasn't wrong in thinking that the land was special, though. When Shane brought in a soil expert to evaluate the land, having his own speculations that the soil was prime for planting, the expert chose the exact same parcel that his great-grandfather had selected over a hundred years previously. These 80 acres of virgin soil are now the McLaughlin family's vineyard, named after the historic town of Canonbah that once bordered the farm of old. In the early 1900s, the town was deserted and all that is left today is the old Canonbah Bridge. While the current generation of McLaughlins is responsible for pioneering this new wine region, they still continue to farm approximately ten thousand Merino sheep that roam freely amongst the vines, aiding with natural pruning to keep the yields low.

Given the leap of faith Shane McLaughlin and his family took from wool to wine, their beloved Merino sheep grace their premium range of wine labels, leaping over the only piece of history still standing where the town once thrived: the Canonbah Bridge.

I believe a wine label has an obligation to relay the vineyard and winemaker's character and story.
—SHANE MCLAUGHLIN
Principal, Canonbah Bridge Wines

CANONBAH BRIDGE WINES
Appellation:	**Western Plains**
State:	**New South Wales**
Country of Origin:	**Australia**
Type of Wine:	**Shiraz**
Web Site:	**www.canonbah.com.au**
Design:	**Ian Kidd Design**
	(now KS Design Studio)
Designer's Web Site:	**www.ksdesign.com.au**

There is an artistry to winemaking that extends to its packaging. What I make, people consume; it's an act of intimacy, like music. How much closer can you get to someone? Contemporary winemakers must be able to convey that artistry and intimacy amid a massive sea of competition.
—CHARLES SMITH
Owner and Winemaker,
K Vintners and Charles Smith Wines

Charles Smith knows what he likes in a girl—fundamentally stable, secure with a cool edginess, pretty, of course, and with the ability to deliver a knee-buckling kiss like the girl next door. Of course, this is no ordinary girl.

Rather, she's a sweetheart that integrates the polarity of a razor's edge together with a round and feminine innocence. While Smith says that girls do kick ass, it is the balanced divergence of his Riesling's characteristics that has this wine named Kung Fu Girl.

Inspired by ancient Chinese martial arts, kung fu encompasses broad fighting styles, but is rooted in a combination of balance, stability, harmony, and strength. Add a female kung fu artist with flare into the mix, and you have the perfect fierce but feminine character for a Riesling with a totally ass-kicking label.

CHARLES SMITH WINES

Appellation:	**Columbia Valley**
State:	**Washington**
Country of Origin:	**United States**
Type of Wine:	**Riesling**
Web Site:	**www.charlessmithwines.com**
Design:	**The Korff Kounsil**
Designer's Web Site:	**www.thekounsil.com**

Château d'Esclans

[Provence-Alpes-Côte d'Azur ❧ France]

Château d'Esclans is inspired by the very magical backdrop of winemaker Sacha Alexis Lichine's châteaux situated amidst the rolling hills and forests of Provence, France. Having almost a mystical aura to the area, Mr. Lichine says that he once had a very surreal experience when he witnessed a deer on the cusp of the forest just as the sun was setting. It was a fantastic moment that conjured images of beauty and strength that were almost ethereal in nature.

It was from this enchanted moment that there emerged a natural association with Lichine's premium wine—from heavenly lands and with the gentle persuasion of a celestial mother of the earth, this magical wine was possible. And what better patron for Lichine's wine than Diana, watcher of the woodlands and wild animals, mother of the earth and goddess of the moon? Like the deer, as well as the wine inside the bottle, the goddess Diana is known for her strength, while remaining a distinctly beautiful figure. She is often referenced visually alongside a deer, just as the Déesse label reveals, and at second glance, a trinity binding the regional spirit of nature through Diana and the antlers of the deer emerging into vines of the earth is unveiled to truly represent the wine inside the bottle.

CHÂTEAU D'ESCLANS (DOMAINE SACHA LICHINE)	
Appellation:	**Côtes de Provence**
Region:	**Provence-Alpes-Côte d'Azur**
Country of Origin:	**France**
Type of Wine:	**Grenache and Syrah Blend**
Web Site:	**www.chateaudesclans.com**
Design:	**Design Bridge**
Designer's Web Site:	**www.designbridge.com**

CHÂTEAU MONTELENA WINERY
[CALIFORNIA ❧ UNITED STATES]

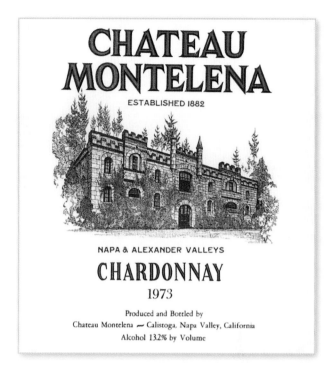

Not much has changed on the Château Montelena wine label over the past thirty-seven years from the first vintage of the estate until today—and that's the way it's meant to be. It's not because the company isn't open to change or is complacent, but rather because the label signifies everything that Château Montelena has been built on—quite literally.

The legacy began in 1882 when entrepreneur Alfred L. Tubbs purchased 254 acres of land at the base of Mount Saint Helena. His vision: to build an estate vineyard and winery that would emulate the quality- and terroir-driven winemaking philosophy of the finest, most celebrated French châteaux. He planted his cuttings from some of the most distinguished European vineyards; imported a French-born and -trained winemaker; built a château—which met the defined requirements of being both a "feudal castle" and "a vineyard estate"—and named it Château Montelena (a contraction of "Mount Saint Helena"), where the vineyard and winery sat at the base of the mountain. The estate thrived until Prohibition, but when it was repealed, the Tubbs family continued to make wine until the property was sold in 1958.

In my experience, the promise of a label is best fulfilled by the wine in the bottle, and the true value of that relationship is determined by whether they buy you a second time.
—JEFF ADAMS
Marketing Director,
Château Montelena Winery

It wasn't until the era of James Barrett that Château Montelena witnessed its renewed renaissance. Under his leadership, the existing vineyard was cleared and replanted with the highest-quality grapes in the valley and upgraded with a modernized facility for his top winemaking and vineyard management team. In 1972, Château Montelena saw its first vintage under Barrett's direction. Four years later, the winery would be on the forefront of the industry when it would pit its 1973 California Chardonnay against the four white Burgundies at the famed Paris tasting that took the world by storm and went down in history.

When the tasting scores were calculated, the French judges assumed that, as usual, it would be the French wines at the helm. However, shockingly, they hadn't chosen one of their own, but rather Château Montelena's Chardonnay and this victory—one of the largest and most famous in wine industry history—truly catapulted Château Montelena and, subsequently, Californian wines onto the international wine stage.

Remaining steadfast with its wine label is a symbol of what Château Montelena represents: America's first grand-cru-caliber château—a working winery built on the premise of making first-class, terroir-driven wines of an Old World-style, but in a New World location. And since this is still its motivation today, why change anything?

CHÂTEAU MONTELENA WINERY
Appellation: **Napa Valley/Alexander Valley**
State: **California**
Country of Origin: **United States**
Type of Wine: **Chardonnay**
Web Site: **www.montelena.com**
Design: **Jeffrey Caldewey (Icon Design Group) and Sebastian Titus**
Designer's Web Site: **www.icondesigngroup.net**

CHERUBINO WINES

[WESTERN AUSTRALIA ✤ AUSTRALIA]

From the Latin phrase meaning "for this purpose," the idiom *ad hoc* is the perfect name for Larry Cherubino's range of the classic Western Australian wines. While the wines are thoughtful interpretations of well-ingrained varietals of Western Australia, his idea to produce them was more "off the cuff" and, in turn, he chose an impromptu name irreverently specific to each blend:

Wallflower, because beauty needn't always be boastful or boisterous. At times, being shy, delicate, and restrained speaks volumes louder, much like his Riesling.

Middle of Everywhere, because though some think that Frankland River is in the middle of nowhere, if you're looking for great Shiraz, Frankland River is at its epicenter—the middle of everywhere.

Etcetera . . ., because when passing by a shop in Melbourne selling gifts, cards, books, trinkets, odds and ends, *etcetera*, Larry thought immediately of his blend of Margaret River Cabernet Sauvignon, Shiraz, and all the other bits and bobs, and knew that the name "Etcetera" would do just fine.

Treehugger, because this Chardonnay hasn't killed any trees in the process by remaining unoaked.

And finally, Hens and Chickens, not just because it's cute, but because of something in the wine world called "millerandage," when grape bunches include berries of different sizes or maturity levels, and have different flavors. Hens and chickens. If you thought it was about the food match, you could be right as well.

While perhaps Larry's choices of names for his wines might have been made spontaneously, his wine label design is completely *ad hoc* and perfect for these very specific wines.

CHERUBINO WINES

Appellation:	**Pemberton**
State:	**Western Australia**
Country of Origin:	**Australia**
Type of Wine:	**Chardonnay**
Web Site:	**www.larrycherubino.com.au**
Design:	**Fusebox Design**
Designer's Web Site:	**www.fusedesign.com.au**

AD HOC

2007 RIESLING
Western Australia

CHERUBINO WINES

Appellation:	**Mount Barker**
State:	**Western Australia**
Country of Origin:	**Australia**
Type of Wine:	**Riesling**
Web Site:	**www.larrycherubino.com.au**
Design:	**Fusebox Design**
Designer's Web Site:	**www.fusedesign.com.au**

AD HOC

2006 SHIRAZ
Western Australia

CHERUBINO WINES

Appellation:	**Frankland River**
State:	**Western Australia**
Country of Origin:	**Australia**
Type of Wine:	**Shiraz**
Web Site:	**www.larrycherubino.com.au**
Design:	**Fusebox Design**
Designer's Web Site:	**www.fusedesign.com.au**

AD HOC

Etc..........................
....
....
....
....
....
....
....
....
....
....

2007 CABERNET SHIRAZ BLEND
Western Australia

CHERUBINO WINES

Appellation:	**Margaret River**
State:	**Western Australia**
Country of Origin:	**Australia**
Type of Wine:	**Cabernet Sauvignon and Shiraz Blend**
Web Site:	**www.larrycherubino.com.au**
Design:	**Fusebox Design**
Designer's Web Site:	**www.fusedesign.com.au**

AD HOC

2008 CHARDONNAY
Western Australia

CHERUBINO WINES

Appellation:	**Pemberton**
State:	**Western Australia**
Country of Origin:	**Australia**
Type of Wine:	**Chardonnay**
Web Site:	**www.larrycherubino.com.au**
Design:	**Fusebox Design**
Designer's Web Site:	**www.fusedesign.com.au**

CHRONIC CELLARS

[CALIFORNIA & UNITED STATES]

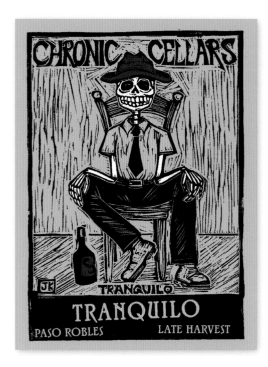

Chronic Cellars was made a reality by two Generation X brothers: one who loved riding waves, the other who was more partial to riding motorcycles, and both who grew up passionate about grapes, having spent their lives working in the family's wine business. Frustrated with the lack of wines that were being made specifically for a new generation of wine consumers, the two had often talked about creating one to fit the bill. This meant not dumbing the wine down, but making it relaxed, approachable, and just good fun.

After a decisive decade spent seriously immersed in every aspect of the industry, the brothers began a joint journey to make their statement within the wine industry. To any non-Gen-Xer, "chronic" will have somewhat of a different definition than what it means to this younger demographic. In this case, "chronic" refers to today's urban definition, meaning "exceptionally likeable," "best of breed," or "as good as it gets." Setting out to make chronically good wines, the brothers aptly chose to call this endeavor "Chronic Cellars."

What's with the Day of the Dead-themed labels? Wanting to study something that didn't involve grapes in college, Jake (one half of Chronic Cellars) gravitated to anthropology. Eventually, he moved to Costa Rica to study pyramids and indigenous peoples. He's traveled the world studying ancient people and has the masks he's picked up along the way to prove it. Coincidentally, the brothers' mutual friend Joe Kalionzes, a fabulous artist, is also greatly inspired by South American influences. When asked to interpret Chronic Cellars, the result was art carved into blocks of wood to produce organic, handprinted wine labels. Sofa king bueno; that's how good this chronic is.

Chronic Cellars makes wines that are unorthodox and fun. We feel that our wine labels, as a reflection of our wines, should be the same.

—JAKE BECKETT
Owner and General Manager,
Chronic Cellars

CHRONIC CELLARS
Appellation: **Paso Robles**
State: **California**
Country of Origin: **United States**
Type of Wine: **Syrah, Grenache, and Petite Sirah Blend**
Web Site: **www.chroniccellars.com**
Art: **Joe Kalionzes**

CHRONIC CELLARS
Appellation: **Paso Robles**
State: **California**
Country of Origin: **United States**
Type of Wine: **Petite Sirah**
Web Site: **www.chroniccellars.com**
Art: **Joe Kalionzes**

CHURCHILL GRAHAM

[PORTO ❧ PORTUGAL]

Modern science has taught us, with reason, that the closer you get to something, the better you are able to see it, to understand it. The details capable of being viewed under the lens of a microscope or through a macro-lensed camera are truly magnificent. However, there are instances when the view from afar actually provides us with the most intimate perspective.

By using aerial photographs, this label has the ability to provide a perspective that actually brings us closer to the majesty of the Douro region in Portugal, something likely less achievable through an up-close analysis. Due to the region's diversity between peaks and valleys and river and land, the imagery actually invokes an immediate association with organic veins of a leaf, symbolic of the vines that are so much a part of the people who live there, and ultimately what is inside the Churchill's bottles.

The Douro region is considered a remarkable feat of nature and an example of man's ability to adapt to a tremendous terrain. The Portuguese were onto something when they demarcated the area in 1756 and almost 250 years later, in 2001, the region was officially designated a World Heritage Site by UNESCO and said to be "the most incredible masterpiece of human labor, equal to the pyramids of Egypt, the Great Wall of China, and the Gothic cathedrals of Europe."

It is the relationship between the land and the people that has enabled the creation of such unnatural splendor. Natural elements caused physical constraints due to narrow valleys, steep slopes, and the river, which led to the need to create conditions favorable for sustainment—hence the production of wine and cultivation of other crops. According to the UNESCO World Heritage Center, the region is "an expression of people's courage and creative genius in understanding the cycles of water and the materials, and of their intense, and almost passionate, attachment to the vine." Further, the region has been called "a collective work of land art." It is this complex and creative mosaic of natural and man-made features that gives the Douro region its spectacular character—viewed most dramatically, impressively, and with an unexpected intimacy from far above and captured on Churchill's wine labels.

CHURCHILL GRAHAM

Appellation:	**Douro**
District:	**Porto**
Country of Origin:	**Portugal**
Type of Wine:	**Red Blend**
Web Site:	**www.churchills-port.com**
Design:	**Interbrand**
Designer's Web Site:	**www.brandchannel.com**

CLOOF WINE ESTATE
[WESTERN CAPE ❧ SOUTH AFRICA]

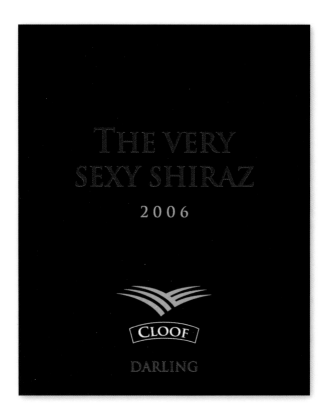

Though the good people at Cloof Wine Estate in Darling, South Africa, don't make a habit of training the palates of their children at an exorbitantly young age, like any line of work, business does tend to waft home with them every once and a while. It even inconspicuously makes its way into children's coveted "story time," somehow.

This is exactly what happened when a very particular Shiraz was found continually on the mind of Oscar Foulkes of Cloof. One evening, while reading a popular children's book by celebrated author Eric Carle to his young child, and with said Shiraz hovering inconspicuously in the back of his mind, an idea instantly came to mind. Carle's most famous book, *The Very Hungry Caterpillar*, has sold millions of copies and is based on an easy and straightforward story that teaches children to recognize the days of the week, how to count to five and, of course, how the caterpillar eats its way through the life cycle to become a butterfly. Translated into forty-seven languages, the message is clear and simple—just what Foulkes was looking for in naming Cloof's new Shiraz.

They could have called it something that absolutely said nothing about this particular wine; something to do with a paddock, a creek, or a meadow. But instead, Foulkes chose to be inspired by and follow Carle's ingenuity by just spelling it out, explaining exactly what was in the bottle: a very sexy Shiraz.

And if the legs on this Shiraz are anything like the legs on Carle's caterpillar that made its way into millions of homes, Cloof's Very Sexy Shiraz is going to be teaching quite a few people about just what happens when you get your hands on and work your way through a cycle of this very sexy Shiraz.

The brand is everything. Not only are you, as wine marketer, vying for the consumer's attention on retail shelves, you are also trying to ensure that the consumer will actually remember your product. The label speaks on your behalf in thousands of locations around the globe. —OSCAR FOULKES
Wine Marketer, Cloof Wine Estate

CLOOF WINE ESTATE

Appellation:	**Darling**
Province:	**Western Cape**
Country of Origin:	**South Africa**
Type of Wine:	**Shiraz**
Web Site:	**www.cloof.co.za**
Design:	**Eleven Creative Team**
Designer's Web Site:	**www.elevenct.co.za**

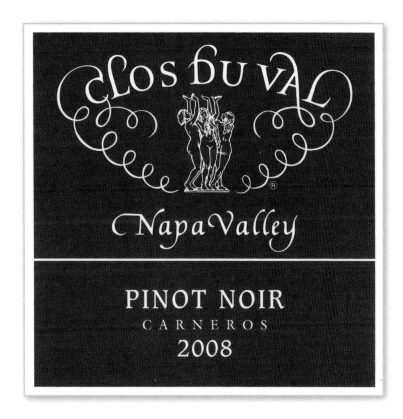

The Clos Du Val winery certainly knows what it takes to host a great gathering. Particularly, it always ensures that Joy, Mirth, and Splendor are around. In fact, this little party-planning trio has had the winery entertaining like Caesar himself since 1972, when Napa Valley owner and pioneer producer John Goelet founded Clos Du Val.

Mr. Goelet, a keen art academic and collector, commissioned a graphic interpretation of a fifteenth-century gilt statue he felt represented the central theme of his wines. Known as "the Three Graces" in Greek mythology, these were the "it girls" of Mount Olympus—goddesses of charm, beauty, human creativity, and fertility. As in Mr. Goelet's statue, which now resides in a permanent collection at the Museum of Fine Arts in Boston, the divine daughters of Zeus (who are most often displayed in celebration with the arms outstretched and wearing their birthday suits, no matter whose birthday it is) have been depicted by a long list of famed artists across a variety of movements including Sandro Botticelli (Early Renaissance), Paul Cezanne (Post-Impressionism), and Raphael (High Renaissance).

Of course, who in their right mind would question capturing the spirit of goddesses responsible for keeping the glasses filled and good times rolling? Clos Du Val certainly hasn't, as indicated on every one of its wine labels.

CLOS DU VAL

Appellation:	**Carneros**
State:	**California**
Country of Origin:	**United States**
Type of Wine:	**Pinot Noir**
Web Site:	**www.closduval.com**
Design:	**John Goelet and Leo Wyatt**

CONO SUR VINEYARDS & WINERY
[O'HIGGINS ✒ CHILE]

On any given day at Cono Sur Vineyards and Winery, approximately eighty employees arrive to work at the vineyards by bike. This isn't because there is a shortage of available cars or alternate transport, but because the bicycle is the preferred means of transportation for many Chileans. Not only that, but it is the chosen means of getting from one point to another in the vineyards. There is no missing the multitude of bikes that are intermittently propped up against the walls and ends of vine rows. Bikes are everywhere. They protect the prized possession of the land that the workers so carefully and affectionately tend to, and they also offer the opportunity to enjoy a relaxing and civilized journey from one place to the next. By using a different bicycle illustration for each wine range, the visuals are each intended to bear an individual message.

On the flagship Cono Sur range, the bicycle represents the company's persistent spirit to always seek out the latest techniques both in the vineyard and the winery that ensure respect for the land and the wine that it produces. On the Organic range, the bicycle on the label pays homage to every Cono Sur worker who rides their bike to and from work every day. The employees take great pride in and are devoted to their work—this dedication is what makes Cono Sur able to fulfill its ultimate commitment of creating top-quality wines while utilizing a clean action plan to protect the environment. The label on the Reserva range *(not pictured)* acts as a lifestyle statement suggesting that the wines are viewed as essential, relaxed, and joyful—the same simple sensations that are felt after a pleasant ride through the Cono Sur vineyards and what the team refers to as getting back to "bicycle basics." After all, it's not only the destination, but also the journey and experience in getting there, that is memorable and that matters.

The Cono Sur Pinot Noir label carries the bicycle as its main icon. It symbolizes Cono Sur's spirit of innovation, passion, commitment, and respect for the environment, as well as its persistence in always finding the latest winemaking techniques in order to take care of the land where the grapes grow.

—BARBARA LE-BERT
Brand Manager,
Cono Sur Vineyards & Winery

CONO SUR VINEYARDS & WINERY	
Appellation:	**Colchagua Valley**
Region:	**O'Higgins**
Country of Origin:	**Chile**
Type of Wine:	**Pinot Noir**
Web Site:	**www.conosur.com**
Design:	**Internal**

CONO SUR VINEYARDS & WINERY	
Appellation:	**Central Valley**
Region:	**O'Higgins**
Country of Origin:	**Chile**
Type of Wine:	**Pinot Noir**
Web Site:	**www.conosur.com**
Design:	**Internal**

THE COST VINEYARD

[OREGON ❧ UNITED STATES]

The Cost family doesn't come from a century of grape farmers or winemakers; it also doesn't have a history in the newspaper industry as the labels may allude to. In fact, the family doesn't particularly like reading the paper religiously (although they all are quite fond of magazines such as the *New Yorker*). And on its Web site, The Cost Vineyard claims to have no real news to report. But while it alleges to have nothing headline worthy, it seems to be doing a pretty good job writing its own wine story nonetheless.

Here's the scoop: The Cost Vineyard is owned and worked by none other than the Cost family themselves. They planted their sustainable Pinot Noir vineyard in 1999 and have tended their own vines to ensure that they kept ultimate control over the quality of fruit that goes into their wines. And maybe this doesn't seem all that newsworthy, but the care and passion this family has for the fruit that represents their unique terroir and microclimate is. After all, as Greg Cost says, "Great wine is never in absence of great fruit." This is true. And news to some.

So maybe the Costs are still under the radar because they don't look for a lot of press. But watch this space. Right now, they may be on the down low, writing their own story, but pretty soon these wines are going to be stirring up a lot of noise, just as their newsworthy labels suggest.

THE COST VINEYARD	
Appellation:	**Willamette Valley**
State:	**Oregon**
Country of Origin:	**United States**
Type of Wine:	**Pinot Noir**
Web Site:	**www.thecostvineyard.com**
Design:	**Sandstrom Design**
Designer's Web Site:	**www.sandstromdesign.com**

THE COST VINEYARD	
Appellation:	**Willamette Valley**
State:	**Oregon**
Country of Origin:	**United States**
Type of Wine:	**Pinot Noir**
Web Site:	**www.thecostvineyard.com**
Design:	**Sandstrom Design**
Designer's Web Site:	**www.sandstromdesign.com**

THE COST VINEYARD	
Appellation:	**Willamette Valley**
State:	**Oregon**
Country of Origin:	**United States**
Type of Wine:	**Pinot Noir**
Web Site:	**www.thecostvineyard.com**
Design:	**Sandstrom Design**
Designer's Web Site:	**www.sandstromdesign.com**

CUMULUS WINES

[NEW SOUTH WALES ❧ AUSTRALIA]

Science class has taught us that with a name like Cumulus, you know that your destination has to be somewhere up in the clouds—but certainly not what would be imagined as a typical location for planting a vineyard. At least, not one without its unforeseen challenges. But growing grapes in climates of high altitude certainly has its advantages—most notably bright, vibrant fruit with intense flavor—which is the best starting point for any winemaking endeavor. Given that the district of Orange in New South Wales boasts the highest and coolest wine regions in Australia, Cumulus Wines certainly has its share of advantages . . . after getting used to the overall climb, that is.

So, Cumulus wines crafted from the grapes sourced at such great heights have been called "Climbing." Not only meant as a testament to their geography, the name also acts as a metaphorical reflection on the great heights of challenge and adventure met in a region characterized by extreme peaks of the extinct volcano, Mount Canobolas. These wines toast their own pursuits, as well as applaud the personal challenges accomplished by others. No matter what the pleasure or achievement, you can always find a blend of nerves and excitement similar to that of taking the blind and fearful leap off a high dive. Hence, the choice of imagery for the Climbing wine label.

Cumulus's vineyard covers so much ground and altitude that it actually crosses two distinct geographic indicators. At up to 2,050 feet, it is designated as in the Orange district, where the grapes are sourced for the Climbing wines. Below that, it falls into the Central Ranges. The grapes for the Rolling wines *(not pictured)* have all been sourced from these lower, though still ambitious (1,870 feet and under) foothills that meander over a thousand acres. The wines pay tribute to the cottony clouds that grace the amazing sunny-sloped site of the vineyards surrounding the town of Orange, and the pride of people that love their land and the lulling rhythm of their rural lifestyle.

CUMULUS WINES	
Appellation:	**Orange**
State:	**New South Wales**
Country of Origin:	**Australia**
Type of Wine:	**Merlot**
Web Site:	**www.cumuluswines.com.au**
Design:	**Emma Griffin (Panel Pop) and Square Circle Triangle**
Designer's Web Site:	**www.panelpop.com and www.sct.com.au**
Art:	**James Ratsasane**
Artist's Web Site:	**www.jamesratsasane.com**

CYCLES GLADIATOR

[CALIFORNIA ❧ UNITED STATES]

Years ago, when William Leigon first saw a 1895 French poster created by G. Massias promoting the Gladiator bicycle, it immediately stuck in the back of his mind as a visually compelling piece of artifact. Not just visually compelling, the poster of the uninhibited French woman riding her *bicyclette velocipede* represented a freedom and lust for life during the magical Belle Époque period. This era was a time when arts and science were at a forefront and perpetuated a sense of renewed times and desire for change. It was during this period that the bicycle, with its modern reengineering, witnessed its golden era by providing the first means of democratic transportation. This accessibility to transportation greatly impacted an individual's freedom of movement and independence—for both men and women.

Gone were the days of petticoats and corsets. Instead, a new, less-conservative style of pantaloons and trousers emerged that provided women with optimal dexterity to take advantage of their newfound freedom on wheels. It was a period of hopefulness and *joie de vivre* witnessed across all social classes.

Similarly, a century later during the last two decades of the twentieth century, it can be said that amidst continuous cycles of change, a comparable evolution occurred in the wine industry—traditions evolved; new ideologies, production methods, and modern advancements in viticulture emerged; and media attention on the benefits of moderate wine consumption as part of a healthy lifestyle was promoted. Further, changes initiated from within the industry led to the greater education of and accessibility to wine for the mass consumer, and not solely an affluent population. In a sense, wine saw a democratization allowing for an approachability that had not been seen as evidently before.

Cycles Gladiator represents movement, cycles of time, nature and, ultimately, change that allow fundamental evolution to occur. Further, winemaker Paul Clifton, in keeping with a spirit of open-mindedness, leads a team of young, physically and socially active individuals in the winery. And a wine label with a bicycle made in the 1890s ridden by a naked French woman—that certainly fits the team's spirit.

**CYCLES GLADIATOR
(HAHN FAMILY WINES)**

Appellation:	**Central Coast**
State:	**California**
Country of Origin:	**United States**
Type of Wine:	**Syrah**
Web Site:	**www.cyclesgladiator.com**
Design:	**CF Napa**
Designer's Web Site:	**www.cfnapa.com**
Art:	**G. Massias**

DADA WINES

[HAWKE'S BAY ❧ NEW ZEALAND]

Dada Wines is a small project between business and life partners Kate Galloway and David Ramonteu. David, having grown up in a farming community in southern France, witnessed the unwavering restrictions of winemaking in the Old World firsthand. He first met Kate in 2000 in New Zealand and eventually moved there permanently so the two could plant some roots together. It was thought that being in the New World, New Zealand would provide a more lenient creative space to produce wines in the style that they wanted, but this hope was soon crushed when the realities of being a small producer competing in a large producer's world set in. Winemaking rules still had to be adhered to, and often, far-reaching wine "propaganda" dictated which wines were deemed the best to drink.

Instead of conforming, David and Kate remained steadfast with determination to try something different, to forge their own path and create wines that were true to themselves and their principals: wines made based on the freedom to be fresh, creative, and unique. They wanted people to drink their wines because they liked the taste, not because of a preconceived notion of what the wine would taste like or because someone deemed authoritative said they should like it.

As such, the labels offer very little information of what is inside the bottle from a varietal or the traditions of regional blend perspective. Rather, by using the name "Dada" David and Kate reference the popular movement found in art and literature that is based deliberately on the negation of traditional artistic values. If others zig, Dada, honoring the early twentieth-century anti-cultural and anti-war movement, zags. "Dada" was apparently originally conceived at random by a group of artists by inserting a piece of paper into the French dictionary and choosing the word it landed on—which was *dada*, meaning "hobbyhorse" or "child's toy." There is also a French colloquialism, "*c'est mon dada*," which simply means "it is my hobby." The premise of Dada is almost a Taoist approach to art—the "way" can be any "way."

At a small company like Dada, you give all of yourself in the creation of the wine, so it follows that the label reflects who you are and what you want people to know of you. It is very intimate. The design will always be captivating if it radiates the true essence of the people behind it and is not purely market-driven.

—DAVID RAMONTEU
Owner and Winemaker, Dada Wines

The Dada movement witnessed a resurgence in the '60s possibly due to a large Dada retrospect held in Paris in 1967. At the time, a seventeen-year-old David, living in France, was heavily influenced by the movement that he has carried with him into adulthood and which has translated to a philosophy in winemaking: Dada Wines is David and Kate's creative space to experiment without boundaries, to demonstrate their courage, to welcome surprise, and to enjoy the unexpected.

DADA WINES

Appellation:	**Havelock North**
Region:	**Hawke's Bay**
Country of Origin:	**New Zealand**
Type of Wine:	**Sauvignon Blanc, Viognier, and Gewürztraminer Blend**
Web Site:	**www.dadawine.co.nz**
Design:	**Inhouse Design**
Designer's Web Site:	**www.inhousedesign.co.nz**

D'ARENBERG

[SOUTH AUSTRALIA ❦ AUSTRALIA]

There has long been a debate between the effects of nature versus nurture—nature being inherent qualities and nurture being experiences. Both impact each of our individual differences in physical and behavioral traits, of course, but the debate being exactly which has a greater influence.

At d'Arenberg, both nature and nurture are treated with equal importance during the winemaking process and are almost reflective of one another. For instance, the natural inhabitants of d'Arenberg's vineyards are indicative of the nurturing provided by the winery. Likewise, the nurturing supports the natural elements of the vineyard that are, in turn, reflected in the wines. Two particular examples of this cooperation can be seen with the fox and lizard, both natural inhabitants of the vineyard ecosystem.

The feral foxes of the region, once accustomed to feeding on the local rabbit delicacies, have had to seek more vegetarian options as the rabbit population has dwindled. As such, they have taken a particular liking to grapes off the vines. The folks at d'Arenberg don't object to the grazers, who aren't considered a nuisance, but rather seen as effective natural crop thinners that actually enhance the quality of the grapes. Further, the grapes keep the foxes' digestive systems regular and in addition to acting as pruners, those multi-talented foxes provide organic fertilization for the soil (albeit with very interesting aromas) due to their untraditional meals. The result: delicious grapes that are picked and handled with the utmost care. This includes having the grapes crushed with a gentle open-mouthed, rubber-toothed crusher, tender foot treading, and gentle basket pressing using nineteenth-century presses. D'Arenberg believes that processing the grapes using the most natural techniques promotes the most enhanced flavor possible in its wines. And you can't get more natural than the feral fox droppings, can you?

Likewise, another inhabitant of the vines, the bearded dragon, enjoys sunning itself on the vineyard posts while inconspicuously watching its insect prey. During harvest, these bathing beauties are so unobtrusive that at times they find themselves en route to the winery along with the bunches of grapes. As d'Arenberg gently nurtures its grapes from vineyard to bottle, the lizards most often make it through their adventure a little shaken, but not particularly stirred due to the gentle teeth of the Demoisy crusher, which allows them to slip through unscathed and head back home after a short adventure. These mild-mannered and highly natural processes also help retain the delicate flavors of the Chardonnay grapes that also make their way through the crush, traveling first class with care and utmost attention, just like the lucky lizards who are proof that nature and nurture do certainly coexist at d'Arenberg.

D'ARENBERG
Appellation: **Adelaide Hills**
State: **South Australia**
Country of Origin: **Australia**
Type of Wine: **Chardonnay**
Web Site: **www.darenberg.com.au**
Design: **Pinnacle Creative**
Designer's Web Site: **www.pinnaclecreative.com.au**

DIEVOLE
[SICILY ❧ ITALY]

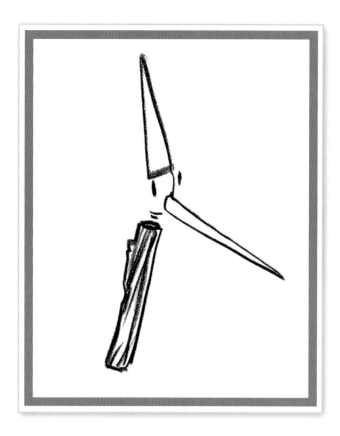

Most people have no idea that one of the world's most beloved books of all times, *The Adventures of Pinocchio*, originated in Italy. The tale was originally written by Italian author Carlo Lorenzini under the pseudonym Carlo Collodi. His pen surname was derived from the small Tuscan town of Collodi where his mother was born. Although Walt Disney's 1940 animated rendition of the story made it the beloved classic tale of the wooden puppet whose nose grew when telling a lie, it all started with the original—a candid and humorous allegorical tale, *Le avventure di Pinocchio*, of Italian origin back in 1881.

While children's literature was a new genre at the time the tale was penned, storytelling itself has long been known as an oral folk art in the Tuscan countryside. Traditionally, stories offered a combination of illustrative narratives while being attentive to the social and moral wisdom of the times. Following suit, Collodi's *Pinocchio* was more of a cultural compass than a fairy tale in the conventional sense. His original tale, however, went on to inspire countless international interpretations and is still one of the most widely read stories, enjoyed today by both children and adults alike.

Dievole honors the heritage of this spectacularly acclaimed classic through the artistry on its Pinocchio wine label. The style of the illustration is reminiscent of the original drawings produced for the book by artist Eugenio Mazzanti in 1883. And while the lessons of Pinocchio can be applied across cultures and in diverse circumstance, there's one cautionary tale to be learnt by all: *in vino veritas*—in wine there certainly is truth. With wine, the nose knows.

	DIEVOLE
Appellation:	**Non-Designated Appellation**
Region:	**Sicily**
Country of Origin:	**Italy**
Type of Wine:	**Nero d'Avola**
Web Site:	**www.dievole.it**
Design:	**Internal**

DIRTY LAUNDRY VINEYARD
[BRITISH COLUMBIA ❧ CANADA]

Once upon a time, there was a little-known vineyard in Summerland, British Columbia, that, at that time, only managed to sell half its annual wine production. After seeing immense potential in the vineyard, new owners purchased what was then known as Scherzinger Vineyards, and decided to put their stamp on this new venture and spice things up. Looking for a name meaningful to both the people and setting of the vineyard, some interesting tidbits on the town were dug up and a dirty little secret was aired as the owners freshened up the name and face of their wines.

As the story goes, in the late 1800s, tired of the interminable work for the Canadian Pacific Railway, one of the fifteen thousand Chinese laborers fled the horrible working conditions to the shores of Summerland, British Columbia. There, he opened a launderette—a seemingly innocent enough service for the locals. His business was quite a success due to an apt location at the busy port of call. And let's face it, clean knickers are kind of a necessity. Having an astute eye for business opportunities, our inconspicuous Chinese launderer couldn't turn a blind eye to the town's dire need for some essential extracurricular activities. Quietly, our entrepreneur expanded his business to include more intimate affairs that went on behind closed doors. Soon enough, the laundry garnered the nickname "the dirty laundry" by the locals, probably because their sheets never came back 100% clean.

The intriguing name brings them in, the naked ladies in the steam of our labels make them smile, and the great wines bring them back for more. . . . —JUDI SKINNER
Sales and Marketing Manager,
Dirty Laundry Vineyard

Thus, with this entertaining regional story as the foundation, a "discrete" label was designed that uses curvaceous and seductive embossed steam plumes rising up from an iconic and sultry red-hot iron. The response: the Dirty Laundry Vineyard became an instant hit with people everywhere airing their own dirty laundry over a glass of good, clean fun.

DIRTY LAUNDRY VINEYARD	
Appellation:	**Okanagan Valley**
Province:	**British Columbia**
Country of Origin:	**Canada**
Type of Wine:	**Gewürztraminer**
Web Site:	**www.dirtylaundry.ca**
Design:	**Brandever**
Designer's Web Site:	**www.brandever.com**

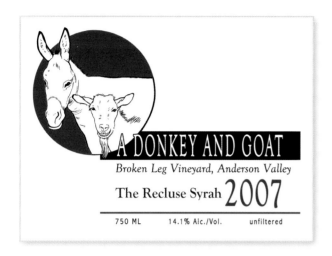

Seeing this wine label, one cannot help but wonder what on earth a donkey and a goat have to do with wine?

The answer: Together, they represent a guiding work philosophy for the winemaking team learnt through a little animal husbandry.

The winery's name, Donkey and Goat, was born through a simple, yet inspiring realization made by the husband-and-wife winemaking duo of Tracey and Jared Brandt while they refined their winemaking skills in Côte Rôtie, France. They found that donkeys are reputed as hardworking animals that have long been used in Mediterranean countries for the tending of the vineyards. And in France, the couple witnessed this firsthand. The vineyard's donkey would spend long days out servicing the vines as an organic weeder. Curiously though, after a laborious day, the donkey would be symbiotically paired, not with another donkey, but instead with a goat. Goats, one of the first animals to be domesticated, are known to be quite civilized. Pairing a notably calmer goat has a naturally relaxing affect on a donkey after a tough day on the job, while the donkey was a nice companion for the goat.

This odd, but admirably functional and balanced coupling became a different way to look at the cooperative work ethic and philosophy of the pair's true 50/50 winemaking partnership. On any given day, either one could be out doing the grunt work of the donkey. At the end of the day, though, the goat would provide support and solace, and the gumption to do it all over again the next day. Thus, both creatures are featured prominently on their wine labels as a reminder that both partners play an equally important role in the success of the couple's joint venture and that the balance achieved from one another is important in both partnership and life.

DONKEY & GOAT WINERY	
Appellation:	**Anderson Valley**
State:	**California**
Country of Origin:	**United States**
Type of Wine:	**Syrah**
Web Site:	**www.adonkeyandgoat.com**
Design:	**Jane Fisher and Colin Frangos (Nadir Novelties)**
Designer's Web Site:	**www.janefisher.net and www.nadir-novelties.net**

DONKEY & GOAT WINERY	
Appellation:	**El Dorado**
State:	**California**
Country of Origin:	**United States**
Type of Wine:	**Red Blend**
Web Site:	**www.adonkeyandgoat.com**
Design:	**Jane Fisher and Colin Frangos (Nadir Novelties)**
Designer's Web Site:	**www.janefisher.net and www.nadir-novelties.net**

DONNAFUGATA

[SICILY ⟩⟨ ITALY]

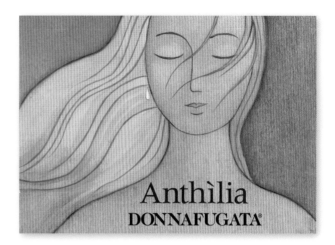

When translated from Italian, the word *donnafugata* means "fleeing woman." To the winemaking Rallo family, particularly the women who play such an important role in their winery, it has meanings layered with history, the arts, and even personal choices. The name was chosen overtly for its historical ties to Queen Maria Carolina, wife of Bourbon King Ferdinand IV, who was forced to take flight from her court in Spanish-ruled Naples during the 1800s due to a siege by Napoleon's army. Fleeing to Sicily, Queen Maria Carolina was given refuge by an Italian prince in his Sicilian palace. This story of Sicilian sanctuary, along with other chronicles and complexities that occurred during the period of *Il Risorgimento*, inspired and have been immortalized in Sicilian author Giuseppe Tomasi di Lampedusa's internationally acclaimed novel, *Il Gattopardo*.

Based on the queen's flight, the author named the palatial sanctuary Donnafugata, which was not only featured as a prominent setting in the book, but was a favored residence of the author himself. It also happens to be located in very close proximity to the Rallo family's winery and vineyards.

The label is fundamental. It must be attractive and visible, and it must be unique—like the wine in the bottle.

—JOSÉ RALLO
Owner, Donnafugata

Not only is the palace a central visual in Donnafugata's wine labels, but it is a name that automatically evokes extraordinary imagery and complexities of Sicily as described by Tomasi. "The story is never-ending," suggests José Rallo, the daughter of matriarch Gabriella Anca Rallo. She says that she first read the book at the tender age of ten years old and has since reread it many times. It offers tales of generational changes, conflict between tradition and innovation, and speaks of the influence that the environment has on a people—themes which can also be certainly applied to winemaking.

Other imagery of the wine labels are reflective of the mysterious and fleeting, including that seen on the Anthìla label, which represent a graphic personification of the vanished ancient Elymian civilization of northwest Sicily. Very often, the images on the label show gentle, refined, elegant, dreaming women who not only represent the wines, but perhaps also the vision of Gabriella Anca Rallo and her bond with the native grapes of Sicily, or the decision of José Rallo to gracefully set aside her success as a performing musician to continue the tradition of her family with Donnafugata.

DONNAFUGATA	
Appellation:	**Contessa Entellina**
Region:	**Sicily**
Country of Origin:	**Italy**
Type of Wine:	**Nero d'Avola**
Web Site:	**www.donnafugata.it**

DONNAFUGATA	
Appellation:	**Non-Designated Appellation**
Region:	**Sicily**
Country of Origin:	**Italy**
Type of Wine:	**White Blend**
Web Site:	**www.donnafugata.it**

Edi Simčič

[Brda ❧ Slovenia]

Gnomes are mythical creatures characterized by their pint-sized stature, their subterranean habitation, and their otherworldly, magical qualities. Traditionally, as reflected on the Edi Simčič Duet wine labels, gnomes are most often envisioned as friendly dwarfs with long, flowing beards that wear bright, cone-shaped hats—think of *Snow White and the Seven Dwarfs*. Legend depicts gnomes as caregivers of the earth, friends of wildlife, charitable, and benevolent, while being innocently mischievous.

As such, a subterranean cellar would be a perfect dwelling place for the likes of these mythical creatures. And the winemaking father-and-son duet of Edi and Aleks Simčič believes that when they leave their laborious days behind them, these keepers of the cellar emerge to create havoc and add a little magic to the cellared wines. The Duet wines age for three years in barrel, which can add up to quite a bit of mischief run amok.

No one is certain as to what exactly happens once the door closes behind them, but whatever it is, it certainly seems to be working just fine. The Simčičs aren't ones to fiend off a little magic, and so pay homage to their magical mates on the Duet wine labels. Listen closely during the dark hours before dawn: You can surely hear that magic at work . . . and maybe more so at play.

EDI SIMČIČ	
Appellation:	**Goriška Brda**
Municipality:	**Brda**
Country of Origin:	**Slovenia**
Type of Wine:	**Merlot, Cabernet Sauvignon, and Cabernet Franc Blend**
Web Site:	**www.edisimcic.si**
Design:	**Studio 22**
Designer's Web Site:	**www.studio22.si**

There is something fascinating and alluring about people who create for a living: artists, chefs, designers, surgeons, and winemakers all seem to have lives that people are particularly interested in. There is almost a sexiness to it, it seems. Likely the only ones who know the reality of the long hours and hard work involved in these so-called "sexy" careers are those doing the work and their loved ones who feel the brunt of their absence.

The Engine Room wine label tells the real story of a day in the life of a winemaker during vintage and reveals the repercussions felt by what is widely known in the industry as the "vintage widow"—left to her own devices as the clock ticks on and the incessant hours of vintage never seem to end. The name "Engine Room" refers to where it all happens at the winery. Where the drive, energy, and craftsmanship take place and where the passion to get through it culminates after the grapes are harvested. Winemaker Hamish Maguire, whose mugshots are featured prominently on the label, coined the term after having answered the winery's phone, "Hello, Engine Room," for years. Luckily, his vintage widow is extremely considerate of his career and hasn't hung up on him yet.

The label was created to grab the attention of a new group. We wanted to capture them with the imagery and then with the quality of the wine without overpowering them with wine-speak. Once they have picked it up off the shelf, we're already halfway there! —ALICIA CALLARY
Sales and Marketing Manager,
Shottesbrooke Vineyards

**ENGINE ROOM
(SHOTTESBROOKE VINEYARDS)**

Appellation:	**McLaren Vale**
State:	**South Australia**
Country of Origin:	**Australia**
Type of Wine:	**Sauvignon Blanc, Chardonnay, and Sémillon Blend**
Web Site:	**www.engineroomwines.com**
Design:	**Mash**
Designer's Web Site:	**www.mashdesign.com.au**

**ENGINE ROOM
(SHOTTESBROOKE VINEYARDS)**

Appellation:	**McLaren Vale**
State:	**South Australia**
Country of Origin:	**Australia**
Type of Wine:	**Shiraz**
Web Site:	**www.engineroomwines.com**
Design:	**Mash**
Designer's Web Site:	**www.mashdesign.com.au**

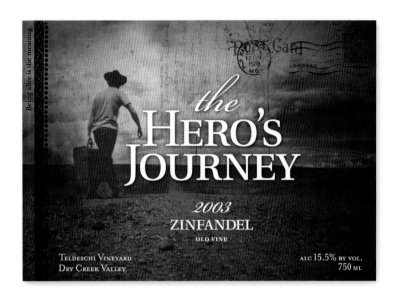

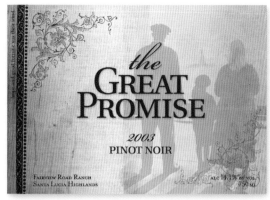

Winemaker Sasha Verhage believes that wine is not an inanimate liquid. In fact, his convictions are so strong that with every bud break through harvest, he believes nature tells a new story, which is captured through his wines. Therefore, he not only calls himself the winemaker and the proprietor of Eno Wines, but the storyteller, as well.

Each vintage, based on the uniqueness of the experience, Sasha chooses a common theme and develops labels that visually represent the journey of the wine. His 2003 suite was based on the life and scholarship of Joseph Campbell told through his book *The Hero with a Thousand Faces*, which has inspired generations of students and artists since it was first published in 1949.

Beyond a binding theme, each wine label is also an intimate reflection on each wine and grape-sourcing vineyard. The Great Promise tells the story of Eno's inaugural vintage from Fairview Ranch Road vineyard in Santa Lucia Highlands, which demonstrated extremely high potential. The Hero's Journey, recounts the arrival of Italian immigrants who planted what they knew best and what reminded them of their heritage as they transitioned their lives to the new lands of Dry Creek Valley some one hundred years ago. The older the vines, the harder they have to work, but what they produce has infinitely more to say. As Sasha puts it, "Anything that comes from 120 years old is heroic." And, despite it being only Sasha's second harvest from the Casatierra Vineyard in Fiddletown, located in Amador County, he felt that the wines from this vineyard had much more wisdom and sophistication than their years. It is for this reason that he called his 2003 Syrah The Old Soul.

With a dedication to both the wine and storytelling, these wine labels are pieces of true epic proportion.

ENO WINES

Appellation:	**Santa Lucia Highlands**
State:	**California**
Country of Origin:	**United States**
Type of Wine:	**Pinot Noir**
Web Site:	**www.enowines.com**
Design:	**Harvest SF**

ENO WINES

Appellation:	**Dry Creek Valley**
State:	**California**
Country of Origin:	**United States**
Type of Wine:	**Zinfandel**
Web Site:	**www.enowines.com**
Design:	**Harvest SF**

ENO WINES

Appellation:	**Fiddletown**
State:	**California**
Country of Origin:	**United States**
Type of Wine:	**Syrah**
Web Site:	**www.enowines.com**
Design:	**Harvest SF**

Eos Estate Winery

[California ✦ United States]

Paso Robles on the Central Coast, with its mineral hot springs, therapeutic waters, apple and almond orchards, oak woodlands, and vineyards a-plenty, is quite a picture. It sounds like it could be heaven on earth.

In fact, legend has it that a mischievous angel did sneak out from within heaven's golden gates to investigate our foreign land and inadvertently lost her way back home. Irked and tired of the endless quest home, the industrious angel crafted her own version of paradise with all the things that she loved most. Coincidentally, these included therapeutic waters, orchards, and woodlands. Absolutely overwhelmed with the beauty of her accomplishment and her new heaven on earth, a tear of the purest joy fell from her eye and delicately landed on the rich and fertile soil of her newfound homeland. In turn, the spirit of the land responded with an equivalent amount of love, and from her soils sprang the strongest vine, growing straight up to the stars and providing a path for the lost angel to find a way back to her celestial life.

And while the lost angel did eventually leave her earthly retreat to return to her home in the heavens, each year she is said to sprinkle down sun-drenched tears that kiss the very vines that helped her find her way in the first place. These glistening tears are a reminder of her harvest of love for our earth and, in particular, the very heavenly Paso Robles. It is out of this affection that the Eos Estate wines are crafted and remembered by the divine angel on its wine labels.

EOS ESTATE WINERY

Appellation:	**Central Coast**
State:	**California**
Country of Origin:	**United States**
Type of Wine:	**Cabernet Sauvignon, Petite Sirah, and Sangiovese Blend**
Web Site:	**www.eosvintage.com**
Design:	**Image Juice**
Designer's Web Site:	**www.imagejuice.net**

Eric Kent Wine Cellars
[California ᴥ United States]

The husband-and-wife owners of Eric Kent Wine Cellars are each curators in their own right. Kent is the keeper and engineer behind the vines and wines, while Colleen is the propagator of unique masterpieces shared with wine lovers through their wine labels.

The pair claim that their best ideas have been inspired over dinner and wine: an engagement ring drawn on a placemat with a blue crayon over pizza and red, and the idea to showcase undiscovered artists on their labels over burgers and Zin. On both accounts, they've been bang on.

In her thirties, Colleen, having worked professionally in advertising, decided to go back to school to obtain a bachelor of fine art in painting and drawing. During her last year of schooling, Kent, also working in advertising as a creative director at the time, decided to follow his passion for winemaking and a memorable evening of drinking wine out of paper cups with burgers brought about the brainstorming of what would be put on the wine labels. Both obviously creative individuals, Colleen and Kent believed that there was a strong relationship between art and winemaking, as they both were a craft unto their own. From Kent's perspective, winemaking is like the art of cooking; from Colleen's perspective, winemaking is like the act of painting. No matter what, when provided with the exact same ingredients—be it legumes, spices, acrylics, oils, or grapes—every individual craftsperson will create something utterly unique.

Given their expansive approach to art, it just made sense to blend their two crafts together by pairing art with their Eric Kent wines—especially since Colleen had so many talented, yet unknown, artist friends.

ERIC KENT WINE CELLARS

Appellation:	**Sonoma County (Non-Designated Appellation)**
State:	**California**
Country of Origin:	**United States**
Type of Wine:	**Syrah**
Web Site:	**www.erickentwines.com**
Art:	**Sharon Eisley**
Artist's Web Site:	**www.sharoneisley.com**

1 km west of Florencia, Caquetá, Colombia, 13 January 1971

<table>
<tr><td colspan="2">ERIC KENT WINE CELLARS</td></tr>
<tr><td>Appellation:</td><td>Sonoma County
(Non-Designated Appellation)</td></tr>
<tr><td>State:</td><td>California</td></tr>
<tr><td>Country of Origin:</td><td>United States</td></tr>
<tr><td>Type of Wine:</td><td>Syrah</td></tr>
<tr><td>Web Site:</td><td>www.erickentwines.com</td></tr>
<tr><td>Design:</td><td>Maggie Taylor</td></tr>
<tr><td>Artist's Web Site:</td><td>www.maggietaylor.com</td></tr>
</table>

<table>
<tr><td colspan="2">ERIC KENT WINE CELLARS</td></tr>
<tr><td>Appellation:</td><td>Sonoma Coast</td></tr>
<tr><td>State:</td><td>California</td></tr>
<tr><td>Country of Origin:</td><td>United States</td></tr>
<tr><td>Type of Wine:</td><td>Chardonnay</td></tr>
<tr><td>Web Site:</td><td>www.erickentwines.com</td></tr>
<tr><td>Design:</td><td>Klea McKenna</td></tr>
<tr><td>Artist's Web Site:</td><td>www.kleamckenna.com</td></tr>
</table>

Our desire is simple: we want the art on the bottle to reflect the same passion and dedication to craft as the wine inside. When the bottle is empty, the art keeps the story alive. By sharing this art with those who might not encounter it in daily life, new stories are inspired with each bottle opened.

—COLLEEN TEITGEN, Curator, and KENT HUMPHREY, Winemaker, Eric Kent Wine Cellars

Hence, unique artwork of diverse media is featured on every new vintage. Not only does this provide their often-undiscovered friends with a captive audience, but it also adds a dual perspective to the couple's venture.

With most artwork and vintages, there are always stories that go alongside. As such, every individual label has its own story told through the artist's visual creation. Kalen's Big Boy Blend was named after the big personality and smiling spirit of Colleen and Kent's young son. Using inspiration from the "little monkey" himself (fittingly born in the Year of the Monkey) and experiences with her own child, artist Sharon Eisley used a unique mixture of media to create this original label.

In another instance, as wine tells the story of the individual terroir from which it is grown, Klea McKenna's artwork also explores the relationship between time, place, and nature. Paticularly as glimpsed on the Eric Kent wine label, Klea has photographed hundreds of specimens of her late father's butterfly collection including the scraps of newspaper, magazines, and letters that the butterflies were wrapped in for nearly forty years. She says that through this inherited material, she was able to tell her father's story, as well as create a conflicted portrait of the times in the late 1960s and early 1970s.

None of the artwork for Eric Kent wines is commissioned. Rather, Colleen chooses artists based on their uniquely compelling work, which adds to a cohesive collection that, just like their product, they like to share with friends, family, and lovers of wine and art everywhere.

ERNA SCHEIN

[CALIFORNIA ✸ UNITED STATES]

While it wouldn't be much of a surprise that Les Behrens likes art (it's quite a reasonable hobby), what might seem a bit off-the-wall is Les's penchant for shopping on eBay. In fact, he likens himself to being a bit of an eBay addict . . . though his family would be more likely to jokingly call it an addiction to "e(vil)Bay."

Les has found some hidden gems while engaged in online shopping sprees, but he says it's mostly useless crap, yet arguably good for something, someone, somewhere.

Take, for example, Les's prized bowling figurine. The statuette, a very rare, sought-after ceramic (in Les's eyes anyways), had the year '62 and the initials "S. H." painted on it. Though maybe just a coincidence, this was a sure sign for Les to make the purchase, given the year '62 was the year of his wife's birth, and S. H., was short for St. Helena, where they live. And so, Les purchased the antique, thinking it would definitely come in handy one day.

And one day it certainly did. In 2006, Les and Lisa of Erna Schein decided that they'd spare an overage of Cabernet Sauvignon that they traditionally wouldn't use instead of selling it off, and make it into something that just jumped out of the glass—luckily with the scent of orchids, violets, and Asian spices, and not bowling alleys. Les admits that his family does enjoy a bowling game for fun every once and a while, and his son does apparently find inspiration in *The Big Lebowski*—sounds like an interesting game to play with the Behrens clan for sure. So don't knock eBay. You never know what you'll find. As the saying goes, "one man's junk is another man's treasure." And the Behrens family's Spare Me wine label is certainly right up this alley. Dude, let's grab a glass and go bowling.

> **We started using art on our labels just for the love of it, but over time it has made a big plus for selling our wine. We hear from our buyers all the time about how much they love our art labels. We did not set out to market our wine this way, but frankly it has worked out very well.**
> —LES BEHRENS
> Owner and Winemaker,
> Erna Schein (Behrens Family Winery)

**ERNA SCHEIN
(BEHRENS FAMILY WINERY)**
Appellation: **Napa Valley**
State: **California**
Country of Origin: **United States**
Type of Wine: **Cabernet Sauvignon and Cabernet Franc Blend**
Web Site: **www.ernaschein.com**
Design: **Brian Nash Design Company**
Designer's Web Site: **www.bndco.com**

ESKADALE VINEYARDS

[SOUTH AUSTRALIA ❧ AUSTRALIA]

Tucked unassumingly amidst the Eskadale Vineyards vines, there is an old, unsuspecting water tank. Thought to simply be a utilitarian eyesore, the locals certainly know better.

Australians are known to be overtly passionate about a few very distinct things, and sport has to be the leader on the list. In the vicinity of Eskadale Vineyards, demonstrating true Aussie character, fierce and longstanding rivalries exist between the neighboring Great Southern Football League teams. Tradition over the last thirty or so years has seen the local winners celebrate their victory by arrogantly flaunting their triumph and painting the Eskadale water tank in their team's respective colors.

And so, David Knight has christened his wine The Winner's Tank and each year, Eskadale pays homage to the victorious team. Whether or not they need the added glory is up for debate, and it's likely the losing team would be against seeing their rivals' mugs plastered all over the bottle shops. The Velvet Sledgehammer label refers to the multiple personalities of the team leader who is always the first one with the paint can. He's sweet as pie off the field, but a dangerous felon once he steps a foot on. Just like this wine, he is the ultimate example of two polarities. Ask David Knight which team he follows and he'll be sure to answer ambiguously and tiptoe around the question . . . after all, the water tank is amidst his vineyards and the players do know where he lives!

ESKADALE VINEYARDS	
Appellation:	**Langhorne Creek**
State:	**South Australia**
Country of Origin:	**Australia**
Type of Wine:	**Shiraz**
Web Site:	**www.oddfellowswines.com.au**
Design:	**Detour Design**
Designer's Web Site:	**www.detourdesign.net.au**

Estate Voyatzi

[West Macedonia ❧ Greece]

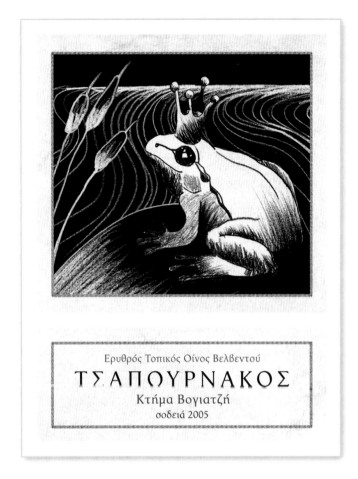

Ερυθρός Τοπικός Οίνος Βελβεντού

ΤΣΑΠΟΥΡΝΑΚΟΣ

Κτήμα Βογιατζή

σοδειά 2005

Most people have heard the classic fairytale of "The Frog Prince."

More or less, the tale is about a spoiled princess who loses her golden ball in a pond. When propositioned by a talking frog to retrieve it, she promises to bring the frog home should he rescue it for her. In her excitement with the return of her golden ball, however, she reneges on her vow and refuses to care for the frog. The persistent frog follows her to the palace and, while sitting down to dinner with her father, the princess hears the frog's plea to make good on her promise, which she ignores. Her father, the king, asks what the ruckus is about. When the princess tells him of the agreement she made with the frog, the king says that if she made a commitment, then she must honor it in the name of her integrity. And so, not being able to disobey her father, she invites the frog in, feeds him, lets him sleep on her pillow, and allows him free range of the palace.

Gradually, the two form a mutual bond and are rarely seen apart. One evening, feeling confident with their relationship, the frog asks the princess if she would kiss him. While she wasn't quite anticipating kissing a frog before a prince, she is willing to take a chance in the name of friendship. And so, she gently picks up her frog and softly puts her smooth pink lips to his that are rough and green. Immediately, a cloud of smoke fills the room with a poof and out of the smoke emerges the most handsome prince she has ever seen, transformed before her very eyes by the touch of her lips. The spell that had been cast on the prince was broken forever and the princess and her prince lived happily ever after.

The moral of the story, as told through the Estate Voyatzi wine label:

Labels are one of the elements that make wine considered to be artwork. A bottle of wine is an aesthetic object that, through the label and by its content, stimulates thoughts, imagination, emotions, and our senses." —Yannis Voyatzis
Oenologist and Vineyardist,
Estate Voyatzi

There exist thousands of grape varietals around the globe and some are not as well known as the "noble" few. The Tsapournakos native grape of Greece is a fine example. Here sits what many might think a "frog," unworthy to touch one's lips. If given the opportunity to release its full potential on the palate, however, it too will transform into an enchanting prince before your eyes. But you'll only know if you open up, kiss a frog, and try it.

ESTATE VOYATZI
Appellation:	**Velventos (Non-Designated Appellation)**
Periphery:	**West Macedonia**
Country of Origin:	**Greece**
Type of Wine:	**Tsapournakos**
Web Site:	**www.ktimavoyatzi.gr**
Design:	**Red Creative**
Designer's Web Site:	**www.redcreative.gr**

ESTATE VOYATZI

[WEST MACEDONIA ❧ GREECE]

This is not a wine bottle.
Αυτό δεν είναι ένα μπουκάλι κρασιού.
Ceci n'est pas une bouteille de vin.

This is not a wine glass.
Αυτό δεν είναι ένα κρασί γυαλί.
Ceci n'es pas un verre de vin.

This is definitely not a pipe.
Αυτό δεν είναι σίγουρα ένα σωλήνα.
Ceci certainement n'est pas une pipe.

ESTATE VOYATZI	
Appellation:	**Velventos (Non-Designated Appellation)**
Periphery:	**West Macedonia**
Country of Origin:	**Greece**
Type of Wine:	**Xinomavro, Merlot, and Cabernet Sauvignon Blend**
Web Site:	**www.ktimavoyatzi.gr**
Design:	**Red Creative**
Designer's Web Site:	**www.redcreative.gr**

ESTATE VOYATZI	
Appellation:	**Velventos (Non-Designated Appellation)**
Periphery:	**West Macedonia**
Country of Origin:	**Greece**
Type of Wine:	**Chardonnay, Roditis, and Batiki Blend**
Web Site:	**www.ktimavoyatzi.gr**
Design:	**Red Creative**
Designer's Web Site:	**www.redcreative.gr**

Ex Nihilo Vineyards

[British Columbia ❧ Canada]

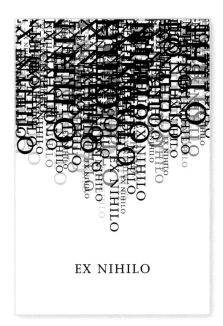

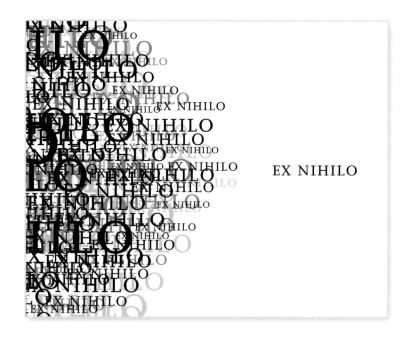

When Jeff and Decoa Harder took their first holiday together to Napa Valley and the Bay Area, they stumbled upon an art gallery in San Francisco where they were immediately moved by a very particular sculpture. The sculpture, entitled *Ex Nihilo*, was an artistic replica of the famed Frederick Hart masterpiece carved into the west façade of the Washington National Cathedral. Hart had been noted as saying, "Art must touch our lives, our fears, and cares—evoke our dreams and give hope to the darkness."

The vision of this sculpture certainly did evoke a dream for Jeff and Decoa as they immediately decided that the name "Ex Nihilo" would be perfect for the winery that they had dreamt of together. *Ex nihilo*, or *creatio ex nihilo*, is Latin that means "created out of nothing," and was well suited for their imagined winery. It perfectly described what it was—created from absolutely nothing. No financiers, no family heritage, no property, no vineyard, no winery, and no grapes. *Niente. Nihilo.* Nothing.

This moment, however, stirred their drive to realize this dream no matter what stakes (or at that moment, lack of stalks!) were against them. Over the next four years, the couple searched high and low and on and off the beaten track for the property that would provide the roots to their dreams. Finally, on their fourth drive along Camp Road, they happened upon a weathered, rickety "for sale" sign, and the Harders knew that they had found their destined piece of land. And so, this couple then seized the day (*carpe diem*) and, together with close friends Jay and Twila Paulson, saw their dream of Ex Nihilo transform *a posse ad esse* ("from possibility to actuality") and now have the wine and labels to show for it. While it may have been born out of nothing, it's certainly not "nothing" anymore.

> **The label and its design are a winery's personal communication piece that positions the wine and brand in the marketplace. Not only is it a message "on" the bottle, but we also hope that it also conveys a message from "inside" the bottle.**
> —Jeff Harder
> Owner, Ex Nihilo Vineyards

EX NIHILO VINEYARDS

Appellation:	**Okanagan Valley**
Province:	**British Columbia**
Country of Origin:	**Canada**
Type of Wine:	**Merlot**
Web Site:	**www.exnihilovineyards.com**
Design:	**Chip Sheean**
Designer's Web Site:	**www.chipsheean.com**

EX NIHILO VINEYARDS

Appellation:	**Okanagan Valley**
Province:	**British Columbia**
Country of Origin:	**Canada**
Type of Wine:	**Riesling**
Web Site:	**www.exnihilovineyards.com**
Design:	**Chip Sheean**
Designer's Web Site:	**www.chipsheean.com**

FAMILLE LIGNÈRES

[LANGUEDOC-ROUSSILLON ❦ FRANCE]

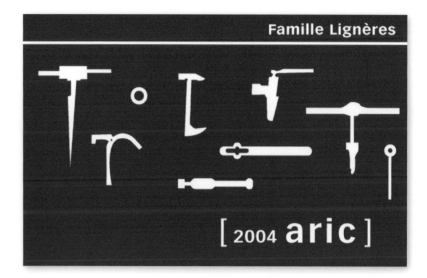

The Lignères family is one with a long history as medical practitioners and scientists. The patriarch, André Lignères, practiced general medicine in the village of Moux, and his wife, Suzette, was the village's pharmacist. Their children followed closely in their footsteps, as Jean is now the village's general practitioner; Paul, a dentist; and Geneviève, a biologist. They do say that the apple doesn't fall far from the tree. In addition, it isn't surprising that this family also have the practice of winemaking coursing through their veins, as winemaking can be traced to their forefathers of the sixteenth century. Today, the younger generation of the Lignères family have taken over what their ancestors began and what their parents continued with the purchase of the estate in 1957.

Though this younger generation is now at the helm, allowing André and Suzette to take a backseat to relax and enjoy the ride, the labels truly pay homage to the winemaking of yesteryear. For instance, the single vineyard wines are based on an authentic antique blackboard that was found hanging in one of the cellars. It seemed to have the dual purpose of a blackboard, and also a storage space where winemaking tools were secured. The passage of time left a distinct outline of the tools, which today provides the visual for the labels. Each of the labels is printed in a color significant to the respective wine inside the bottle and each has been named for an antiquated story that binds them to the region or the Lignères family.

The Aric wine label, for instance, is named for the famed Alaric, king of Visigoths, who ruled from AD 395 to 410, and was the first Germanic leader to seize the city of Rome. "Alaric" literally means "king of all," and the mountain that provides a spectacular backdrop to the Lignères estate has been named in his honor. The Lignères family still deliberate over whether Alaric knew of the majesty of the wines that the mountain possessed—and if he had, would he still have decided to storm Rome in AD 410, or would he have lived out a royal life of regal wines on the mountain?

The Pièce de Roche wine label *(not pictured)* carries a slightly more modern tale, dating back to 1890. It was then that the Lignères grandfather asked his best friend, Louis Roche, to plant this extraordinary parcel of land with sixteen thousand Carignan vines, which he did. In southern France, that which is thought to be the prized jewel of an estate is habitually called *"la pièce."* The Pièce de Roche label pays tribute to Mr. Roche's part in farming these spectacular grapes, literally, "the rock" *(la roche)*, or gem, of the estate.

In the 1920s, Louis Lignères regularly drove his Berliet barrel-carrier truck at the steady rate of 6.8 miles an hour from Alaric Mountain to Lourdes, in order to deliver wines. The journey was one that required patience, as the resolute winemaker traveled twenty-two hours to ensure that his wines were distributed to the people. Upon entrance to the town, he would take pride in signaling his arrival to the villagers with the Berliet's characteristic horn. The Famille Lignères Le Signal label *(not pictured)* touts the grandfather's tenacity and commitment to his wines, and the family's enjoyment far and wide as it continues the tradition today—though not transporting its wines behind the wheel of an antique Berliet anymore.

<table>
<tr><td colspan="2">FAMILLE LIGNÈRES</td></tr>
<tr><td>Appellation:</td><td>Languedoc-Roussillon</td></tr>
<tr><td>Region:</td><td>Languedoc-Roussillon</td></tr>
<tr><td>Country of Origin:</td><td>France</td></tr>
<tr><td>Type of Wine:</td><td>Carignan, Mourvèdre, and Syrah Blend</td></tr>
<tr><td>Web Site:</td><td>www.familleligneres.com</td></tr>
<tr><td>Design:</td><td>Paul Lignères</td></tr>
</table>

FARMGATE WINES
[HAWKE'S BAY ᭏ NEW ZEALAND]

FARMGATE

Hawkes Bay
2006 ~ CHARDONNAY
NEW ZEALAND WINE

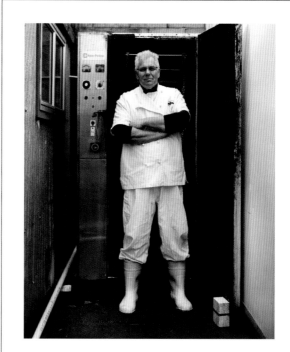

FARMGATE

Hawkes Bay
2007 ~ GEWURZTRAMINER
NEW ZEALAND WINE

When you look at the labels of Farmgate Wines, you are looking at a celebration of the heart and soul of the local community that not only produces the wines, but those who create the distinctive foods and flavors of the region. Terroir literally extends beyond the tangibility of the land and its character, to the intangibility of the people and culture of a region.

The farm gate is a place that everyone knows. It's "at the end of the dirt road at the beginning of a long driveway." It's a place where locals come together to provide everyday authentic tastes of the land, lovingly produced by real people. The concept is quite simple: a community of like-minded neighbors who share the same values.

The Farmgate Wines labels portray a connection between land, the people who farm it, and their combined passions in a raw and authentic manner. Through the wines, one can vicariously taste the place and one is able to meet the unique kinsmen that characterize Hawke's Bay, New Zealand. Through these convincing wine labels, it feels like being right there at the Hawke's Bay farm gate.

FARMGATE WINES	
Appellation:	**Hawke's Bay**
Region:	**Hawke's Bay**
Country of Origin:	**New Zealand**
Type of Wine:	**Chardonnay**
Web Site:	**www.farmgatewines.co.nz**
Design:	**Alt Group**
Designer's Web Site:	**www.altgroup.net**

FARMGATE WINES	
Appellation:	**Hawke's Bay**
Region:	**Hawke's Bay**
Country of Origin:	**New Zealand**
Type of Wine:	**Gewürztraminer**
Web Site:	**www.farmgatewines.co.nz**
Design:	**Alt Group**
Designer's Web Site:	**www.altgroup.net**

F A R M G A T E

Hawkes Bay
2007 - SYRAH
NEW ZEALAND WINE

F A R M G A T E

Hawkes Bay
2007 - SAUVIGNON BLANC
NEW ZEALAND WINE

FARMGATE WINES

Appellation:	**Hawke's Bay**
Region:	**Hawke's Bay**
Country of Origin:	**New Zealand**
Type of Wine:	**Syrah**
Web Site:	**www.farmgatewines.co.nz**
Design:	**Alt Group**
Designer's Web Site:	**www.altgroup.net**

FARMGATE WINES

Appellation:	**Hawke's Bay**
Region:	**Hawke's Bay**
Country of Origin:	**New Zealand**
Type of Wine:	**Sauvignon Blanc**
Web Site:	**www.farmgatewines.co.nz**
Design:	**Alt Group**
Designer's Web Site:	**www.altgroup.net**

F A R M G A T E

Hawkes Bay
2007 - MERLOT
NEW ZEALAND WINE

F A R M G A T E

Hawkes Bay
2008 - VIOGNIER
NEW ZEALAND WINE

FARMGATE WINES

Appellation:	**Hawke's Bay**
Region:	**Hawke's Bay**
Country of Origin:	**New Zealand**
Type of Wine:	**Merlot**
Web Site:	**www.farmgatewines.co.nz**
Design:	**Alt Group**
Designer's Web Site:	**www.altgroup.net**

FARMGATE WINES

Appellation:	**Hawke's Bay**
Region:	**Hawke's Bay**
Country of Origin:	**New Zealand**
Type of Wine:	**Viognier**
Web Site:	**www.farmgatewines.co.nz**
Design:	**Alt Group**
Designer's Web Site:	**www.altgroup.net**

FAT BASTARD

THIERRY & GUY

FAT *bastard*™

SHIRAZ

Remarkably full bodied

Fat Bastard was born out of a memory-making experiment between friends, Thierry Boudinaud, a re-nowned French winemaker, and Guy Anderson, a rebel in the wine industry from England. The two had been collaborating on various wine projects for some time, and Anderson had flown to France to taste their latest vintage. It was cold and damp in the cellar, but the plentiful barrel samples tasted and the convivial conversational kept the friends warm well into the night. The following morning, Thierry told Guy that he had another wine to try, an experimental one. Though they had tasted hundreds of wines the evening before, nothing had that big "wow factor" that blew either of them away. And what was one more wine to begin a day that had gotten off to a delinquent start anyway? Barely dried out from merriment put to bed only a few hours earlier, back to the cellar they went to taste Thierry's experimental wine that had been left to sit on the lees (a fancy term for yeast cells) for an extended period of time.

Neither friends anticipated what happened next—it was a dramatic departure from what they had tasted the night before. With one sip, this wine knocked them over with its rich, round palate. Staring at each other in awe for what seemed like at least five minutes, Thierry, with his passionate and characteristic articulation, finally broke the silence in exclamation.

"Now *zat* is what you call eh phet bast-ard!"

Guy reacted with such a booming laugh they reckon even the neighbors in the next village heard it. Guy had used the cheeky British phrase "fat bastard" before, but had never heard his friend use it—and the endearing French accent made it so much more comical. After trying more of the wine to reconfirm its majesty, the two friends knew that this was the wine that they needed to share with wine lovers on both sides of the pond and beyond. Of course, there could only be one viable name for it—Fat Bastard.

Wonder where the hippo on the label comes from? That still remains a little unclear. Certainly not indigenous to France or England, perhaps it just made its way onto the label haphazardly as a symbol of what the two like to call "living large," which should include indulging in big, fat wines every now and again.

**FAT BASTARD
(CLICK WINE GROUP)**

Appellation:	**Languedoc-Roussillon**
Region:	**Languedoc-Roussillon**
Country of Origin:	**France**
Type of Wine:	**Shiraz**
Web Site:	**www.fatbastardwines.com**
Design:	**The Fat Bastard Wine Company**

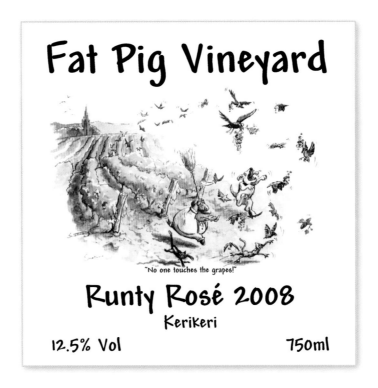

Winemaker Bruce Soland says he has always been a bit fascinated by pigs. And the Soland family—which includes a champagne-colored Labrador named Moey, a Devon Rex cat named Miss Manky (because it is said to be the mangiest thing around), Stiffy the rat, and three chickens named Chook, Chook, and Chook—has always had a pig on the farm. At one point, the family had two pigs, but the animals got too greedy when the kids came around to feed them. It was decided at that point that one fat pig, named Jenny Craig, was more manageable than two greedy pigs.

Typically, the family raises what it calls a "long white" pig on the farm that it likes to fatten up, as this type of pig has a bonus: an extra rib. This suits the Soland family just fine, as they all particularly like ham and bacon, but don't do pork chops—they sure do enjoy their "spare" ribs, though.

Aside from being a culinary staple, the Solands' fat pig is known to protect the vines by intimidating the birds that flock to eat the grapes. In the name of these rotating family pets that bring them so much gastronomic pleasure, they have named their vineyard and wines Fat Pig, and have honored them on their label.

Across the road, the Solands have neighbors who also have a vineyard—in fact, they have also followed in the Soland family's footsteps and have not one pig, but two. It is for this reason (and not after the indigenous Morepork owl), that they have named their own winery "More Pork," as they have one more pork than the Solands. It's not certain what they have included on their wine labels, but it seems safe to surmise they've showcased a plurality of pork just to playfully one-up the Solands.

FAT PIG VINEYARD

Appellation:	**Kerikeri**
Region:	**Northland**
Country of Origin:	**New Zealand**
Type of Wine:	**Rosé**
Web Site:	**www.fatpig.co.nz**
Design:	**Scott Tulloch**

FESTIVAL '34

[CALIFORNIA ❧ UNITED STATES]

How could one imagine the world without the ability to enjoy a glass of luxurious fermented fruit of the vine? In this day and age, it just seems impossible. But from 1920 through 1933, the United States witnessed the dark days of Prohibition. During this period, the sale, manufacture, and transportation for the purpose of consumption of all alcoholic beverages was legally banned as mandated by the 18th Amendment to the U.S. Constitution. American tables were deemed dry. The continued desire for alcoholic beverages only led to the increase in organized crime, bootlegging of booze, and secret gatherings at underground establishments called "speakeasies," named so because bartenders would covertly serve drinks to patrons and in turn tell them to be quiet, not raise suspicions, and "speak easy." In 1925, New York alone had anywhere from 30,000 to 100,000 speakeasy clubs active at any given time.

There became ways to maneuver around the legal implications of the ban with the passing of the Cullen-Harrison Act in 1933. This allowed small amounts of wine to be made at home or in wineries and sold legally for consumption during religious ceremonies. Of course, one can imag-

FESTIVAL '34
(FOSTER'S WINE ESTATES)
Appellation: **Central Coast**
State: **California**
Country of Origin: **United States**
Type of Wine: **Chardonnay**
Design: **The Launch Point**
Designer's Web Site: **www.thelaunchpoint.com**

FESTIVAL '34
COLLECTION

CABERNET SAUVIGNON
CENTRAL COAST
APPELLATION

FESTIVAL '34
COLLECTION

MERLOT
CENTRAL COAST
APPELLATION

**FESTIVAL '34
(FOSTER'S WINE ESTATES)**

Appellation:	**Central Coast**
State:	**California**
Country of Origin:	**United States**
Type of Wine:	**Cabernet Sauvignon**
Design:	**The Launch Point**
Designer's Web Site:	**www.thelaunchpoint.com**

**FESTIVAL '34
(FOSTER'S WINE ESTATES)**

Appellation:	**Central Coast**
State:	**California**
Country of Origin:	**United States**
Type of Wine:	**Merlot**
Design:	**The Launch Point**
Designer's Web Site:	**www.thelaunchpoint.com**

ine the rise in the number of devout—likely increasing their pious celebration from once a week to a very "religious" routine honored on a daily basis.

Regardless of illegal activity and the 1933 amendment, the years of Prohibition were detrimental to the decline of the wine industry, which saw the grapes of wrath close many winery doors. When the 18th Amendment was repealed with the ratification of the 21st Amendment on December 5, 1933, there certainly was reason to celebrate. And celebrate they did, from September 21 through September 23, 1934, where the first vintage seen in California wine country since Prohibition was commemorated with a harvest festival. People came from all over to partake in this monumental event, which was hailed as Festival '34.

The Festival '34 wines remember this historical event, which ended the dark days of Prohibition and are doing their part to keep that celebration going. They even believe that Repeal Day should be a national holiday observed annually on December 5. The Festival '34 wine labels pay homage to real personalities who played integral roles in the inaugural post-Prohibition harvest: the Blonde Giant, who lent a helpful hand to many wineries each day at harvest; the Three Jakes, who were leaders at the time in California's wine community; and the beautiful Ethel Byers, the main attraction at the St. Helena Vintage Festival of 1934, where she donned a dress made entirely of the prized grape clusters from the most highly valued vintage since 1920.

Fiasco Wines

[Marlborough ∾ New Zealand]

Winemaker Aaron Thompson and his wife Jacinda Thompson completely understand that life is full of little challenges that, at times, require a fine balancing act. For them, the art of balance crops up particularly during vintage.

Each year, the good people at Fiasco Wines say that they are faced with a few unexpected fiascos at vintage. Anyone who has worked vintage knows that it can be trying during the best of times. The reality is that mistakes do happen. Disasters do occur. Calamities often come a-callin'. But while things mightn't always go right, some supposed wrongs aren't always a bad thing. At Fiasco Wines, the Thompson family sets out with passionate intentions and daily zest to face the battles of coping with the uncontrollable nature of the elements. Despite the challenges, the family has decidedly learnt to roll with vintage punches, and this calm-under-fire attitude seems to have enabled it to bottle only the best of it.

So here's a bit of advice from those who have seen their share of fiascos, big and small:

Wine labels are a clue, a temptation for our customers' curiosity. We went with something unconventional so that people will stop and question it, read on further, and hopefully make a connection. For Fiasco Wines, that connection is a realization that this wine company is keeping it real. New World winemaking and life in general can be a fun-filled fiasco!

—Jacinda Thompson
Owner, Fiasco Wines

Don't always get hung up on rules. Instead, embrace and enjoy the ebbs and flows of life with a little bit of lighthearted laughter and good people to share the memories with. Practice standing on one foot on top of a barrel with a glass of wine in hand—don't forget to breathe and you'll be all right. This, dear friends, as the Fiasco label says, is no tall tale.

FIASCO WINES

Appellation:	**Marlborough**
Region:	**Marlborough**
Country of Origin:	**New Zealand**
Type of Wine:	**Sauvignon Blanc**
Web Site:	**www.fiascowines.co.nz**
Design:	**Abbie Taylor Design**
Designer's Web Site:	**www.abbietaylordesign.co.nz**

FINCAS PATAGÓNICAS

[MENDOZA ❦ ARGENTINA]

Renowned Argentine doctor Patricia Ortiz decided that she needed a change in life after many years of a successful medical practice. The accomplished doctor was looking for a whole new challenge. Along with her husband, lawyer Jorge Ortiz, Patricia had enjoyed being an avid tourist of wines and thought that a change that complemented this passion would be a fabulous pursuit.

Opportunity knocked in 2003, and it knocked loudly. Owning a vineyard already in Valle de Uco, and with the purchase of the Tapiz vineyard and winery, as well as Kendall Jackson (now collectively called Fincas Patagónicas), the Ortiz family took its passion for wine to a whole new level. Life as they knew it changed dramatically from vines to wines when they turned their *love* of wine into to a *life* of wine.

Given this was really Patricia's baby (a "baby" the size of 2,131 acres), she took the helm and regularly commuted from Buenos Aires to the Mendoza region to run Fincas Patagónicas. Jorge, on the other hand, continued to practice law and, more often than not, found that he was left to his own devices in Buenos Aires.

When the time came to name the new Fincas Patagónicas range of wines, said to be so good they'd blow your head off, Patricia thought it only appropriate to salute the man who was "*todo solo*," or all alone, because their lives were turned upside down by the exciting endeavor. The wine labels are a hu-morous play on the Spanish word *solo* (the letter *z* is a reverse *s*, which is where "*zolo*" came from!), with Jorge's hat being blown off because of his unlimited access to these great wines. Jorge has adapted rather well to his overturned life of, at times, frequent solitude. And while he does spend much time on his own, it has been said that that hasn't reduced his enjoyment of the family's wine—he seems to have certainly has lost quite a few hats, just as the Zolo wine labels indicate.

FINCAS PATAGÓNICAS	
Appellation:	**Valle de Uco**
Province:	**Mendoza**
Country of Origin:	**Argentina**
Type of Wine:	**Malbec**
Web Site:	**www.tapiz.com.ar**
Design:	**Boldrini & Ficcardi**
Designer's Web Site:	**www.bfweb.com.ar**

FIRST DROP WINES

[SOUTH AUSTRALIA ✤ AUSTRALIA]

First Drop Wines is a creative collaboration between mates Matt Gant and John Retsas. Having worked together at one of Australia's mega-wine producers, the two decided to go it alone and craft the wines they wanted to drink—and that were equally as fun to make. The two friends, avid cricket supporters with a passion for grapes, thought that "first drop," a well-known term for cricket's first batsman who traditionally scores considerable runs, would be a great name for their joint venture. Together, it felt like they were taking the "first drop" in their careers.

The two strive to make wines that are easy to drink and not just put on a pedestal. Much like a mother's breast milk, the boys say their Shiraz "slips down easily" without much of an effort. Aussies in particular view Shiraz almost as a lifeline, just as mother's milk is to a newborn babe. Pure and delicious, this Shiraz is meant to go down intuitively and effortlessly. Who can argue with that?

Once you've gotten Mother's Milk in you, the next step is 2%—with 2% Albariño "phat" in this funked up Shiraz. And next up, after you've graduated from that, there's First Drop Mother's Ruin, which plays off artist William Hogarth's famed print *Gin Lane*, a depiction of the immense effect that cheap gin had on English society, especially in London during the 1730s. Government records have documented that the average Londoner drank 14 gallons of spirit a year. Much of the gin was drunk by women—leaving children neglected and running rampant, while wet nurses were feeding it to babies to soothe them—and bootleggers were known to peddle the alcohol under fancy names such as Cuckold's Comfort, Ladies' Delight, and Knock Me Down (which it certainly did). It is said to have left men impotent and women sterile.

While the boys of First Drop don't suggest the tomfoolery of drinking 14 gallons of Mother's Ruin, buyer beware: It will go down smoothly and taste delicious. It is sheer magnificence in moderation—the definition of which is certainly open for individual interpretation.

We have a laugh with our packaging, that's the First Drop way, but it's just as important to us that the booze is kick-ass, and has a true sense of variety and place.

—JOHN RETSAS, General Manager, and MATT GANT, Winemaker, First Drop Wines

---

FIRST DROP WINES

Appellation:	**Barossa Valley**
State:	**South Australia**
Country of Origin:	**Australia**
Type of Wine:	**Shiraz**
Web Site:	**www.firstdropwines.com**
Design:	**Mash**
Designer's Web Site:	**www.mashdesign.com.au**

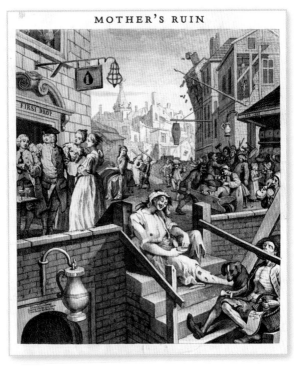

MOTHER'S RUIN

FIRST DROP WINES

Appellation:	**Barossa Valley**
State:	**South Australia**
Country of Origin:	**Australia**
Type of Wine:	**Shiraz**
Web Site:	**www.firstdropwines.com**
Design:	**Lure Creative**
Designer's Web Site:	**www.lurecreative.com.au**

FIRST DROP WINES

Appellation:	**McLaren Vale**
State:	**South Australia**
Country of Origin:	**Australia**
Type of Wine:	**Cabernet Sauvignon**
Web Site:	**www.firstdropwines.com**
Design:	**Mash**
Designer's Web Site:	**www.mashdesign.com.au**

FIVE ROWS CRAFT WINE OF LOWREY VINEYARDS

[ONTARIO ❧ CANADA]

In 1869, David Jackson Lowrey founded Lowrey Vineyards by meticulously choosing a parcel of land on what is called St. David's Bench. Here, he planted some of the first fruit crops in the area. Since then, five generations of the Lowrey family have tended the land with a concerted effort of farming with kindness, honesty, and reverence, which has resulted in a land that has continually been abundant.

The tradition of grape growing took a turn in 1984, when Howard Wesley Lowrey was urged by the region's "grandfather of wine," Karl Kaiser, to rip up the Lowrey livelihood (Concord juice grapes) and replant with *vitis vinifera* (wine grapes). Taking an immense leap of faith, the Lowreys' first five rows of Pinot Noir were planted and have successfully provided award-winning fruit to customer wineries ever since.

Wes Lowrey, the fifth in the Lowrey grape-growing family lineage, hadn't planned to follow in the family's fruitful footsteps and instead chose to study microbiology. Soon after his science degree was completed, he realized that while science was appealing to him, being constrained to a sterile and uncreative laboratory was not. He decided to turn to the land he had grown up on and worked as a young boy, the difference being they weren't the same old juice vines anymore.

It was then, in the summer of 2001, while working in those old, first five rows of Pinot Noir vines that Wes knew that the only way to thoroughly enjoy working this land and their vineyard would be for him to eventually produce his own wine from their bountiful fruit. The vision of crafting a premium, small-batch artisan wine, while still amply providing fruit to their loyal clients, was born right there and then.

> For me, the label represents the last physical contact I will have with each bottle of my wines. I like to hand-label every bottle, then admire it briefly to reflect on the journey to that point. If the label fails to move me personally or relate its wine's story, then my product would be incomplete. —WES LOWREY
> Winemaker and Labeler,
> Five Rows Craft Wine of
> Lowrey Vineyards

The name "Five Rows" and the respective labels reflect this vision made while standing amongst those first five precious and sage rows of vines. It is also a nod to the four generations prior to Wes, who, because of their gifts and care of the earth, would allow Wes to make his mark and, of course, keep him out of that boring lab.

FIVE ROWS CRAFT WINE OF LOWREY VINEYARDS

Appellation:	**St. David's Bench**
Province:	**Ontario**
Country of Origin:	**Canada**
Type of Wine:	**Pinot Gris**
Web Site:	**www.fiverows.com**
Design:	**Insite Design**
Designer's Web Site:	**www.insitedesign.ca**

THE FOLK MACHINE

[CALIFORNIA ❦ UNITED STATES]

The Folk Machine is Kenny Likitprakong's subsequent creation to his initial solo journey on the open road making wine under his proprietary company, Hobo Wine. A visual reflection of Likitprakong's inspiration found in decades of growing up in skate and surf culture, The Folk Machine wine labels are a means of visual art. With a lack of information overload, the artistic labels enable individual assessments made about his wines to be based on the enjoyment of the wine because of taste, and not because of preconceived notions that we all unintentionally carry about different varietals, blends, places, and appellations. These acquired beliefs can often bias the personal impressions of a wine on one's own palate, and therefore dissuade an honest experience by routinely seeking wine out based on other's opinions without even being aware of it.

The label is a story, a chance to express something and reach out to people. We work with artists that we like and admire, themes and ideas that mean something to us, and styles that inspire us. We try to use the label to explore our backstories and feelings, and we are constantly transforming our labels to keep up with the ways our lives and wines change.
—KENNY LIKITPRAKONG
Owner and Winemaker,
The Folk Machine

The Folk Machine wine labels are as free-spirited as Kenny's own wanderlust. Likitprakong says the wines are experimental and, consequently, both the wines and the labels reflect a sense of uncompromising exploration and change based on the adventure and expression of the winemaking each year. By keeping technical information to a minimum, it allows those who are adventurous enough to take a surprise journey and see where they end up.

THE FOLK MACHINE	
Appellation:	**Non-Designated Appellation**
State:	**California**
Country of Origin:	**United States**
Type of Wine:	**Red Blend**
Web Site:	**www.hobowines.com**
Design:	**Landonsea**
Designer's Web Site:	**www.landonsea.com**

THE FOLK MACHINE	
Appellation:	**Non-Designated Appellation**
State:	**California**
Country of Origin:	**United States**
Type of Wine:	**White Blend**
Web Site:	**www.hobowines.com**
Design:	**Landonsea**
Designer's Web Site:	**www.landonsea.com**

THE FOREIGN AFFAIR WINERY

[ONTARIO ❧ CANADA]

the
Foreign Affair
Riesling 2007
VQA NIAGARA PENINSULA VQA

Work may have brought Len and Marisa Crispino to Italy, but true love brought Italy home with them to Canada.

During the early 1990s, the Crispino family lived as Canadian expatriates in Milan, Italy, while Len was on a work term. During this period, they all became enamored with living simple joys as transplanted locals. Particularly, they became besotted with the Amarone-styled wines that were prevalent in the northern part of the country. They even let their minds wonder how they would be able to bring this distinct Italian craftsmanship back home with them when it was time for their return—clearly this captivation with the wine was more than a holiday fling.

After saying goodbye to Italy, the Crispinos returned home to find themselves unexpectedly contemplating their lives as they once knew them. They evaluated what passions they intended to surround themselves with in order to continue living the fullest life possible. Back came memories of that unique, foreign style of wine that

THE FOREIGN AFFAIR WINERY
Appellation:	**Niagara Peninsula**
Province:	**Ontario**
Country of Origin:	**Canada**
Type of Wine:	**Riesling**
Web Site:	**www.foreignaffairwine.com**
Design:	**Brandever**
Designer's Web Site:	**www.brandever.com**

Ti Amo

THE FOREIGN AFFAIR WINERY
Appellation: **Niagara Peninsula**
Province: **Ontario**
Country of Origin: **Canada**
Type of Wine: **Cabernet Franc**
Web Site: **www.foreignaffairwine.com**
Design: **Brandever**
Designer's Web Site: **www.brandever.com**

Abbraccio

THE FOREIGN AFFAIR WINERY
Appellation: **Niagara Peninsula**
Province: **Ontario**
Country of Origin: **Canada**
Type of Wine: **Sauvignon Blanc**
Web Site: **www.foreignaffairwine.com**
Design: **Brandever**
Designer's Web Site: **www.brandever.com**

What's in a label? A label excites the senses. It invites us to experience further into the soul of the wine. A well-designed label tells the story in a suggestive, provocative, and compelling way.

—LEN and MARISA CRISPINO
Owners, The Foreign Affair Winery

had captured both of their hearts and silently urged them to bring their interpretation of the craftsmanship to Ontario, Canada. Which is exactly what they did. The Crispinos planted 40 acres of their beloved Amarone-style vines, and after three years of tender loving care and devotion to the fruit, they harvested their first crop in 2004.

The Crispinos, now the local experts on the craft of the traditional Amarone style, have brought an authentic piece of Italy to the Niagara Peninsula. Their chosen name and wine labels, The Foreign Affair, bridges the gap between the Crispinos' love for two very different countries and cultures, ultimately culminating with a very special blending of the two: the foreign landscape of Italy, where the life-altering affair with Amarone began and, in contrast, the local Canadian fauna indicative of where their roots are and where the next chapter of the romance continues to unfold. The turbulent skies represent the tumultuousness of life that is often the best catalyst for change. For the Crispinos, Amarone-styled wine in Canada—now *that's* amore!

FORREST WINES

[MARLBOROUGH ❧ NEW ZEALAND]

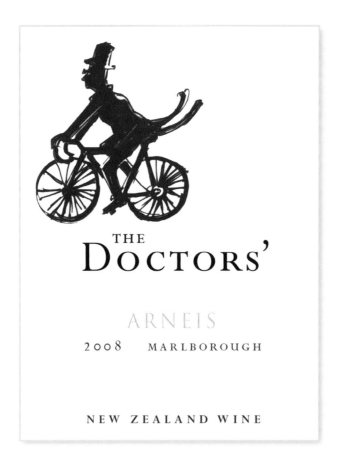

The saying "an apple a day keeps the doctor away" takes on a slight variation with the Forrest Wines The Doctors' label, named after owners John and Brigid Forrest. Both coming from very successful medical careers (John, a neurobiologist, and Brigid, a general practitioner), the esteemed doctors have long agreed with the philosophy that wine, taken in moderation, has many health benefits. Studies have actually indicated that the health advantages can reach far and wide, implicating both physical and emotional wellness. Not only does wine act as a social gatherer, but it also has been said to combat the hardening of arteries, increase good cholesterol, decrease the instance of and the slowing of the progression of a variety of cancers, and act as an antioxidant, amongst other positive effects.

Consequently, the Forrests have spent extensive time researching wine and its relation to health, and they have developed a series of wines based in winemaking innovation and alternative techniques and varietals to make lower-alcohol-styled wines that can be enjoyed (in moderation) on a daily basis. Hurrah! Particularly, the relatively unknown grape varietal Arneis, native to Piedmont, Italy, has been brought to the forefront in The Doctors' range for its natural lower acidity levels and crisp floral notes, making it not only a joy to drink, but a healthy choice, too.

The imagery selected for The Doctors' wine label pays homage to Dr. John Forrest's tendency towards exercising creativity in his innovation. The image of a mad scientist in a Seuss-like style of illustration is indicative of the doctors' lightheartedness, while constantly striving for invariable excellence both as doctors and with their wines.

According to these esteemed health experts, a glass of wine a day should help keep illness away, but it won't necessarily keep The Doctors' away.

FORREST WINES

Appellation:	**Marlborough**
Region:	**Marlborough**
Country of Origin:	**New Zealand**
Type of Wine:	**Arneis**
Web Site:	**www.forrest.co.nz**
Design:	**Harvey Cameron Advertising**
Designer's Web Site:	**www.hca.co.nz**

FORREST WINES

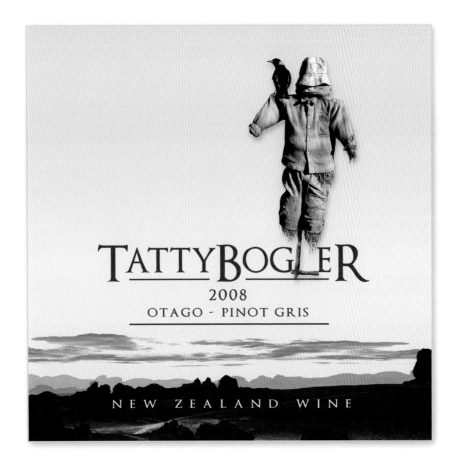

Otago is considered to be the heart of the Scottish expatriate community in New Zealand. Having two vineyards in the region, winemaker Dr. John Forrest decided to salute his Scottish ancestors and pioneers of the region who paved (or ploughed) the way for today's regional success.

Scarecrows are one of the most recognized identities of the rural landscape and are identified with farming internationally. To the Scots, a more familiar word for scarecrow is a "Tatty Bogler." Traditionally erected in the potato fields (tatty fields), they were meant to ward off birds, typically crows known best for destroying the crops, while also being annoying and noisy when they congregated.

(Coincidentally, The Scarecrow in the classic 1939 American film *The Wizard of Oz* was played by actor Ray Bolger, likely destined for the role given his last name, an anagram of the Scottish word for scarecrow, "bogler.")

To this day, many farmers still use scarecrows in their fields. This is a practice that the Forrests follow not only to guard the vines from destructive birds, but also because the scarecrow is known to be a deterrent of interference from evil spirits. As such, to honor the Scots of yesteryear and the good riddance made by the friendly scarecrow, a traditional tatty bogler graces this Forrest wine label.

FORREST WINES

Appellation:	**Otago**
Region:	**Otago**
Country of Origin:	**New Zealand**
Type of Wine:	**Pinot Gris**
Web Site:	**www.forrest.co.nz**
Design:	**Harvey Cameron Advertising**
Designer's Web Site:	**www.hca.co.nz**

FRANÇOIS LURTON

[CASTILE AND LEÓN ❧ SPAIN]

You know the words—the curse words and phrases that if heard by your mother, your mouth would be full of soap in the blink of an eye. In some contexts, though, there just aren't any other words to use. Granted, if used in the wrong context, these words can mean something very, very wrong, but in the right context and culture, they can mean something very, very good—like a double entendre. It seems like all languages have them, but the relative meaning can definitely get lost in translation from one language to the next.

Take the phrase "*de puta madre*," for instance. Without knowing the context, *puta* would translate from Spanish to "f——k" in English, and *madre* would translate to "mother." The two put together translates to . . . well, you know. However, in Spanish slang, the phrase actually leans more so to mean the English equivalent and less-offensive exclamation, "holy s——t."

Most commonly throughout Spain, the saying actually is not derogatory at all. In fact, it is said to suggest that something is extremely good, especially appealing, or exceptionally desirable. It can be applied to people, situations, things, experiences, and even really good wines—"*Ese vino es de puta madre*," or, "This wine is so f——ing good!"

When François Lurton was working on his wines in Spain, he crafted one in the style of many of the old cellar masters who used to make *solera* wines, or sweet wines, that were aged in the sun. He used overripe Verdejo grapes and aged the wine in custom, 100-liter barrels to increase the contact of the wine with the wood. Almost forgotten, the wines in these made-to-measure barrels were tasted two years later. When François's cellar master tasted the wine, he exclaimed, "*De puta madre, que bueno!*" which, like the wine, left a lasting impressing on François and inspired a wine label representing something very, very good.

So if you are ever caught in what is thought to be an inappropriate language predicament, tell the *de puta madre* story and it will be sure to get you out of hot water—and hopefully into some wine.

FRANÇOIS LURTON

Appellation:	**Rueda**
Community:	**Castile and León**
Country of Origin:	**Spain**
Type of Wine:	**Verdejo**
Web Site:	**www.francoislurton.com**
Design:	**Thomas Berthon Design**
Designer's Web Site:	**www.monsieur-tom.com**

François Lurton Le Pas de la Mûle wines are made in the Roussillon region of France. Here, the grapes for the wine are sourced from very old Grenache vines planted in rugged terrain on the top of a small, hilly part of the vineyard.

Technically, the label needs to fulfill a single objective: to identify the product. This distinguishes our wine from our competitors. But, more importantly, it evokes what is in the bottle, conveys an emotion, and stimulates the senses before the cork is pulled. It is this anticipation that plays a key role in the pleasure of enjoying wine. —VIVIANA VECCHIONE Marketing Manager, François Lurton

Historically, this area acted as a pass (or *pas* in Catalan, due to Roussillon's proximity to the Spanish border) through the mountain, at the foothills of the Corbières separating Aude from the Pyrénées-Orientales. Most of the passes were high and difficult to navigate. Today, you can often still see the worn tracks grooved out of the stone by the well-trodden route of the mules, which have not changed for centuries. These treacherous passes were once significant for communication, trade, and war.

Today, luckily for the mules, most major passes have been replaced with proper roads or railways. However, you are still able to hike the numerous passes in this beautiful region for which the Mas Janeil Le Pas de la Mûle wine label commemorates.

FRANÇOIS LURTON

Appellation:	**Côtes du Roussillon-Villages**
Region:	**Languedoc-Roussillon**
Country of Origin:	**France**
Type of Wine:	**Grenache, Syrah, and Mourvèdre Blend**
Web Site:	**www.francoislurton.com**
Design:	**Gabriel Despagne Design**
Designer's Web Site:	**www.ggetdd.com**

FROG'S LEAP

[CALIFORNIA ❧ UNITED STATES]

The delicacy of frog's legs isn't solely limited to French cuisine. In fact, in the early twentieth century, farming frogs in the United States was a lucrative commerce that often had the stock sold out prior to even being reared and raised. A 1934 edition of the popular how-to magazine *Modern Mechanix* offered step-by-step instructions on how to get rich farming frogs. One of such breeding facilities was once located along Mill Creek in Rutherford, California, but was eventually converted to a vineyard for farming grapes.

When the Williams family purchased the property that would become home to its winery, an old ledger revealed the land's hopping history in the frog industry at the turn of the century. The records indicated that frogs were raised and sold at $0.33 per dozen, most likely to Victorian-era gourmets.

Prior to the purchase of this historical frog-farming facility, John Williams worked at a then-little-known wine outfit called Stag's Leap Wine Cellars. After the property purchase in 1981, John crafted the family's first vintage with grapes borrowed from Stag's Leap—the grapes making a literal and figurative "leap" from one winery to the other. Graphic designer Chuck House, not widely known at the time, either, designed the inaugural 1981 vintage label for "a couple hundred bucks and a couple cases of wine," effectively instating the name "Frog's Leap" to the winery.

Over a quarter of a century later, little has changed about the Frog's Leap wine label—though the designer and winery have quite a few accolades under their belts now. John Williams still runs the family's winery estate with sustainable farming practices, an utmost respect for their natural surroundings, and a commitment to honorable stewardship of the land—all with a "whimsical exuberance" that is summed up best by the Williams family motto: "Time's fun when you're having flies." With this kind of attitude, there's no doubt that Frog's Leap winery is a feeding frenzy for frogs and wine lovers alike.

FROG'S LEAP	
Appellation:	**Rutherford**
State:	**California**
Country of Origin:	**United States**
Type of Wine:	**Sauvignon Blanc**
Web Site:	**www.frogsleap.com**
Design:	**Chuck House (Icon Design Group)**
Designer's Web Site:	**www.icondesigngroup.net**

Giant Steps/Innocent Bystander

[Victoria ❧ Australia]

750mL

When the owners of and creative forces behind Giant Steps/Innocent Bystander, Phil and Alison Sexton, had their first child, the duo appropriately named a very special wine, only made during very warm and exceptional years, after him.

Now, it's natural for children who are born to winemaker parents and who grow up amongst the vines to get their hands dirty and learn the language of grapes at a very young age. The vineyards, the workers, the winery—it is what they come to know almost through osmosis. Harry was no different. Of course, as any inquisitive boy would, and knowing the lay of the vineyard land, Harry decided that it was time for him to be more involved in his wine at the age of eleven. After all, it had his name on it, didn't it?

Feeling that he was slightly too young to be consulting on the winemaking side of things, Phil and Alison suggested Harry "consult" on a new look for *his* label. As such, from the 2005 vintage onwards, the big and bold Giant Steps wine blend, made from the highest slopes of the Sexton vineyard, became true to its name with artwork handcrafted, like the wine, by the little monster himself.

GIANT STEPS/INNOCENT BYSTANDER

Appellation:	**Yarra Valley**
State:	**Victoria**
Country of Origin:	**Australia**
Type of Wine:	**Red Blend**
Web Site:	**www.giant-steps.com.au**
Art:	**Harry Sexton**

In the late 1990s, the idea for Goats do Roam was born while well-known South African winemaker Charles Back was attending a wine-tasting event. Sitting with his United Kingdom importer at the time, the two were discussing his wine-producing farm in the Western Cape province, which dates back to 1693 and had also become home to hundreds of Swiss goats used for the production of over thirty exotic cheeses.

Charles also loosely mentioned that he was interested in launching a blended wine based on the vineyard's primary varietal, Shiraz, and others, including Grenache and Carignan. After a few glasses of wine, Charles returned to regaling about the herd of goats that roamed his property like *they* owned it. He told a story about how, once, the gate of the goat tower was left open, and the goats eagerly freed themselves and helped themselves to the ripest berries. Eventually, the two men laughed about the quip, "Goats do roam," as a name for the blend they had previously spoke about and, consequently, the first vintage was released in 1998 using Rhône varietals.

While the name may be taken as a friendly jab at French wines, it was never meant to be. Back has said that in order not to be viewed as another "critter" label, he produced a wine that would exceed expectations and authentically represent the pride he had in the capability of South African wine. Furthermore, the fact that there really is a very true story behind the la-

THE GOATS DO ROAM WINE COMPANY (FAIRVIEW)

Appellation:	**Paarl/Agter-Paarl/Stellenbosch**
Province:	**Western Cape**
Country of Origin:	**South Africa**
Type of Wine:	**Red Blend**
Web Site:	**www.goatsdoroam.com**

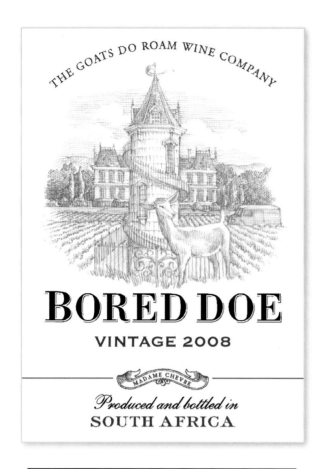

THE GOATS DO ROAM WINE COMPANY (FAIRVIEW)
Appellation: **Stellenbosch/Darling/Paarl Mountain**
Province: **Western Cape**
Country of Origin: **South Africa**
Type of Wine: **Red Blend**
Web Site: **www.goatsdoroam.com**

THE GOATS DO ROAM WINE COMPANY (FAIRVIEW)
Appellation: **Paarl/Agter-Paarl/Swartland**
Province: **Western Cape**
Country of Origin: **South Africa**
Type of Wine: **Shiraz and Viognier Blend**
Web Site: **www.goatsdoroam.com**

bel that involves roaming goats that actually do produce the largest amount of exotic cheese in South Africa certainly corroborated the Goats do Roam label design.

The wines with the garish yellow label adorned with a goat achieved much success, perhaps due to the approachability of its name and the subsequent enjoyment of the distinct South African flavor inside the bottle. However, there were some that vehemently opposed Goats do Roam's success. Namely, the French government, who sued Charles Back and issued a cease-and-desist letter in 2004 under the premise that the name "Goats do Roam" was creating a confusing situation in the marketplace and was also a blatant insult to the French appellation of Côtes du Rhône. Although the legal fees surmounted $100,000, Back was unwilling to lose the "Goats" versus "Côtes" battle.

Deciding to take another approach, Charles Back assembled a troop of Goats supporters and marched to the French consulate in South Africa, flanked with placards and adorned with goat masks and regalia promoting their "don't buck with us" message. Charles Back personally knocked on the front door and presented the consulate with a 3-liter bottle of wine, a selection of their estate cheeses, and a mammoth bag of goat manure—perhaps to "fertilize" their relationship in the hopes that it would grow more friendly. The French government quietly disappeared from their once-aggressive allegation. The silence was deafening. When approached by the press requesting a statement, the French declined to comment. Needless to say, the goats continue to roam and on any given day, you can still always find some authentic Goat Roti to enjoy while sitting back, relaxing, and savoring a little Bored Doe.

GRIFFIN WINES

[SOUTH AUSTRALIA ❧ AUSTRALIA]

The Griffin family has owned what it calls "The Farm" for over thirty years. The original 118-acre piece of scrub and pasture proved perfect for cattle, and those cattle eventually had a total of 235 acres of pasture to graze. In the mid-1990s, however, cattle prices were low and the family was running quite a large herd. The family's Kuitpo neighbors, with their heads in the clouds, decided to start planting grapes.

At over 1,000 feet above sea level, Kuitpo is challenged by some adverse conditions that make viticulture difficult. However, the region also boasts some amazing fruit. The challenge seemed worth it for the Griffins, who embraced the transition wholeheartedly as lovers of the outdoors. And together as a family, Trevor, Val, Mark, and Tim, along with the family's three dogs, all dug in to convert the cattle yard into a vineyard.

In 2002–2003, the 66-acre vineyard was being run entirely by the family. Trevor Griffin says that at Easter, which falls anywhere from the end of March to early April from year to year and coincides with harvest, the family "works like convicts." This is a very funny way of describing it. Especially coming from the *Honorable* Trevor Griffin, who retired from the South Australian Parliament in 2002 after twenty-five years as a member of Legislative Council and who, for a considerable period of time, held the role of state attorney general.

A true family operation, the Griffin family harvests over two hundred tons of grapes during each vintage. They are involved with every single aspect of the vineyard, from maintenance to wine production to the marketing of their wines. The wine labels reflect the importance of the involvement each member (Val's label has to be coming next?) and the joy it brings to them as a family, right down to the dogs, Bear and Hamish, who are in absolute heaven on "The Farm."

Like a magnet, one is drawn to the design of the label and its equally important narrative as a physical representation of the unique qualities of the wine. The Griffin label reflects commitment by family, elegance of style, and passion seeking to transmute the best from the soil, the vine, and the fruit into the bottle.
—TREVOR GRIFFIN
Owner, Griffin Wines

GRIFFIN WINES
Appellation:	**Adelaide Hills**
State:	**South Australia**
Country of Origin:	**Australia**
Type of Wine:	**Chardonnay**
Web Site:	**www.griffinwines.com**
Design:	**Black Squid Design**
Designer's Web Site:	**www.blacksquid.com.au**

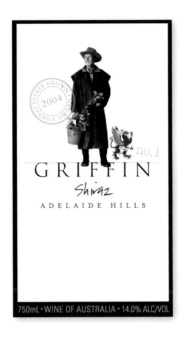

GRIFFIN WINES

Appellation:	**Adelaide Hills**
State:	**South Australia**
Country of Origin:	**Australia**
Type of Wine:	**Shiraz**
Web Site:	**www.griffinwines.com**
Design:	**Black Squid Design**
Designer's Web Site:	**www.blacksquid.com.au**

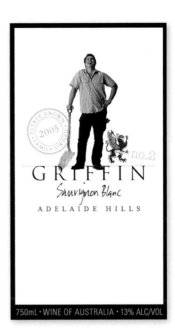

GRIFFIN WINES

Appellation:	**Adelaide Hills**
State:	**South Australia**
Country of Origin:	**Australia**
Type of Wine:	**Sauvignon Blanc**
Web Site:	**www.griffinwines.com**
Design:	**Black Squid Design**
Designer's Web Site:	**www.blacksquid.com.au**

GRIFFIN WINES

Appellation:	**Adelaide Hills**
State:	**South Australia**
Country of Origin:	**Australia**
Type of Wine:	**Pinot Noir**
Web Site:	**www.griffinwines.com**
Design:	**Black Squid Design**
Designer's Web Site:	**www.blacksquid.com.au**

GRIFFIN WINES

Appellation:	**Adelaide Hills**
State:	**South Australia**
Country of Origin:	**Australia**
Type of Wine:	**Merlot**
Web Site:	**www.griffinwines.com**
Design:	**Black Squid Design**
Designer's Web Site:	**www.blacksquid.com.au**

GUT OGGAU

[BURGENLAND ❧ AUSTRIA]

GUT OGGAU
WILTRUDE
(SÜSS)

In the province of Burgenland, Austria, you will find Gut Oggau, a biodynamic vineyard where wine is a family affair. Not only because the husband-and-wife team of Eduard Tscheppe and Stephanie Tscheppe-Eselböck works to produce authentic wines in its own modern style, but because of the extended family of wines that it has created together.

Each wine "born" at Gut Oggau has its own distinctive personality or temperament, while still being tied together in familial unity through regional flavors. The wines have been given traditional Austrian names adopted from the history of the former owners of the property, and each wine will tell you a different story about its history and character. With the youngest generation "still in puberty," as Eduard says, they might speak of fresh, fruity, and vibrant flavors. Their "parents," or the second generation, are elegant wines who have aged and now have some more experience in life to speak about through their full bodies and relaxed demeanors. The first generation is made of very special wines and has many tales to tell about how they have been pampered with nineteenth-century oak presses and the wisdom gained from their deeper aging process.

The design of the label or the bottle is the first thing that catches your eye; it can attract or distract you. For us, it is important that the design tells the story behind the wine and fits the concept, so it makes sense as one. There is no worse thing than a perfectly designed bottle filled with a wine you can't enjoy. —STEPHANIE TSCHEPPE-ESELBÖCK and EDUARD TSCHEPPE
Owners, Familie Tscheppe-Eselböck

At Gut Oggau, the focus is on biodynamic farming and supporting its unique biotope. Instead of protecting the vines per se, it looks to strengthen and preserve the unique character of each plant. And, of course, all the wines are treated like children—"You can't love one more than another," Eduard assures. The same amount of love and energy has been dedicated to each offspring in their own way. As such, each "child" has its own personal label to boast the personality of what's on the inside.

**GUT OGGAU
(FAMILIE TSCHEPPE-ESELBÖCK)**

Appellation:	**Oggau**
	(Non-Designated Appellation)
State:	**Burgenland**
Country of Origin:	**Austria**
Type of Wine:	**Sweet**
Web Site:	**www.gutoggau.com**
Design:	**Jung von Matt/Donau**
Designer's Web Site:	**www.jvm.com**

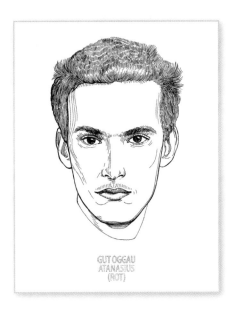

**GUT OGGAU
(FAMILIE TSCHEPPE-ESELBÖCK)**

Appellation:	**Oggau**
	(Non-Designated Appellation)
State:	**Burgenland**
Country of Origin:	**Austria**
Type of Wine:	**Red**
Web Site:	**www.gutoggau.com**
Design:	**Jung von Matt/Donau**
Designer's Web Site:	**www.jvm.com**

**GUT OGGAU
(FAMILIE TSCHEPPE-ESELBÖCK)**

Appellation:	**Oggau**
	(Non-Designated Appellation)
State:	**Burgenland**
Country of Origin:	**Austria**
Type of Wine:	**White**
Web Site:	**www.gutoggau.com**
Design:	**Jung von Matt/Donau**
Designer's Web Site:	**www.jvm.com**

**GUT OGGAU
(FAMILIE TSCHEPPE-ESELBÖCK)**

Appellation:	**Oggau**
	(Non-Designated Appellation)
State:	**Burgenland**
Country of Origin:	**Austria**
Type of Wine:	**White**
Web Site:	**www.gutoggau.com**
Design:	**Jung von Matt/Donau**
Designer's Web Site:	**www.jvm.com**

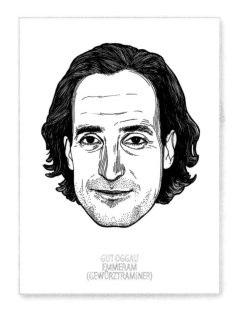

**GUT OGGAU
(FAMILIE TSCHEPPE-ESELBÖCK)**

Appellation:	**Oggau**
	(Non-Designated Appellation)
State:	**Burgenland**
Country of Origin:	**Austria**
Type of Wine:	**Gewürztraminer**
Web Site:	**www.gutoggau.com**
Design:	**Jung von Matt/Donau**
Designer's Web Site:	**www.jvm.com**

HAPPY CAMPER WINES

[CALIFORNIA ❧ UNITED STATES]

Stuffy, stale, and pretentious are words sometimes associated with the conservative, indoor wine-consumption experience. Why stay inside when the expanse of nature beckons and offers a much more compelling backdrop and experience? Happy Camper Wines celebrates the freedom available in the great outdoors, the appreciation for living landscapes, and the adventures, camaraderie, and memories to be made with friends when sharing a bottle of wine. Be it on the beach, in the desert, in the forest, in your own backyard, or even with the windows wide open and a picnic blanket spread out on your living room floor, the opportunities are endless.

The retro-styled camper emblazoned on the Happy Camper wine labels is a true piece of Americana, using the iconic Airstream trailer that was created by Wally Byam during the Great Depression as its inspiration. It started when Byam worked as an advertising copywriter for the *Los Angeles Times*. Not enjoying working for someone else, he decided to open up his own shop and publish do-it-yourself guides for home carpenters and builders. He stumbled upon an article on how to build a camping trailer and bought the article for publication.

People immediately embraced the notion of building their own campers, but it wasn't long, however, before letters of complaint started flowing in due to the less-than-perfect DIY plans. An industrious Byam, determined to fix the problem, abandoned the article and started building trailers of his own in the backyard. He rewrote the article and sold it to *Popular Mechanics* in order to finance his new full-time occupation: building camper trailers. Neighbors started paying attention. Word spread and eventually his custom model experiments were sought out for sale under the name "Airstream." Byam went on to live his philosophy, "see more, do more, live more," and created the largest group of owners in RV history, the Wally Byam Caravan Club, as he led camper caravans all over the world.

The classic image of the Airstream is a symbol of adventure, discovery, and exploration. According to the Recreational Vehicle Industry Association (RVIA), one in ten American vehicle owners also owns a recreational vehicle, otherwise known as an RV.

The world is a big place with lots of space to explore—and, like many other things, it is always better done in the company of good friends and wine.

HAPPY CAMPER WINES

Appellation:	**Non-Designated Appellation**
State:	**California**
Country of Origin:	**United States**
Type of Wine:	**Chardonnay**
Web Site:	**www.happycamperwines.com**
Design:	**Buster O'Connor**
Designer's Web Site:	**www.verdeo.tv**

Hard Row to Hoe Vineyards

[Washington ❧ United States]

A "hard row to hoe" is a tongue-in-cheek play on an old idiom applied to a piece of local history in Lake Chelan, the region where Judy and Don Phelps's vineyard sits on its shores in Manson, Washington. The vineyard moniker is an homage to a colorful local account of old escapades as reminisced by some of the elder local natives.

As the grapevine story goes, around 1924, the Edgemont Lodge was built a few miles up from Lucerne, in an area appropriately named Point Lovely. At this time, the Grand Coulee Dam was also being built. When construction of the dam tapered off in the early '30s, some of the Coulee "dames" moved down to Edgemont Lodge to provide "service" to the miners in a newly operational Howe Sound mine in Lucerne.

The label is the face of the winery that everyone sees and, hopefully, remembers. Having only one chance for a first impression, it is important for the label to open the door of intrigue within the mind, thus luring the consumer to select that bottle from the sea of bottles.

—Don Phelps
Proprietor, Hard Row to Hoe Vineyards

Wanting to capitalize on the booming enterprise in his own way, one Manson resident initiated a rowboat taxi service from Lucerne to Point Lovely, ensuring that those that required "servicing" indeed got the ministrations that were duly desired. Of course, none of the miners wanted to miss that boat. Discovering the adulterous activity, the misdemeanant miners' wives stole the boat and attempted to burn down the brothel, eventually succeeding at razing it to the ground in 1940.

Hard Row to Hoe Vineyards remembers the naughtiness of the region's bygone eras and reflects the handiwork of Judy and Don Phelps done together in their vineyards, along the rows in a sea of grapes, with a hoe (not "ho"!) in hand.

HARD ROW TO HOE VINEYARDS	
Appellation:	**Wahluke Slope**
State:	**Washington**
Country of Origin:	**United States**
Type of Wine:	**Cabernet Sauvignon, Merlot, and Syrah Blend**
Web Site:	**www.hardrow.com**
Design:	**Brandever**
Designer's Web Site:	**www.brandever.com**

Henry's Drive Vignerons

[South Australia ❧ Australia]

Long before locomotives were pervasive, when the establishment of the farm and wine industry of South Australia was at its peak during the 1800s, horse-drawn coaches traveled hundreds of miles over rough terrain to transport passengers and deliver mail. These regular routes were called "drives," and the coachmen became well known and were respected by passengers and mail recipients alike for being an essential service critical to the community's daily life. In the southeastern area of South Australia, the region's coach service proprietor and mail contractor was Mr. Henry John Hill, whose coach not only regularly carried the mail and members of the laity, but also the parson as he made his way around the district doing the things that all good parsons do.

Of course, it wasn't solely pleasantries on Henry Hill's drives. Particularly, an incident in 1863 scandalized one of the region's local townships, a few miles away from today's Padthaway, when bushranger bandit John Montford, wielding a pistol and handkerchiefed in disguise, held up the mail coach and took flight with an excess of £75. He didn't make it very far, though. Still yielding the handkerchief with the cut eyeholes in his swag, he was convicted for his crime.

On the very land where Mr. Henry John Hill conducted his coach drive, three generations of Longbottoms have driven the growth of the family's vineyards more recently. Staying connected to the land and the people who hoofed it before them, the Longbottoms have remembered them in the chosen name of their winery, Henry's Drive. They also pay tribute to the good parson, the convicted thief, and the thousands of letters that traveled the drive, but never made it to their rightful homes, deemed "dead letters." A dead letter office employs the only people with the authority to open undeliverable mail and are still in service today. The Dead Letter Office label salutes those deciphering postal clerks tasked with uncovering the details to right the routes of thousands of wayward letters each and every year.

HENRY'S DRIVE VIGNERONS

Appellation:	**Padthaway**
State:	**South Australia**
Country of Origin:	**Australia**
Type of Wine:	**Cabernet Sauvignon**
Web Site:	**www.henrysdrive.com**
Design:	**Parallax Design**
Designer's Web Site:	**www.parallaxdesign.com.au**

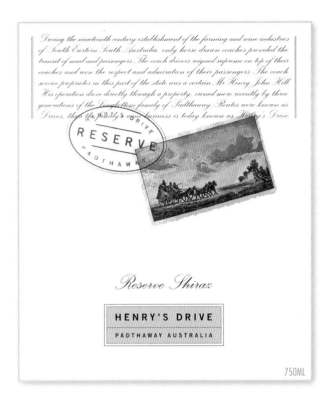

Reserve Shiraz

HENRY'S DRIVE

PADTHAWAY AUSTRALIA

750ML

HENRY'S DRIVE VIGNERONS

Appellation:	**Padthaway**
State:	**South Australia**
Country of Origin:	**Australia**
Type of Wine:	**Shiraz**
Web Site:	**www.henrysdrive.com**
Design:	**Parallax Design**
Designer's Web Site:	**www.parallaxdesign.com.au**

PADTHAWAY
PARSON'S FLAT
SHIRAZ · CABERNET

750ML

HENRY'S DRIVE VIGNERONS

Appellation:	**Padthaway**
State:	**South Australia**
Country of Origin:	**Australia**
Type of Wine:	**Shiraz and Cabernet Sauvignon Blend**
Web Site:	**www.henrysdrive.com**
Design:	**Parallax Design**
Designer's Web Site:	**www.parallaxdesign.com.au**

Dead Letter Office

750ML

HENRY'S DRIVE VIGNERONS

Appellation:	**Padthaway/McLaren Vale**
State:	**South Australia**
Country of Origin:	**Australia**
Type of Wine:	**Shiraz**
Web Site:	**www.henrysdrive.com**
Design:	**Parallax Design**
Designer's Web Site:	**www.parallaxdesign.com.au**

THE HESKETH WINE COMPANY
[SOUTH AUSTRALIA ✖ AUSTRALIA]

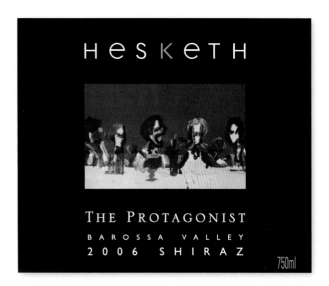

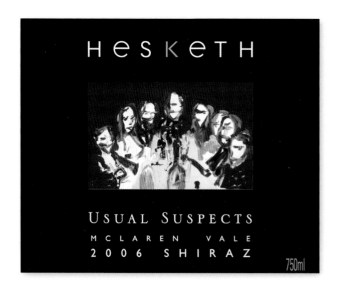

Winemaker Jonathon Hesketh says that wine is like a condiment—it's a food that needs to be packaged to reflect what's inside. Unfortunately, samples that could provide you with insight can't be put on labels, but art that reflects all that the wine is can be. Further, art (unlike words) can be appreciated and interpreted across diverse cultures without any translation whatsoever.

Brought up with wine from an early age, Jonathon learnt that the wine industry, while global, was also very small. After a successful career, Jonathon and his wife, Trisha, decided to launch their own wine label as negotiants. The wines made by the Heskeths followed a shared, three-part winemaking philosophy: "Wine is a social lubricant that should be enjoyed with food, friends, and healthy conversation."

The artwork for the labels was first discovered in 2000 on the head table at a wedding celebration of two of the Heskeths' friends. There was an immediate gravitation toward the modern style of work and the message of shared merriment between friends. The piece was coined "The Protagonist" as a reflection of what Barossa Valley Shiraz has been for the Australian wine industry—the merrymaker.

As for The Usual Suspects, this image is a direct representation of Jonathon and his best mates, who Trisha calls "the usual suspects." We all have them; the ones you enjoy your wine, food, and healthy conversation with on a regular basis. By selecting these works of art for their wine labels, the Heskeths are able to communicate their winemaking philosophy in a manner that all—no matter what race, religion, language, or nationality—can easily understand.

Labels are important—not because of what they say about the wine, but because of what they say about the drinker. We want our wines to look good on your table, and to make you look good! However, that counts for nothing if the quality in the bottle doesn't exceed the quality of the packaging. Disappointment is, after all, directly proportional to expectation! —JONATHON HESKETH
Owner, The Hesketh Wine Company

THE HESKETH WINE COMPANY

Appellation:	**Barossa Valley**
State:	**South Australia**
Country of Origin:	**Australia**
Type of Wine:	**Shiraz**
Web Site:	**www.heskethwinecompany.com.au**
Design:	**Tucker Creative**
Designer's Web Site:	**www.tuckercreative.com.au**
Art:	**Hamish Macdonald**

THE HESKETH WINE COMPANY

Appellation:	**McLaren Vale**
State:	**South Australia**
Country of Origin:	**Australia**
Type of Wine:	**Shiraz**
Web Site:	**www.heskethwinecompany.com.au**
Design:	**Tucker Creative**
Designer's Web Site:	**www.tuckercreative.com.au**
Art:	**Hamish Macdonald**

HIGHFLYER WINES

[CALIFORNIA ❧ UNITED STATES]

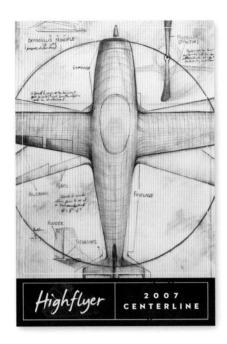 

Not many people are able to boast that they can be anywhere within an hour or two in the state of California, which spans 163,696 square miles and has a length of 770 miles from the northern tip to the southern, especially given the state's reputation for severe traffic congestion. In addition, try working in a different location anywhere in the state of California on a daily basis, and still make it home in time for dinner each night. Traveling by ground, it would be impossible, but by air is another story. But who does that, besides John Travolta or Clint Eastwood? Well, a certain high-flying winemaker by the name of Craig Becker does.

The idea was triggered when Craig was consulting in 1999 with one of his clients, who just happened to have a runway in the middle of their vineyard. This spawned his idea to investigate an alternate means of commuting to and from work each day and, as such, he has been able to blend two of his passions together, piloting his own Cessna 182 Skylane and making wine, without any boundaries in terms of vineyard sources or varietal styles.

Labels create emotion, setting a stage for a hopeful memory. It is in the label that you find pride, passion, or purpose. It paints a place, a tradition, or simply sculpts the impression of the winery.

—DAVID ZUROWSKI
Marketing Director, Highflyer Wines

Each of the Highflyer wine labels illustrates Craig's unique ability to be just about anywhere in California with as much ease as jumping in a cab and zipping across town, though his cab has wings and Craig just happens to be the driver. The labels also provide an impression of the style of wine in each bottle. For instance, the Centerline Red blend is a no-holds-barred assembly of the most proportional wine and likewise, the label features an illustration playing on Leonardo da Vinci's famous drawing, the *Vitruvian Man*, based on the principals of architect Vitruvius Pollio.

HIGHFLYER WINES

Appellation:	**Napa Valley**
State:	**California**
Country of Origin:	**United States**
Type of Wine:	**Red Blend**
Web Site:	**www.highflyerwines.com**
Design:	**Plumbline Studios**
Designer's Web Site:	**www.plumbline.com**
Art:	**Christopher Paddock**

HIGHFLYER WINES

Appellation:	**Napa Valley**
State:	**California**
Country of Origin:	**United States**
Type of Wine:	**Viognier**
Web Site:	**www.highflyerwines.com**
Design:	**Plumbline Studios**
Designer's Web Site:	**www.plumbline.com**
Art:	**Christopher Paddock**

HOFFMAN CELLARS
[CALIFORNIA ❧ UNITED STATES]

It's an unusual task to come up with a name for something that is part of your own blood, sweat, and tears, but that you feel needs to tell more than is capable with just your name. Such was the case with Brian Hoffman's personal wine venture. In looking for an adjacent designation to be paired with Hoffman Cellars, Brian and friends appropriately drank the fruits of their own labor and, sure enough, the perfect name did unfold.

The television was on in the background—a history show that Brian says was about something just old enough to be considered history, but young enough to relate to and they found their name. Or rather, it found them.

During the first years of the 1900s, a forlorn work camp existed in the dusty Mojave Desert, where some four-to-eight-hundred railroad workers called this camp home. They were unfortunately accustomed to the endless heat and exhausted by the long hours of physical drudgery. Founded on a once-Mormon settlement, the camp's past may have been the premise of its legal abstinence from anything remotely fun: No alcohol, no gambling, and definitely no philandering allowed. Naturally, these realities didn't make the camp a breeding ground of merrymaking.

But then a building went up. And more followed. Then streets were built, two of them to be exact. These streets, First and Ogden, became the cornerstone of the beginnings of the town of Las Vegas. And within the confines of these streets and a few flimsy buildings, a well-deserved distraction from the drudgery of daily life at the camp emerged. It was here, in what was called the area of Block 16, that drinking, gambling, laughing, cavorting, "companionship," and music all were legal. And, boy, did the spirit of the camp change! But by the time World War II was underway, Block 16 and its infamous revelry were abandoned for the greater good and, eventually, a changed economy. Today, Block 16 is a little-known piece of unconventional Nevada history.

So, what does this Napa Valley wine have to do with the carousing of a far-off, red-light district from yesteryear? In the physical sense, they have absolutely nothing in common. But if you think about it, nothing much has changed despite the distance in time and space. We all long for the same things. Perhaps on different levels and in different quantities, but we all have the same innate desire to seek out a sense of togetherness and pleasure. And maybe a splash of a little naughty tucked in there, too. (Hoffman did, taking his now-wife to Sin City on their second date!) After all, we're only human—we all want our own Block 16.

So, as Brian Hoffman says, "Pull a cork, sit back, and watch the night either fall apart or come together." It's what life is all about.

HOFFMAN CELLARS
Appellation: **Napa Valley**
State: **California**
Country of Origin: **United States**
Type of Wine: **Cabernet Sauvignon**
Design: **Lisa Hobro Design**
Designer's Web Site: **www.lisahobrodesign.com**

HOLUS BOLUS

[CALIFORNIA ❧ UNITED STATES]

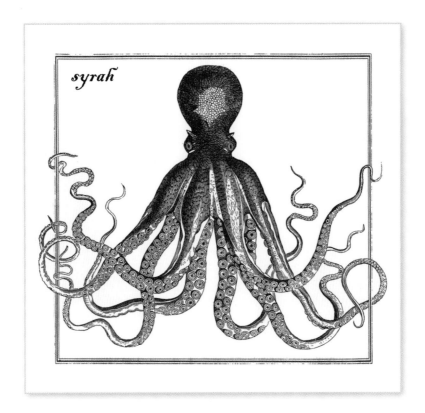

Holus-bolus. It's a real word. In fact, it's a word that has been around since the 1800s. In 2003, however, this little-known word became the perfect fit for four friends starting a wine label together.
Peter Hunken, Chad Melville, and Jim Knight met in 1997 while working the grape harvest at Lafond Winery and Vineyards. They hit it off easily and quickly. Peter Hunken eventually moved on to become assistant winemaker at Stolpman Vineyards, where he met Sashi Moorman, who effortlessly joined the mix. The friends soon realized that they shared similar views on life, wine, and winemaking and with this perfect mix of parallels, the idea of a shared wine venture was born.

Needing a name and finding one that was significant for the foursome turned out to be more difficult than ever anticipated. After days of brainstorming without progress, the collective of friends (and now winemaking partners) sat down over some great wine and drank on it. Although the creative juices were flowing, literally and figuratively, they still remained dissatisfied with the options on the table. In a desperate attempt, they succumbed to a dusty, but faithful, old dictionary. Randomly, they flipped through the pages and read words and definitions aloud. When, by chance, they hit "holus-bolus," the foursome simultaneously knew that they had struck gold. Holus-bolus defined means "altogether," which is exactly what they were—friends jointly making wine, shoulder-to-shoulder and together, fulfilling their dreams. Four partners, four even better friends, together like the tentacles of a single octopus, eight hands working together seamlessly. That's Holus Bolus.

HOLUS BOLUS

Appellation:	**Santa Ynez Valley**
State:	**California**
Country of Origin:	**United States**
Type of Wine:	**Syrah**
Web Site:	**www.piedrasassi.com**
Design:	**Heroist**
Designer's Web Site:	**www.heroist.com**

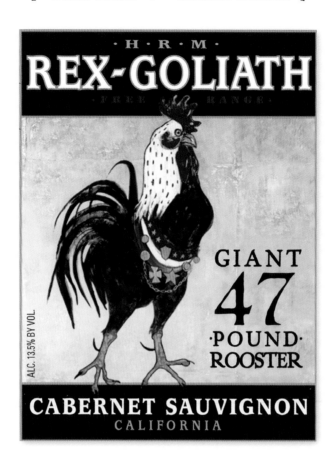

Legend has it that there was once a rooster of epic size that traveled with a Texas circus at the turn of the twentieth century. He was the circus's prized possession and so the rooster was appropriately named HRM (His Royal Majesty) Rex Goliath as a reflection of his goliath weight—47 lbs. To put it in perspective, a typical full-grown rooster today weighs between 5 and 8 lbs. Being over six times the average size gave the circus suitable authority to hail him as the "World's Largest Rooster." People traveled from near and far to gawk at the feathered creature who displayed himself ostentatiously from his circus roost. In true rooster fashion, a cocky portrait painted in his likeness was displayed splendidly above him.

Hahn Estates, the originators of HRM Rex Goliath! Wines, saw a vintage poster of the famed rooster hanging in the Pick and Shovel Café in Murphys, California, and after a little pecking about, realized the curious and fascinating tale. Given that the Hahn Estates label was already adorned with a beloved rooster honoring the family's European heritage (the German meaning for *hahn* is "cock"), it was seen as the perfect anecdote for a new range of wines. In 2002, Rex Goliath was reborn. The original poster was purchased from the Pick and Shovel Café and now a meticulous replication of the vintage circus banner that reportedly once hung over the king cock's throne nobly graces the label.

HRM REX GOLIATH! WINES (CONSTELLATION WINES U.S.)	
Appellation:	**Non-Designated Appellation**
State:	**California**
Country of Origin:	**United States**
Type of Wine:	**Cabernet Sauvignon**
Web Site:	**www.rexgoliath.com**
Design:	**Vintage Poster (Updated in 2008 by HKA Design)**
Designer's Web Site:	**www.hkadesign.com**

The black sheep. You know the one. The one that is just a little different than the rest. The one that stands out in the crowd. The one that's in a category of their own.

From a very early age, Hugh Hamilton was called "the rascal" by his father, and it's been said that it wasn't always a term of endearment. Well, the rascal followed in the family footsteps and went on to become a skilled winemaker. Five generations of winemakers, and then along he came to stir things up. He always liked doing things his own way and making wine was no different. This earned Hugh the reputation of being "the black sheep" of the Hamiltons by both family members and industry peers alike. Never one to take things too seriously, Hugh added the illustration of a black sheep on his back wine labels to represent his nickname and enjoy a little inside joke with himself.

When his marketing-savvy daughter, Mary, arrived on board, she felt Hugh's labels needed a facelift. She envisioned something fresh, but something that would also remain timeless. Using her father's convivial personal icon would tell a true story and also be reflective of the values on which he built the company. It also benefitted from being a humorous and engaging concept that resonated with people across oceans and cultures.

No longer an inside joke, the modernly classic Hugh Hamilton wine labels provide interesting characters said to be named after his friends, but perhaps they may just be different facets of Hugh's own personality. Either way, they are characters that everyone can in some way or another associate with be it a Rascal, a Jekyll, or a Hyde.

After all, the label says it the best, "Every family has one," and at Hugh Hamilton Wines, they certainly come in a varietal of characters.

A wall of wine confronts people when they visit a wine store. Strong design that jumps off the shelf will stand out in a sea of sameness, but the label really works when a simple design coveys the story of the wine, the place, and the people—that's when you have something unique!
—MARY HAMILTON
CEO, Hugh Hamilton Wines

HUGH HAMILTON WINES

Appellation:	**McLaren Vale**
State:	**South Australia**
Country of Origin:	**Australia**
Type of Wine:	**Shiraz and Viognier Blend**
Web Site:	**www.hamiltonwines.com.au**
Design:	**Ian Kidd Design (now KS Design Studio)**
Designer's Web Site:	**www.ksdesign.com.au**

IMAGERY ESTATE WINERY

[CALIFORNIA ❧ UNITED STATES]

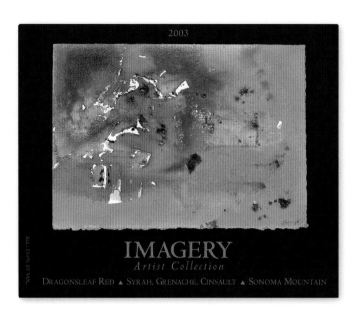

In 1982, artist Bob Nugent met winemaker Joe Benziger, surprisingly not over the tasting of a *wine flight*, but when the two broke up a *fistfight* at a polo match both were attending. The two eventually reconnected over a more civilized lunch and the conversation understandably found its way to discussing one another's respective crafts, and how the two creative art forms with different palates could provide a synergistic collaboration in some manner. The opportunity presented itself not long after in the form of one of Benziger's wines. Benziger had produced a singular Chardonnay that he didn't want to blend with anything else and felt that it required an individual wine label to represent its exceptional character. Nugent was asked to design an equally characteristic wine label that ended up consisting of Nugent's grape cluster triptych, a continuous piece of thematic artwork over three wine labels. The wine sold out within a month.

Soon, the fast friends invited another artist to create an original piece of artwork for the label of another character wine. This time, the artist Tim McDowell included Benziger's Parthenon, a unique feature that sits atop the property, looking down on it with a vigilant eye. And so, the Imagery Estate Artist Collection was inaugurated, and each subsequent piece of commissioned artwork would yield the Benziger icon in some artistic form.

The artwork chosen for Imagery's Artist Collection is not just any old art. Likewise, the wine in the bottles is not just any old wine. Rather, these Imagery Estate wines were considered to be Benziger's most experimental wines with the utmost individualistic personality—like works of art themselves. The art, reproduced in label format, is said by art critic Donald Kuspit in the foreword of *Imagery: Art for Wine* to "confirm the originality of the wines with which they are associated."

It has been over two decades that the acclaimed American artist and professor emeritus at Sonoma State University, Bob Nugent, has curated the Imagery Estate Artist Program in collaboration with Joe Benziger and the Benziger family, resulting in one of the largest and most impressive original wine label art collections in the world. Nugent's keen eye and creative vision have been responsible for commissioning artwork from the most elite, international artist community and has comprised of invitations extended to both young and burgeoning artists, as well as well-tenured masters.

Each artist brings their own inspiration and is given the utmost freedom with their creative execution, the only stipulation being the inclusion in some creative interpretation of Benziger's iconic Parthenon—said to be a symbol of "enterprise, aspiration, and integrity" by Kuspit. The rest is up to the experience and expression of each artist—with absolutely no qualification of their artwork required. Not in any way reflective of an interpretation generated by tasting of the Imagery Estate wines, each piece of artwork has its own intimate story. Bob Nugent adds that each piece of art also initiates another cherished experience for himself and Joe Benziger, who interpret the art together and assign it to the wine they feel each beautifully handcrafted creation is best suited for or most closely associates with—which ultimately results in wines graced with a synergistic and artful complimentary label.

IMAGERY ESTATE WINERY

Appellation:	**Sonoma Mountain**
State:	**California**
Country of Origin:	**United States**
Type of Wine:	**Syrah, Grenache, and Cinsault Blend**
Web Site:	**www.imagerywinery.com**
Art:	**Bob Nugent**
Artist's Web Site:	**www.nugentandcompany.com**

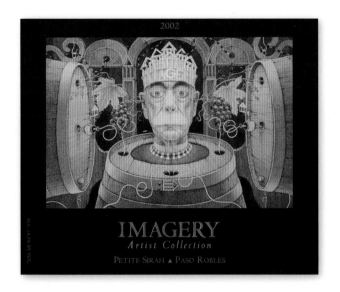

IMAGERY ESTATE WINERY

Appellation:	**Paso Robles**
State:	**California**
Country of Origin:	**United States**
Type of Wine:	**Petite Sirah**
Web Site:	**www.imagerywinery.com**
Art:	**Dominic Dimare**

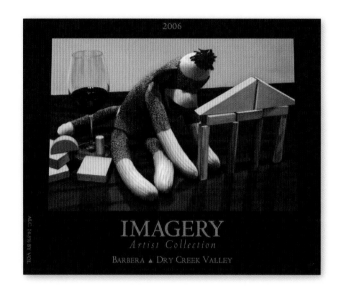

IMAGERY ESTATE WINERY

Appellation:	**Dry Creek Valley**
State:	**California**
Country of Origin:	**United States**
Type of Wine:	**Barbera**
Web Site:	**www.imagerywinery.com**
Art:	**Robert Durham**

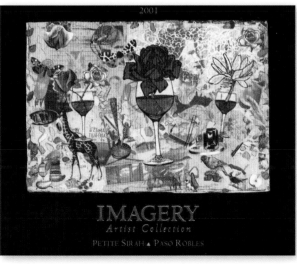
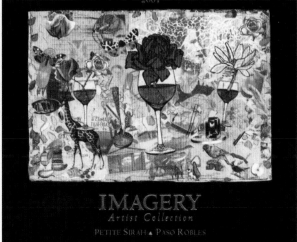

IMAGERY ESTATE WINERY

Appellation:	**Paso Robles**
State:	**California**
Country of Origin:	**United States**
Type of Wine:	**Petite Sirah**
Web Site:	**www.imagerywinery.com**
Art:	**Jane Hammond**
Artist's Web Site:	**www.janehammondartist.com**

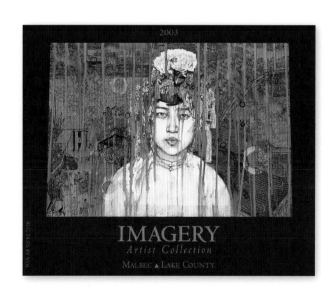

IMAGERY ESTATE WINERY

Appellation:	**Lake County (Non-Designated Appellation)**
State:	**California**
Country of Origin:	**United States**
Type of Wine:	**Malbec**
Web Site:	**www.imagerywinery.com**
Art:	**Hung Liu**
Artist's Web Site:	**www.kelliu.com**

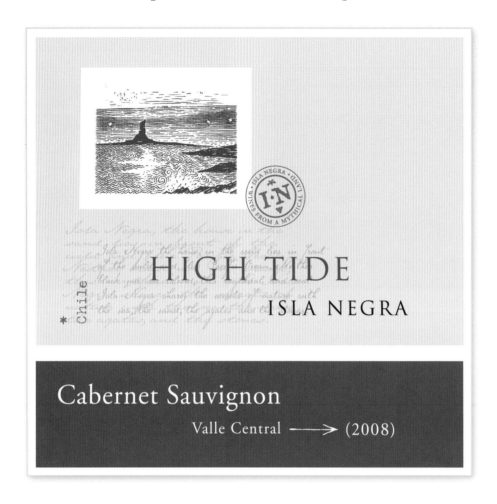

The planet Earth is geographically expansive, and in every corner we are blessed with magical places to explore. Isla Negra is one of those mystical places.

Though the word *isla* is Spanish for "island," Chile's Isla Negra is not actually an island, but instead, a cozy coastal town named for its outcropping of black rocks that appear island-like from off-shore. This small village is a gathering spot for Chile's artistic and mystical side. Here, people are relaxed, open-minded, and have often been inspired creatively through many art forms.

Perhaps the most well-known resident of Isla Negra was the 1971 Nobel laureate, Chilean poet and politician, the late Pablo Neruda, who made the sleepy village his home and eventual resting place. His home overlooked the Pacific Ocean's rapid rise and fall, and the waves that are the crown of Isla Negra's magic.

As this enchanted place inspired Neruda and those that followed, it has also stirred an expression of creative experimentation in this range of wines, whose labels represent the beauty found in the captivating place that is Isla Negra.

	ISLA NEGRA WINES	
Appellation:	**Central Valley**	
Region:	**O'Higgins**	
Country of Origin:	**Chile**	
Type of Wine:	**Cabernet Sauvignon**	
Web Site:	**www.islanegrawines.com**	
Design:	**Internal**	

JAQK Cellars

[California & United States]

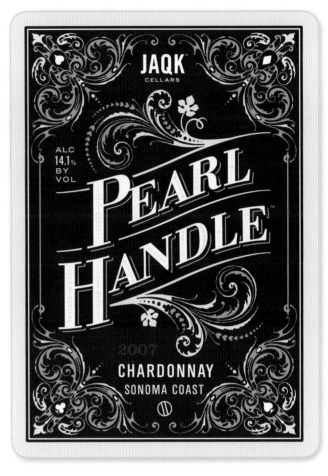

The folks at JAQK Cellars have some good advice. It's simple: do what you love. This is the guiding philosophy that Craig MacLean, Katie Jain, and Joel Templin have built JAQK wines on. While the premise seems easy enough, it appears a majority of the working population just doesn't seem to get it. But if you do what you love, if you do what you're passionate about, work really isn't work anymore because it is so enjoyable. It's almost like, dare we say . . . play?

JAQK Cellars is based on this fresh, "work-free" ideal: doing what is inspiring to you so inevitably work, as most of us know it, is really obsolete.

For the trio behind JAQK, this means that Craig gets dirty in the vineyards, wearing gumboots and courting an intimate relationship with his vines, inevitably coaxing the best juice possible from them. And while Joel and Kate like their juice as much as Craig, their love for the stuff falls more to the front-end, enjoying a bottle (or two) of wine gregariously with friends.

So while Craig is tending to his fruit, Katie and Joel can be found entertaining themselves in their studio, Hatch Design, where they craft brand identities, render stylish and sophisticated typography, and develop both elegant and effective communications that really make the world a more beautiful place. When all three of them are left to their own devices, it undoubtedly means less work and more play.

The perfect storm within the wine industry is one where the overall brand experience and packaging is just as impressive as what's in the bottle. Both need to deliver in order to succeed in this overly saturated category.
— Joel Templin
Founder, JAQK Cellars

This concept has been bottled in every one of JAQK's wines. Perhaps if their roles were reversed—Craig was left to develop the branding and packaging, and Katie and Joel were in charge of pruning the vines, harvesting the grapes, and making the wine—things mightn't be so fun. But together, each member of the team works in their element producing quality wines and having a boatload of fun—the way work ought to be.

Of course, the first vintage and bottling can be a little risky, but that, too, is all part of this crew's recreation—tempting fate, but trusting good fortune and tasting a whole lot of wines. According to JAQK Cellars, the only risk is not taking the time to play a little. Its wine bottles, with no gamble on the design (given who designed them), act as a reminder to unwind, let loose, and play—no matter what your age or game is.

JAQK CELLARS	
Appellation:	**Sonoma Coast**
State:	**California**
Country of Origin:	**United States**
Type of Wine:	**Chardonnay**
Web Site:	**www.jaqkcellars.com**
Design:	**Hatch Design**
Designer's Web Site:	**www.hatchsf.com**

JELLY ROLL WINES
[CALIFORNIA ❧ UNITED STATES]

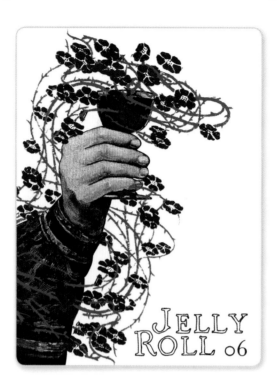

As music fans go, Jim Knight was dedicated. Like other Deadheads, he loyally followed the Grateful Dead to about sixty of their shows a year, participating in a total of 167 live shows in total. When he realized that he was paying for university classes he wasn't attending (given the band's rigorous touring schedule), he postponed his studies at the University of Southern California. When Jerry Garcia died in 1995, Knight's life on the road as a devotee dwindled and he looked for something else he loved in order to evolve himself professionally. He found it in wine.

Three years after working at Lafond Winery and Vineyards, he joined his family's Los Angeles retail business—aptly, The Wine House. Tasting twenty-five to fifty wines a day (and they call this work), he was well on his way to developing quite a discriminating palate. In 2001, he decided to get his hands dirty and made a wine that was based on his own appreciation of flavors, and tastes that made magic on his own palate.

In naming his wine, he called on something to which he had consistently been devout—music. Long gone were his days as a Deadhead, but from that, as well as his tenure of fifteen years as a hand percussionist in various bands and formal study of Latin and Afro-Cuban percussion, spawned an appreciation for music that truly ranges a full spectrum.

From lyrics found in songs by Van Morrison such as "And It Stoned Me," and the Grateful Dead's "Dupree's Diamond Blues," amongst others, an interest flourished in the legendary Jelly Roll Morton (although it is debatable whether these references of jelly roll were actually alluding to the father of jazz versus something a little more carnal!). Regardless, out of this appreciation came a desire to pay tribute to the 1920s Dixieland piano player whose name was also befitting for a juicy Syrah wine.

Not only does the name of his wine have deep personal significance, but also the imagery can be related to Knight on multiple levels. The hand holding the chalice is reminiscent of the 1975 cult favorite *Monty Python and the Holy Grail*, and is a symbol of Knight's fabulous sense of humor. The roses are a tribute to the Grateful Dead, but the way they dance on the vines are like music notes dancing on sheet music—a symbol of Knight's deep appreciation for all music.

JELLY ROLL WINES

Appellation:	**Santa Ynez Valley**
State:	**California**
Country of Origin:	**United States**
Type of Wine:	**Syrah**
Design:	**Heroist**
Designer's Web Site:	**www.heroist.com**

JIM BARRY WINES

[SOUTH AUSTRALIA ❧ AUSTRALIA]

SILLY MID ON
SAUVIGNON BLANC SEMILLON

SILLY MID ON
SAUVIGNON BLANC SEMILLON

The Jim Barry Cover Drive and Silly Mid On wine labels are reflections of true sporting legacy found in the fruit farmed on the fields of the old Penola cricket grounds, located on the edge of Coonawarra, South Australia. These grounds, which were converted into vineyards decades later, saw their first ball bowled and the classic cover drive of the local champions in 1950. When the pitch retired from play in the early 1990s, Jim Barry purchased the legendary 30-acre cricket ground and repurposed it as a Cabernet Sauvignon vineyard in 1997—ensuring that the original pavilion be retained by planting the vines around the actual pitch, and salvaging this piece of Coonawarra culture. While this was the first "play" by the Barry family in Coonawarra, whose viticultural heritage lay in Clare Valley, interest in the region had begun back in 1947 when he met friend Sam Wynn, of Wynns Coonawarra Estate.

Jim Barry Wines is heavily steeped in tradition. The patriarch, Jim Barry, graduated with the seventeenth oenology diploma from Roseworthy Agricultural College in South Australia (now Roseworthy Campus at the University of Adelaide), Australia's first college of this caliber, established in 1883. There, he also played cricket in the Roseworthy first XI. He moved to South Australia in 1947, where he became the first qualified winemaker in Clare Valley working at the Clarevale Cooperative. By 1959, he had developed his first vineyard and in 1974, built the winery. Today, Barry's name, synonymous with high-quality Riesling and Shiraz, as well as his passion for viticulture, has been carried on by four of the six Barry children, including managing director Peter Barry and winemaker Mark Barry.

The first wine in the Coonawarra cricket series was named after the game's signature "cover drive." In 2005, a partner was added with Silly Mid On. "Silly mid on" is a cricketing position located ridiculously close to the batsman that requires prime reflexes, and sheer lunacy—a silly position to play on the pitch, but a on a wine label, it's a very Aussie way to introduce and educate non-aficionados to critical Australian sporting culture via another important aspect of all things Aussie: wine.

	JIM BARRY WINES
Appellation:	**Clare Valley/Adelaide Hills**
State:	**South Australia**
Country of Origin:	**Australia**
Type of Wine:	**Sémillon and Sauvignon Blanc Blend**
Web Site:	**www.jimbarry.com**
Design:	**Parallax Design**
Designer's Web Site:	**www.parallaxdesign.com.au**

	JIM BARRY WINES
Appellation:	**Clare Valley/Adelaide Hills**
State:	**South Australia**
Country of Origin:	**Australia**
Type of Wine:	**Sémillon and Sauvignon Blanc Blend**
Web Site:	**www.jimbarry.com**
Design:	**Parallax Design**
Designer's Web Site:	**www.parallaxdesign.com.au**

JIM BARRY WINES

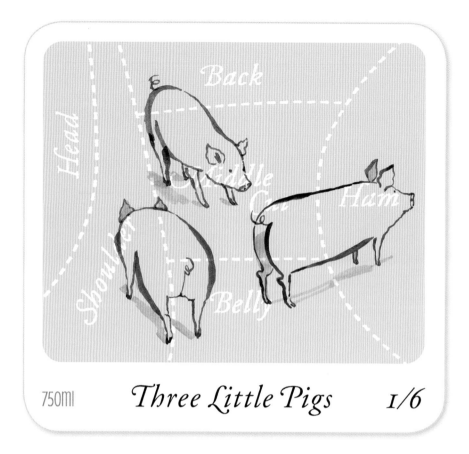

750ml   *Three Little Pigs*   1/6

Here's a story of three little pigs—but not the ones made popular by the nineteenth-century nursery tale. Rather, it's a tribute paid to three pampered pork reared in Peter Barry's own backyard.

Peter Barry says he acquired a particular taste for succulent Spanish *bodega* prosciutto while on a trip to Spain back in 1999 and in turn became quite "serious about pigs." Upon his return home to Clare Valley, he purchased his first piglets. Here, the pigs are truly pampered in the "comfortable surroundings of a cozy sty constructed from a converted dairy" and with regular diet supplements including a snout-watering selection of leftovers from Barry's friend and green grocer, the ironically named John Hams.

With the motto, "a happy pig is a tasty pig," Barry has continued his part-time pig farming on an annual basis, sharing his homegrown fare with friends and family, and even honing his skills curing his meats in his cellar in Armagh.

The importance of a label is to draw attention to the wine. Wine labels will change and evolve over periods of time—we have changed some of our labels three or four times—not all labels are forever. —PETER BARRY
Managing Director, Jim Barry Wines

In 2004, Barry produced a blend of Shiraz and Cabernet Sauvignon with a complimentary splash of Malbec, which calculatingly softened the blend and made it more favorable for the delicate taste of pork. Launched in 2007, which appropriately was the Year of the Pig in the Chinese zodiac calendar, Barry's labels pay tribute not only to the art of food and wine pairing, but also to his revolving pig-pen filled with personalities including pork chop, tenderloin, and ham hock!

JIM BARRY WINES
Appellation: **Clare Valley**
State: **South Australia**
Country of Origin: **Australia**
Type of Wine: **Shiraz, Cabernet Sauvignon, and Malbec Blend**
Web Site: **www.jimbarry.com**
Design: **Parallax Design**
Designer's Web Site: **www.parallaxdesign.com.au**

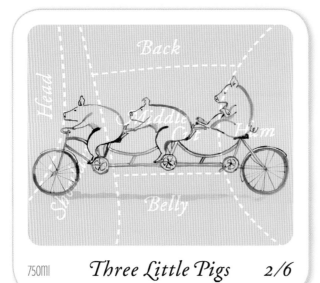

Three Little Pigs   2/6

750ml

JIM BARRY WINES

Appellation:	**Clare Valley**
State:	**South Australia**
Country of Origin:	**Australia**
Type of Wine:	**Shiraz, Cabernet Sauvignon, and Malbec Blend**
Web Site:	**www.jimbarry.com**
Design:	**Parallax Design**
Designer's Web Site:	**www.parallaxdesign.com.au**

Three Little Pigs   3/6

750ml

JIM BARRY WINES

Appellation:	**Clare Valley**
State:	**South Australia**
Country of Origin:	**Australia**
Type of Wine:	**Shiraz, Cabernet Sauvignon, and Malbec Blend**
Web Site:	**www.jimbarry.com**
Design:	**Parallax Design**
Designer's Web Site:	**www.parallaxdesign.com.au**

Three Little Pigs   4/6

750ml

JIM BARRY WINES

Appellation:	**Clare Valley**
State:	**South Australia**
Country of Origin:	**Australia**
Type of Wine:	**Shiraz, Cabernet Sauvignon, and Malbec Blend**
Web Site:	**www.jimbarry.com**
Design:	**Parallax Design**
Designer's Web Site:	**www.parallaxdesign.com.au**

Three Little Pigs   5/6

750ml

JIM BARRY WINES

Appellation:	**Clare Valley**
State:	**South Australia**
Country of Origin:	**Australia**
Type of Wine:	**Shiraz, Cabernet Sauvignon, and Malbec Blend**
Web Site:	**www.jimbarry.com**
Design:	**Parallax Design**
Designer's Web Site:	**www.parallaxdesign.com.au**

JOHANNESHOF CELLARS

[MARLBOROUGH ❧ NEW ZEALAND]

Sunday drives—you never know where they'll take you, which is half the fun.

Edel Everling, a fifth-generation winemaker from Germany, was traveling in New Zealand when she first met Warwick Foley. After connecting on many things the two had in common, Edel returned to study toward her degree in viticulture and oenology in Germany, and Warwick consequently followed and became a visiting student. There, the two cemented their friendship quickly and would take meandering Sunday drives (when not studying) to explore the countryside. On one occasion, the two visited an area close to Edel's hometown and came upon the town where famed German silhouette artist Ernst Moritz Engert grew up. On that day, the town was celebrating Engert with an exhibit of his art and the two friends purchased an exhibition booklet of Engert's works as a keepsake.

Some years later, Edel and Warwick's relationship evolved into a partnership and they started a winery in New Zealand together. Whilst unpacking their books from boxes shipped over from Germany, there appeared the Engert exhibition booklet from that casual Sunday drive taken together years prior. Flipping through the book in commemoration, an image jumped out at the two and they noticed that it was the only piece of work that had been done in the theme of good company and merriment of drink. This particular piece was a creative interpretation from Shakespeare's *The Tempest* and they thought it to be a wonderful visual for their wine label.

The artwork is not only reminiscent of their time spent together at school in Germany, but also symbolic of the wines made together in New Zealand. Edel and Warwick also felt that the label communicates that Johanneshof Cellars wines are perfect for enjoying in any situation, no matter where the wind takes you.

A wine label is the first point of contact with a wine, like the first few seconds one meets a person. It will smile at you, draw your attention, intrigue you, fascinate you, or simply leave you cold and make you move on to another. So as winemakers, we ought to choose carefully, for the story we like to tell about our wine starts with what our label tells you. —EDEL EVERLING
Co-Owner and Winemaker,
Johanneshof Cellars

JOHANNESHOF CELLARS
Appellation: **Marlborough**
Region: **Marlborough**
Country of Origin: **New Zealand**
Type of Wine: **Gewürztraminer**
Web Site: **www.johanneshof.co.nz**
Art: **Ernst Moritz Engert**

JUSTIN Vineyards & Winery

[California ❦ United States]

The Orphan was born twice, and twice born out of tragedy. But the third time it arrived, it was a charm. The first disaster for Justin and Deborah Baldwin, owners of JUSTIN Vineyards and Winery, was of a natural persuasion. It arrived in the form of a 6.5 Richter-scaled earthquake on December 22, 2003, at 11:15 AM, causing an estimated $300 million in damages for the region of Central California. It was amongst this rubble that two hundred barrels of JUSTIN's much-noted, premium, handcrafted Bordeaux blends were lost, just days before the holidays festivities. Needing to replenish the dwindling stock of wines lost, but with consequently little wine left to do so given the circumstances, The Orphan was born. This stand-alone unblended (or "orphaned") wine came to the rescue and saved the dwindling shelves from being empty. It was thought that it would be the only life that this orphan would live.

Sadly, tragedy struck again for JUSTIN. This time, however, it was in the form of the suspected arson of a 240,000-square-foot wine storage facility. Its Northern California warehouse, Wines Central, was leveled by a fire, taking with it an estimated five hundred thousand cases of rare vintages and, in some cases for an unfortunate number of Bay Area wineries and private collectors, their entire inventories went up in smoke. It was in this fire that the Baldwins took a second punch, again losing seventeen thousand cases of their primary wines. The strength of the unsuspecting Orphan was resurrected to support the loss.

The next time the Baldwins would meet The Orphan would be once more out of tragedy. But this time, however, instead of loss, they would show the true giving spirit at JUSTIN in the form of a temporary adoption. Taking in one of Hurricane Katrina's displaced victims, this orphan was pleased to help out and integrate into the Baldwins' welcoming team. One night, while the Baldwins shared their home and hospitality with this New Orleans native, the concept of their next "bottled baby" was conceived—not to be an orphan, but instead an astute partner that would embody the strength of The Orphan wine, but with the wisdom of things past that would be called The Savant *(not pictured)*.

JUSTIN VINEYARDS & WINERY	
Appellation:	**Paso Robles**
State:	**California**
Country of Origin:	**United States**
Type of Wine:	**Cabernet Sauvignon and Syrah Blend**
Web Site:	**www.justinwine.com**
Design:	**Kraftwerk Design**
Designer's Web Site:	**www.kraftwerkdesign.com**

K Vintners

In the eyes of winemaker Charles Smith, this wine is divine. So, what on earth do you call a wine that's going to knock you off your feet and, as Charles Smith says, "Bring you to your knees singing 'sweet baby Jesus, hallelujah!'"?

Since it was by the grace of his own alchemy that this little liquid miracle came to be, the only thing fitting for the label would be something reverent. Or maybe *irreverent* in the case of Charles Smith, as he modeled himself in the Big Guy's likeness and called it The Creator. You can't get much holier than that. With a wine like this and a label to boot, a couple glasses in, one can almost expect to become a fallen angel.

Amen.

K VINTNERS	
Appellation:	**Walla Walla Valley**
State:	**Washington**
Country of Origin:	**United States**
Type of Wine:	**Cabernet Sauvignon and Syrah Blend**
Web Site:	**www.kvintners.com**
Design:	**The Korff Kounsil**
Designer's Web Site:	**www.thekounsil.com**

KATARZYNA ESTATE

[STARA ZAGORA ❧ BULGARIA]

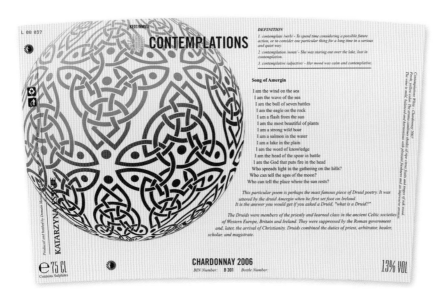

Snuggled up in front of a crackling fireplace on a snowy evening; watching the pitter patter of rain on the windowsill on a lazy Sunday afternoon; flowing curtains and a warm, grassy breeze on a summer's eve; with friends, or taking a moment of solitude; reflecting; thinking; daydreaming. . . .

The Katarzyna Estate wine labels provide a series of starting points for these meandering thoughts and evocative conversations. No matter where, no matter when, the rituals are universal: full glasses, contemplations, and conversation. Drink on it. Think on it. Expand your mind and your palate. Take a look at these labels and you will certainly discover something new, and the conversation will never get old.

KATARZYNA ESTATE	
Appellation:	**Stara Zagora**
Province:	**Stara Zagora**
Country of Origin:	**Bulgaria**
Type of Wine:	**Chardonnay**
Web Site:	**http://katarzyna.bg/**
Design:	**Stefan Gyonev**
Designer's Web Site:	**www.tatau.org**

KATARZYNA ESTATE	
Appellation:	**Stara Zagora**
Province:	**Stara Zagora**
Country of Origin:	**Bulgaria**
Type of Wine:	**Cabernet Sauvignon, Merlot, and Mavrud Blend**
Web Site:	**http://katarzyna.bg/**
Design:	**Stefan Gyonev**
Designer's Web Site:	**www.tatau.org**

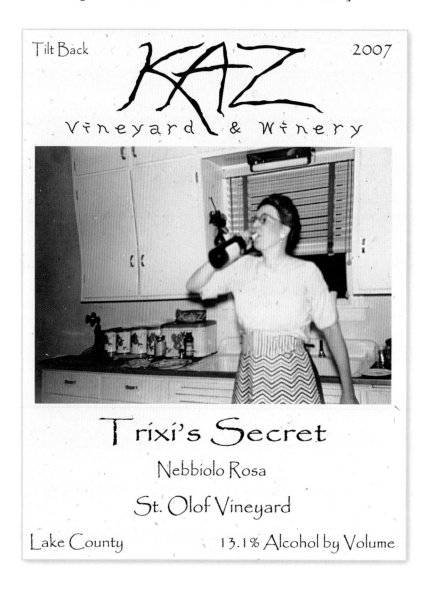

Tilt Back   2007

KAZ
Vineyard & Winery

Trixi's Secret

Nebbiolo Rosa

St. Olof Vineyard

Lake County   13.1% Alcohol by Volume

Bigger is not better in the case of Kaz Vineyard and Winery, which set out to be Sonoma Valley's smallest boutique winery from the get-go. Though small, there is nothing petite about the personality behind this fine tour de force, which of course is reflected in the charismatic Kaz labels. Given Richard Kasmier's (Kaz Sr.) panache with and penchant towards less commercial and more unique varietals—such as Lenoir, De Chaunac, Carignan, Malbec, and Barbera, to name a few—there is no doubt that the wines need equally inimitable labels, for which there is no shortage of as the Kaz troop abounds with familial creative flair.

Take the Rumble label, for instance. This creative collaboration has the entire family involved and includes a layout and naming by son Ryan (Kaz Jr.),

A bottle of wine is more than the drink itself. It's a full package where taste, smell, and visual aesthetics culminate in a unique experience. I work at the tasting room from time to time, and I get my biggest thrill when someone has a reaction to the label images and names, and what's on their tongue.   —RYAN KAZ
Marketing Team of One, Kaz Winery

KAZ VINEYARD & WINERY
Appellation:	**Lake County (Non-Designated Appellation)**
State:	**California**
Country of Origin:	**United States**
Type of Wine:	**Nebbiolo Rosé**
Web Site:	**www.kazwinery.com**
Design:	**Ryan Kaz Design**
Designer's Web Site:	**www.ryankazdesign.com**

Hoarded   2003

KAZ
Vineyard & Winery

Rumble
100% Carignane

East Hopland Vineyards

Sonoma County   13.8% Alcohol by Volume

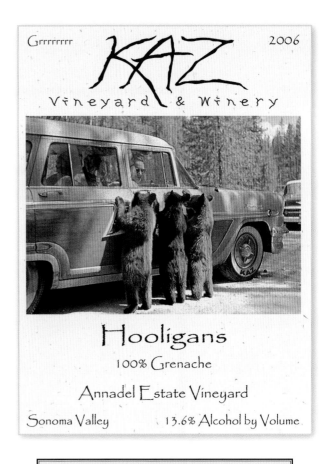

Grrrrrrrr   2006

KAZ
Vineyard & Winery

Hooligans
100% Grenache

Annadel Estate Vineyard

Sonoma Valley   13.6% Alcohol by Volume

KAZ VINEYARD & WINERY

Appellation:	**Sonoma County (Non-Designated Appellation)**
State:	**California**
Country of Origin:	**United States**
Type of Wine:	**Carignan**
Web Site:	**www.kazwinery.com**
Design:	**Ryan Kaz Design and the Kasmier family**
Designer's Web Site:	**www.ryankazdesign.com**

KAZ VINEYARD & WINERY

Appellation:	**Sonoma Valley**
State:	**California**
Country of Origin:	**United States**
Type of Wine:	**Grenache**
Web Site:	**www.kazwinery.com**
Design:	**Ryan Kaz Design**
Designer's Web Site:	**www.ryankazdesign.com**

hand-coloring of the photo by his wife Sandi (Mrs. Kaz), photography by Kaz Sr. himself—taken when he was just ten years old (just a little foreshadowing that he would go on to become a very successful commercial photographer)—all while daughter Kristin was cracking the whip. The photo itself provides even more nostalgic and sentimental value to the label as the man in the white shirt is actually Richard Kasimer's father, the first one to use the family's term of endearment: Kaz.

Each of the wine label images is selected specifically with an individual wine in mind. Hooligans was chosen for its playful spin on a Grenache wine that shocks you with a burst of bright energy with its aromas and flavors of citrus fruit, despite its being light in color—not what you'd necessarily expect, much like these furry hooligans creeping up on you.

Bring in Trixi! She's a character that was found by Mrs. Kaz in an old family album and who was affectionately named Trixi. A true swigger, Trixi certainly could knock back a slew of wine straight from the bottle. Consequently, the fruity but dry style of wine that this label represents is known by many to be a bottle quaffer, tipped back straight from the source in true Trixi style.

Each of the Kaz wine labels also has a hidden salute to the Kaz clan—sometimes so small that even the Kazes themselves can't find it. Kaz Vineyard and Winery is certainly a fun family affair. Through the wine and the labels, the family members are able to marry their creative talents together and truly personify the Kasmier spirit in and on the bottle.

Behind absolutely anything great, there lies a team of ignored workers that, though given little credit, are the backbone of getting things done no matter what. Known as the "pee ons," grunts, or lackeys, they are most often underappreciated despite their critical importance. Who knows if anyone ever even sees them or even knows that they exist unless they are being balked at to take care of something or another. Though neglected, these shit-kickers are worth their weight in gold, kind of like the iconic Blundstone boots that Australian lackeys wear. Blundstones are know to be "hardworking boots for hardworking men," which is just what a lackey is—a damn-good hard worker.

Much like the lackey of Australian wine varietals, Shiraz has been known as the go-to grape for absolutely anything because it is always hardworking and will never fail to get the job done. Black-tie or barbeque, Shiraz always delivers.

The Lackey wine label by Kilikanoon Wines, with its image of the iconic Blundstone, gives a nod to all the minions out there who are pivotal to the wine industry and beyond, and who come through every time, no matter what.

KILIKANOON WINES	
Region:	**Clare Valley**
State:	**South Australia**
Country of Origin:	**Australia**
Type of Wine:	**Shiraz**
Web Site:	**www.kilikanoon.com.au**
Design:	**Signature Labels**
Designer's Web Site:	**www.signaturelabels.com.au**

KILLIBINBIN WINES

[SOUTH AUSTRALIA ❦ AUSTRALIA]

When it came time to revamp the Killibinbin Wines label, winemaker Wayne Anderson knew that the marketplace was extremely crowded and that it would almost take a murderous act to cut through the clutter. While he wanted to stand out, it was also important for the labels to say something more about his philosophy and personality that was reflected in his wines through his winemaking.

Here was a good start: at the end of the day, wine is a drink and it should be fun, not scary. Giving his design firm free reign, they played off the name of the estate, "Killibinbin," an Australian word meaning "to shine." Taking this into consideration, along with Wayne's appreciation of old movie posters and not wanting to be too serious about grape juice, these deadly labels appeared and Wayne knew they would definitely cause a stir. Just the murderous act he was looking for.

> The function of the wine label is to grab the consumer's attention, to arouse their curiosity, to make them take the next step of actually picking up the bottle. But it also goes far deeper, giving little clues about the personalities of those behind the wine and helping to forge a bond between the maker and the drinker.
>
> —WAYNE ANDERSON
> Proprietor, Killibinbin Wines

And while drinking Killibinbin wines isn't scary, harvesting on a steep cliff proved to be for one Killibinbin vineyard hand. And so, the Scaredy-Cat label particularly honors this member of the team who lost his courage driving his harvester halfway along the very first row of the extremely steep slopes of the Tallagandra vineyard. Leaving his harvester behind and Killibinbin in a lurch, the cowardly lion slunk off to find his courage and his bollocks.

The Killibinbin wines are sharp and shiny. Some call them killer. The same certainly can be said about their wine labels.

KILLIBINBIN WINES	
Appellation:	**Langhorne Creek**
State:	**South Australia**
Country of Origin:	**Australia**
Type of Wine:	**Shiraz and Cabernet Sauvignon Blend**
Web Site:	**www.killibinbin.com.au**
Design:	**Mash**
Designer's Web Site:	**www.mashdesign.com.au**

KILLIBINBIN WINES	
Appellation:	**Adelaide Hills**
State:	**South Australia**
Country of Origin:	**Australia**
Type of Wine:	**Cabernet Sauvignon and Malbec Blend**
Web Site:	**www.killibinbin.com.au**
Design:	**Mash**
Designer's Web Site:	**www.mashdesign.com.au**

KRINKLEWOOD BIODYNAMIC VINEYARD
[NEW SOUTH WALES ❦ AUSTRALIA]

Prior to planting their biodynamic vineyard, the Windrim family's Krinklewood property in New South Wales was home to a herd of over sixty Limousin cattle.

Limousin cattle are a breed native to the Limousin and Marche regions of France. While the earliest herd book has been recorded as being established in 1886, the breed has likely been around for much longer. Perhaps even 20,000 years longer based on the drawings of cattle found in the Lascaux caves near Montignac, France, which were discovered in 1940. The complex caves have since become world-famous for these prehistoric cave paintings. The images are estimated at being 16,000 years old and are mostly images in true likeness of some of today's large domesticated animals. Of these drawings, many have a remarkable likeness to today's Limousin cattle.

As an acknowledgment of Krinklewood's Limousin cattle heritage and the important role they play in the biodynamical fertilization of the vineyard's soils, Krinklewood looked to the cattle's prehistoric ancestors and the famous cave drawings for its wine label's inspiration. Looking for a younger, more bullish brother for their mature wines, it made sense to modernize the beloved image of the traditional Krinklewood cattle. While Limousin are known to be docile and do roam the property at their leisure, the cheekier, more adolescent version of the cattle seen on this wine label is wildly alive, like the wine—accessible and ready to be grabbed by the horns and given a go.

KRINKLEWOOD BIODYNAMIC VINEYARD	
Appellation:	**Broke Fordwich**
State:	**New South Wales**
Country of Origin:	**Australia**
Type of Wine:	**Verdelho, Sémillon, and Chardonnay Blend**
Web Site:	**www.krinklewood.com**
Design:	**The Collective Design Consultants**
Designer's Web Site:	**www.thecollective.com.au**

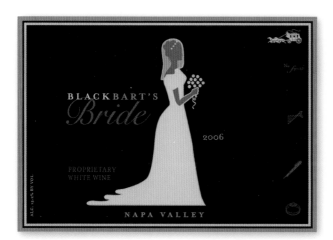

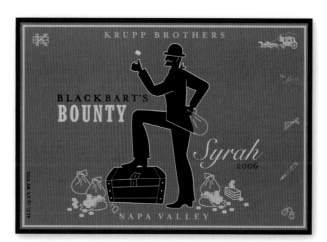

In Napa Valley, above the Stags Leap District, there is a parcel of land that is known for its valued vines. Back in the late 1800s during the days of the Wild West, however, these very grounds bore witness to a string of stagecoach robberies at the hand of thieving bandits.

Unlike most of the horsebacked thugs, there was one refined rogue who was quite gentlemanly when it came to intercepting the transport of cash and gold stagecoach cargo. Due to his sophisticated manner during the hold-ups, as well as his finely tailored attire, polished appearance, and oft, a signature poem left behind at the scene of the crime, he soon took on a legendary status. Charles Earl Bolles, or as he came to be known, Black Bart, robbed his first stagecoach in 1875. This would prove to be the first of his many daring robberies "courteously orchestrated" until 1883, where his last coach robbery occurred fittingly at the exact site of his inaugural thievery.

The label is a window to the soul of the wine within by providing clues to the personality and quality of both the wine and the vintner. A great label sets the stage for the tasting experience to come. —DR. JAN KRUPP
Proprietor, Krupp Brothers

Today, treading (or rather, trellising) where Black Bart successfully and repeatedly robbed his riches, sits the aptly named Stagecoach Vineyard, owned by Dr. Jan Krupp and his brother, whose name coincidentally is Bart. Considering that Bart Krupp is known to often be elusively absent from the vineyard, it made this series of refined and sophisticated wines that much more fun to label. Bart's Bride is a seductive blend with a label that pays homage to the bandit's poor wife, who was abandoned for her husband's exciting illegal activities. His last letter to her was in 1871, and after a long period without any further correspondence, she assumed him dead.

KRUPP BROTHERS	
Appellation:	**Napa Valley**
State:	**California**
Country of Origin:	**United States**
Type of Wine:	**Marsanne, Viognier, and Chardonnay Blend**
Web Site:	**www.kruppbrothers.com**
Design:	**Michael Mabry Design**
Designer's Web Site:	**www.michaelmabry.com**

KRUPP BROTHERS	
Appellation:	**Napa Valley**
State:	**California**
Country of Origin:	**United States**
Type of Wine:	**Syrah**
Web Site:	**www.kruppbrothers.com**
Design:	**Michael Mabry Design**
Designer's Web Site:	**www.michaelmabry.com**

KRUPP BROTHERS

[CALIFORNIA ❧ UNITED STATES]

From the age of seven, Jan Krupp knew that he felt at home in the garden. But when the time came for him to pursue his career, his propensity for plants was put aside as he successfully studied to practice medicine. At the end of his studies, Dr. Jan Krupp set up shop in the San Francisco Bay area, where he also first indulged his senses in the fabulous flavors of wine. Quickly, he was transformed from an amateur enthusiast into a committed oenophile.

Striking a balance between his medical practice during the week and his wine passion on the weekends, Dr. Krupp experimented with winemaking, which proved to be encouraging with wins at various local competitions. For fifteen harvest seasons, he would refine his winemaking skills with every vintage.

In 1991, the full-time doctor and part-time viticulturist got back to his green-thumbed roots by planting his first 41 acres of Cabernet Sauvignon and Merlot. Four years later though, 750 acres on the south side of Pritchard Hill was on the market and nothing could stop Dr. Krupp from achieving his next goal. With no legal right of access, no known water or power source, clearing the scrub would prove to be the easiest part of the endeavor. Engaging his brother, Bart Krupp, the two men had the foresight and certainty that the rocky, intense soils were perfect conditions for farming grapes of the highest quality.

One hundred and thirty-five legal documents later, with the right to construct a road, the first 100 acres of Stagecoach Vineyard was underway. Over the next four years, another 400 acres was added, and in 1999, the Krupp Brothers winery saw its inaugural vintage.

The Doctor label remembers where Dr. Krupp started as a young physician in San Francisco and his respect and commitment to science in various forms. The Advocate label is a tribute to Stacy Krupp, whose tireless legal counsel was pivotal (over one hundred and thirty-five legal documents pivotal!) to the realization of Stagecoach Vineyard and the Krupp Brothers winery.

<table>
<tr><td colspan="2">KRUPP BROTHERS</td></tr>
<tr><td align="right">Appellation:</td><td>Napa Valley</td></tr>
<tr><td align="right">State:</td><td>California</td></tr>
<tr><td align="right">Country of Origin:</td><td>United States</td></tr>
<tr><td align="right">Type of Wine:</td><td>Red Blend</td></tr>
<tr><td align="right">Web Site:</td><td>www.kruppbrothersestates.com</td></tr>
<tr><td align="right">Design:</td><td>Michael Mabry Design</td></tr>
<tr><td align="right">Designer's Web Site:</td><td>www.michaelmabry.com</td></tr>
</table>

<table>
<tr><td colspan="2">KRUPP BROTHERS</td></tr>
<tr><td align="right">Appellation:</td><td>Napa Valley</td></tr>
<tr><td align="right">State:</td><td>California</td></tr>
<tr><td align="right">Country of Origin:</td><td>United States</td></tr>
<tr><td align="right">Type of Wine:</td><td>Petit Verdot, Merlot, and Malbec Blend</td></tr>
<tr><td align="right">Web Site:</td><td>www.kruppbrothersestates.com</td></tr>
<tr><td align="right">Design:</td><td>Michael Mabry Design</td></tr>
<tr><td align="right">Designer's Web Site:</td><td>www.michaelmabry.com</td></tr>
</table>

LaVigne Wine Estate

[Western Cape ✤ South Africa]

Robert Jorgensen wanted a little music in his life. Rather than fall back on the profession of a previous life as a sound engineer, Jorgensen decided to set the "score" higher.

A Norwegian native, Jorgensen traveled to Franschhoek, South Africa, on holiday, and while some people return home with T-shirts as souvenirs, Jorgensen returned home with a vineyard. He now spends six months a year in South Africa pursuing an "interest" in wine.

Having such an affinity for music, Jorgensen has taken a melodic approach to crafting his wines. Studies that have been done by Japan's Dr. Masaru Emoto are said to demonstrate that music can have positive effects on water molecules. Since 1999, Emoto has published various books depicting that water, when exposed to music in a liquid state, will form beautiful crystal formations visible when frozen.

Given Jorgensen's personal involvement with the art of sound, as well as his openness to such studies suggesting the positive reactions that music has on water—wine's composition being more than 80%—LaVigne Wine Estate decidedly plays classical music continuously in the barrel cellar.

With the belief that the maturing wines will benefit in a "harmonic" way, Jorgensen explains, special care is taken to ensure that music makes its way into the oak barrels twenty-four hours a day, seven days a week. Because of a 56-decibel loss of volume on its way in to the barrels, the music must be played very loudly to compensate—higher than 90 decibels of sound pressure, which is a fancy way of saying . . . very loud. The speed of sound found in LaVigne wines is approximately 1,480 meters per second—four times higher than in air. This apparently helps disperse the pressure waves inside optimally and allows all the wine an equal ear. If this theory is correct, it could be said that LaVigne wines truly provide a step in the right direction of happier living through the consumption of happier wines, which in this case is not only music to the ears, but to the mouth, too.

LAVIGNE WINE ESTATE

Appellation:	**Franschhoek**
Province:	**Western Cape**
Country of Origin:	**South Africa**
Type of Wine:	**Shiraz**
Web Site:	**www.lavigne.co.za**
Design:	**Fireworks Design**
Designer's Web Site:	**www.designbyfireworks.com**

LAVIGNE WINE ESTATE

Appellation:	**Non-Designated Appellation**
Province:	**Western Cape**
Country of Origin:	**South Africa**
Type of Wine:	**Red Blend**
Web Site:	**www.lavigne.co.za**
Design:	**Fireworks Design**
Designer's Web Site:	**www.designbyfireworks.com**

LE VILLAGE DU SUD

[LANGUEDOC-ROUSSILLON ❧ FRANCE]

At the foot of Mont Tauch in southern France, the remote village of Tuchan can be found romantically set amidst vineyards. Here, the small village of eight hundred is a paradise that seems unscathed by its historical hardships and even less affected by modern efficiencies (which they might actually consider modern "inefficiencies"). This small village, which for centuries saw its fair share of invasions, violence, and plagues, has certainly come out on top, despite being at the foot of a mountain. Here, the simple and sleepy (but rich and meaningful) lives of the villagers prevail.

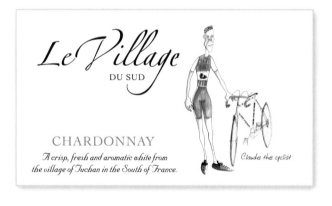

Tuchan is a working village that lives off and rallies around a grape growing co-operative. The Mont Tauch Le Village du Sud wine labels tell the story of Tuchan through the very real personalities known in the village—each with a wine genuinely reflective of their distinct characteristics and contributions to the livelihood and spirit of the village. Just like in any true community, it is not unusual to know everyone by first name and spend sunny afternoon gossiping and generally watching the world go by.

Bien sur, c'est la vie!

LE VILLAGE DU SUD (MONT TAUCH)	
Appellation:	**Fitou**
Region:	**Languedoc-Roussillon**
Country of Origin:	**France**
Type of Wine:	**Pinot Noir**
Web Site:	**www.villagedusud.com**
Art:	**Tim Bulmer**
Artist's Web Site:	**www.timbulmerartist.com**

LE VILLAGE DU SUD (MONT TAUCH)	
Appellation:	**Fitou**
Region:	**Languedoc-Roussillon**
Country of Origin:	**France**
Type of Wine:	**Chardonnay**
Web Site:	**www.villagedusud.com**
Art:	**Tim Bulmer**
Artist's Web Site:	**www.timbulmerartist.com**

Roland the Café owner

**LE VILLAGE DU SUD
(MONT TAUCH)**

Appellation:	**Fitou**
Region:	**Languedoc-Roussillon**
Country of Origin:	**France**
Type of Wine:	**Merlot**
Web Site:	**www.villagedusud.com**
Art:	**Tim Bulmer**
Artist's Web Site:	**www.timbulmerartist.com**

Sophie the Flower Seller

**LE VILLAGE DU SUD
(MONT TAUCH)**

Appellation:	**Fitou**
Region:	**Languedoc-Roussillon**
Country of Origin:	**France**
Type of Wine:	**Rosé**
Web Site:	**www.villagedusud.com**
Art:	**Tim Bulmer**
Artist's Web Site:	**www.timbulmerartist.com**

Danièle the Waitress

**LE VILLAGE DU SUD
(MONT TAUCH)**

Appellation:	**Fitou**
Region:	**Languedoc-Roussillon**
Country of Origin:	**France**
Type of Wine:	**Sauvignon Blanc**
Web Site:	**www.villagedusud.com**
Art:	**Tim Bulmer**
Artist's Web Site:	**www.timbulmerartist.com**

LEVIATHAN WINES

[CALIFORNIA ❧ UNITED STATES]

Leviathan Wines was born out of contrast. While developing wine labels for the elegant and feminine Favia wines, designer Michael McDermott threw in a thematic detour to ensure that the path they were taking was the most optimal route to follow. By incorporating a very dark wild card that took the diabolical name "Leviathan," it became clear that in this particular war between masculine and feminine, a delicately designed Favia label was the absolute right choice.

Leviathan, which at the time was simply a word and placeholder, was anything but forgotten, though it lay dormant until the right time presented itself again. As it happened, some time later, winemaker Andy Erikson produced a very big—even monstrous—wine with not a delicate, feminine grape in its body. Out slinked the ever-appropriate Leviathan, with the face of a formidable and intimidating sea creature, big in spirit, bold in character, and abundant in body. It was just the wine that this label had been waiting for to consume.

My job is to create a wine that will evoke a certain feeling in the person who tastes it. Similarly, a label can lead you in and set the stage for the experience. I feel like the Leviathan label mirrors the style of the wine: bold, vibrant, and mysterious. I definitely think that the package adds to the enjoyment.

—ANDY ERICKSON
Winemaker and Owner, Leviathan Wines

LEVIATHAN WINES

Appellation:	**Non-Designated Appellation**
State:	**California**
Country of Origin:	**United States**
Type of Wine:	**Red Blend**
Web Site:	**www.leviathanwine.com**
Design:	**Michael McDermott**
Designer's Web Site:	**www.retifex.com**

LILLIAN WINERY

[CALIFORNIA ᗯ UNITED STATES]

Winemaker Maggie Harrison always thought that she would name a daughter after her late maternal grandmother, Lillian, to venerate all that was endearing about her: her strength, charm, generosity, humor, and epical nature. As it turns out, Maggie says, she got a winery before a daughter.

At first, the project was actually going to be called Little Bird Vineyards. What else would they call it? Little Bird seemed appropriate enough considering Maggie had been quite at home in the nest of Manfred and Elaine Krankl of Sine Qua Non winery for almost nine years, not wanting to take flight on her own despite their gentle nudging. But as true nurturing parents do, they continually urged her to spread her wings and make something of her own, which she was more than capable of. Maggie says endearingly that she was essentially kicked out of the nest.

Once soaring on her own, she put some thought into her own endeavor. Knowing that she would never be capable of making a small, hesitant wine, Maggie had always strived, however, to achieve a certain balance or "levity," as she says, in terms of style and architecture, inspired by the wines of France. She aimed for a wine of considerable finesse without thinness, despite the manner in which the varietal was often structured (closer to home and away from her French inspiration).

For this reason, the feather of a crow—a big and powerful bird, yet with a lightness to its wing—was chosen as the label's visual reminder of her continual strive to make a buoyant wine without the lethargy of an overly robust grape. And the Little Bird moniker just didn't seem to fit with the feather. Since the winery and the subsequent wines created from her first grapes were everything that she could have wanted to create in her first independent wine, the name bestowed to it would be that of Lillian. Strong. Charming. Generous. Epic. And with a strong sense of humor, which is always needed when it comes to the tackling of all "firsts."

LILLIAN WINERY

Appellation:	**Santa Barbara County (Non-Designated Appellation)**
State:	**California**
Country of Origin:	**United States**
Type of Wine:	**Syrah**
Web Site:	**www.lillianwinery.com**
Design:	**Heroist**
Designer's Web Site:	**www.heroist.com**

Longboard Vineyards

[California ❧ United States]

Today, the two personal passions of winemaker Oded Shakked go hand in hand.

Some years ago, though, one wouldn't have existed without the happenstance brought about by the other.

Born at the edge of the Mediterranean, Oded was in the water by the tender age of two months. He went on to become one of the first surfers in the waters just north of Tel Aviv, Israel. Later, having such a strong affinity with surfing, he even began making surfboards. While riding the waves on vacation in Portugal, he took a sip that would change the direction of his life forever—he happened to stumble upon wine when he realized that it was often a better choice than drinking the local water—and he became an instant devotee. That discovery is where the journey towards his second great passion began, leading him ultimately to Sonoma County, where he now is a skilled craftsman, a second time around.

Today, taking time for both of his pursuits, Oded has found that balance, harmony and, of course, nature are prevalent in both his passions. Whether surfing or making wine, acting in accordance with nature (instead of against it) is the magic that makes the music.

The Longboard Vineyards labels pay tribute to what he has discovered is important in life—wine, waves, and a whole lot of soul.

> **If we want to experience something beyond wine as a commodity, we must adopt the view that everything we do says something about us. Thus, we must study the label for clues about what to expect in the bottle: conformity, individuality, corporate formula, narcissism, extreme creativity, or a mix of all.**
>
> —Oded Shakked
> Winegrower, Longboard Vineyards

LONGBOARD VINEYARDS	
Appellation:	**Russian River Valley**
State:	**California**
Country of Origin:	**United States**
Type of Wine:	**Cabernet Sauvignon**
Web Site:	**www.longboardvineyards.com**
Design:	**Firefly Creative**
Designer's Web Site:	**www.fireflycompany.com**

LONGBOARD VINEYARDS	
Appellation:	**Russian River Valley**
State:	**California**
Country of Origin:	**United States**
Type of Wine:	**Sauvignon Blanc**
Web Site:	**www.longboardvineyards.com**
Design:	**Firefly Creative**
Designer's Web Site:	**www.fireflycompany.com**

LOS PINOS RANCH VINEYARDS
[TEXAS ✤ UNITED STATES]

Cellared at Los Pinos Ranch Vineyards / Pittsburg, Texas
Ph 903-855-1769 www.LosPinosRanchVineyards.com
Artwork © Brown & Bigelow Inc.

Sweet Rodeo Red
750ml   Texas Table Wine   13% Alc./Vol.

Nothing says "heart of Texas" more than a good, old-fashioned rodeo. And they've certainly been known to happen under the influence of this particular Los Pinos Ranch Vineyards wine. Therefore, something very fun, a little frisky, and with a lot of cowgirl spunk seemed just right for the wine label.

This vision couldn't have been better actualized than through the iconic illustration by the legendary Gil Elvgren. Gil Elvgren has been acclaimed as the most important pin-up artist of the twentieth century. Having a career that started in the 1930s and spanned over forty years, he was best known for his calendar pin-up illustrations produced for Brown and Bigelow, as well as other commercial art, most notably for twenty-five years of advertising illustration for Coca-Cola. Today, through the Los Pinos Ranch Vineyards wine labels, his pin-up proliferation lives on.

Los Pinos Ranch Vineyards takes a rather avant-garde approach to wine. Therefore, we advocate the idea that wine, and certainly the labels, should be fun! —JEFF SNEED Owner and Winemaker, Los Pinos Ranch Vineyards

With a label like this, one is sure to be smitten at first glance. In fact, this innocent Sweet Rodeo Red is also known to be a lucky little Love Potion No. 9 with lots of success stories under its belt. The fact is, true to its sweet rodeo label, this wine has been known to get people to throw caution to the wind. After a bottle (or two), the folks at Los Pinos Ranch have seen just about everything . . . including first-timers saddling up and bucking it up bronco-style by the end of the night. Giddy up!

LOS PINOS RANCH VINEYARDS

Appellation:	**Pittsburg (Non-Designated Appellation)**
State:	**Texas**
Country of Origin:	**United States**
Type of Wine:	**Red Blend**
Web Site:	**www.lospinosranchvineyards.com**
Art:	**Gil Elvgren**
Artist's Web Site:	**www.gilelvgren.com**

THE LOST HIGHWAY PROJECT

[VICTORIA ❧ AUSTRALIA]

In 2000, passionate wine enthusiast and importer Ronnie Sanders found himself driving down a dark, deserted highway between Olympia and Walla Walla, Washington, in solitude. There were no lights on the road and it was eerily desolate when, all of a sudden, it unexpectedly and absurdly started to rain down on this expansive and arid terrain. It felt almost like a surreal scene from one of David Lynch's films, and Ronnie almost looked to see if Renee Madison or Alice Wakefield was sitting in the backseat unbeknownst to him.

It was here on this remote highway, in the solitude of the night, alone with nothing but his own thoughts and a thundering storm, that Ronnie recalled his tasting earlier that day with winemaker Bob Andrake. Bob had introduced him to a huge Malbec wine that just didn't have anything to be blended with it. Quite taken with the wine, Ronnie thought of purchasing it, but didn't really have anything to do with it. As he drove for those five-plus hours feeling like he was in a scene from *Lost Highway*, his wine project using that very Malbec was envisioned.

Each year since, Ronnie has collaborated with a different winemaker to develop a distinct, one-of-a-kind and one-time-only wine in a small allotment. There would be no timeline, no real cor-

As a kid, I would buy records based solely upon whether I thought the album art was cool or not. As I segued into adulthood, I held wine labels to the same standard. People are always apt to grab a bottle of wine that looks interesting and tells a story through the design of a great label. After that, it's the wine's job to do its part and keep the fans coming back. —RONNIE SANDERS
Owner, The Lost Highway Project

porate objective, and no "route" to getting there. Creative exploration, passion, and innovation for the wine would be the only drive of the project. As he would work with craftsmen to create the unique wines, he would also work with visual artists equally inspired with imagination to develop the labels. Each wine would be a journey unto its own and he would label it The Lost Highway Project.

THE LOST HIGHWAY PROJECT

Appellation:	**Macedon Ranges**
State:	**Victoria**
Country of Origin:	**Australia**
Type of Wine:	**Pinot Noir**
Web Site:	**www.vsimports.com**
Art:	**Justin Hampton**
Artist's Web Site:	**www.justinhampton.com**

People who meet winemaker Matt Berson always comment on how romantic his life must be. But he knows all too well that the vintner's life is much more than a picnic in a vineyard on a sunny day.

Yes, there is the passion, the artistry, and an intense pride for the craft. There is also the joy of sharing the handcrafted wines with friends and family, especially when paired with food at the table—a marriage that turns wine into pure magic. And, yes, there is the occasional picnic.

On the other (squalid) hand, and contrary to the perception of the romanticism of producing fine wine, we have the stained purple hands, muddy knees, the twelve-plus-hour days lasting weeks on end, the damp socks, and bruised shins—all evidence that a stroll through the vineyard isn't always a walk in the park.

Though much hardship may come with the profession, there is a devotion to this polarized passion that ultimately keeps winemakers doing what they love to do most: making their best possible wine. When Matt was faced with the challenge of naming his first wine, a challenge that can only be compared to the naming of a child, it was the dichotomy of his craft and a love for literature that struck a chord. His favorite short story by J. D. Salinger, entitled "For Esmé—with Love and Squalor," was the source of his wine's name. An appreciation for the author's skillful technique—required to shape a poignant tale with only an agonizingly few words—seemed to parallel his own approach to the art of making wine. With the clean visual of freshly washed linen, a symbol of a simpler life—lovely or squalid—Matt felt that he had found an evocative sense of beauty that befittingly matched his wines and the fervor he feels creating them.

LOVE & SQUALOR WINE	
Appellation:	**Willamette Valley**
State:	**Oregon**
Country of Origin:	**United States**
Type of Wine:	**Riesling**
Web Site:	**www.loveandsqualorwine.com**
Design:	**Bluelist Communications**
Designer's Web Site:	**www.bluelist.net**

MAC FORBES WINES
[VICTORIA ❧ AUSTRALIA]

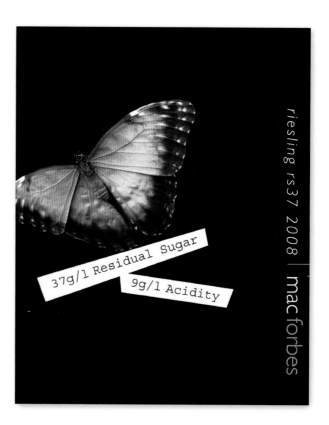

The Strathbogie Ranges in Australia is a place of exceptional beauty graced with mystical woodlands, cascading waterfalls set amidst ferned glades, dramatically rugged hillsides, and awesome, scenic vistas. It is also known for its plentiful native wildlife, which includes an abundance of unique butterfly species—the state of Victoria is said to actually have over one hundred and forty different varieties.

Much like the transformation from grape to wine, butterflies first travel through a lifecycle whereby they change from less-enticing caterpillars into elegant insects that need little more than sunshine and flowers to be happy. Further, while caterpillars are at times considered pesky vineyard foes, the butterfly is a harmless friend to the vineyard ecosystem.

The highly aromatic Riesling varietal is known to express floral notes, making it a perfect friend for the region's butterflies. Known also to be a "terroir-expressive" grape, Mac Forbes Wines uses butterflies native to the region as a face for the wines—a perfect match for these Rieslings that showcase their region's natural beauty in every sip.

MAC FORBES WINES	
Appellation:	**Strathbogie Ranges**
State:	**Victoria**
Country of Origin:	**Australia**
Type of Wine:	**Riesling**
Web Site:	**www.macforbes.com**
Design:	**Thanissorn**
Designer's Web Site:	**www.thanissorn.com**

MAC FORBES WINES	
Appellation:	**Strathbogie Ranges**
State:	**Victoria**
Country of Origin:	**Australia**
Type of Wine:	**Riesling**
Web Site:	**www.macforbes.com**
Design:	**Thanissorn**
Designer's Web Site:	**www.thanissorn.com**

M.A.D.

Many would consider M.A.D. just that—an illogical investment by three friends living in what many consider a non-wine consuming country: China. The reality is that the pursuit of this wine venture, while seemingly mad, is actually quite sound. Based on three friends' insatiable love of Pinot Noir and further, the trifecta's leader's intimate knowledge of Australian wines, the trio were led down the right path from the get go.

Partnering with friend and vintner Sandro Mosele (from Port Phillip Estates in Victoria), the Pinot-philes—Michael, Andrew, and David, who are professional colleagues-turned-friends—invested in the project together and released a Pinot Noir in China under the moniker M.A.D. (for Michael, Andrew, and David).

Andrew, who is currently based in Shanghai as the fine wine manager for the most influential wine importer in China, ASC Fine Wines, says that he dragged his other friend, Chris, into the project to insure that the label captured what they were looking for. Coincidently, Chris's design studio is called The Asylum, which gave him fair play to exercise his lunatic talent on the absolutely M.A.D. wine label.

M.A.D.	
Appellation:	**Mornington Peninsula**
State:	**Victoria**
Country of Origin:	**Australia**
Type of Wine:	**Shiraz**
Design:	**The Asylum**
Designer's Web Site:	**www.theasylum.com.sg**
Art:	**Agathe Bailliencourt**

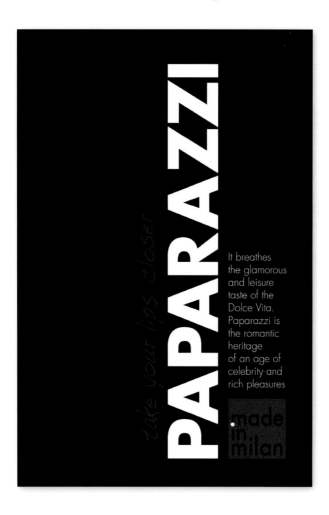

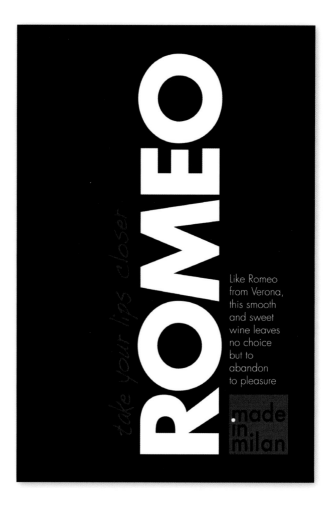

Italians. They've got quite the reputation. They are known for being romantic, eccentric, impassioned, fashionable, and the ultimate purveyors and practitioners of rich and hedonistic pleasure.

Beauty, sex, food, and wine—does there really need to be anything else? It's what many people think Italians are all about. And while it's *not* all that Italians are about, there is an absolute truth to this enviable, pleasure-seeking lifestyle of Italian people that is often emulated but never duplicated.

The Madeinmilan wines offer a cheeky escape for those dreaming of *la dolce vita*, a glimpse inside Italian life if even just for an evening. Each wine label offers a bit of Italian character for which the country and its nationals have become known and loved for: romance, boldness, and elegant extravagance.

It's been said that everyone has a little Italian in them. Madeinmilan wines, in true cheeky Italian style, tempt you to turn fantasy to reality simply by taking a sip.

Go on. Take a sip and let your inner Italian out. You know you want to.

MADEINMILAN	
Appellation:	**Non-Designated Appellation**
Region:	**Emilia-Romagna**
Country of Origin:	**Italy**
Type of Wine:	**Lambrusco**
Web Site:	**www.madeinmilanwine.com**
Design:	**Fabio Bressan (Pop My Pet)**
Designer's Web Site:	**www.popmypet.com**

MADEINMILAN	
Appellation:	**Non-Designated Appellation**
Region:	**Emilia-Romagna**
Country of Origin:	**Italy**
Type of Wine:	**Cagnina di Romagna**
Web Site:	**www.madeinmilanwine.com**
Design:	**Fabio Bressan (Pop My Pet)**
Designer's Web Site:	**www.popmypet.com**

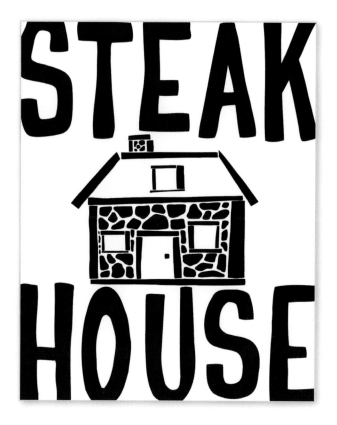

After returning home from living in Europe for over eleven years, touring with big stars and generally living the rock-and-roll lifestyle, Charles Smith decided to go back to something that he always loved: wine.

Noticing that many wines he came across had $20 worth of label, but failed to meet the price or label expectation by giving the customer only 50¢ worth of wine inside, he decided to switch things up a bit and do just the opposite—make a wine that had $20 worth of juice but with a 50¢ label. A good wine, but without the fluff that would inflate the price; the kind of wine that you would have on hand to serve at your house.

Staying true to the cause, he drew the label and picked a name that everyone would surely know—perhaps the most common wine terms in the world, "house wine" and "table wine."

Nothing fancy. Nothing that would break the bank.

Rather, it's all about the wine and the simple things that make drinking it special: friends, family, and plenty of good times at home and around the table. As Charles says, *"Mi casa es su casa"*: "My house is your house."

THE MAGNIFICENT WINE COMPANY (PRECEPT WINE BRANDS)	
Appellation:	**Columbia Valley**
State:	**Washington**
Country of Origin:	**United States**
Type of Wine:	**White Blend or Red Blend**
Web Site:	**www.magnificentwine.com**
Design:	**The Korff Kounsil**
Designer's Web Site:	**www.thekounsil.com**

THE MAGNIFICENT WINE COMPANY (PRECEPT WINE BRANDS)	
Appellation:	**Columbia Valley**
State:	**Washington**
Country of Origin:	**United States**
Type of Wine:	**Cabernet Sauvignon**
Web Site:	**www.magnificentwine.com**
Design:	**The Korff Kounsil**
Designer's Web Site:	**www.thekounsil.com**

MAGPIE ESTATE

[SOUTH AUSTRALIA ❧ AUSTRALIA]

 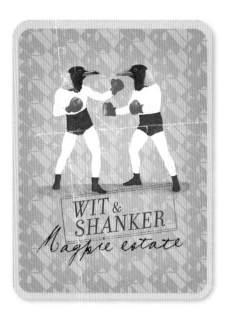

What happens when you get two sport-loving men together? They sit around having a laugh and talk sports incessantly, remembering the most obscure facts and re-enacting pivotal play-by-play moments from games past.

What happens when you get two sport-loving men together and one happens to be a winemaker and the other a wine negotiant? They sit around having a laugh, talking sports incessantly while tasting copious amounts of their favorite varietals, and then decide to make wines that they like to drink together and name them after their favorite footie teams.

This is almost what happened in 1993 when Noel Young, a wine merchant with a "cracking palate" from England met Rolf Binder, a sought-after winemaker from South Australia. Both shared a passion for Rhône grape varietals that, at the time, were the underdogs in the wine industry. We all know that Aussies often hold a cultural soft spot for the underdogs, so it didn't take much to convince Rolf. With Noel being a huge fan of the Aussie rules football team Collingwood (officially nicknamed "The Magpies"), and Rolf being a former player for the Tanunda Magpies, it appeared that they had their venture's name: Magpie Estate.

The sport-fanatic oenophiles' philosophy is to make quality wines that have complex flavor, but are fun, exceed expectations, and made to drink—and drunk not merely for competition. The labels are equally entertaining, and definitely exceed expectation if you can decipher the two mates' twisted inside jokes often arrived at after a couple of beverages. Rumor has it that some of the labels pay homage to neglected male appendages and that Wit and Shanker is more than just a tribute to Cabernet Sauvignon. So, no matter what age or occupation, the Magpie Estate wine labels suggest one other thing for sure: boys will always be boys.

At Magpie Estate, we have a lot of fun making these wines and we want people to enjoy them. Our labels are somewhat irreverent, but also intriguing and fun, humorous even, which I think is essentially what we are trying to do and what we are about.
—NOEL YOUNG
Partner, Magpie Estate

MAGPIE ESTATE	
Appellation:	**Barossa Valley**
State:	**South Australia**
Country of Origin:	**Australia**
Type of Wine:	**Mourvèdre**
Web Site:	**www.magpieestate.com**
Design:	**Mash**
Designer's Web Site:	**www.mashdesign.com.au**

MAGPIE ESTATE	
Appellation:	**Barossa Valley**
State:	**South Australia**
Country of Origin:	**Australia**
Type of Wine:	**Cabernet Sauvignon**
Web Site:	**www.magpieestate.com**
Design:	**Mash**
Designer's Web Site:	**www.mashdesign.com.au**

How does one go from the world of Hollywood to the world of wine? When it means adding more than just your name to a label, it takes more than just money.

Martin Malivoire has decades of tenure in the film industry in special effects, but he began his relationship with wine in the 1970s when he was traveling to renowned wine regions of the world to expand his knowledge and grow his personal wine cellar. In 1994, while working on the set of *Trapped in Paradise* in Niagara-on-the-Lake, Ontario, Martin took an interest in the idea of purchasing a vineyard property as a weekend holiday home. Encouraged by his partner, Moira, the purchase would not only be a commitment to their mutual interest in wine, but a deep commitment to each other. After diligent research, the couple decided on a site below the escarpment in the Beamsville Bench appellation in 1995, where Malivoire's Moira Vineyard now sits.

Now, when one thinks of Hollywood and the movie industry, there are certain stereotypes that immediately come to mind. These call forth unfortunate words such as superficiality, pretension, and artificiality, and suggest a certain numbness and selfishness often required to survive in a dog-eat-dog world. Martin is certainly the largest exception to the stereotype. You can feel his polar opposition to the generalized industry norm in his energy, and see it in his utter approachability; he is a man alive with generosity, humility, and respect for people and nature. In fact, he wouldn't so much as even step on a ladybug—the Malivoire symbol of enjoyment of and commitment to the environment.

A good label engages a consumer before the wine is tasted. A great one seems at home on its chosen bottle and lingers in the mind long after the bottle is empty.
—MARTIN MALIVOIRE
Proprietor, Malivoire Wine Co.

MALIVOIRE WINE COMPANY	
Appellation:	**Niagara Escarpment**
Province:	**Ontario**
Country of Origin:	**Canada**
Type of Wine:	**Rosé**
Web Site:	**www.malivoire.com**
Design:	**Scott Thornley + Company**
Designer's Web Site:	**www.stcworks.ca**

MALIVOIRE WINE COMPANY	
Appellation:	**Niagara Peninsula**
Province:	**Ontario**
Country of Origin:	**Canada**
Type of Wine:	**Gamay**
Web Site:	**www.malivoire.com**
Design:	**Scott Thornley + Company**
Designer's Web Site:	**www.stcworks.ca**

MANDALAY ROAD

[WESTERN AUSTRALIA ❧ AUSTRALIA]

When Bernice and Tony O'Connell thought of retiring from their professional lives in education and science, they were looking for a big change.

With the purchase of the inland property in the beautiful Preston Valley in Western Australia, they knew, as beach lovers, there would need to be another draw for them to enjoy their time there. At first, they thought of cherries, and then of apples, and then the memory of one of Bernice's tennis friends waxing lyrical about how fabulous it was to sit on the veranda of their Margaret River property, sipping wine and watching the sun set through the vines resurfaced from years gone by. And so, the decision was made to plant vines of the "just enough for us to enjoy" varietal. But when it was discovered that a dam had to be constructed in order to nourish these "just enough for us to enjoy" vines, it seemed a costly endeavor for a mere acre of grapes. "Just enough for us" became "might as well put more in," and the adventure was underway.

For six years, Bernice and Tony spent weekends commuting to and from their holiday home that, in reality, was a whole lot of work and very little holiday at the time. Eventually, they transitioned from Perth to permanent residence at the holiday homestead and there were no more long commutes at the weekend. The grapes planted had been thriving and the O'Connells had been quite content selling their crops to neighboring wineries. That all changed when one vintage arrived and the winery saw grapes left on the vines due to a shortage of bins sent to be filled. Not wanting to leave the grapes just hanging helplessly on the vines and inevitably going to waste, the O'Connells saw their first vintage. And one vintage became two, and two became three. Now, they no longer wait for the bins to arrive from neighboring wineries. Instead, they have their own label, Mandalay Road, which is in fact where the vineyard sits—a long way from Mandalay in Burma, but with a similar story of change and haulage of sorts.

The original Mandalay, far from the shores of Western Australia, didn't actually exist where the city resides today. In fact, it was the Burmese King Mindon who said that in order to fulfill a Buddhist prophecy, it was required that he move the entire royal city of Amarapura to the base of Mandalay Hill.

Labels are the forerunner of the taste experience for the wine drinker. They titillate and entice, and in that process give an impression of the vignerons who have produced the wine.

—BERNICE O'CONNELL
Owner, Mandalay Road

And in 1857, the transition was actually made entirely on the backs of elephants in order to found the Buddhist metropolis that would celebrate the 2,400th jubilee of Buddhism. Almost one hundred and forty years later, the O'Connells made a pilgrimage of sorts to their own new Mandalay. The Mandalay Road label art bridges a gap of time and geographical space between both journeys, and recognizes the similarities of plight, fortitude, and determination in the face of the unknown.

MANDALAY ROAD

Appellation:	**Geographe**
State:	**Western Australia**
Country of Origin:	**Australia**
Type of Wine:	**Zinfandel**
Website:	**www.mandalayroad.com.au**
Design:	**Barbara Harkness**
Designer's Web Site:	**www.harknessdesign.com.au**

MARTIN ESTATE

[CALIFORNIA & UNITED STATES]

At the age of twelve, a young Greg Martin spotted an antique 1863 Colt revolver at a Northern Californian thrift shop. Having an immediate pull towards the allure of the pistol, he immediately asked his mother if he could purchase the $15 collector's item. His mother replied by saying that he could buy the gun if he could negotiate a price of $10. The industrious twelve-year-old succeeded, and it was here that began a lifelong love affair with historical arms, armor, and dealing in antique auctions—all before he could even shave. At the same young age, as a result of his restaurateur parents, Martin was more exposed to the food and wine industry than the average kid, and also had easy access to grapes from the nearby property. An inquisitive child, Martin began making "wine" at an early age by picking his own grapes and experimenting.

With a keen eye for coveted pieces, Martin began scouring flea markets and antique and thrift shops, effectively uncovering aspirational and sought-after items and turning a profit by reselling them to other collectors. Concurrently, Martin says that as he grew into a teenager, he was quite adept at the science of winemaking. Both of these young amusements would be the foundation of Martin's entire career. As he matured, his dealings in antiques evolved to a more grandiose scale. In 1985, Martin purchased the entire William Parker Lyon Pony Express Museum in order to acquire three coveted pieces. This resulted in the onset of a relationship with Butterfield Auction House (now Bonham and Butterfields) where he would spend sixteen years consulting as director of arms and building the division to the largest of its kind internationally.

Martin split his time between his San Francisco home atop Telegraph Hill and a country home in the Napa Valley town of Rutherford. The historic country home dated back to 1887 and was once the H. H. Harris Winery, producing wines until 1909, at which point it ceased to exist. Never imagining going back to his adolescent interest in winemaking, it was actually the local Rutherford Planning Commission that brought Martin back to it in a roundabout way. Wanting to build a 16-foot fenced gate on the property that houses some of Martin's prized collection, he was informed that only commercial properties could have fenced surroundings of that height. A determinedly single-minded Martin responded by planting 8 acres of grapes, hiring a winemaker, bonding his new winery ninety-one years after its last vintage and put up his gates.

The Martin Estate wine labels bring both of Greg's lifelong passions together, both of which he says can be compared to time capsules: objects of fantasy that have the ability to transport you to another time and another place just by different means. After all of his collecting, Martin says that his favorite piece is still that first 1863 Colt, though the same perhaps cannot be said of his first wine.

MARTIN ESTATE	
Appellation:	**Rutherford**
State:	**California**
Country of Origin:	**United States**
Type of Wine:	**Cabernet Sauvignon**
Web Site:	**www.martinestate.com**
Design:	**Greg and Pietra Martin**

Matsu

[Castile and León ᔍ Spain]

The Japanese word *matsu* has a simple definition when translated into English; it means "to wait." This moderate mindset provides a perfect framework for Vintae's modern wine project that uses sustainable viticulture and advanced biodynamic agriculture as a means to emulate values of the Japanese culture, namely respecting and conserving both nature and the elements. In this manner, the vineyards produce wines that are all natural from crops that are cultivated in a form that is completely ecologically friendly—meaning not using any chemicals, synthetic herbicides, insecticides, or fungicides. Nature is left to run its course and thus made "to wait" in order for the wine's fullest potential to be achieved at every stage of the process.

"Waiting," however, is not idle in nature. In fact, it involves building a strong relationship between farmers and the vines in order to understand and respect the ebb and flow of the natural growth cycle. This takes work and can be traced through soiled hands and sun-kissed skin that comes from nurturing the vines on a daily basis.

The Matsu wine labels carry the themes of waiting and purity on its labels. They contain raw imagery of the sincere faces of the rural farmers who dedicate their lives to the tending of the vineyards and who so intimately work with nature day in and day out. Each wine has been paired with an image of the most fitting farmer according to the style and personality of wine on their respective labels.

	MATSU **(VINTAE)**
Appellation:	**Toro**
Community:	**Castile and León**
Country of Origin:	**Spain**
Type of Wine:	**Tinta de Toro (Tempranillo)**
Web Site:	**www.vintae.com**
Design:	**Moruba**
Designer's Web Site:	**www.moruba.es**

MATSU
(VINTAE)

Appellation:	**Toro**
Community:	**Castile and León**
Country of Origin:	**Spain**
Type of Wine:	**Tinta de Toro (Tempranillo)**
Web Site:	**www.vintae.com**
Design:	**Moruba**
Designer's Web Site:	**www.moruba.es**

MATSU
(VINTAE)

Appellation:	**Toro**
Community:	**Castile and León**
Country of Origin:	**Spain**
Type of Wine:	**Tinta de Toro (Tempranillo)**
Web Site:	**www.vintae.com**
Design:	**Moruba**
Designer's Web Site:	**www.moruba.es**

MAYBACH FAMILY VINEYARDS
[CALIFORNIA ∽ UNITED STATES]

2006 MATERIUM.

Maybach
FAMILY VINEYARDS

Look up the word "materium" in the dictionary and it will offer few clues. "Maybach," on the other hand needs no definition for many, particularly for car aficionados.

The Maybach name and the luxury vehicles associated with it began with an underprivileged young Wilhelm Maybach, who was a child of a German orphanage. While odds were stacked against him, this particular orphanage provided industrial education opportunities to its inexperienced residents through factory apprenticeships. Involving himself in this program, the young Maybach demonstrated tremendous talent that didn't go unnoticed, especially by Werner Factories design director Gottlieb Daimler. By the time Maybach was nineteen, the two had embarked in business together and Maybach would remain Daimler's invaluable partner until Daimler's death in 1900.

As Daimler's chief engineer, Maybach designed the first high-speed internal combustion engine—a precursor to his invention of the first motorcycle—and was credited with creating the earliest Mercedes vehicle in Germany.

Following in his father's footsteps and continuing to build the family legacy, Karl Maybach also became a visionary engineer, developing the first high-speed diesel engine and successfully built motors that would enable legendary Zeppelin airships to circumnavigate the globe during the '20s and '30s. However, Karl is possibly most identified with designing the Maybach luxury sedan, which earned him international recognition.

Eventually, the Maybach family established themselves in San Francisco, California, and the lineage continued to grow. After his own successful career, Wilhelm's great-great-grandson, Chris Maybach, felt a calling to reinstate his family's roots in luxury goods. The obvious—cars—wasn't an option, as DaimlerChrysler now owns the Maybach name. Instead, Chris turned to his roots—*rootstalks* to be precise. While beginning a new chapter in the family's history, he was sure to elegantly observe the longstanding traditions of craftsmanship, quality, and individuality that have presented themselves as equally in Maybach wines as Maybach cars.

We didn't want the label to look like a real-estate brochure—a staged piece of property. Instead, the idea was to evoke a feeling or a memory. The label leaves something to the imagination. —CHRIS MAYBACH
Owner, Maybach Family Vineyards

The hand-illustrated image of the garage that would have traditionally housed the famed cars is homage to the family's heritage. "Materium" is a toast to the current Maybach generation's *mater*, the granddaughter of Wilhelm Maybach. It is also an echo of the word *motorenbau*, the name of the company founded by Karl Maybach, and is Latin for "earthly realm"—a gentle reminder that even the finest of wines are still fundamentally material and should not be put on an ethereal pedestal.

MAYBACH FAMILY VINEYARDS

Appellation:	**Oakville**
State:	**California**
Country of Origin:	**United States**
Type of Wine:	**Cabernet Sauvignon**
Web Site:	**www.maybachwines.com**
Design:	**Bob Johnson Design & Art**
Designer's Web Site:	**www.johnson-design.com**

M BY MICHAEL MONDAVI
[CALIFORNIA ❧ UNITED STATES]

Michael Mondavi's winemaking roots run deep—both literally and figuratively. A third-generation winemaker, Michael has spent over four decades at the forefront of the industry. While he has essentially "done it all," it is the winemaking that he has always been passionate about. M by Michael Mondavi is indisputably Michael's return to doing what he loves best and getting back to his roots, including those from deep within the soils of his Animo Vineyard in the Foss Valley of Atlas Peak. Fittingly, the vineyard's name means "spirit" or "soul," when translated from the Mondavi family's native Italian.

Michael follows a philosophy that has evolved from his grandmother's sage advice, recommending that he make wines that just taste good and not wines that are merely expensive and solely for purchase by wealthier customers. He says that to follow this philosophy, the most important thing when making his wines is not the château, not the winery, and not the winemaker. Rather, it is the guiding force of the terroir and the almighty graces of Mother Nature that should be the foundation and core of every wine. Each wine should have a true sense of time and place.

Of critical importance, according to Michael's guiding principle, is the unique terroir of the Animo Vineyard and the high quantity of volcanic rock and little organic matter that is found within the soils. Respecting the individuality of the land and being meticulous at every stage of the process, from all-natural growing through bottling, is an indication of the utmost dignity of the land, the grapes, and Mother Nature, which ultimately ends in an elegant glass and an invitation to always come back for a second—certainly just what his grandmother had advised him that a good wine should do.

Wanting to capture his admiration for terroir and the strength of the vines in a contemporary manner, Michael engaged renowned fashion designer Karen Joyce to create a contemporary interpretation of just what is at the core of Mondavi's roots, secured not only in the depths of his soils, but in his soul as well.

**M BY MICHAEL MONDAVI
(THE MICHAEL MONDAVI FAMILY)**

Appellation:	**Napa Valley**
State:	**California**
Country of Origin:	**United States**
Type of Wine:	**Cabernet Sauvignon**
Web Site:	**www.mbymichaelmondavi.com**
Design:	**Karen Joyce**
Designer's Web Site:	**www.joyceimage.com**

MEGALOMANIAC
[ONTARIO ❧ CANADA]

The fact that John Howard named his retirement project Megalomaniac is diametrically ironic. As the story goes, after selling his first venture in wines, Vineland Estates, Howard thought that he should undertake a "small project" of his own to keep him out of trouble. And as small projects go, he purchased a 100-acre parcel of prime property for his new vineyard. It seemed only natural to name it as his own: The John Howard Vineyard. Close friends, having full license and lacking the tiptoe of tact, denounced that he was "another [profanity withheld] megalomaniac," Howard recounts. His friends joked about it because they also knew that what was behind the wines was nothing such. The ironic wisecrack stuck and Megalomaniac it was.

In fact, rather than megalomaniac self-indulgence, the backbone of the wines was built on a foundation to help children heal. The purchase of each of Howard's wines helps the Kids' Health Links Foundation in Canada, which he is a founder of. The foundation enables children in medical care to join the Upopolis private social community that connects young hospital patients to their friends, family, schools, and other children suffering from similar circumstances. Further to this small probity, Howard has been known to volunteer at children's orphanages while on holiday in Africa.

Though the clever Megalomaniac wine labels are plays on self-centered personalities, the wines certainly aren't self-serving. While the surface story is about naming the wines with his moniker, upon closer inspection, there is certainly so much more to this Megalomaniac than meets the eye.

Buying and selling wines should be a fulfilling experience and not martyrdom. The label should reflect the spirit and constancy to purpose of the producer as well as the anticipation of the client. In essence, it should threshold joy for both.
—JOHN HOWARD
Proprietor,
John Howard Cellars of Distinction

MEGALOMANIAC (JOHN HOWARD CELLARS OF DISTINCTION)	
Appellation:	**Niagara Peninsula**
Province:	**Ontario**
Country of Origin:	**Canada**
Type of Wine:	**Chardonnay**
Web Site:	**www.megalomaniacwine.com**
Design:	**Brandever**
Designer's Web Site:	**www.brandever.com**

MEGALOMANIAC (JOHN HOWARD CELLARS OF DISTINCTION)	
Appellation:	**Niagara Peninsula**
Province:	**Ontario**
Country of Origin:	**Canada**
Type of Wine:	**Pinot Noir**
Web Site:	**www.megalomaniacwine.com**
Design:	**Brandever**
Designer's Web Site:	**www.brandever.com**

MEGALOMANIAC
(JOHN HOWARD CELLARS OF DISTINCTION)

Appellation:	**Niagara Peninsula**
Province:	**Ontario**
Country of Origin:	**Canada**
Type of Wine:	**Merlot**
Web Site:	**www.megalomaniacwine.com**
Design:	**Brandever**
Designer's Web Site:	**www.brandever.com**

MEGALOMANIAC
(JOHN HOWARD CELLARS OF DISTINCTION)

Appellation:	**Niagara Peninsula**
Province:	**Ontario**
Country of Origin:	**Canada**
Type of Wine:	**Cabernet Sauvignon**
Web Site:	**www.megalomaniacwine.com**
Design:	**Brandever**
Designer's Web Site:	**www.brandever.com**

MEGALOMANIAC
(JOHN HOWARD CELLARS OF DISTINCTION)

Appellation:	**Niagara Peninsula**
Province:	**Ontario**
Country of Origin:	**Canada**
Type of Wine:	**Cabernet Franc Icewine**
Web Site:	**www.megalomaniacwine.com**
Design:	**Brandever**
Designer's Web Site:	**www.brandever.com**

MEGALOMANIAC
(JOHN HOWARD CELLARS OF DISTINCTION)

Appellation:	**Niagara Peninsula**
Province:	**Ontario**
Country of Origin:	**Canada**
Type of Wine:	**Sauvignon Blanc**
Web Site:	**www.megalomaniacwine.com**
Design:	**Brandever**
Designer's Web Site:	**www.brandever.com**

Mendocino Wine Co.

[California ✶ United States]

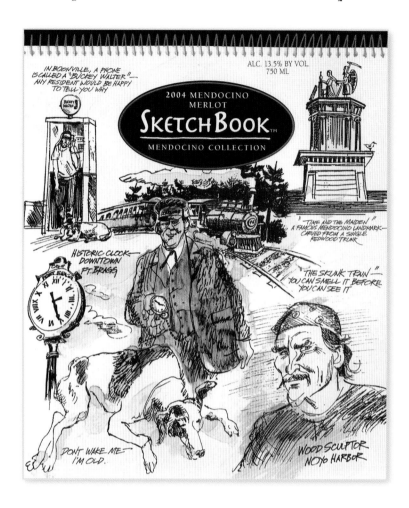

Take a look around your neighborhood. You know the usual suspects—the people, the local haunts, and the unique charm that creates the character that makes one neighborhood different from the next. And Mendocino is a perfect example of a place that truly sets itself apart from any other because of its natural beauty, free-spirited residents, and the eclectic and plentiful hidden gems that often only a native would likely know.

The Mendocino Wine Company Sketchbook wine collection provides that touch of insider information that ensures that even if you aren't from Mendocino, you still get to feel like a local. The labels' illustrations were sketched by two regional talents—Bill Shields and Randy Grochoske—who, with sketchbooks in hand, left nothing unexplored in the county. They combed the streets and the backroads, roamed with tourists, became one with the locals, witnessed harvest and ocean fishing, strolled the harbors, and visually documented the beauty and simple charm that is Mendocino.

Through the label artwork, one is able to meet distinctive local characters that embody the spirit of the Mendocino County community. Once an intimate artist's colony, Mendocino is said still to hold on to its neighborly feel that is characterized by a touch of hippie and creative expression.

Ask anyone in Mendocino County what a "Buckey Walter" or a "skunk train" is. They'll tell you the story. You'll get to know the people and place so well, you'll be packing your bags to move in. The next thing you know, it'll be you that's become part of the local scenery.

MENDOCINO WINE CO.

Appellation:	**Mendocino**
State:	**California**
Country of Origin:	**United States**
Type of Wine:	**Merlot**
Web Site:	**www.mendocinowineco.com**
Art:	**Bill Shields and Randy Grochoske**
Artist's Web Site:	**www.billshieldsart.com**

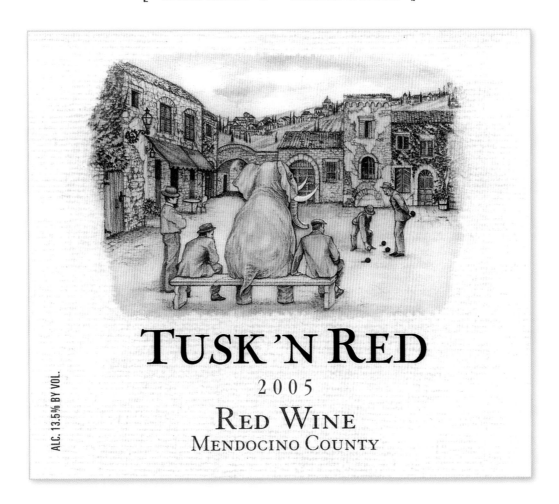

Having a vision of a traditionally styled wine, while using a mixture of multiple New World varieties, inspiration was sought in the legends and traditions of the Old World for this Mendocino label. At first glance, Tusk 'N Red seems simply an amusing play-on-words that fits with the wine's Tuscan style. But think again. This clever label is historically and culturally evocative of its Tuscan muse.

Most people associate bocce, which is one of the oldest known games to mankind, with the Italian culture. Even today, Italian men regularly congregate to pass time throwing balls while fervently engrossing themselves in the debates of politics, religion, life, and love. Where does the elephant fit into the equation? Well, at one point, long before bocce, elephants also figured into Italian history. The warrior Hannibal Barca, who defeated the Romans in a series of battles, marched his army (including thirty-seven war elephants) into northern Italy circa 218 BC. They traveled to battle from Iberia, over the Pyrenees, and then over the Alps. It was a bit of a walk.

The label, taking cues from the wine it houses, is classically illustrated in Old World style, but with New World curiosity. You can almost imagine yourself sitting amidst the unforgettable architecture, engrossed in a game of bocce, sipping a smooth glass of red, with what just happens to be an elephant next to you!

But don't stare at the elephant. As they say at Mendocino Wine Company, "It's not polite. And it makes him nervous!"

MENDOCINO WINE CO.	
Appellation:	**Mendocino**
State:	**California**
Country of Origin:	**United States**
Type of Wine:	**Red Blend**
Web Site:	**www.mendocinowineco.com**
Design:	**Rae Huestis Design**

Patrick McNeil and Craig Becker are the men behind Michael Austin Wines. When it came to naming their combined endeavor, they chose to combine their two middle names, creating the moniker for their joint project. Instead of getting twisted in a knot trying to explain the unique name, they decided to use it to their advantage and have some fun.

Together with their agency, Hatch Design, Patrick and Craig took a trip down memory lane and told stories about their long-standing friendship. These reminiscent days of old—beginning at Mater Dei High School (where the two first met) and through each achieving individual career paths in wine marketing and winemaking, respectively—have been told through their quirky alter ego. Though Michael Austin's adventures are filled with a significant amount of whimsy (for instance, it is said that he grew up in a monastery in Europe, was raised by a pack of wild nuns, and taught to survive on a diet of wine and cheese), each of the tall tales on the labels also hints at stories all with a bit of truth to them that are both memorable and meaningful for the two friends.

MICHAEL AUSTIN WINES
Appellation: **Napa Valley**
State: **California**
Country of Origin: **United States**
Type of Wine: **Cabernet Sauvignon**
Web Site: **www.highflyerwines.com**
Design: **Hatch Design**
Designer's Web Site: **www.hatchsf.com**

MICHAEL AUSTIN WINES
Appellation: **Napa Valley**
State: **California**
Country of Origin: **United States**
Type of Wine: **Syrah**
Web Site: **www.highflyerwines.com**
Design: **Hatch Design**
Designer's Web Site: **www.hatchsf.com**

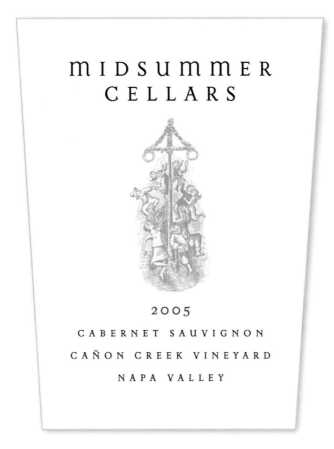

M idsummer in Sweden is said to be a magical time of the year when the sun spends little time dipped below the horizon. Though it is a short season, it is a festive period that is taken full advantage of before the crisp coolness of winter creeps back in and the days become more dark than light.

It was during this time that Sally and Rollie Heitz took their initial trip to the lake district of Sweden to visit longtime friends. Here, during the midsummer's "celebration of life," they were romanced by the local traditions that came alive at the end of June when the maypole is raised to welcome summer and the season of fertility. Despite the brevity of the season, the Swedish summer is bursting with greenery and flowers perfect for making adornments abound on the maypole.

While the Heitzes already had a wine label, they couldn't help but feel that the festivities during that special holiday were those that should be remembered and that would translate to the perfect sentiments they'd want to share about their wines. The Midsummer Cellars label was created using the historic maypole that likely dates back as far as the sixteenth century, and is a symbol of good times, good friends, and fabulously festive memory-making. It should be enjoyed and appreciated not just when dancing around the maypole in Sweden, but anywhere and everywhere on a regular basis because life is meant for celebrating.

MIDSUMMER CELLARS

Appellation:	**Napa Valley**
State:	**California**
Country of Origin:	**United States**
Type of Wine:	**Cabernet Sauvignon**
Web Site:	**www.midsummercellars.com**
Design:	**Paladin Wine Marketing**
Designer's Web Site:	**www.paladinwine.net**

Mission Hill Family Estate
[British Columbia 🙖 Canada]

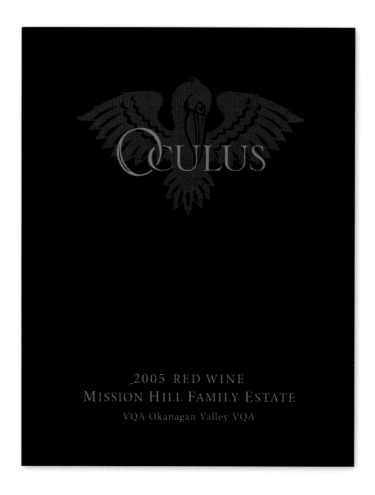

Those who have visited British Columbia's Mission Hill winery will rave of its opulence and the immense attention to detail that Okanagan Valley advocate Anthony von Mandl took while spending six years transforming his winery into what is now the landmark Mission Hill Family Estate. One of the obvious details consistent throughout the winery is the omnipresence of the pelican. Taken from the von Mandl family crest, the pelican can be seen in the design of some of the winery's grandiose elements, such as its inclusion on the 7,500-pound, hand-chiseled keystone that greets visitors upon arrival and the pelican-inspired weathervane sitting atop the twelve-story bell tower, right down to the more subtle, but equally exquisite, craftsmanship of the carved pelican door handles. The pelican's significance within the crest, as well as its presence throughout the winery, offers the protection, nurturing, and charity that the pelican is often associated with.

Von Mandl's pelican also graces the bottle of the Mission Hill Oculus wine label. The winery, an architectural masterpiece, does in fact boast its own oculus, which is the only source of natural light into the eight-hundred-barrel underground cellar. When paired with the von Mandl emblem, the *oculus* (Latin for "eye") implies that this highly selective and coveted flagship wine is protected through the constant custody of the pelican's vigilant watch.

MISSION HILL FAMILY ESTATE

Appellation:	**Okanagan Valley**
Province:	**British Columbia**
Country of Origin:	**Canada**
Type of Wine:	**Red Blend**
Web Site:	**www.missionhillwinery.com**

MOLLYDOOKER WINES

[SOUTH AUSTRALIA ∞ AUSTRALIA]

Sarah and Sparky Marquis first met in 1987 while studying winemaking in South Australia and, immediately having a connection, married in 1991. The couple says that their lives have been a journey along an "enchanted path" that has, most recently, led them to a "carnival of love" with their joint winemaking venture, Mollydooker Wines. A family-run business, Mollydooker focuses on living a good life filled with love and friendships.

Each bringing unique abilities to winemaking, Sarah and Sparky say that they blend those qualities together to ultimately craft wines to the best of both their capabilities. Similarly, these wines bring together the separate personalities of two distinct varietals, the result being strength in combined character.

When put together side by side, the Enchanted Path and Carnival of Love wine labels create one whole image signifying the joyful party that is their joint life. With characters from their Lefty series (which reflects true tales from Sarah and Sparky's lives growing up left-handed) put together with images of loved ones, these labels are a celebration of their journey together in life, love, and their partnership in winemaking.

MOLLYDOOKER WINES	
Appellation:	**McLaren Vale**
State:	**South Australia**
Country of Origin:	**Australia**
Type of Wine:	**Shiraz**
Web Site:	**www.mollydookerwines.com**
Design:	**Mash**
Designer's Web Site:	**www.mashdesign.com.au**

MOLLYDOOKER WINES	
Appellation:	**McLaren Vale**
State:	**South Australia**
Country of Origin:	**Australia**
Type of Wine:	**Shiraz and**
	Cabernet Sauvignon Blend
Web Site:	**www.mollydookerwines.com**
Design:	**Mash**
Designer's Web Site:	**www.mashdesign.com.au**

Mollydooker Wines

After spending endless amounts of time making acclaimed wines for other people, the husband-and-wife winemaking duo of Sarah and Sparky Marquis knew the time had come to achieve something of their own. Of course, coming up with a name that represented both themselves and their joint passion proved difficult.

One lunch, however, while sitting at the office's dining table, colleagues tossed about possible names for their wines, all the while knocking elbows between righties and lefties. The idea of "left hand/right brain" came up. The name wasn't ideal, but given that both Sarah and Sparky are left-handed, as was almost half their team, the concept seemed to be the "right" fit!

Cuddy-wifter, scoochy, squiffy, corrie-pawed; these are some of the eighty-eight words found in the English language used to describe being a left-hander. But as Sparky's father, Leigh, pointed out, nothing says "lefty" in Australian better than "mollydooker"—they had their name.

For thousands of years, people showing the slightest left-handed tendencies have been ostracized, and, even further, they have been associated with witchery, sorcery, and devil worship. Throughout history, left-handers have so often been aligned dexterously with social awkwardness (French: *gauche*, "left") and ineffectiveness (French: *mal*, "badly"; *à*, "to"; *droit*, "right"; *à droit*, "properly"), as well as being unlucky, wicked, or evil (Latin: *sinistro*, "left") that it is embedded deep into our language. Up until the late twentieth century, children were often dissuaded from using their left hands in order to better fit into a right-handed world.

Wine is an art, a culmination of the passion, desires, and personalities of those who create it. The label is the visual expression of these things that can make the whole experience as memorable and enjoyable as it should be. —SARAH MARQUIS CEO and Winemaker, Mollydooker Wines

Even the simplest of things in life like doorknobs, car gearboxes, and can openers have been designed with left-to-right wrist motion by right-handers for right-handers.

The Mollydooker Lefty label series is reminiscent of Sarah and Sparky's own personal experiences of being left-handed: Sparky's inclination to step all over Sarah when dancing with his "two left feet," and the time he spent as a left-handed waiter, opening bottle after bottle of wine with a traditional corkscrew—some-

MOLLYDOOKER WINES
Appellation: **McLaren Vale**
State: **South Australia**
Country of Origin: **Australia**
Type of Wine: **Verdelho**
Web Site: **www.mollydookerwines.com**
Design: **Mash**
Designer's Web Site: **www.mashdesign.com.au**

MOLLYDOOKER WINES

Appellation:	**McLaren Vale**
State:	**South Australia**
Country of Origin:	**Australia**
Type of Wine:	**Shiraz**
Web Site:	**www.mollydookerwines.com**
Design:	**Mash**
Designer's Web Site:	**www.mashdesign.com.au**

MOLLYDOOKER WINES

Appellation:	**McLaren Vale**
State:	**South Australia**
Country of Origin:	**Australia**
Type of Wine:	**Cabernet Sauvignon**
Web Site:	**www.mollydookerwines.com**
Design:	**Mash**
Designer's Web Site:	**www.mashdesign.com.au**

MOLLYDOOKER WINES

Appellation:	**McLaren Vale**
State:	**South Australia**
Country of Origin:	**Australia**
Type of Wine:	**Merlot**
Web Site:	**www.mollydookerwines.com**
Design:	**Mash**
Designer's Web Site:	**www.mashdesign.com.au**

MOLLYDOOKER WINES

Appellation:	**McLaren Vale**
State:	**South Australia**
Country of Origin:	**Australia**
Type of Wine:	**Shiraz, Carbernet Sauvignon, and Merlot Blend**
Web Site:	**www.mollydookerwines.com**
Design:	**Mash**
Designer's Web Site:	**www.mashdesign.com.au**

thing "righties" certainly take for granted.

Now Sarah, Sparky, and the mollydookers on their team can add their names to a long list of some of the most talented, brilliant, and creative people in history who have been known to be left-handers. The list is extensive: Leonardo da Vinci, Michelangelo, Helen Keller, Henry Ford, Lewis Carroll, and Oprah Winfrey, for a drop in the bucket. Clearly these mollydookers are in the right company!

MONTES

[O'Higgins ✺ Chile]

In 1987, four friends—Aurelio Montes, Douglas Murray, Pedro Grand, and the late Alfredo Vidaurre—started the Montes company on a "wing and a prayer." The wings, however, weren't those of a plane, but the personal belief that the wings of angels carried the friends through every stage of their endeavor. After twenty years of successfully operating the pioneering Chilean winery, it has become clear to the friends that its success has been garnered, at times against the odds, by divine inspiration.

From where does this belief of angels stem? For Douglas Murray, his belief in "extremely busy and dedicated angels" looking after him stemmed from his "adventurous and often accident-prone" spirit. Yet always coming out unscathed, how could angels not be looking after him?

Angels are the mantra of Montes wines, their symbolic philosophy and, in turn, have always adorned their wine labels. When Montes was to launch their Folly label—a fun, but equally serious wine—the question was: How would they communicate this contradiction effectively so both extremities were balanced together? Immediately, Murray was given another example of Montes' angel intervention and instigated the crossing of paths between himself and the artist-genius Ralph Steadman, who had visited Murray's native Chile in 1992.

As timing would have it, Steadman arrived during a period when Chileans retreat for the holidays, leaving Steadman and his family without a tour guide upon their arrival. Murray immediately stepped in and graciously offered to show the Steadmans *his* Chile, the place where he was born and the place that molded his character—the Atacama Desert, the driest desert in the world. It's so dry that no plant or insect life exists there, and with conditions so similar to that of the moon, NASA even tested its moon vehicles in the region. While many people see this desert as a place of nothingness, those who know it intimately, and those with artist's eyes, see it as a place of splendor and very much a part of the vastness of Chile's character.

Indeed, Ralph Steadman did see this perspective and, upon return to the United Kingdom, felt such an emotional pull towards the desert that, in order to "exorcize" it, he madly painted for days—landscapes of this memorable, inhospitable land juxtaposed with the grace of bountiful beauty found in its color, mountain diversity, and expansive skies filled to the brim on starry nights.

MONTES

Appellation:	**Colchagua Valley**
Region:	**O'Higgins**
Country of Origin:	**Chile**
Type of Wine:	**Syrah**
Web Site:	**www.monteswines.com**
Art:	**Ralph Steadman**
Artist's Web Site:	**www.ralphsteadman.com**

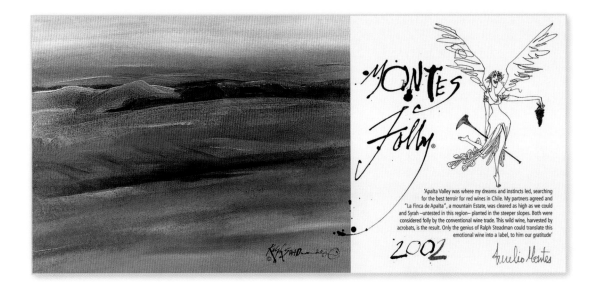

MONTES

Appellation:	**Colchagua Valley**
Region:	**O'Higgins**
Country of Origin:	**Chile**
Type of Wine:	**Syrah**
Web Site:	**www.monteswines.com**
Art:	**Ralph Steadman**
Artist's Web Site:	**www.ralphsteadman.com**

MONTES

Appellation:	**Colchagua Valley**
Region:	**O'Higgins**
Country of Origin:	**Chile**
Type of Wine:	**Syrah**
Web Site:	**www.monteswines.com**
Art:	**Ralph Steadman**
Artist's Web Site:	**www.ralphsteadman.com**

Of this artistic furor, Murray knew nothing. He had no idea that his new friend sent from the heavens had been so inspired by the desert until years later, when he reconnected with Steadman to see if the artist would consider providing his mastery for their new Folly wine project. Before Murray could even get the words out, Steadman had him convinced to "pop round" to England to discuss. Of course, Murray couldn't decline a visit with his old friend and, upon arrival, he was presented with eleven original paintings and simply told to take them. He couldn't believe his eyes or the majesty of the interpretation of his land. It is these images, which now include paintings from Ralph Steadman's subsequent visits to other majestic corners of Chile, that adorn the Montes Folly labels, along with a very characteristic sketch (in true Steadman style) of Montes' guardian angel—an illustration of nature and the divine at work together, just like Montes wines.

MOUNT EDWARD

[OTAGO ❧ NEW ZEALAND]

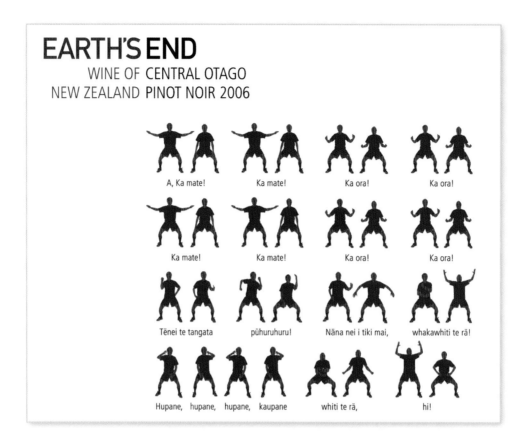

Many countries are known to include a national dance as part of their cultural tradition. No dance, however, is as unique and as instantly recognizable as New Zealand's *"Ka Mate"* *haka. Haka*, which is a broad term for Maori dance, uses the entire body in a complex physical interpretation of New Zealand's cultural soul. More so than any other feature of Maori culture, it demonstrates a fierce expression of the passion and identity of the indigenous people of the country. The *"Ka Mate"* haka has been exposed to the greatest extent internationally by New Zealand's All Blacks rugby team, given their precise and well-respected performances prior to each match.

Intending to launch a force to be reckoned with in the wine industry, it was suggested that Mount Edward use the nationally treasured *"Ka Mate"* haka on its label when developing the new branding—a notion that just about literally made hearts stop.

Mount Edward's immediate response: unfathomable.

But soon, it realized that hearts don't just stop for anything. Mount Edward knew that undoubtedly this was precisely the essence required to represent the flavors unique to New Zealand found in Mount Edward wine. Soon thereafter, a trip was planned to the Maori tribe that originated the art form to request their honored permission. The tribe gave its blessing to share the *"Ka Mate"* spirit of the people. Now, the Mount Edward Earth's End wine labels proudly share the much-revered symbol of New Zealand pride with nationals, rugby fans, and wine enthusiasts alike.

> As a wine label, I would rather be discussed, debated, opined over, chewed about at length, and ultimately spat out than never be talked about at all. If one side doesn't like you, others most certainly will, so stand up and be counted for something.
>
> —DUNCAN FORSYTH
> General Manager and Winemaker,
> Mount Edward

MOUNT EDWARD

Appellation:	**Central Otago**
Region:	**Otago**
Country of Origin:	**New Zealand**
Type of Wine:	**Pinot Noir**
Web Site:	**www.mountedward.co.nz**
Design:	**Brandever**
Designer's Web Site:	**www.brandever.com**

Muster Wine Co.
[South Australia ❧ Australia]

Barossa **Muster**

M

Mataro Mourvedre Monastrell | 06

Muster

Riesling | 08

Wrangling, herding, cowboy-ing. These are all different terms that mean the same thing—essentially, the rounding up of livestock on foot, on horse, by vehicle, or even aircraft. A "muster" is the equivalent term used in the antipodean countries of Australia and New Zealand. These stockmen still play a significant role in the isolated countryside, where they often ride for long days herding cattle.

David Muster, true to his surname, is an authentic Aussie musterer, although a non-traditional one. His "mustering" involves the rounding up a different type of "live stalk." Instead of herding cattle or sheep, this muster, after twenty years working for others in the wine industry, decided that it was about time he tried his hand at herding in grapes from some of the best stock around and making his own wine. Of course, given the task at hand and the coincidence of his last name, it made sense to call it exactly what it was—a gathering of grapes. Visually, the imagery depicts a traditional muster in an artistic style that could be interpreted as grape vines entwined together, a true sense of what wine really is: unique flavors of the grapes and terroir mustered up and tangled intimately together in each vintage.

MUSTER WINE CO.	
Appellation:	**Barossa Valley**
State:	**South Australia**
Country of Origin:	**Australia**
Type of Wine:	**Mataro, Mourvèdre, and Monastrell Blend**
Web Site:	**www.musterwineco.com.au**
Design:	**Asylum Graphic Design**
Designer's Web Site:	**www.refuge.com**

MUSTER WINE CO.	
Appellation:	**Barossa Valley**
State:	**South Australia**
Country of Origin:	**Australia**
Type of Wine:	**Riesling**
Web Site:	**www.musterwineco.com.au**
Design:	**Asylum Graphic Design**
Designer's Web Site:	**www.refuge.com**

NEW NORCIA ABBEY CELLARS

[WESTERN AUSTRALIA ✺ AUSTRALIA]

Wine has held an association with many religious orders for a long time. So long, that there are references to the holy drink in ancient books of worship and ceremony.

Australia's only monastic community bears no exception. The father of this monastic community's beliefs, Saint Benedict (born circa AD 480 in the district of what is today's Norcia in Umbria, Italy), is said to have stated that wine was not a suitable drink for devout monks in his compilation of monastic teachings and principles. However, he was unable to convince his contemporaries, and contrary to his beliefs, monks have since been continually tied to the vine, especially from a winemaking standpoint.

The winemaking tradition in New Norcia dates back to the accidental founding of the monastic town in 1846 by Dom Rosendo Salvado and fellow Benedictine Dom Joseph Serra. Upon arrival, olive trees and vines were planted for the growing monastery's own consumption. The original plantings, a hectare in scale, gradually increased to four hectares by the mid-1870s. In 1875, Salvado went back to his native Spain and returned to the Australian monastic town with cuttings to improve the vineyards of New Norcia. The community also owned some experimental plantings approximately 30 miles away at Wyening, which seemed to be providing a superior outcome, and so Salvado's successor, Bishop Torres, concentrated his viticulture efforts there.

During this period (circa 1909), the juice from the 40 acres of vineyard was pressed at Wyening and the 8,000–9,000 gallons were then transported to New Norcia for fermenting and aging. Wine evolved from solely a monastic item of consumption to being sold to the local farmers and the Italian clearing workers. Focus on the quality was increased with the building of a new winery, the continual planting of vines, and the engagement of the monastery's first non-ecclesiastic vigneron, Austrian Gustel Schwarzbach. Schwarzbach ushered New Norcia Abbey to its finest wine producing years, and was at the helm for some twenty-five years.

During the 1970s, however, the quality of the soils declined with salinity problems. Because of Schwarzbach's advanced age, a decision was taken by the community to close the vineyard and winery with the last vintage of their proprietary wine bottled in 1973. The monastery then returned to purchasing wines produced by others for its own consumption.

However, despite the some thirty years that passed with the monastery operating this way, times changed, and the community began to see a drastic increase in tourism. In turn, an increase in hospitality at New Norcia Abbey led to an unanticipated decision to bring back the Benedictine abbey wines. And once again, the monks at New Norcia are able to share their wines— a beverage of saints, not sinners—and proudly indicate their wines' providence and philosophy of *pax*, or "peace," on the resurrected and restored wine label.

NEW NORCIA ABBEY CELLARS
Appellation:	**Frankland River**
State:	**Western Australia**
Country of Origin:	**Australia**
Type of Wine:	**Shiraz**
Web Site:	**www.newnorcia.wa.edu.au**
Design:	**Public Creative**
Designer's Web Site:	**www.publiccreative.com.au**

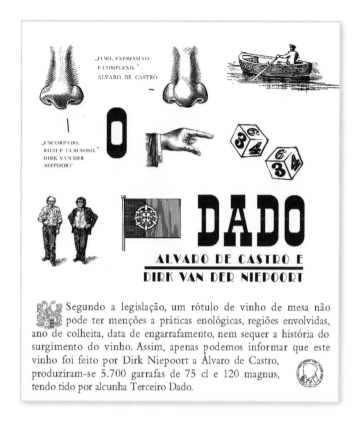

D ado was inspired by an old imaginative idea of Dirk Niepoort's father, Rolf. The idea of making the perfect wine by blending diverse grapes characteristic of two distinct regions together was almost impractically idealistic given Portugal's wine classification regulations. Though the blending of grapes from diverse regions is uncommon, Dirk says that it was the easiest part of the project—the most difficult was overcoming the legal issues of labeling the wine. The label had to tell the story of the wine without actually being able to include the specifications on the label. It was a feat he was able to overcome by creating a label that visually defined what the wine was all about.

Along with Álvaro de Castro from Dão, the collaboration brought together and blended a unique flavor profile to showcase the freshness and elegance that is typical of the Dão region, and the concentration and fine tannins that are characteristic of the Douro region. As the wine was made from a multiregional blend, the only qualified classification was that of Portuguese table wine, whereby there could be no mention of regions involved, grapes blended, or vintage. However, by using visual references that include illustrations of both the winemakers and their respective noses, with a quote from each of them describing the broad (but typical) flavor profile from each of their relevant regions, a Portuguese flag, and a pair of dice, it is clear that this wine was a gamble that both winemakers were willing to take.

What matters is what is in the bottle. If what is in the bottle is outstanding, the label should also be standing out. —DIRK NIEPOORT
Proprietor, Niepoort (Vinhos)

NIEPOORT (VINHOS)

Region:	**Dão/Douro**
District:	**Viseu/Porto**
Country of Origin:	**Portugal**
Type of Wine:	**Red Blend**
Web Site:	**www.niepoort-vinhos.com**
Design:	**Alessandri Design**
Designer's Web Site:	**www.alessandri-design.at**

Niepoort (Vinhos)

[Porto ❧ Portugal]

The easy drinking wines in this Niepoort range have been blended with grape varietals indigenous to Portugal and specifically characteristic of the Douro region, such as Touriga Franca, Touriga Nacional, Tinta Amarela, Tinta Barroca, and Tinto Cão. Because these grape varietals aren't as typical outside their native country as the big five—Merlot, Cabernet Sauvignon, Pinot Noir, Sauvignon Blanc, and Chardonnay—Dirk Niepoort had a series of entertaining and approachable (and sometimes slightly stereotypical) visuals developed to storyboard wine consumption situations representing characteristics of the country where the potentially unknown Portuguese wines were to be purchased.

Using local artists and humorous vignettes, these labels suggest that while the wines may be big and bold in nature, wine in general should not be taken too seriously. Rather, wine should always provide exceptional company at a table, adding a component of lightheartedness and fun that people can relate to and enjoy anywhere—no matter what type of grape or where it is being consumed. At the end of the day, life, laughter, and a good glass of wine speak an international language known in every culture.

NIEPOORT (VINHOS)	
Appellation:	**Douro**
District:	**Porto**
Country of Origin:	**Portugal**
Type of Wine:	**Red Blend**
Web Site:	**www.niepoort-vinhos.com**
Design:	**Alessandri Design**
Designer's Web Site:	**www.alessandri-design.at**
Art:	**Frédéric Janin**

NIEPOORT (VINHOS)	
Appellation:	**Douro**
District:	**Porto**
Country of Origin:	**Portugal**
Type of Wine:	**Red Blend**
Web Site:	**www.niepoort-vinhos.com**
Design:	**Alessandri Design**
Designer's Web Site:	**www.alessandri-design.at**
Art:	**Bill Plympton**

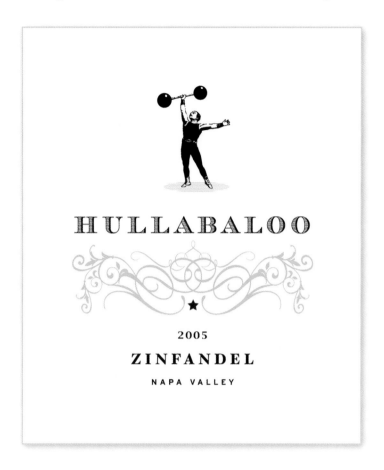

When Nine North Wine Company was presented with a stupefying opportunity to get its hands on some seriously impressive old-vine Zinfandel grapes, it was an opportunity not to say no to. Despite the fact that Zinfandel hadn't traditionally been the company's thing, nor the fact that it might cause a bit of a stir with the old-timers who'd been making Zinfandel for ages, Nine North just couldn't pass the grapes up.

Not wanting to rock the proverbial boat, it was sworn to secrecy to not divulge where the premium fruit had been sourced. And so, just as it couldn't say no, the company's lips were sealed. After all, no one should be shamed for something this good—and it was sure to create a huge "hullaballoo" amongst Nine North's industry peers.

To honor the strength in character of these risk-taking growers that went out on a limb to sell their grapes to newcomers, as well as to celebrate the mighty, old-vine Zinfandel grape, Nine North Wine Company chose the image of an iconic strongman for its label. Coincidentally, Zinfandel grapes "muscled" their way to California in the 1840s and exhibited their great size and bold flavor simultaneous to when these strongmen were creating their own uproars by demonstrating their amazing feats of strength. The Hullaballoo wine label allows the two to come together to show off their combined "flex appeal."

NINE NORTH WINE COMPANY
Appellation:	**Napa Valley**
State:	**California**
Country of Origin:	**United States**
Type of Wine:	**Zinfandel**
Web Site:	**www.ninenorthwines.com**
Design:	**Chip Sheean**
Designer's Web Site:	**www.chipsheean.com**

NINE NORTH WINE COMPANY

[CALIFORNIA ❧ UNITED STATES]

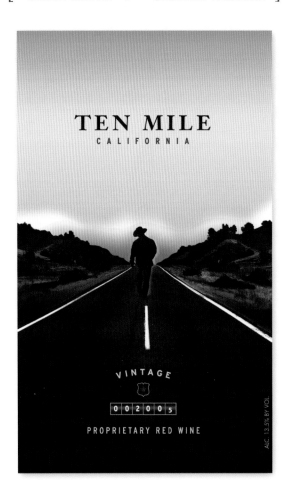

In the early 1800s, the West was considered a vast region, wildly unspoiled, and therefore unknown and unconquered by Eastern settlers of the United States. By 1840, pioneers began the perilous journey to the Wild West of California, nostalgic for the simpler life they'd enjoyed before becoming victim to the overpopulated East Coast cities. In the West, they imagined escape, financial security, a new start, and the dream of Manifest Destiny's propaganda.

Against the odds, they traveled determinately by wagon, by horse, and often harrowingly by foot at an average pace of ten tiresome miles per day. Many didn't make it, and those who did found an unfortunate waning of the Gold Rush and what was promised as an open road to prosperity, now almost at a dead end.

Rather than digging for gold, with unceasing determination they sought richness from the land, instead, to build their own potential through vines and the liquid gold of California wine. Here, they planted Zinfandel, Petite Sirah, Carignan, and Barbera—bold grapes that reflected their bold ambitions. Some 140 years later, the Nine North Ten Mile label pays tribute to these ancestral pioneers who traveled from afar—even down a broken road of dreams—to pave their way and those of generations to come via a route they never had imagined.

After almost twenty years in this business, it has become abundantly clear to me that there are very many world-class vineyards, wineries, winemakers, and wines, but there are very few talented storytellers that can truly capture the art, essence, and emotion of a wine brand and its label design.

—JAMES HARDER
Owner, Nine North Wine Company

NINE NORTH WINE COMPANY

Appellation:	**Non-Designated Appellation**
State:	**California**
Country of Origin:	**United States**
Type of Wine:	**Red Blend**
Web Site:	**www.ninenorthwines.com**
Design:	**Chip Sheean**
Designer's Web Site:	**www.chipsheean.com**

ODD ONE OUT WINERY

[VICTORIA ❧ AUSTRALIA]

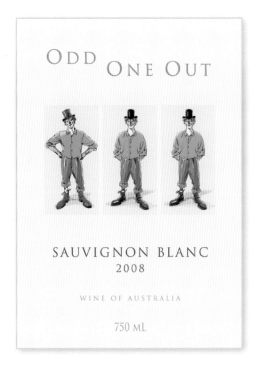

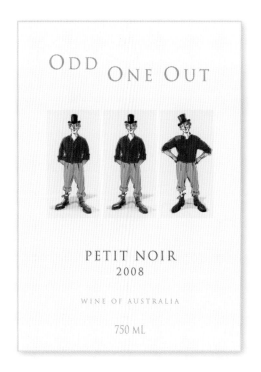

John Ellis's life could have turned out very differently. Growing up in a family of Methodist beliefs, abstinence from alcohol was the norm for the future wine industry maverick. As they say, "What you don't know won't hurt you." This seemed the case for John. That is, until he tried the stuff. What he found out when he tasted it was that what he now knew didn't hurt him; it just made him the odd man out of the family. Especially when he became a winemaker, and then even more so, when he married into the fourth generation of one of Australia's most famous winemaking families. That certainly was a first.

As a winemaker, John was blessed with entrepreneurialism, insight, and very strong intuition. Despite his family's belief system, he became a minister of the vine and always danced to his own beat, which pushed him to always be a step ahead of his contemporaries. This individualism saw John pioneer astounding firsts, such as bringing cool-climate Chardonnay to the forefront, making the first Cabernet-Merlot blend in the country, and initiating the production of world-class sparkling wines in Australia—as well as many committee appointments, awards, and accolades that are simply too long to list.

To think that this all might not have happened if he hadn't risked following his gut, despite the alienation it may have caused. The Odd One Out wine label, illustrated by renowned Australian artist Nigel Buchanan, celebrates John's spirit of individuality and legendary courage to "stand out in a crowd," both within the wine community and as a personality all on his own.

**ODD ONE OUT WINERY
(HANGING ROCK WINERY)**

Appellation:	**Strathbogie Ranges/King Valley/ Kilmore (Non-Designated Appellation)**
State:	**Victoria**
Country of Origin:	**Australia**
Type of Wine:	**Sauvignon Blanc**
Web Site:	**www.oddoneout.com.au**
Design:	**Depot Creative**
Designer's Web Site:	**www.depotcreative.com.au**
Art:	**Nigel Buchanan**
Artist's Web Site:	**www.nigelbuchanan.com**

**ODD ONE OUT WINERY
(HANGING ROCK WINERY)**

Appellation:	**Macedon Ranges**
State:	**Victoria**
Country of Origin:	**Australia**
Type of Wine:	**Petit Noir**
Web Site:	**www.oddoneout.com.au**
Design:	**Depot Creative**
Designer's Web Site:	**www.depotcreative.com.au**
Art:	**Nigel Buchanan**
Artist's Web Site:	**www.nigelbuchanan.com**

OLIVER'S TARANGA VINEYARDS
[SOUTH AUSTRALIA ✎ AUSTRALIA]

Living a nomadic lifestyle during one's formative years in the winemaking business is often viewed as an extension of formal education and almost a rite of passage. Traveling the globe and working harvest in different countries provides exposure to different skills and craft forms, and offers new perspectives and rich experiences for those in passionate pursuit of winemaking tutelage. Inevitably, such adventurous episodes away from home influence a young winemaker's own style of winemaking subtly, profoundly, or anywhere in between. Of course, it isn't just the objective learnings that affect the traveling student and laborer. It is also the people, the places, the personal experiences, and the memories made that are deeply influential.

The Oliver's Taranga Expatriate wine label is reminiscent of winemaker Corrina Rayment's own journey and adventure from her home in Australia to California, while seeking to broaden her winemaking education at the University of California at Davis. While she studied, she immersed herself happily in a foreign life for two years. Just as many travelers collect memorabilia along their routes, this wine label is a collection of nostalgia reminiscent of her time spent exploring away from home: the beautiful town of Healdsburg; driving her borrowed, shiny-blue 1980 180Z BMW sportscar; Italian-styled vineyard picnics with the Gallo family; Halloween; hiking in Yosemite; The Oakville Grocery; the view from the old gunnery above the Golden Gate Bridge; peacocks in the neighboring vineyards; and spending time with new friends, industry legends, and people passionate about wine that she met from all corners of the earth. Learning, learning, learning from so many great people, all the while carrying a piece of her grandmother's art as a reminder of home.

Submerged in a completely new life allows you to open up to fresh perspectives and grab hold of worldly experiences along the way. For Corrina, each of her experiences has been sketched in her memory. Now back in Australia, Corrina sends an interpretation of her cherished moments in the U.S. back to her home away from home in the form of liquid love, including her precious memories imprinted on the Expatriate label.

OLIVER'S TARANGA VINEYARDS

Appellation:	**McLaren Vale**
State:	**South Australia**
Country of Origin:	**Australia**
Type of Wine:	**Shiraz**
Web Site:	**www.oliverstaranga.com**
Design:	**Tucker Design**
Designer's Web Site:	**www.tuckercreative.com.au**

OPUS ONE
[CALIFORNIA ❧ UNITED STATES]

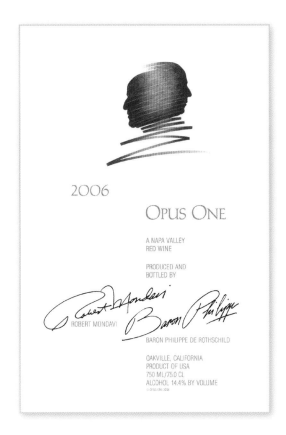

In 1970, two of the world's highest regarded international wine industry personalities—renowned Napa Valley vintner Robert Mondavi and Baron Philippe de Rothschild, the patriarch of one of Europe's greatest aristocratic families—met for the first time in Hawaii. It was here that the baron initially suggested a joint venture. Eight years later, Mondavi would be invited to Bordeaux where the two made the first international joint venture in wine a reality.

Given the combined endeavor, bound by the rich heritage of both celebrated vintners, a story needed to be told that would be representative of their united traditions and innovations that were to be incorporated into this single wine. The new partners decided that a name of Latin origin would allow for easy recognition in both English and French and, shortly thereafter, Baron Philippe suggested the name "Opus," a musical term meaning "the work of a composer." Two days later, the addition of the word "one" was decided upon, solidifying the concept of a true "first work," for the men together.

Visually inspired by the Roman god Janus—who represents contemplations of the past and future, and who was celebrated at the beginning of the planting season and again at harvest—the fusion of individual silhouetted profiles provides a symmetrical balance between the two winemaking partners. Originally, both vintners were looking inward at each other with each of their respective noses creating the illusion of a wine goblet. However, the final design revealed each man looking towards his respective nation: Mondavi, west to the United States, and Rothschild, east to France.

Though both celebrated vintners have passed, the Opus One name has remained steadfast in its association with the joint venture of two of the world's preeminent vintners, and it is likely the label will remain unchanged as homage to these passionate pioneers. Together, they ventured to make a singular wine of perfection unlike either of their own parent wines; a wine that would stand alone in spirit and quality.

OPUS ONE	
Appellation:	**Napa Valley**
State:	**California**
Country of Origin:	**United States**
Type of Wine:	**Red Blend**
Web Site:	**www.opusonewinery.com**
Design:	**Pate International**
Designer's Web Site:	**www.pateinternational.com**

THE ORGANIZED CRIME WINERY
[ONTARIO ❧ CANADA]

^{the}**Organized Crime**
2006 Gewürztraminer

^{the}**Organized Crime**
2006 Chardonnay Musqué

When one hears the term "organized crime," the last thing that likely comes to mind is church music.

But in Beamsville, Ontario, where The Organized Crime Winery is located, there is a sordid tale told about how the winery got its name, and it certainly involves church music. As the story goes, the winery sits in a reverent region—not only because of its heavenly view, but because of the devout residents who once lived there.

In the 1900s, there lived two Mennonite communities side by side, one known for its conservative views and the other for its progressive beliefs. The latter congregation refused to adhere to the strict religious doctrines and instead introduced a blasphemous pipe organ into the community and even, heaven forbid, music and singing to their devout celebrations. Of course, this act of profanity infuriated the more God-fearing conservatives who, in turn, conspired to steal the organ and put an end to such sacrilege. They succeeded by breaking into their rival's most sacred space, collectively snatching the immoral instrument, and throwing it into the region's Twenty Mile Creek.

The Organized Crime wine labels are a eulogy to the region's rich and rebellious history remembered through the winery's faith in the nectar of the gods.

THE ORGANIZED CRIME WINERY	
Appellation:	**Beamsville Bench**
Province:	**Ontario**
Country of Origin:	**Canada**
Type of Wine:	**Gewürztraminer**
Web Site:	**www.organizedcrimewine.com**
Design:	**Brandever**
Designer's Web Site:	**www.brandever.com**

THE ORGANIZED CRIME WINERY	
Appellation:	**Niagara Peninsula**
Province:	**Ontario**
Country of Origin:	**Canada**
Type of Wine:	**Chardonnay Musqué**
Web Site:	**www.organizedcrimewine.com**
Design:	**Brandever**
Designer's Web Site:	**www.brandever.com**

THE ORGANIZED CRIME WINERY

Appellation:	**Beamsville Bench**
Province:	**Ontario**
Country of Origin:	**Canada**
Type of Wine:	**Pinot Noir**
Web Site:	**www.organizedcrimewine.com**
Design:	**Brandever**
Designer's Web Site:	**www.brandever.com**

THE ORGANIZED CRIME WINERY

Appellation:	**Beamsville Bench**
Province:	**Ontario**
Country of Origin:	**Canada**
Type of Wine:	**Sauvignon Blanc**
Web Site:	**www.organizedcrimewine.com**
Design:	**Brandever**
Designer's Web Site:	**www.brandever.com**

THE ORGANIZED CRIME WINERY

Appellation:	**Beamsville Bench**
Province:	**Ontario**
Country of Origin:	**Canada**
Type of Wine:	**Syrah**
Web Site:	**www.organizedcrimewine.com**
Design:	**Brandever**
Designer's Web Site:	**www.brandever.com**

THE ORGANIZED CRIME WINERY

Appellation:	**Niagara Peninsula**
Province:	**Ontario**
Country of Origin:	**Canada**
Type of Wine:	**Merlot and Cabernet Franc Blend**
Web Site:	**www.organizedcrimewine.com**
Design:	**Brandever**
Designer's Web Site:	**www.brandever.com**

ORIN SWIFT CELLARS

[CALIFORNIA ❦ UNITED STATES]

Dave Phinney grew up in Southern California, where he was exposed to a juxtaposition of cultures. At home, both of his parents were academics and made art and culture accessible to Dave as a young boy. While most boys his age were being gifted with skateboards, Dave was given an etching of Goya's *The Little Prisoner*, which he has cherished since. On the other side of his upbringing outside of his home life, Dave was exposed to the reality of Southern California's large population of ex-cons. He formed an interest in the raw art form of inmates' tattoos that expressed and symbolized records of the wearer's personal history and, often, criminal accolades.

Originally intending a career in law or politics, Dave ditched the conventional while studying abroad in Florence, Italy, after his roommate, who was from an old wine family in Sonoma Valley, planted the brilliant idea: "Why not get into the wine business?" Upon his return home, he preoccupied himself with all things *vitis vinifera*, and found a professor in the agriculture department at the University of Arizona who was also keen on growing grapes (in the middle of the desert!). Dave worked at a fine wine shop, where he says he learnt the hard stuff—actually selling wine, because it wasn't always going to sell itself—and worked his first harvest at Michael Mondavi's winery during the night shift. With only this single harvest under his belt, he began Orin (his father's middle name) Swift (his mother's maiden name) Cellars. When it came time to label his first wine, he chose to reproduce the art that he had admired since he was a child: *The Little Prisoner*.

For a future release, the idea of incorporating convict tattoo art together with the imagery of authentic working hands on his label inspired him. When Phinney's daughter, Angeline, who had never been exposed to the French language, started calling butterflies *"papillons,"* the name of the wine took flight.

While Dave Phinney may have just happened upon winemaking by chance, his wine labels certainly reflect purpose, binding together his professional pursuits, personal history, and his interest in arts and cultural together seamlessly.

ORIN SWIFT CELLARS	
Appellation:	**Napa Valley**
State:	**California**
Country of Origin:	**United States**
Type of Wine:	**Red Blend**
Web Site:	**www.orinswift.com**
Design:	**Dave Phinney**

ORIN SWIFT CELLARS	
Appellation:	**Napa Valley**
State:	**California**
Country of Origin:	**United States**
Type of Wine:	**Red Blend**
Web Site:	**www.orinswift.com**
Design:	**Dave Phinney**

With a name like Sebastiani, there's no denying an Italian heritage. And if you're a winemaker, like August Sebastiani, president of The Other Guys, making an Italian-styled wine is almost a given. Inspired by "Mambo Italiano," the song most famously sung by both Dean Martin and Rosemary Clooney, this wine's label was born, reminiscent of quaint cafés tucked away amidst romantic, cobble-stoned streets, tables adorned with checkered cloths and dripping Chianti candles, and the sounds and smells of succulent Italian cuisine. It is even imaginable that under a ceiling of stars, lovers dance in the hot, humid air of the night. This wine label effortlessly takes you back to a time when life was easy, when dancing the night away and sipping a glass of easy drinking wine often would leave you wishing the evening would never end.

Wine labels sell the first bottle off the shelf, and we all know how important first impressions are. That said, it's the wine quality that sells the second bottle. If the quality isn't there, you've got nothing. It won't matter what your label looks like.

—AUGUST SEBASTIANI
President, The Other Guys
(Don Sebastiani Family of Companies)

**THE OTHER GUYS
(DON SEBASTIANI FAMILY OF COMPANIES)**

Appellation:	**Non-Designated Appellation**
State:	**California**
Country of Origin:	**United States**
Type of Wine:	**Red Blend**
Web Site:	**www.togwines.com**
Design:	**Internal**

**THE OTHER GUYS
(DON SEBASTIANI FAMILY OF COMPANIES)**

Appellation:	**Non-Designated Appellation**
State:	**California**
Country of Origin:	**United States**
Type of Wine:	**White Blend**
Web Site:	**www.togwines.com**
Design:	**Internal**

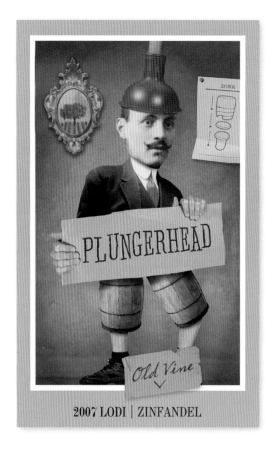

The Other Guys has provided a whole new perspective to what has been most often frowned upon as just a dirty, old plunger.

Of course, this plunger is not the one that you'll find in the restroom, and it certainly isn't dirty or old. In fact, this wine was aptly named after its own innovative bottle closure, the showstopper of wine closures, the Aussie-invented "zork." While having some of the same features of a cork, it is also the furthest thing from it. With the convenience of a screw cap, but the feel and pop of a cork, this little stumpy-shaped plastic plunger garnered the endearing nickname "plungerhead" around the Sebastiani winery. The nickname stuck.

When creative development for this particular wine rolled around, Don Sebastiani Sr. ("the Big Guy," and father of Mia and August, the ones in charge of the Sebastiani family's The Other Guys wines) made a great recollection of a wine label concept previously discussed. The label concept had been a hit, but not right for the original wine it had been presented for. After all, who could forget "the label with the guy and the plunger on his head," as Mr. Sebastiani reminded everyone. Originally depicting a man with a World War II-styled helmet and a screw attached to it, the slightly distorted screw/helmet combination paved way for this revised and perfectly plungered label rendition to pop back up quite appropriately for the wine at hand.

This label, with its unforgettable name and equally as impressive imagery, is a true conversation piece. If the evening starts out with a little Plungerhead, one can only imagine where it will go from there.

THE OTHER GUYS
(DON SEBASTIANI FAMILY OF COMPANIES)
Appellation:	**Lodi**
State:	**California**
Country of Origin:	**United States**
Type of Wine:	**Zinfandel**
Web Site:	**www.togwines.com**
Design:	**M Space**
Designer's Web Site:	**www.mspacedesign.com**

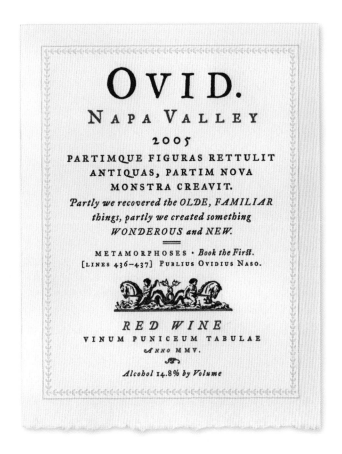

The owners of Ovid, Mark Nelson and Dana Johnson, share two passions. On the one hand, a fond appreciation for antiquated cultures, particularly that of the Romans, and the works of the Roman poet Publius Ovidius Naso, who wrote famed verses on love, seduction, seasons, and change. Of his works, they have admired the eminent and expansive *Metamorphoses*, wherein Ovid epically engages the reader on the subject of transformation in various forms.

And, on the other, more contemporary hand, they also share an appreciation of fine food and wine, particularly that of Napa Valley.

When deliberating what to call their wine label, their mutual appreciation of Ovid's works came to mind. Given that the fundamental nature of winemaking is, in fact, that of transformation—or, as Nelson and Johnson eloquently suggest on their Web site, "a metamorphosis of grapes into something sublime"— the name of their shared and admired Ovid seemed entirely fitting. It indicates the essence of their wines: layered, complex, experimental, and recalls the spirit and uniqueness of the place—much like the poet himself reflected upon Rome. Fittingly, the Ovid label bridges together mutual interests—the old and the new—and also speaks to their vision of winemaking, phrased with an evocative quotation from Ovid's *Metamorphoses* that they translate as: "Partly we recovered the *olde*, *familiar* things, partly we created something *wonderous* and *new*."

	OVID
Appellation:	**Napa Valley**
State:	**California**
Country of Origin:	**United States**
Type of Wine:	**Red Blend**
Web Site:	**www.ovidwine.com**
Design:	**Madeleine Corson Design**
Designer's Web Site:	**www.madeleinecorsondesign.com**

OWEN ROE WINERY
[WASHINGTON ❧ UNITED STATES]

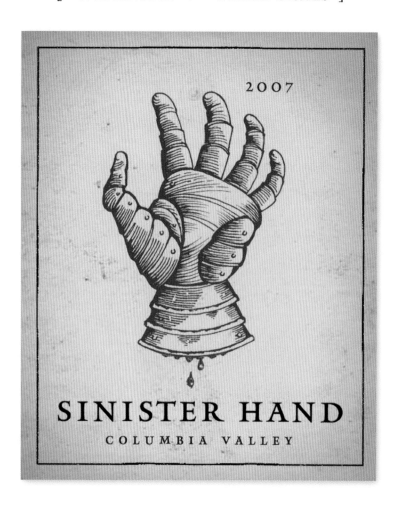

When winemaker David O'Reilly contemplated the name of his winery and the wines he was crafting, he knew without a doubt that the name had to be personal—a reflection of his ancestral roots and the land where he came from. He also wanted something that would reflect a blend of old traditions passed along to new ones that would both be paramount in the crafting of his wines.

Being of the Irish O'Reilly clan and having the natural Irish propensity for telling tales (both long and short), he knew his wine labels needed to tell *his* story. As a result, each of his wines and labels are marked with an ancestral name and tale of significance.

Owen Roe O'Neill, an Irish patriot during the seventeenth century, was said to have been one of the greatest Irish leaders ever and was revered by both friend and foe alike. He dedicated his life to the plight of upholding just political equality and freedom—radical thinking for the time. Given the patriot's commitment to greatness, attributing O'Reilly's wines to the Owen Roe moniker provides a tie not only to his heritage, but a level of meticulous excellence that is strived for on a daily basis in everything that they do at the winery. A reflection of this solid patriotism for the homeland is extended beyond the name to every piece of label artwork that dresses the prideful wines commemorating his ancestors.

OWEN ROE WINERY

Appellation:	**Columbia Valley**
State:	**Washington**
Country of Origin:	**United States**
Type of Wine:	**Merlot and Cabernet Franc Blend**
Web Site:	**www.owenroe.com**
Art:	**Martha Williams**

Likely one of the most memorable of the Owen Roe wine labels is O'Reilly's Sinister Hand Rhône blend. The Sinister Hand wine label tells the "cutting" story of the courage of Owen Roe O'Neill and is considered by contemporary O'Neills to be one of the most prevailing and relevant Irish symbols today. Representing his clan in a competition, it was agreed that the first of the warriors to land on the untouched

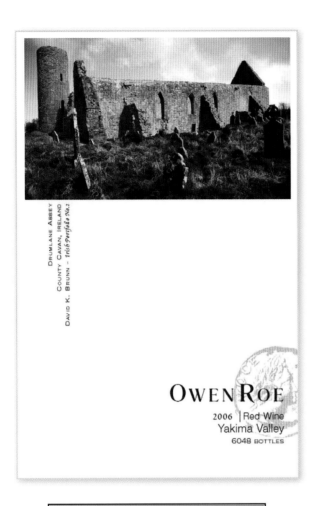

DRUMLANE ABBEY
COUNTY CAVAN, IRELAND
DAVID K. BRUNN – *Irish Portfolio No.2*

OWEN ROE

2006 | Red Wine
Yakima Valley
6048 BOTTLES

CLOGH OUGHTER CASTLE
COUNTY CAVAN, IRELAND
DAVID K. BRUNN – *Irish Portfolio No.1*

OWEN ROE

2006 | DuBrul Vineyard
Cabernet Sauvignon

OF 9216 BOTTLES

OWEN ROE WINERY

Appellation:	**Yakima Valley**
State:	**Washington**
Country of Origin:	**United States**
Type of Wine:	**Red Blend**
Web Site:	**www.owenroe.com**
Art:	**David K. Brunn**

OWEN ROE WINERY

Appellation:	**Yakima Valley**
State:	**Washington**
Country of Origin:	**United States**
Type of Wine:	**Cabernet Sauvignon**
Web Site:	**www.owenroe.com**
Art:	**David K. Brunn**

---

soils of the northeastern tip of Ireland would claim the rights to that land. As the brave warrior was rowing feverishly against his ghastly opponents, he saw that he was falling dramatically behind. The valiant Roe responded to his lag as only a heroic and fearless warrior would do, and chopped off his left (or *sinistra*, in Latin) hand and plummeted it ashore to ensure that he touched down first and thus, his clan would claim the land as the rules outlined. This prideful image has been emblazoned on the O'Reilly family crest for ages.

The gorgeous imagery captured by photographer David K. Brunn for the Owen Roe labels captures sacred snapshots of historical Irish patriotism including Drumlane Abbey in County Cavan—a place of refuge for many for almost one thousand years until its destruction by Oliver Cromwell—and the remains of Clough Oughter castle where the great Owen Roe O'Neill eventually perished in 1649.

Each of the labels represents a reminder of the principles once lived by the O'Reilly clan. In turn, David O'Reilly endeavors for excellence in every bottle of Owen Roe wine and always aims to meet expectations in the eyes of his ancestors.

PERISCOPE CELLARS

[CALIFORNIA ✎ UNITED STATES]

When Brendan Eliason envisaged the face of his wines, he knew the identity would not be based on his last name or some geographic place to which he had no connection. Having always gravitated towards the academic realms of science and art, he definitely knew that his wine would be a creative reflection of himself both in and outside the bottle. Eliason also imagined an urban space where both of his passions, wine and art, could come together in a relaxed and non-intimidating atmosphere. When he happened upon an old World War II submarine repair facility in Emeryville, his vision unfolded right before his eyes. Industrial in nature and steeped in California's unique maritime history with the U.S. Navy and Submarine Force, it was just the space he had been looking for.

Likewise, the chosen name of his wines and winery, Periscope, offers not only a view through the porthole to a unique aspect of California's history, but also to his 7,000-square-foot wine facility that includes both a vibrant, urban-chic tasting space, as well as room for art installations. In fact, one of the first pieces of art ever hung on the walls of Periscope Cellars was an original Picasso, provided for a fundraising auction benefiting children displaced by the war in Iraq.

Each of Eliason's vintages offers a unique look "under the sea" through the Periscope Cellars porthole, a merging of fine art and the art of wine, synchronized with a piece of the region's history.

There are many rational reasons to choose engaging artwork for your wine. To me, none of them really matter. Wine is an emotional drink; it has the power to be personal, evocative, and to linger in your memory. If your artwork does not meet these same standards, you are doing a disservice to the wine inside.
—BRENDAN ELIASON
Owner and Winemaker, Periscope Cellars

PERISCOPE CELLARS
Appellation: **Non-Designated Appellation**
State: **California**
Country of Origin: **United States**
Type of Wine: **Red Blend**
Web Site: **www.periscopecellars.com**
Art: **J. B. Lowe**
Artist's Web Site: **www.jblowe.com**

PERISCOPE CELLARS
Appellation: **Non-Designated Appellation**
State: **California**
Country of Origin: **United States**
Type of Wine: **Red Blend**
Web Site: **www.periscopecellars.com**
Art: **J. B. Lowe**
Artist's Web Site: **www.jblowe.com**

Winemaker Paul Petagna chose the girl. Despite carrying around an image of exactly what he had been envisioning for years and had fondly grown attached to, he still chose the girl over the tattoo. On numerous occasions while Paul had been dating "the girl" (now his wife), the topic had arisen about Paul's strong desire to get a tattoo. However, the now-Mrs. Petagna was obviously less-than-enthusiastic, as Paul's skin remains un-inked. He finally realized that his efforts were futile, but rather than becoming disparaged, he decided to get creative with how he went about getting his beloved tattoo. In order to have his way, he chose to have it created for his first baby: his first wine. Made with his own hands, it was the closest thing to his own body.

The wine named Diovolo (Italian for "devil") is now graced with his long-desired dragon tattoo and juxtaposed against Dio (Italian for "God"), which is joined by a tiger illustrated in the same style (perhaps illustrative of the polarity between Paul and his wife when it came to this certain artwork matter). Ask each of them who won the war of the tattoo, however, and they'll each give you a different answer.

PETAGNA WINES

Appellation:	**McLaren Vale**
State:	**South Australia**
Country of Origin:	**Australia**
Type of Wine:	**Shiraz and Cabernet Sauvignon Blend**
Web Site:	**www.petagnawines.com**
Design:	**TypeSpace**
Designer's Web Site:	**www.typespace.com.au**

PETAGNA WINES

Appellation:	**McLaren Vale**
State:	**South Australia**
Country of Origin:	**Australia**
Type of Wine:	**Grenache, Shiraz and Mataro Blend**
Web Site:	**www.petagnawines.com**
Design:	**TypeSpace**
Designer's Web Site:	**www.typespace.com.au**
Art:	**Nahum Ziersch**

PETER LEHMANN OF THE BAROSSA

[SOUTH AUSTRALIA ❧ AUSTRALIA]

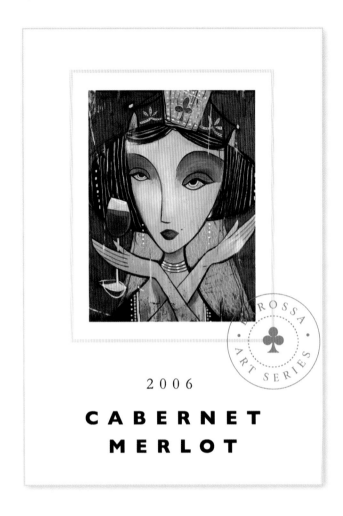

2006

CABERNET
MERLOT

Peter Lehmann is referred to affectionately as "the baron of Barossa" with good reason. His story, quite noble in nature, was born on a gamble.

At the age of seventeen, still wet behind the ears, Peter began what would become an illustrious career at the Yalumba winery. In 1960, he became the winemaker and manager at Saltram Estates, where he remained devoted for twenty years. While there, he built many strong friendships with local grape growers as he moved Saltram from crushing four hundred tons of grapes to a magnificent six thousand tons. That's a lot of grapes, and certainly a lot of friendships. The grape growers respected Peter for his honest dealings and knew that his word was as good as gold to their businesses.

You taste with your eyes. Every package should evoke a sensation of expectation that heightens the visual taste buds to over-deliver for the occasion. —KARIN SEJA
Managing Director, KS Design Studio

However, in the late 1970s, hardship fell on many Australian grape growers when faced with the harsh realities of the overproduction of grapes. To resist the strain, the multinational that owned Saltram at the time directed Peter Lehmann to renege on his good word and previously arranged grape orders—directions that no honorable man would uphold.

Instead, he bought the grapes himself. Wine was made, sold, and a multitude of growers—his friends—were salvaged from financial ruin. As Sal-

---

**PETER LEHMANN OF THE BAROSSA
(HESS FAMILY ESTATES)**

Appellation:	**Barossa Valley**
State:	**South Australia**
Country of Origin:	**Australia**
Type of Wine:	**Cabernet Sauvignon and Merlot Blend**
Web Site:	**www.peterlehmannwines.com.au**
Design:	**KS Design Studio**
Designer's Web Site:	**www.ksdesign.com.au**
Art:	**Dan Tompkins**

2007

MERLOT

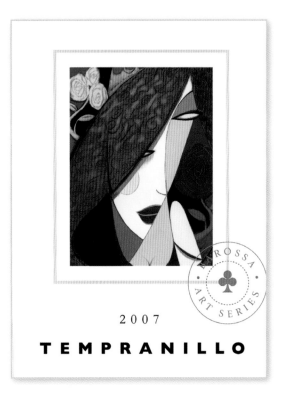

2007

TEMPRANILLO

**PETER LEHMANN OF THE BAROSSA
(HESS FAMILY ESTATES)**

Appellation:	**Barossa Valley**
State:	**South Australia**
Country of Origin:	**Australia**
Type of Wine:	**Merlot**
Web Site:	**www.peterlehmannwines.com.au**
Design:	**KS Design Studio**
Designer's Web Site:	**www.ksdesign.com.au**
Art:	**Edwina White**

**PETER LEHMANN OF THE BAROSSA
(HESS FAMILY ESTATES)**

Appellation:	**Barossa Valley**
State:	**South Australia**
Country of Origin:	**Australia**
Type of Wine:	**Tempranillo**
Web Site:	**www.peterlehmannwines.com.au**
Design:	**KS Design Studio**
Designer's Web Site:	**www.ksdesign.com.au**
Art:	**Dan Tompkins**

tram's landscape continued to change and the livelihoods of the growers and their vineyards were perpetually questioned, Peter chose to give it a go on his own. With his pursuit of risky business, he decidedly called his company Masterson, based on his admiration of the author Damon Runyon, whose short stories inspired *Guys and Dolls* and included fictional gambler Sky Masterson. Barossan artist Rod Schubert, who designed the label, is said to have been adamant that the queen of clubs is the gambler's card. Lehmann concurred and it stuck.

In 1982, they changed the name of the company from Masterson to the gambler's own moniker, Peter Lehmann of the Barossa, but kept the queen of clubs logo. The logo has now evolved into many different renditions of the same face. Since 1995, young Australian artists have been commissioned to interpret the wines visually, defining the character of each individual wine in the series through their interpretation of the club queen on the wine labels.

As for Peter Lehmann himself, he is known to enjoy a good card game and actually plays cribbage every day with his wife, Margaret. Demonstrating that he needn't rely solely on his lucky queen of clubs to be a winner, the pair once took a gamble on a game against the champions of Wales—and won of course.

Over the past thirty years, the queen of clubs has become the public face of our wines. In 1995, we commissioned young artists to re-interpret the queen of clubs in the context of the variety of tastes, flavors, bouquets, and defining characters of the wines being crafted at the time. This innovative concept bridged the art of winemaking with the art of painting, resulting in a striking collection of dynamic images and an engaging link with wine lovers around the world.

—PAUL TURALE
Global Marketing Manager,
Peter Lehmann of the Barossa

PHILIP SHAW

[NEW SOUTH WALES ❧ AUSTRALIA]

THE IDIOT
by philip shaw
shiraz 2007
orange, australia

750 ml

Driven, crazy, clumsy, spontaneous, serious, focused, playful, passionate, devilish, dry-witted, innovative, thoughtful, respectful, a barrel of fun.

These are some of the complimentary characteristics attributed to winemaker Philip Shaw. To sum it up, like the wines he crafts, he is a distinct character who has many layers to his personality that simply attract people to him. It is this spirit that makes people want to work hard for him and just want to generally be in his presence.

THE DREAMER
by philip shaw
viognier 2008
orange, australia

750 ml

PHILIP SHAW

Appellation:	**Orange**
State:	**New South Wales**
Country of Origin:	**Australia**
Type of Wine:	**Shiraz**
Web Site:	**www.philipshaw.com.au**
Design:	**Emma Griffin (Panel Pop)**
Designer's Web Site:	**www.panelpop.com**
Art:	**Nior**
Artist's Web Site:	**www.niorart.com.au**

PHILIP SHAW

Appellation:	**Orange**
State:	**New South Wales**
Country of Origin:	**Australia**
Type of Wine:	**Viognier**
Web Site:	**www.philipshaw.com.au**
Design:	**Emma Griffin (Panel Pop)**
Designer's Web Site:	**www.panelpop.com**
Art:	**Ghostpatrol**
Artist's Web Site:	**www.ghostpatrol.net**

THE ARCHITECT
by philip shaw
chardonnay 2008
orange, australia

750 ml

THE CONDUCTOR
by philip shaw
merlot 2007
orange, australia

750 ml

PHILIP SHAW	
Appellation:	**Orange**
State:	**New South Wales**
Country of Origin:	**Australia**
Type of Wine:	**Chardonnay**
Web Site:	**www.philipshaw.com.au**
Design:	**Emma Griffin (Panel Pop)**
Designer's Web Site:	**www.panelpop.com**
Art:	**Miso**
Artist's Web Site:	**www.cityofreubens.com**

PHILIP SHAW	
Appellation:	**Orange**
State:	**New South Wales**
Country of Origin:	**Australia**
Type of Wine:	**Merlot**
Web Site:	**www.philipshaw.com.au**
Design:	**Emma Griffin (Panel Pop)**
Designer's Web Site:	**www.panelpop.com**
Art:	**Acron**

The Philip Shaw Character Series affectionately highlights his many alter egos, and what others say are his strengths as both an individual and vintner. Of course, the reality is that, with the exception of one character that he vehemently beseeched be included, he modestly denies most of it.

Each of the Character Series wine labels visually depicts these alter egos through the art of some of Victoria's most talented contemporary street artists. The visuals mightn't overtly explain Shaw's figuratively split personalities, so here's the inside scoop: The Dreamer is a reflection of Shaw's aspirations of owning his own vineyard, which to some might have seemed a lofty goal, even perhaps out of his league. But for Philip Shaw, if he can dream it, he can achieve it.

Although Philip would never suggest himself to be likened with the talent of a conductor, anyone who has witnessed him orchestrate a team knows that he is able to make beautiful music by instilling his team members with the confidence to work independently, as well as integrate harmoniously. It's almost like a symphony when each individual is able to work in their element to produce wonderful wines—thus, The Conductor.

While it may be hard to conceive having enough head or heart space to accommodate another passion, Shaw has endless energy to devote to what he loves. After his vines, wines, family, and friends, Philip also possesses a serious fascination, appreciation, and knowledge of the world of architecture and spends time outside his world of wine exploring, educating himself, and experimenting within this ulterior creative outlet. The Architect wine label applauds the joy Philip takes in expanding his knowledge and creativity through various extracurricular interests, especially his absorption in architecture and design

Given his disdain with being characterized in the same light as professionals he holds in very high regard, and his extreme humility towards being praised for his innate talent and personality, it was with great difficulty that these labels were created. Philip agreed to the Character Series wine labels only by insisting strictly on the inclusion of one final character that he likens himself to, though an absolute misnomer to everyone else—The Idiot.

PHILIP SHAW
[NEW SOUTH WALES ❧ AUSTRALIA]

PHILIP SHAW N°17

PS·N°17   MERLOT CABERNET
          FRANC CABERNET 2005   750ml
          Orange, Australia

Philip Shaw has a thing for numbers. Each of the wines bearing his name has one that has personal meaning to him. For instance, he calls his Chardonnay No. 11 because that is the number given to his south-sloping dream plot. Away from the sun, it is one of the coolest in the vineyard and perfect for Chardonnay. He calls his Merlot, Cabernet Franc, and Cabernet blend No. 17 because if you add the plots where the fruit is sourced from together (2, 3, 5, and 7), you'll get 17. His Sauvignon Blanc is called No. 19 as a tribute to a good friend, the late Albert Chan, whose birthday was on August 19. His prized Shiraz is called No. 89 because that was the year the vines were planted. His Pinot Noir—ah, the Pinot Noir—is called No. 8 because when he decided that he wanted to extend his Philip Shaw range to include Pinot Noir, those playing devil's advocate asked him what his gambling number was, given Pinot is not known to thrive in the region. He said, "No. 8," also a Chinese number of luck. The gamble was obviously in the favor of the Chinese.

The other interesting aspect of the Philip Shaw Number Series is that each vintage is adorned with a custom illustration done literally on the fly, which is a testament to Shaw's lightheartedness.

The label's job is to introduce the wine, stimulate the imagination, or remind someone of past enjoyments. At its best, a wine label is truthful, intriguing and, in the end, proudly overshadowed by the leading act.
—EMMA GRIFFIN
Designer, Panel Pop

PHILIP SHAW

Appellation:	**Orange**
State:	**New South Wales**
Country of Origin:	**Australia**
Type of Wine:	**Merlot, Cabernet Franc, and Cabernet Sauvignon Blend**
Web Site:	**www.philipshaw.com.au**
Design:	**Emma Griffin (Panel Pop)**
Designer's Web Site:	**www.panelpop.com**

KOOMOOLOO VINEYARD
EST IN 1988, ALTITUDE ~900M

PHILIP SHAW

Appellation:	**Orange**
State:	**New South Wales**
Country of Origin:	**Australia**
Type of Wine:	**Various**
Web Site:	**www.philipshaw.com.au**
Design:	**Emma Griffin (Panel Pop)**
Designer's Web Site:	**www.panelpop.com**
Art:	**Tobias Röttger**
Artist's Web Site:	**www.tobiasroettger.de**

PHILIP SHAW

Appellation:	**Orange**
State:	**New South Wales**
Country of Origin:	**Australia**
Type of Wine:	**Various**
Web Site:	**www.philipshaw.com.au**
Design:	**Emma Griffin (Panel Pop)**
Designer's Web Site:	**www.panelpop.com**
Art:	**Callum Addis**

About a week out from vintage, Philip's creative designer, Emma Griffith, chooses an artist and flies them up to Orange for a full day and night for an intimate Philip Shaw vintage experience. In turn, each artist interprets the vintage events through their integration and involvement with the vintage team. Each illustration is Shaw's salute to his team, through a quirky and memorable illustrative snapshot of the year's overall experiences in the vineyards and at the winery.

For instance, in the first vintage illustration, the plane parked at the base of the vineyard slopes is a toast to the plane that Philip was a passenger of while conducting research on the region's potentiality for a vineyard. Though its engine nearly seized, this was the plane that successfully flew over Orange and led Philip eventually to purchase his property. The character floating against the glass doors of the yellow house? That's Sam; he worked in the vineyard and helped out in the winery. He's wearing a jumpsuit as a reflection of his personality—always laughing and happy-go-lucky. In every illustration, there is always a menagerie of vineyard animals who, in a roundabout way, indirectly contribute to the wine's character. Philip is the one in the ballet shoes—ask him about his unique style of dance and in particular . . . the dance he performed on Pitt Street.

As for the rest, probably best to visit and experience it for yourself. You won't be disappointed. You might even find yourself on a vintage label one day.

Peter Hunken and Sashi Moorman. Peter and Sashi. Piedrasassi.

Seemingly, this unique name is just a creative play on the names of the two winemakers and owners of Piedrasassi wines, but there is actually more meaning to it than meets the eye. In Spanish, *piedra* means "rock." In Italian, *sassi* means "stones." These two winemakers consequently share a deep appreciation for the wines of both Spain and Italy, as well as the belief that in vineyards, rocks and stones provide the soil with a critical foundation for growing the grapes needed to produce quality wines.

The Piedrasassi wine label features the image of a Native American sling—a primitive weapon whose ammunition is none other than a humble rock or stone. The record for slinging a stone is 437.1 meters, as indicated in the *Guinness Book of World Records*, set by Larry Bray in Loa, Utah, on August 21, 1981. The most famous sling story told, however, you probably recall from the Bible. The renowned story tells the tale of the battle between the unarmored shepherd David, who defeated the monstrous warrior Goliath with nothing but the precision of his handiwork with stone and sling.

A sling, in the precise hands of an expert, together with a lowly stone or rock has unassuming might, never to be underestimated. Just like artisan wineries against the big goliaths. Armed with intense passion, commitment, and premium fruit—they are a rock solid force to be reckoned with.

PIEDRASASSI	
Appellation:	**Lompoc (Non-Designated Appellation)**
State:	**California**
Country of Origin:	**United States**
Type of Wine:	**Syrah**
Web Site:	**www.piedrasassi.com**
Design:	**Heroist**
Designer's Web Site:	**www.heroist.com**

PIERI WINES

Those in the wine industry know that attempting to make the centuries-old tradition of Amarone-style wine is risky business. It is, however, worth the game of chance when you get it right.

The reputation of risk comes from its precarious production method. This form of winemaking is lengthy in time and dicey due to the reliance on Mother Nature—who is quite hard to predict even on the best of days! Amarone wines are the only ones that are enough of a gamble to be vinified using "raisined," or dried, grapes. Ever tried making grape juice out of a raisin? Winemakers almost have to hold their breath until the wine is in the barrels, but even then it can be a total game of chance.

Traditionally, the grapes are harvested just prior to being fully ripe to preserve their level of acidity. They are then left to shrivel patiently—or, as the Italians say, *rasinate*—a method actually invented by the Romans. It is this drying of the grapes that allows for a high concentration of sugars that can then convert into alcohol during the fermentation process. Moreover, there a substantially lower yield of juice from the successfully dried grapes, meaning you must use more grapes to produce the same amount found in one regular glass of wine. This draws out the fermentation process, increasing the risk of spoilage or faults to the wine.

Andrew and his family recognize that making this style of wine is an absolute game of chance, and that is exactly what they have chosen to call their wines, the Italian word *azzardo*, meaning "gamble," and *occasione*, meaning "chance." The Azzardo label depicts Andrew's father, who passed down the tradition of Amarone-style winemaking to his son from days spent in his hometown of L'Aquila in Italy. He is shown taking a gamble and playing cards with his Italian friends with what just happens to be the original hustler's (Paul Newman) body. The Occasione label showcases a traditional scene from the 1930s of a group of kids sitting around shooting craps—the ultimate game of pure chance.

While making this Amarone-style wine does involve its risks, if you get your hands on a bottle, consider yourself lucky. You'll agree it's a winner every time, no matter what the odds.

PIERI WINES	
Appellation:	**McLaren Vale**
State:	**South Australia**
Country of Origin:	**Australia**
Type of Wine:	**Shiraz**
Design:	**Mash**
Designer's Web Site:	**www.mashdesign.com.au**

PIERI WINES	
Appellation:	**McLaren Vale**
State:	**South Australia**
Country of Origin:	**Australia**
Type of Wine:	**Shiraz**
Design:	**Adam Hooper**

PRINCE HILL WINES
[NEW SOUTH WALES ❧ AUSTRALIA]

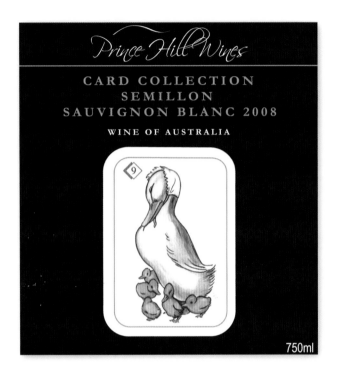

The Prince family's foray into wines began when its ancestor, James Prince, arrived in Mudgee, New South Wales, in the late 1800s. Upon arrival, he worked the land and lived in the homestead where the current Prince Hill winery now sits. A century later, the Prince family still owns some of the land around the winery and keep James Prince's pioneering spirit alive through their involvement in the region's wine industry.

The Card Collection remembers James Prince through precious heirloom cards that once provided hours of amusement for children during the late 1800s. As was customary at the time, books and games were designed to instruct as well as entertain, and were sent over from Great Britain. The Schwarzer Peter playing cards are an example of the scholarly type of diversions children were once fond of.

In the 1960s, a collection of two hundred books and fifty games once enjoyed by the children of the region were donated to the Children's Literature Research Collection at the State Library of South Australia. These precious cards remain on display in the State Library today and also grace these Prince Hill labels as a welcome to the warm, approachable wines, as well as a toast to those, both young and old, who worked (and played) on and around the estate in the past.

PRINCE HILL WINES	
Appellation:	**Mudgee**
State:	**New South Wales**
Country of Origin:	**Australia**
Type of Wine:	**Chardonnay**
Web Site:	**www.princehillwine.com**
Art:	**Vintage Art by Pix**

PRINCE HILL WINES	
Appellation:	**Mudgee**
State:	**New South Wales**
Country of Origin:	**Australia**
Type of Wine:	**Sémillon and Sauvignon Blanc Blend**
Web Site:	**www.princehillwine.com**
Art:	**Vintage Art by Pix**

PURE LOVE WINES

[SOUTH AUSTRALIA ❧ AUSTRALIA]

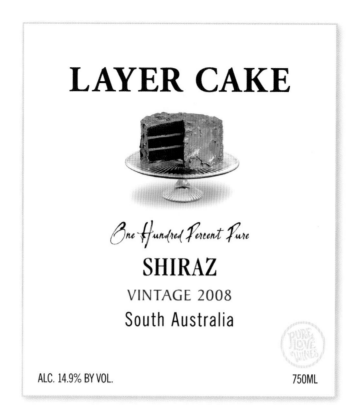

LAYER CAKE

One Hundred Percent Pure

SHIRAZ

VINTAGE 2008

South Australia

ALC. 14.9% BY VOL.   750ML

While growing up, vintner Jayson Woodbridge's weekends involved the traditional visit to his grandparents for Sunday dinner. When he arrived, his grandmother could always be found in the kitchen baking, inevitably constructing her famed triple-layer cake. As a young boy of five, Jayson would sit at the counter fixated on the pride his grandmother took in crafting her cakes using homemade jams, fluffy icing, and moist layers, expertly stacked to perfection.

His grandfather, who made and enjoyed wine for eighty years, would often join and put a miniature wine glass in front of Jayson to give him a different lesson on layers. To a young Jayson, it was explained that in order to make wines, there were many ingredients, just like in his grandmother's cakes. Visible at the top were the grapes, fruit that grew on the vines and vines that attached to the rootstalk that dug into the earth. The earth's soils had layers of essential nutrients and, if prepared correctly, the wines made from the fruit fed by the soils would also show layers of flavor. These flavors were reflective of the nutrients the soil provided—the grapes could taste like mocha, chocolate, and hints of spice. His grandfather always advised him to never pass up a good piece of cake and just the same, never to pass up a good wine.

For Jayson, layer cake has always been symbolic of the handmade artistry taught to him by his grandparents. Now Jayson handcrafts of his own Layer Cake wines that fully express the stratums of the soils from which they are harvested and produced, just as he remembers those lessons learnt long ago by his wise grandparents on the labels.

> **For the winemaker, nothing stands above the wine in the bottle. The label is a canvas and a completely different medium for the winemaker to speak directly to people who love wine, now and in the future. It allows us to convey a message, perhaps a belief, an ethos, or a feeling; it is a window into the mind of the winemaker.**
>
> —JAYSON WOODBRIDGE
> Winemaker, Pure Love Wines

PURE LOVE WINES	
Appellation:	**McLaren Vale**
State:	**South Australia**
Country of Origin:	**Australia**
Type of Wine:	**Shiraz**
Web Site:	**www.layercakewine.com**
Design:	**Jayson Woodbridge and Mash**
Designer's Web Site:	**www.mashdesign.com.au**

QMS GROUP

[CALIFORNIA ✎ UNITED STATES]

According to winemaker Quincy Steele, wine is a linguistic medium. It speaks volumes of its beginnings in the soil and specific terroir, and moves through the growing seasons, harvesting, and then winemaking, right to the glass in your hand. We talk about it, we write about it, and there is always an explanatory story in its experience.

The Writer's Block series of wines is a project that father Jed and son Quincy began with the intention of bottling a small amount of Mendocino County Pinot Noir and Lake County Syrah. Having just graduated from college with a double major in history and English literature under his belt, Quincy Steele gravitated towards those experiences immediately close to him and fresh in his mind. Namely, a year-long course on the history and theory of the novel, as well as to two close friends who were already working writers. The friends had spoken previously about engaging in a joint project of sorts and this seemed the opportune time. The concept: a writer's block, from multiple perspectives.

The idea was that the wines would each be made each from a single block of a vineyard and then layered with the addition of a linguistic and storytelling label. Each label includes individually interesting, entertaining, and evocative prose from a single writer suffering from writer's block and being tempted by the bottle. Was it not Homer who wrote in *The Odyssey*, "The wine urges me on, the bewitching wine, which sets even a wise man to singing and to laughing gently and rouses him up to dance and brings forth words which were better unspoken"? Wine is a creative lubricant that opens the mind and coaxes out words that, in its absence, may have never been.

Quincy Steele says that the label is meant to portray a historical aspect of wine, while the image of Shakespeare associates wine with language, storytelling and, of course, the ubiquitous writer's block—a shared ailment that knows no boundaries between men, women, creators, writers, and artists. It, like the enjoyment of wine, is more a fraternity than a disparity between all creative and passionate souls.

The culture of wine labels is a constantly changing universe of history, tradition, and values. We can remember or forget a label, wine, or related company, but we must always pass through the threshold first. Good wine labels give us directions to go further, quietly urge us, and direct us over always new bridges.

—QUINCY MCANDREW STEELE
Winemaker, QMS Group

QMS GROUP (STEELE WINES)

Appellation:	**Lake County (Non-Designated Appellation)**
State:	**California**
Country of Origin:	**United States**
Type of Wine:	**Syrah**
Web Site:	**www.steelewines.com**
Design:	**Michele LeBlanc**
Designer's Web Site:	**www.leblancdesign.net**

QUIXOTE WINERY

[CALIFORNIA ✎ UNITED STATES]

Aworking winery: An approachable place where people would easily enjoy themselves when they visited; a place that didn't take itself too seriously, and allowed a little magic and whimsy to live freely—two things that are often lacking in an industry that revolves wholeheartedly around the pleasures of grape "juice"—a place where people just simply smile upon arrival and take a little piece of magic with them when they depart. This was the unambiguous vision of Carl Doumani—an anomaly in what is often seen as quite a staunch industry.

Happenstance would have it that, while contemplating this change of direction after thirty-five years tenure in the industry, Doumani would stumble upon the eclectic sculptural work of Friedensreich Hundertwasser and knew that the iconic and revered Austrian artist, architect, philosopher, sculptor, and environmentalist was the ideal creative collaborator to realize his archetypal winery.

Hundertwasser, though enchanted with the Stags' Leap Ranch, had provisions that would inevitably drive the winery to become the quintessence of Doumani's dream: no straight lines, roofs planted with grass and trees, the building capped with a golden turret. Last, but certainly not least, color had to be king—absolutely unheard of for an industry where constraint in color had historically ruled.

Doumani took the leap and a close friendship ensued as the two worked together to plan and build the rare and remarkable winery from 1988 to 1998. The winery was designated "Quixote," a Seuss-like wonderland fit for Alice. Whimsy is certainly obvious in the broken ceramic tiles, an assortment of found objects, a living roof, deliberately uneven floors, postmodern rounded columns, minarets, and no right angles (with the necessary exception for the cellar in the basement). Don't let the fanciful environment fool you—the winemaking at Quixote is not taken as lightheartedly as its surroundings. But that doesn't mean that they don't have fun making it!

The wine label, also designed by the late Hundertwasser, is a fanciful reflection of the philosophy the winery was built on by quixotic industry visionary Carl Doumani.

	QUIXOTE WINERY
Appellation:	**Napa Valley**
State:	**California**
Country of Origin:	**United States**
Type of Wine:	**Red**
Web Site:	**www.quixotewinery.com**
Art:	**Friedensreich Hundertwasser**
Artist's Web Site:	**www.hundertwasser.at**

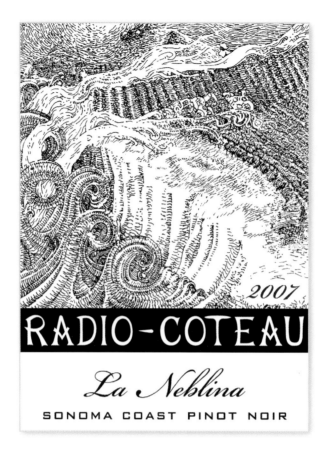

The colloquial or conversational term *"radio-coteau"* is most commonly used in France's northern Rhône region. It was first introduced to winemaker Eric Sussman while working on multiple projects in the mid-1990s in Burgundy at Domaine Comte Armand and Domaine Jacques Prieur. The term, which literally translates to "broadcasting from the hillside," has a definition similar to the English equivalent, "word of mouth."

This informal phrase resonated deeply with Sussman and was a strong reflection of his belief in the traditional methods of grape growing and winemaking passed on organically through oral tradition from one generation to the next. When embarking on his own venture in 2002, the term was redolent of Sussman's inspiration more so by the characteristics and location of the land rather than strictly driven by grape varietal. The realization of Sussman's visionary, coastal cliffside farming sources allowed his non-interventionist winemaking philosophies and techniques to materialize "from the hillside."

This label is an artistic interpretation of Sussman's treasured northern coast of the western Sonoma County region, captured in time and place and broadcast through his bottles of wine. The artist, Jeffrey Baker, was an old university mate who had created labels for Eric's earliest experiments in winemaking while studying agriculture at Cornell. Coming full circle, Sussman tracked Baker down in 2002 and commissioned him to artistically interpret his more current coastal cliffside venture that is Radio-Coteau.

RADIO-COTEAU

Appellation:	**Sonoma Coast**
State:	**California**
Country of Origin:	**United States**
Type of Wine:	**Pinot Noir**
Web Site:	**www.radiocoteau.com**
Art:	**Jeffrey Baker**

RAVENSWOOD WINERY

[CALIFORNIA ❦ UNITED STATES]

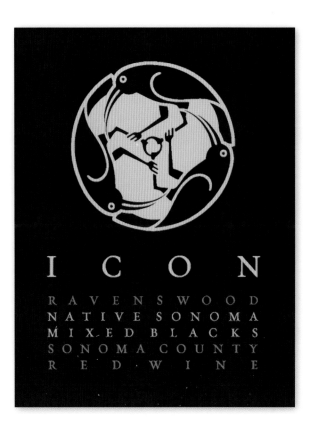

Joel Peterson sunk his life savings of $4,000 into his inaugural Ravenswood Winery fledgling. Having learnt the nuts and bolts of winemaking, he set out to purchase his first vintage's grapes, pre-paying for four tons and scheduling to have help loading them onto his truck once harvested. When he arrived at the vineyard, however, the only thing that was moving were the dark clouds in the sky above him. Not a soul in sight, there he was with four tons of uncovered grapes, a truck, and only his own hands to beat the rain; a race against Mother Nature's ticking clock. Fifty pounds at a time, Joel saved his grapes from rot with nothing but his two hands, and a little pluck, wit, and sheer determination.

All the while, he was in the company of two massive ravens perched in the tree providing a canopy over his truck. Try as he might, he wasn't able to block out their incessantly nagging squawks. Initially extremely annoyed, especially under the circumstances, Joel tried to wish them away. As the night wore on though, bleeding hands and exhaustion set in and Peterson began looking at his trickster watchdogs with a kinder eye. By one thirty in the morning, having narrowly escaped the rain, he was actually thinking fondly of his feathered friends. Though Mother Nature may not have been on his side, the Native American mythological heroes certainly were. And so it was: his first crush.

Months later, when it came time to give this first-born wine a name and label, he immediately thought of the ravens that were watching over him that cloudy night. Though the name "Raven's Wine" just didn't seem right, he knew that the ravens definitely needed to play a part in it. Drawing on his enjoyment of opera and reminiscence of a particular hero from *Lucia di Lammermoor,* with whom he definitely associated with during this time of turbulence, he looked to this character for his name—Sir Edgardo di Ravenswood. Ravenswood ultimately drowns in quicksand during the opera and Peterson quite identified with the feeling; starting a winery kind of felt the same to some degree. His two feathered tricksters were also integrated into the name, and so it would be that Peterson bestowed the name "Ravenswood" upon his wines.

The ultimate piece of the Ravenswood story, however, came long after Joel Peterson's initial Zinfandel crush. For the thirty years that he had been nurturing a relationship with his prized Zinfandel grapes, he never actually knew their history: The Zinfandel grapes were first imported by a horticulturalist in the 1820s to a section of Queens, New York, eerily called none other than . . . Ravenswood.

**RAVENSWOOD WINERY
(CONSTELLATION WINES U.S.)**

Appellation:	**Sonoma County (Non-Designated Appellation)**
State:	**California**
Country of Origin:	**United States**
Type of Wine:	**Zinfandel, Petite Sirah, and Carignan Blend**
Web Site:	**www.ravenswoodwinery.com**
Design:	**Voicebox Creative**
Designer's Web Site:	**www.voiceboxsf.com**
Art:	**David Lance Goines**
Artist's Web Site:	**www.goines.net**

RED CAR WINE

[CALIFORNIA ❧ UNITED STATES]

It's amazing where a shared Hollywood history, a common interest in cigars and wine, and a little Chinese food can take two friends.

Carroll Kemp had been hankering to get out of Hollywood and into a joint wine venture with good friend Mark Estrin for some time. Despite already giving up on his cinematic pursuits, Estrin continued to resist a persistent Kemp. One day, however, while enjoying some Chinese together at Panda Express, things literally unfolded in Kemp's favor through the sheer fate found in a fortune cookie.

"The venture you are thinking of will bring you wealth and fame," it read.

Not even the most precautionary person could turn a blind eye to what the universe was saying. Kemp and Estrin made their decision there and then, and Red Car Wine was born.

Beyond their shared passion for wine, the two also shared a commonality in storytelling. Witnessed first during their time spent in Hollywood, as a producer and screenwriter, respectively, it then evolved into a natural element of their winemaking partnership with a seamless shift in media—from big screen to a slightly smaller space, and motion picture to still art. The pair exhibited an amazing capacity to unravel tales told in the form of a continuous novella from one vintage and varietal to the next.

The name "Red Car Wine" was coined as a tribute to the Pacific Electric streetcars that provided Southern California with transportation during the first sixty years of the twentieth century. This was also the golden era of film in Hollywood and these iconic red cars are reminiscent of a romanticized time and place in Los Angeles history. While the wines weave together the intricate stories of the soil, vines, climate, and weather of each vintage and territory, the wine labels expound each story and allow the wine enthusiast to ride the train with an existentialist in the Trolley series, step into the ring with an aging boxer in The Fight *(not pictured)*, or get involved with a femme fatale in Amour Fou *(not pictured)*, amongst other compelling dramas to which Red Car Wine has no shortage of.

RED CAR WINE	
Appellation:	**Sonoma County (Non-Designated Appellation)**
State:	**California**
Country of Origin:	**United States**
Type of Wine:	**Syrah**
Web Site:	**www.red-car-wine.com**
Design:	**Marc Hauser**
Designer's Web Site:	**www.hausercreative.com**

RED HEADS STUDIO

[SOUTH AUSTRALIA ✑ AUSTRALIA]

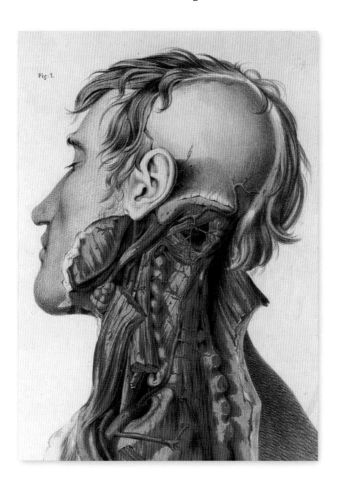

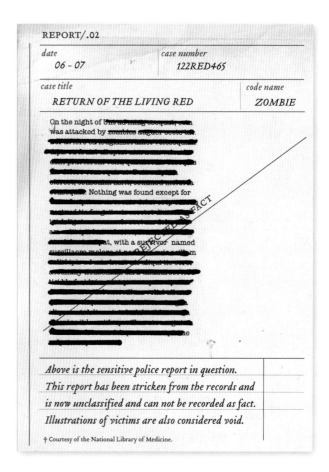

Above is the sensitive police report in question.

This report has been stricken from the records and is now unclassified and can not be recorded as fact.

Illustrations of victims are also considered void.

† Courtesy of the National Library of Medicine.

The wine label to the winemaker heralds the finale of a long and often drawn-out process of bringing together the components of a beautiful wine. For the consumer, the wine label represents the commencement of their wine experience. It is at this point that they begin to understand the heart and soul of the bottle they are holding in their hand. —SIMON WEST
Managing Director,
Fullglass Management

This Red Heads Studio wine is thick and juicy and made from a once-dead varietal, Touriga Nacional, and the interminably alive Cabernet Sauvignon. Touriga, a notoriously black-fruited variety native to Portugal, was planted in Australia at the turn of the century by Portuguese immigrants who combined it with their signature, fortified-styled wines.

In recent years, these syrupy-thick winemaking vines were pulled up in favor of other more conventional and accepted varietals. Safe varietals. Less-dangerous varietals. However, Red Heads Studio, villainous winemakers that they are, has dug deep in the depths of vine land and found some of the last vineyards producing this dearly departed fruit. The vines themselves are said to look lifeless, but regardless of their inanimate façade, once resur-

rected, they still bear fruit with an extreme concentration of flavor.

This wine, raised from the dead like a fiendish zombie, is called Return of the Living Red and is said to be "thicker than blood" and hold "more body than a city morgue and more tannin than a mouthful of fishhooks." Now that sounds just deadly, and the labels very obviously corroborate the evidence.

RED HEADS STUDIO

Appellation:	**Non-Designated Appellation**
State:	**South Australia**
Country of Origin:	**Australia**
Type of Wine:	**Cabernet Sauvignon and Touriga Nacional Blend**
Design:	**Mash**
Designer's Web Site:	**www.mashdesign.com.au**

RED HEADS STUDIO

[SOUTH AUSTRALIA ❧ AUSTRALIA]

There's one on every street: a family pet, once cherished, but now left abandoned to live out its days in the backyard. It's a bleak fate without the necessities of warmth, companionship and, least of all, grooming. Throw the dog a bone only every now and then and this is what you end up with: a family pet gone feral!

Like the once-adored family pet, the grape varieties in Red Heads Studio Yard Dog wine, previously praised, have more recently been overlooked for something a little more exalted. But just like yard dogs, these grapes just don't succumb to a lack of interest. They may lose their reverence while the others are favored, but these old mutts are champs. The neglect builds spirit, the festering allows fermenting and, eventually, like the feral dog, these varietals fight back with character.

Ask the oh-so-cryptic winemaker and Lynch fan Justin Lane how they ended up with this yin and yang mixture of a ferocious-looking whippet set against delicate pink-and-orange polka dots. He'll leave you hanging with something obscure about who killed Laura Palmer and the midget in the red room. . . . Now figure that one out.

RED HEADS STUDIO	
Appellation:	**McLaren Vale**
State:	**South Australia**
Country of Origin:	**Australia**
Type of Wine:	**Petit Verdot, Merlot, and Cabernet Sauvignon Blend**
Design:	**Mash**
Designer's Web Site:	**www.mashdesign.com.au**

RED HEADS STUDIO	
Appellation:	**McLaren Vale**
State:	**South Australia**
Country of Origin:	**Australia**
Type of Wine:	**Chardonnay, Sémillon, and Gewürztraminer Blend**
Design:	**Mash**
Designer's Web Site:	**www.mashdesign.com.au**

RED ZEPPELIN WINERY

[CALIFORNIA ❧ UNITED STATES]

LA MORT DU ROI

Anyone who has had the pleasure of being in the company of winemaker Stillman Brown has likely met alter ego Swilly Idol, the louder than life, fun-loving, party-throwing personality who is anything but a wallflower. It is no secret that Stillman Brown/Swilly Idol is a bit of a music fanatic and, in fact, this fanaticism goes hand in hand with his wine, proven particularly by one of his Red Zeppelin wine labels, which can boast one of the most outrageous images ever to legally appear on a bottle of wine.

Using a wine label as a humor IQ test isn't exactly common, and it's certainly not practical marketing, so I don't know what grand generalities I could spout that wouldn't be undermined by the La Mort Du Roi label itself.
                    —STILLMAN BROWN
                    Owner and Winemaker,
                    Red Zeppelin Winery

While feeding his fascination with a certain rock-and-roll deity, fueled by a visit to Graceland, Stillman is said to have had a near-religious experience with the King himself. Graceland welcomes millions of visitors a year, but on this particular day, the historical property was relatively quiet and Stillman was able to tour the home at his leisure. Not wanting to pollute his intimate experience with the King, he opted to ditch the pre-recorded ramblings of Presley's life and, instead, took in everything at his own pace. It

was on this visit that Stillman heard that famed, rolling Southern drawl saying, "Stillman, I should have drank more wine"—perhaps instead of making less healthy decisions that are speculated to have led to *le mort du Roi*. How different life might have been for our beloved King. It is because of this Graceland experience and intimate exchange with the King himself that Stillman (or was it Swilly?) commissioned the painting that honors Elvis on this Red Zeppelin wine label.

RED ZEPPELIN WINERY

Appellation:	**Paso Robles**
State:	**California**
Country of Origin:	**United States**
Type of Wine:	**Syrah and Alicante Bouchet Blend**
Web Site:	**www.redzeppelinwinery.com**
Art:	**Robert Cochran**

ROAD 31 WINE CO.

[CALIFORNIA ❦ UNITED STATES]

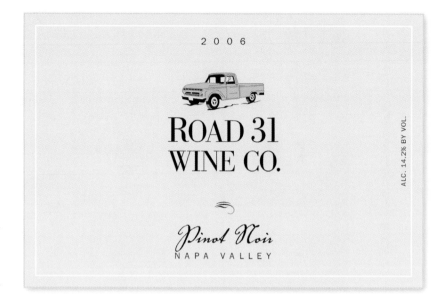

Kent Fornter, winemaker and owner of Road 31 Wine Company, was bequeathed a 1966 green Ford pickup truck by his late grandfather. By adorning his wine labels with the truck, he honors the true heart and soul of wine—not the snobby, white-linened dining-room experience, but the farmer's right hand, the truck. Just about the time when he considering what to name his wines, he was home having lunch with his grandmother and she told him the story of the '66 Ford as they looked out on it through the window.

Kent's grandmother, Mary, was born and raised in a small town in southwestern Kansas. At the age of sixteen, her mother arranged an introduction between Mary and a respectable young lad, as you did in those days. Mary packed up her things and traveled to Fredona, in southeastern Kansas. Upon arrival, she found out that the meeting wasn't to be, as the lad was still out working the wheat-harvest loop. Now, working the wheat harvest loop isn't like your everyday nine-to-five job—wheat harvesters followed the crops from Oklahoma to Colorado, then to Nebraska and onto Kansas, working the loop as the wheat matured. Since Mary had traveled all the way to Fredona, the parents of the wheat-harvesting lad felt terribly responsible and thought it indecent for Mary to be wandering the strange city herself. So they assigned her with a chaperone, a close friend of the family's named Loren.

Unbeknownst to the wheat-harvesting lad's family, Mary and Loren had a grand old time together until the news arrived that the original fella was on his way home. The new couple decided it would be best for Mary to immediately return home in the hopes of avoiding a disastrous situation, and promises were made to write to each other daily. When Mary returned home, write she did, but not a single letter arrived from Loren as promised.

One evening, weeks later, she suddenly heard rocks at her window. When she opened the shutters, to her surprise, Loren was standing there and yelling up that he had come to do what he said he'd do in all of his letters. It didn't take long to put it all together. As it turns out, in the very first letter that Loren wrote to Mary, he'd mentioned that he would be traveling west to a Methodist church camp, and would call to see Mary and hopefully pick up the pieces of their lost love. Of course, Mary's mother intercepted that first letter and, finding out that it was from a strange boy, she kiboshed all other letters from getting through. Loren said it didn't matter, and that he was still there to do what he'd said he'd come to do: marry her.

Because that same harvest loop that had brought them together was now going to take them apart from each other the very next day, the amorous couple got hitched that night in 1937. And in 1966, the couple purchased the green Ford pickup and in it they finally went on their honeymoon to Niagara Falls. In 1986, Loren passed away and Kent has been working harvests with his grandfather's green '66 pickup ever since.

ROAD 31 WINE CO.

Appellation:	**Napa Valley**
State:	**California**
Country of Origin:	**United States**
Type of Wine:	**Pinot Noir**
Web Site:	**www.road31.com**
Design:	**Karen Templer**
Art:	**Mignon Khargie**
Artist's Web Site:	**www.zand2ohs.com**

ROCK 'N ROLL WINE

[CALIFORNIA ✤ UNITED STATES]

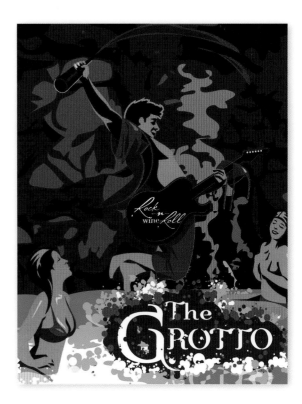

If you are having a party, this is what you need to be the host with the most.

Rock 'n Roll Wine started off as its own small party—the coming together of an intimate group of friends that explored wine casually, but always with high-octane energy and tons of roll-on-the-floor laughter. Word of the fun-filled evenings eventually got around and after opening their arms to more and more revelers, the group no longer had the ability to get together in a living room to learn about and taste wines.

In October 2003, building on the popularity of the once-casual classes, the Rock 'n Roll Wine series was developed. It is an alternative and approachable means to explore the characters of different wines while pairing the tastes with different musical genres, right down to specific songs. Rock 'n Roll groupies continued to flourish, and founder Chris Hammond and partner Sonny Barton gave the crowds what they wanted . . . more! More music, more concerts, more parties, and all with more wine tastings.

The Rock 'n Roll wine labels reflect their rock-and-roll style of wine as interpreted through music. The Grotto red blend promises to be a "voluptuous vixen"—best enjoyed in your "favorite silk jammies or velvet jumpsuit" and accompanied with the salacious sounds of Prince's "Kiss," the Cure's "Close to Me," or the Doors' "Peace Frog." And Reggae Rhapsody would be best enjoyed in a string bikini or in your wetsuit after catching a wave and while listening to Bob Marley's "Stir It Up," Sublime's "What I Got," or Jimmy Cliff's "The Harder They Come." Don't believe it's better with the right tune? Throw a jumpsuit on, pull a cork, crank up the tunes, and you'll see for yourself.

ROCK 'N ROLL WINE	
Appellation:	**Non-Designated Appellation**
State:	**California**
Country of Origin:	**United States**
Type of Wine:	**White Blend**
Web Site:	**www.rnrwine.com**
Design:	**M3 Advertising Design**
Designer's Web Site:	**www.m3ad.com**

ROCK 'N ROLL WINE	
Appellation:	**Non-Designated Appellation**
State:	**California**
Country of Origin:	**United States**
Type of Wine:	**Red Blend**
Web Site:	**www.rnrwine.com**
Design:	**M3 Advertising Design**
Designer's Web Site:	**www.m3ad.com**

ROCLAND ESTATE

[SOUTH AUSTRALIA ❧ AUSTRALIA]

The expression "Kilroy was here" is a piece of popular culture that was often left as an anonymous mark in the form of a graffitied doodle of the distinctive cartoon "Kilroy" peeking out over a wall. Speculation has it that this piece of visual culture first emerged by way of an American shipyard inspector during World War II, James J. Kilroy. It has been suggested that the mark acted as Inspector Kilroy's signatory work audit. The builders whose work he was inspecting were paid based on their individual number of completed rivets. At they end of each shift, they were to mark where they had left off and, accordingly, where the next worker would pick up. Dishonest workers realized that they could easily be paid a higher wage if they began work before the arrival of the inspector, erased the chalk marking of the previous worker and remarked it some rivets back, thereby taking extra credit for work done by another laborer.

To curtail this crookery, J. J. Kilroy apparently began heavily marking "Kilroy was here" at each chalkmark. Ships at this time were released into service not yet having been painted and therefore, it is possible that when sealed areas were accessed for maintenance, the unexplained marking was found. Thousands of servicemen are anticipated to have been exposed to the strange insignia, then adopting it as their own, leaving this stamp of presence on surfaces of all kinds where they'd visited, were stationed, or had occupied. "Kilroy was here" holds no geographic boundaries and has traveled across the globe, morphing into different personas, but always means the same thing: "I was here. I'm leaving my mark."

While the fad ended in the 1950s, people the world over are still guilty of scrawling "I was here"

We try to create labels that eclipse competitors by nurturing a sense of anticipation and excitement, therefore enticing the consumer to eagerly await the fruits of our labors hiding under its veil of mystery.

—FRANC ROCCA
Managing Director and Owner,
Rocland Estate

all over the place. Rocland Estate has revitalized this piece of popular culture through its wine labels, suggesting that, in some way, we all leave our mark in this world. For Rocland Estate, its wines are a mark of time, place, people, and history. Each of the labels include a visual of the estate's proprietors, the Rocca family, with a missing piece of the puzzle—begging the question, who is this phantom Rocca, never to be seen, but always around?

ROCLAND ESTATE	
Appellation:	**Barossa Valley**
State:	**South Australia**
Country of Origin:	**Australia**
Type of Wine:	**Shiraz**
Web Site:	**www.roclandestate.com**
Design:	**Barbara Harkness**
Designer's Web Site:	**www.harknessdesign.com.au**

Root: 1

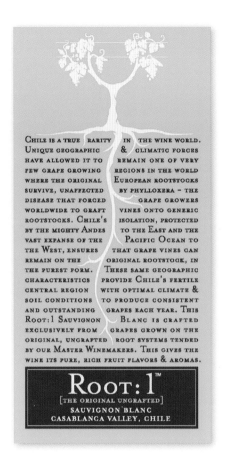

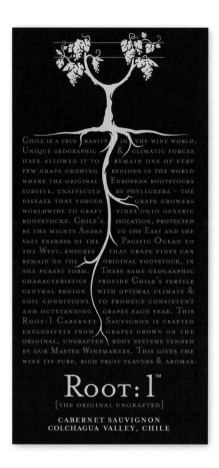

In the late 1860s, phylloxera, a villainous aphid-like insect, arrived in Europe attacking the vulnerable *vitis vinifera* rootstalk. As a result of the epidemic, substantial European vineyards, most notably in France, were obliterated. The obnoxious parasite was resistant to boundaries and spread throughout the continent and to other parts of the world including Australia, New Zealand, and South Africa, devastating vineyards along the way and taking a serious toll on the wine industry.

In order to revive the obliterated vines, the most appropriate solution seemed to graft the *vitis vinifera* species of grapevines onto more resistant American rootstalk as phylloxera was native to North America and American stalks remained unaffected against the pest. Luckily, grafting the root system didn't hybridize or interfere with the development of the grapes.

Chile was one of the few places that remained unscathed by the phylloxera attack. Given that European *vitis vinifera* grapevine species were introduced by Spanish colonists approximately a century prior to the aphid outbreak, many of Chile's vines are in fact original European rootstalk, never having been touched by phylloxera. Root: 1 wine is made from original, ungrafted vines and, as a result, has this incredible differentiator highlighted on the wine bottles.

ROOT: 1 **(CLICK WINE GROUP)**	**ROOT: 1** **(CLICK WINE GROUP)**
Appellation: **Casablanca Valley**	Appellation: **Colchagua Valley**
Region: **Valparaíso**	Region: **O'Higgins**
Country of Origin: **Chile**	Country of Origin: **Chile**
Type of Wine: **Sauvignon Blanc**	Type of Wine: **Cabernet Sauvignon**
Web Site: **www.root1wine.com**	Web Site: **www.root1wine.com**
Design: **Turner Duckworth**	Design: **Turner Duckworth**
Designer's Web Site: **www.turnerduckworth.com**	Designer's Web Site: **www.turnerduckworth.com**

Roshambo Winery

[California ☙ United States]

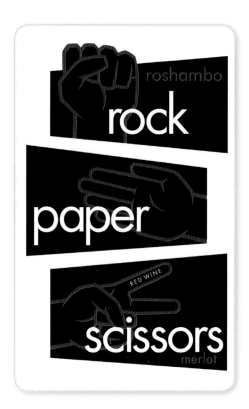

The children of Frank Johnson spent many a summer lulling about their late grandparents' vineyard—hanging out with their cousins, just being kids, and loving the grapes it produced (and wine, which they were introduced to once they got older). When Naomi Brilliant's grandparents passed away, the question was, "What are we going to do with all those grapes?"

Feeling an innate calling back home, Naomi knew that she would be the one to continue her late grandfather's dream of a family vineyard. When it came to evolving the name of the vineyard, trials upon trials of names just didn't seem to fit. Eventually, something very elemental to her past came to mind, which led the way.

The story starts with Naomi's grandfather's son—her dad—Tom Johnson. Tom Johnson, a PhD in anthropology with a focus on children's culture and games, traveled to Japan to further his post-doctorate research. While studying in the small village of Kuwakubo, Tom befriended a young boy named Kazuo Wachi, who initiated an introduction between Tom and his older sister, Kimie. Smitten, and with a couple of games for adults that he pulled out of his back pocket, the two soon married. A few years later, the couple moved to Tokyo with their children, Naomi and Morgan. Like other children (and adults!) in Japan, Naomi and Morgan looked to the respectable and gentle form of conflict resolution found in *jan, ken, pon*; *schare, schtal, papier*; *muk, chi, ba*; rock, paper, scissors; and otherwise known as *rochambeau* or, in phonetic English, roshambo!

When Naomi remembered this significant part of her upbringing and what it meant to their family, she thought that there couldn't be a more playful and unpretentious name for a vineyard whose motto is, "Fighting for fun in a winery world." The Roshambo wine labels celebrate the Californian roots and Japanese heritage of the Johnson family's third generation, admiring Naomi's father's academic pursuits, as well as her mother's Japanese culture.

	ROSHAMBO WINERY
Appellation:	**Dry Creek Valley**
State:	**California**
Country of Origin:	**United States**
Type of Wine:	**Sauvignon Blanc**
Web Site:	**www.roshambofarms.com**
Design:	**Calyx Design**
Designer's Web Site:	**www.calyxdesign.com**

	ROSHAMBO WINERY
Appellation:	**Dry Creek Valley**
State:	**California**
Country of Origin:	**United States**
Type of Wine:	**Merlot**
Web Site:	**www.roshambofarms.com**
Design:	**Calyx Design**
Designer's Web Site:	**www.calyxdesign.com**

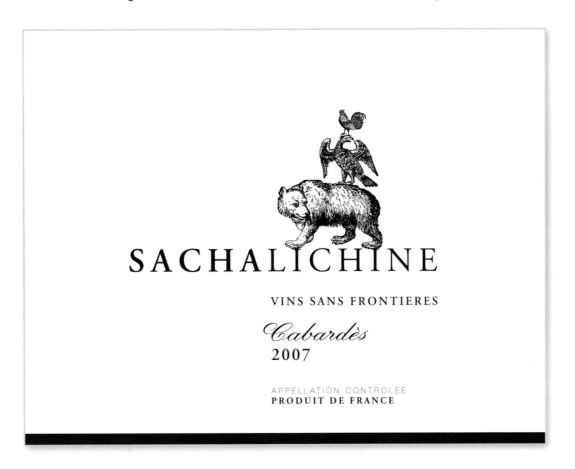

Sacha Alexis Lichine is a winemaker who knows no borders.

Born in Margaux, France, to a Russian father—the famed Alexis Lichine—Sacha moved to New York with his mother when he was just a young boy. He attended school on the East Coast and would holiday with his father, who owned two acclaimed properties in Bordeaux, back in France. Winemaking was obviously in his blood. However, despite the legacy of his late father, who was an exceptionally influential and omnipresent figure within the French wine industry, Sacha has done well at creating his own providence, looking outside of Bordeaux to the sunnier parts of France, namely Provence, to fulfill his wine destiny.

Never forgetting his roots or his family's influential wine heritage, however, Sacha's Vins Sans Frontières (or, "wines without borders") label pays homage to this cosmopolitan winemaker's background and the influence it has made on his international wine vision. Living in Chicago when not in Provence or Bordeaux, Sacha is definitely a man of the world, with projects even in the southern hemisphere. As such, the bear on the label salutes his Russian roots, the American eagle, what he considers representative of his nationality, and the rooster, a symbol of his passion for France—all experiences that are blended together in his past, present, and future and experienced through his wines without borders.

SACHA LICHINE

Appellation:	**Cabardès**
Region:	**Languedoc-Roussillon**
Country of Origin:	**France**
Type of Wine:	**Red Blend**
Web Site:	**www.sachalichine.com**
Design:	**Design Bridge**
Designer's Web Site:	**www.designbridge.com**

SCARECROW WINE

[CALIFORNIA ✺ UNITED STATES]

After a celebrated career as a commercial photographer, beginning with the sale of his first photograph at the tender age of fifteen and spanning upwards of two decades, Bret Lopez decidedly left life as a globe-trotting professional photographer to establish his own sense of place and put down some roots. He remembered with nostalgia that there truly was "no place like home" when visiting his late grandfather, J. J. Cohn, at his summer home during the holidays as a young boy. Not wanting to lose the family vista, Grandpa Joe summoned him home once again, but this time as a grown man.

The J. J. Cohn Estate, however, wasn't just any old vineyard in Rutherford. Rather, it was a "patch of earth" with a famously fabled past. Convinced by his neighbor, John Daniel Jr., to plant 80 acres of Cabernet vines that he promised to purchase, Cohn went ahead and planted the vines. His grapes were subsequently pinnacle to Daniel's famed Inglenook wines of the post-war era and, more recently, have been used in the acclaimed wines of Opus One, Niebaum-Coppola, Duckhorn, Insignia, and Etude.

It wasn't just the grapes that made the estate special though. It was actually J. J. Cohn himself, a self-made film icon highly instrumental in the making of some of the most beloved family film classics of Hollywood's golden age, such as *Ben-Hur*, *Gigi*, *Mutiny on the Bounty*, and most of all, an all-time favorite to this day, *The Wizard of Oz*, a screen adaptation of L. Frank Baum's novel. Of course, featured prominently in the film was the endearing Scarecrow, who accompanies Dorothy on her way to the Emerald City in the hopes of seeking out a brain. The Scarecrow, however, was actually the smartest of Dorothy's travel companions and the one who, in the end, is entrusted with the ruling of the Emerald City in the Wizard of Oz's absence.

It is the icon of this optimistic, spirited, charming character who's "clever as a gizzard" that is truly loved internationally that honors the late J. J. Cohn. His remarkable life has certainly left a legacy somewhere over the rainbow for grandson Bret Lopez, his longtime partner and muse Mimi De Blasio, and all those involved in continuing his passionate pursuit of excellence now seen in the craftsmanship of Scarecrow Wine.

SCARECROW WINE

Appellation:	**Rutherford**
State:	**California**
Country of Origin:	**United States**
Type of Wine:	**Cabernet Sauvignon**
Web Site:	**www.scarecrowwine.com**
Design:	**Vanderbyl Designs**
Designer's Web Site:	**www.vanderbyldesign.com**

SCARPETTA WINE
[FRIULI-VENEZIA GIULIA ∾ ITALY]

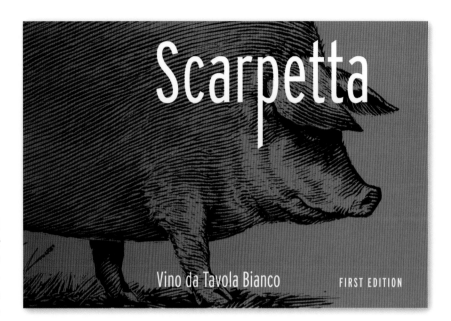

Call it timing, call it luck, call it happenstance. Whatever it was, the paths of Bobby Stuckey and Lachlan Mackinnon-Patterson crossed while both were employed in 2001 at the world-renowned The French Laundry in Yountville, California. Likewise, in a chance meeting Stuckey met Richard Betts while Betts was completing a master's in geology and Stuckey was then employed at Brix in Flagstaff, Arizona. Though fortune may have introduced the men, food and wine would grow their friendships and, eventually, a partnership in the business of gastronomic pleasure.

Stuckey and Mackinnon-Patterson were first to travel to and develop an intimate love affair with the Friuli-Venezia Giulia region in Italy. So deep was this affection and appreciation that the pair launched Frasca Food and Wine in Boulder, Colorado, a celebration of Friuli's favored style of fare, rich in culinary tradition. Here, the two decorated James Beard Foundation Award winners would shine with Stuckey, master sommelier, as wine director and Mackinnon-Patterson as chef. Eventually, Betts, having made a career in wine as a master sommelier himself, was convinced to travel with them to experience Friuli's culinary crossroads firsthand. This geographical intersection has provided the foods of Friuli with a unique combination of Italian, Austrian, Hungarian, Slovenian, and Croatian influences. Though Viennese sausages, goulash, and even strudel can be found in the region, it is Friuli's own unique gastronomy and almost innate understanding of the symbiotic relationship between food and wine that are the most noteworthy.

Prosciutto di Parma holds nothing above one of Friuli's "designated" delights. With the government-enforced regulations on the production of prosciutto di San Daniele, it is assured that the highest level of quality is met for every piece of prosciutto, big or small. Prosciutto is just the beginning of the miracle of meats in Friuli. Sausages, pancetta, musetto—no piece of succulent pork is squandered. Of course, there are also the wines. Stuckey may even venture to say that it is in Friuli that you will find the greatest white wine region in all of Italy.

Given the strength of their relationships with the locals and their fondness of both the food and wine of the region, it seemed only fitting to have a Friulian-styled wine, made specifically to be shared back home at Frasca, thus almost enabling their patrons a culinary venture without the boarding fare. Welcome Scarpetta Wine. "Scarpetta" comes from the traditional Italian phrase *fare la scarpetta*, meaning that something tastes so lovely that any scraps are mopped off the plate with bread. The only thing that could possibly be put on the label was the most revered delicacy of Friuli, the beloved pig, and the perfect match for the wine. Scarpetta wine, good to the last taste—from the plate and the glass.

SCARPETTA WINE

Appellation:	**Prepotto (Non-Designated Appellation)**
Region:	**Friuli-Venezia Giulia**
Country of Origin:	**Italy**
Type of Wine:	**White**
Web Site:	**www.scarpettawine.com**
Design:	**Miko McGinty**
Designer's Web Site:	**www.mikomcginty.com**
Art:	**Antar Dayal**
Artist's Web Site:	**www.dayalstudio.com**

THE SCHOLIUM PROJECT
[CALIFORNIA ✎ UNITED STATES]

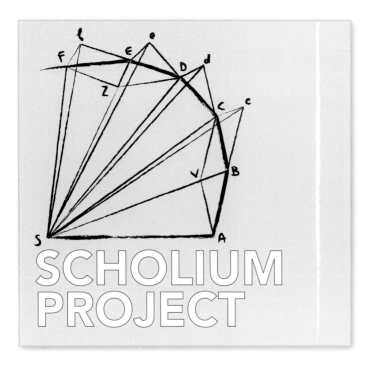

Abe Schoener came to wine academically, but not through conventional study. It was actually while on sabbatical from teaching that this scholar of Ancient Greek philosophy found his passion for winemaking. With no formal scholarship (in the study of grape growing and winemaking, that is), the ever-inquisitive Schoener first got his hands dirty through an internship at Stag's Leap Wine Cellars. Thereafter, trading tutelage for tutelage, Schoener home-schooled winemaker John Kongsgaard's son in exchange for teachings on the study of winemaking. Schoener proved to be a fabulous teacher and a great student himself. After time spent as Kongsgaard's successor as winemaker at Luna Vineyards, he decided it was time to begin his own wine project, Scholium.

Scholium, a derivative from the Greek *scholion*, which shares the same root as "school" and "scholarship," is said by Schoener to be a modest study that has been undertaken as a pedagogic activity for the pure sake of learning and understanding. Schoener says that wine has the remarkable ability to be a portable study of soil, vineyard, vintage, and fermentation. Philosophically, he says that his study revolves around the activity of winemaking, which includes a subset of activities including everything from analyzing and attending to the vineyard and vines, choosing when to pick the grapes, and experimenting with fermentation practices. When the wines are sent out into the world of the unknown, they then set about a second set of possible activities, independent of the winemaking that can be both experiential and experimental in nature. Schoener says that "beyond the essential bacchic activities that almost any wine can inspire," his aim is that his wines will rouse the feeling of complexity, incite a sense of decay, decomposition, and transformation and, ultimately, invite a sense of happiness and joy.

As philosophy is a study of discovery, so is Schoener's The Scholium Project. Like academia, it is conjectural and looks beyond convention in its wisdom of winemaking—which, like anything based on the unknown, is often criticized. Regardless of the potentiality for critique, like a true academic maverick is driven to investigation and to continue forging new ideas, Schoener accepts his errs and celebrates his successes that are at the core of his journey in discovering great wines.

His wine label remembers the advent of his winemaking study spent tutoring Kongsgaard's son, Alex. Though the two spent time studying a wide variety of subject matter, together they spent a year examining Newton with the end result being Alex's ability to articulate the principals of the very diagram that graces Schoener's wine label, the first proposition of Newton's *Principia*. Over their time spent together, Schoener saw the young scholar come full circle starting off as a student, becoming a friend, evolving into an apprentice of sorts and, eventually, transitioning into a teacher himself in Schoener's pursuit of winemaking study.

THE SCHOLIUM PROJECT

Appellation:	**Sonoma Mountain**
State:	**California**
Country of Origin:	**United States**
Type of Wine:	**Sauvignon Blanc**
Web Site:	**www.scholiumwines.com**
Design:	**Abe Schoener**

SETANTA WINES

[SOUTH AUSTRALIA ✦ AUSTRALIA]

When winemakers Sheilagh and Tony Sullivan set out to produce their first vintage in 2001, the question, "What's in a name?" was called into play. Sheilagh, a first-generation Aussie of Irish descent, and her husband Tony, a second-generation Kiwi (also of Irish descent) knew that their ties to Ireland were a very strong commonality that provided a rich sense of place for both of the partners.

Sheilagh grew up in a household where their Irish heritage was part of everyday life and fondly remembers her late mother recounting tales of the mighty Irish folk hero Cúchulain to her as a young girl. When the time came to name the Sullivan wines, it was intuitive to gravitate to something that not only was traditionally Irish, but tied to her mother as well. The name "Sétanta" is actually the given name of Cúchulain as a child, before he set out to become revered as the "Hound of Ulster" in ancient Ireland. From here, each wine has been attributed to a specific portion of the Cúchulain saga based on its style and character, thus becoming a visual voice for the wine.

As a foundation, the Sullivans chose the honorable name Cúchulain for their own prized hero, Shiraz. As the legend has it, on the night that Sétanta was bestowed his name, Culain the Smith was hosting a tributary evening for the king at his fort. Believing that all his guests had arrived, Culain let his guard dog out to watch over the property while the festivities went on inside. Late for the gathering, a young Sétanta came face to face with the guard dog. As the dog lunged toward him, the young warrior fearlessly fought and slayed the beast. Almost immediately, the doors of the fort opened and a mortified Culain knelt by the beast, dismayed. Having raised this hound on his own, he was pained by the slaughter—and now without a guard for his fort. Ancient prophecy had it that when the hounds of Culain died, so too would the clan of Culain. Without another guard dog to immediately replace him, Culain was distraught at his fate. Sétanta asked if there was no other hound to replace his attacker and Culain said that there was only one pup, a mere ten days old. The young warrior then offered to guard the fort until this pup was mature enough to take over. It was then that he was named and became known amongst warriors, nobles, and commoners as Cú Chulain, or "the Hound of Culain," the boy with the larger-than-life strength and character—which can also be said of Australian Shiraz.

Each of the Setanta wines designates a characteristic tale told through its respective label and offers a visual reminder of the Sullivan family's heritage in a traditional Irish storytelling manner.

SETANTA WINES

Appellation:	**Adelaide Hills**
State:	**South Australia**
Country of Origin:	**Australia**
Type of Wine:	**Shiraz**
Web Site:	**www.setantawines.com.au**
Art:	**Anelia Pavlova**
Artist's Web Site:	**www.aneliapavlova.net**

SIBLING RIVALRY WINE

[ONTARIO ❧ CANADA]

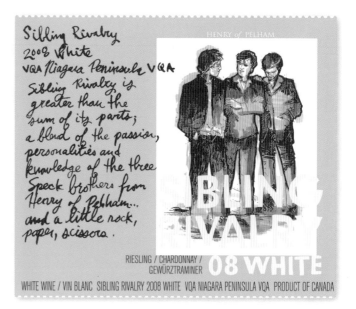

Growing up in a household with three brothers might be a bit chaotic at times. And there certainly was nothing different in the Speck household. But despite the sibling rivalry and brotherly competition, the three boys got on well enough to help their parents plant the family's first plot of vineyard land in 1982 while they were just young lads aged 16, 13, and 8 years old, respectively. They called these weekends and summer holidays of fruitful labor "Camp Farm."

After pulling up their ancestors' original vineyards planted a century and a half earlier, the boys, together with their friends, planted the initial 65 acres of what is now the Speck family's Henry of Pelham Estate over a few summers. An additional 100 acres would be planted afterwards. Daniel Speck says that despite the grueling work, it was paradise for the brothers.

Eventually, the time came for the brothers to set off to university—each attending St. John's College in Annapolis, Maryland, to study philosophy and science. They all had plans for a future that involved professions off of the vineyard since they had each done their due diligence getting the farm up and running—it was time to expand each of their respective horizons.

During the last year of eldest brother Paul's studies (and the first year of vintage for the family), Mr. Speck unfortunately fell ill. Paul agreed to put his studies on hold for a year to return to the farm in order to ensure the smooth operation of the winery and a successful first vintage. Before he knew it, that one year turned into four, and the second brother in line, Matt, made the same pledge. Again, years went by and it was time for the youngest of the brothers to graduate. Following in his brothers' footsteps, Daniel decided to help out for one more year on the farm as well. He says that was ten years ago.

So, for the past ten years, the Speck brothers have each worked in different capacities on the vineyard and in the winery. They may not have always seen eye-to-eye, but have found ways to work things out like any siblings. Their good, vigorous conversations and debates seem to steer them to a place that would not have been possible if there was merely one of them going it alone. Each brother has brought a different passion, personality, knowledge, and philosophy to the business, which together has created an inspired partnership through diversity.

Wine labels are part style, part fad; style is forever, while fads fade. Between the two poles, we want to be close to the middle with our new label design. Having said that, we keep a cool sense of style and aesthetically pleasing design in mind with all of our labels. —DANIEL SPECK
Owner, Sibling Rivalry Wine

The sum is greater than the independent parts, or as brother Paul says it best, "What would the Rolling Stones be without Keith Richards?" With this Henry of Pelham Family Estate wine, the Speck brothers feel that everyone has had their way. While it may have taken some serious sibling rivalry to get here, there has also been some serious sibling *revelry* as well. This is what the Sibling Rivalry wine label is all about.

**SIBLING RIVALRY WINE
(HENRY OF PELHAM FAMILY ESTATE)**
Appellation:	**Short Hills Bench**
Province:	**Ontario**
Country of Origin:	**Canada**
Type of Wine:	**Riesling, Chardonnay, and Gewürztraminer Blend**
Web Site:	**www.siblingrivalrywine.ca**
Design:	**Insite Design**
Designer's Web Site:	**www.insitedesign.ca**

SIDE JOB CELLARS

[CALIFORNIA ❧ UNITED STATES]

STEFANI VINEYARD
Dry Creek Valley
Zinfandel
2006

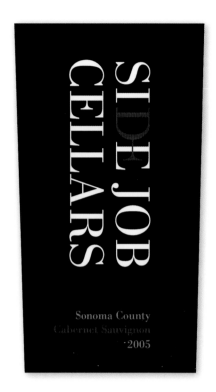

Sonoma County
Cabernet Sauvignon
·2005

Jeff Lubin drives a Mazda, but he didn't used to. Once, he blazed through the Californian countryside in his pride and joy, a 1999 C5 Corvette coupe. "Once," being the operative word.

Jeff climbed his way up in the wine world earning his merits in the "school of hard knocks," as he says. He began on the floor of one of the premium wine shops in Beverly Hills. This initiated a prosperous path from wine retailer to wholesaler, then from supplier to sales manager. Eventually, he was awarded a wine marketer's dream job at Ravenswood Winery.

During Jeff's twenty-fifth year in the industry, he decided that after spending his entire career supporting other people's brands, it was time to package up his twenty-five years of experience and try his hand at something of his own. Not wanting to throw caution to the wine, he decided to throw in the keys to his prized possession instead—his C5 Corvette. Ouch.

While this was a very sad day in the Lubin household (though maybe just for Jeff), the parting of his precious car allowed him to start SideJob Cellars—on the side of his full-time job—with the high hopes that one day, he could make a go of it on a full-time basis and still keep food on the family table, while living out his dream.

Now a few vintages in with SideJob, Jeff has managed to do just that. While he says it has most definitely been worth the sacrifice, it doesn't mean that he still doesn't think of his old beauty. He still looks for her around the neighborhood, even just to take her for just one last spin. As an homage, his wine labels are graced with a C5 keychain, the keys that enabled Lubin to turn his daydream into his dream job.

	SIDEJOB CELLARS	
Appellation:	**Dry Creek Valley**	
State:	**California**	
Country of Origin:	**United States**	
Type of Wine:	**Zinfandel**	
Web Site:	**www.sidejobcellars.com**	
Design:	**Thermostat**	
Designer's Web Site:	**www.youaregettingwarmer.com**	

	SIDEJOB CELLARS	
Appellation:	**Sonoma County**	
	(Non-Designated Appellation)	
State:	**California**	
Country of Origin:	**United States**	
Type of Wine:	**Cabernet Sauvignon**	
Web Site:	**www.sidejobcellars.com**	
Design:	**Thermostat**	
Designer's Web Site:	**www.youaregettingwarmer.com**	

SINE QUA NON

Amongst the thousands of wine labels that are created each year, there are few that can rival those that grace the bottles of Sine Qua Non's acclaimed wines. Like his highly coveted wines, each of Manfred Krankl's labels is a sought-after, handcrafted masterpiece, created by the winemaker himself. The intimate hands-on approach to both his winemaking and the identity Krankl bestows upon each of his wines is a true mark of an artist.

Despite the cult status of Krankl's wines, he says that winemaking has never defined him as an individual and that he has many other interests that contribute to who he is—namely music, motorcycles, art, his children, and the love of his life, Elaine. It is obvious that his deep affection for Elaine, along with the importance of his family and friends, greatly influences his inspired wine label artwork, which more often than not includes intimate, hidden messages to his muse. Further, his art also commemorates cherished experiences and whimsical tales that are tied thoughtfully to each individual wine that the label fronts.

Given Krankl's belief that each wine deserves its own identity, much like the naming of a child, each original hand-etched piece of artwork is never duplicated. While some may have once criticized Krankl for changing his label design for each wine born anew with each vintage, those same people may now be thinking again and saluting him as a savvy marketer. The reality is, however, that marketing wasn't really the original objective. Krankl makes wines the way he likes, and packages them the way he likes—with pure heart. And because words written by no one other than Krankl himself can do the stories behind them justice, it is best to leave it that Krankl's wines and labels literally are *sine qua non*—something utterly indispensable.

SINE QUA NON	
Appellation:	**Non-Designated Appellation**
State:	**California**
Country of Origin:	**United States**
Type of Wine:	**Grenache**
Art:	**Manfred Krankl**

SINE QUA NON	
Appellation:	**Non-Designated Appellation**
State:	**California**
Country of Origin:	**United States**
Type of Wine:	**Roussanne**
Art:	**Manfred Krankl**

SINE QUA NON

Appellation:	**Non-Designated Appellation**
State:	**California**
Country of Origin:	**United States**
Type of Wine:	**Grenache**
Art:	**Manfred Krankl**

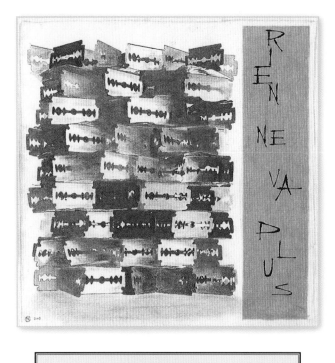

SINE QUA NON

Appellation:	**Non-Designated Appellation**
State:	**California**
Country of Origin:	**United States**
Type of Wine:	**Roussanne**
Art:	**Manfred Krankl**

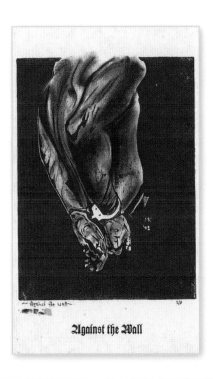

SINE QUA NON

Appellation:	**Non-Designated Appellation**
State:	**California**
Country of Origin:	**United States**
Type of Wine:	**Syrah**
Art:	**Manfred Krankl**

SINE QUA NON

Appellation:	**Non-Designated Appellation**
State:	**California**
Country of Origin:	**United States**
Type of Wine:	**Grenache**
Art:	**Manfred Krankl**

SLEIGHT OF HAND CELLARS

[WASHINGTON ❧ UNITED STATES]

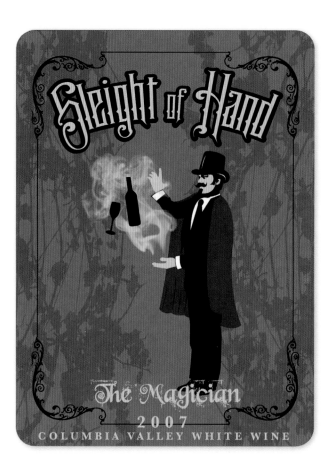

Sleight of Hand Cellars came about at the hand of little magic—the coincidence of three people being at the same place, at the same time, and sharing the same passion.

After a chance meeting, Jerry and Sandy Solomon, two wine enthusiasts, fell under the deft spell and charisma of winemaker Trey Busch. Like magic, the three kindred spirits were almost immediately collaborating to create wine in their shared vision.

The name of their small but crafty winery, Sleight of Hand Cellars, was inspired not only by the alchemy between the newly formed threesome and the spellbinding wines, but also an appreciation for vintage magic posters and Pearl Jam's song of the same name that spoke personally to Busch.

The labels were designed with true magic in mind by Phelyx Hopkins, a professional magician, mentalist, illusionist and . . . graphic designer. "Sleight of hand" is a term for techniques of trickery used by magicians to beguile an audience, and often takes years to master. Comparable to winemaking in many ways, this "sleight of hand" is dexterous rather than deceptive, and crafty rather than cunning. As the labels suggest, these are purely magical wines.

SLEIGHT OF HAND CELLARS	
Appellation:	**Walla Walla Valley**
State:	**Washington**
Country of Origin:	**United States**
Type of Wine:	**Rosé**
Web Site:	**www.sofhcellars.com**
Design:	**Phelyx Hopkins**
Designer's Web Site:	**www.phelyx.com**

SLEIGHT OF HAND CELLARS	
Appellation:	**Columbia Valley**
State:	**Washington**
Country of Origin:	**United States**
Type of Wine:	**Gewürztraminer**
Web Site:	**www.sofhcellars.com**
Design:	**Power Slide Design Co.**
Designer's Web Site:	**www.powerslidedesign.com**

"Slow living" is by no means a new premise. While the Slow Movement and benefits of this lifestyle philosophy have created recent awareness, the same message has actually been around since the time of Aesop. Aesop is said to have been the first source of the tortoise and the hare fable, which provided a lesson that "the slow but steady wins the race." However, today, with technology providing the means to increase the quantity of actions and reactions on a daily basis at the expense of quality, it is rare that we ever stop to smell the roses. (Unless, of course you are a florist.)

On the surface for many, the concept of "slow living" might mean that everything should be done simply at a slower pace. The reality is, however, that things that are meant to be done quickly are, in fact, done quickly. And further, it does not reject progress of advancements by any means. At the center of the Slow Movement philosophy are really two words: mindfulness and balance. This means taking the time to live a thoughtful and purposeful life, and making quality-based decisions rather than quantity-based decisions, as they so often present themselves in multiple aspects of life.

Slowine is a collaborative project initiated by Paul Cluver along with a collection of vineyards that surround the towering Groenland Mountain. Together, this collective shares its expertise, grapes, and an appreciation for slow living. The region is also the site of South Africa's first wine and biodiversity project—the Green Mountain Eco Route. The collaboration, rather than being formulaic, is an exploration and respect of diversity and the possibilities it presents. Slowine embraces the philosophies of slow living, including using only regional grapes and allowing the fruit to express itself most naturally without manipulation, to create a forced flavor profile. Slowine also believes in keeping the wine as accessible as possible to ensure that a wide population can afford to enjoy it—with food, with friends, and at whatever the pace may be.

Inspired by what is often associated with slow, Slowine uses an image of Groenland Mountain's indigenous tortoise on its label as a reminder of and invitation for everyone to stop and take time out to slow down, so you don't miss out on life.

**SLOWINE
(VILLIERSDORP COOPERATIVE)**
Appellation:	**Overberg**
Province:	**Western Cape**
Country of Origin:	**South Africa**
Type of Wine:	**Cabernet Sauvignon**
Web Site:	**www.slowine.co.za**
Design:	**Anthony Lane Design and Brimstone Design**
Designer's Web Site:	**www.anthonylane.co.za and www.brimstonedesign.com**

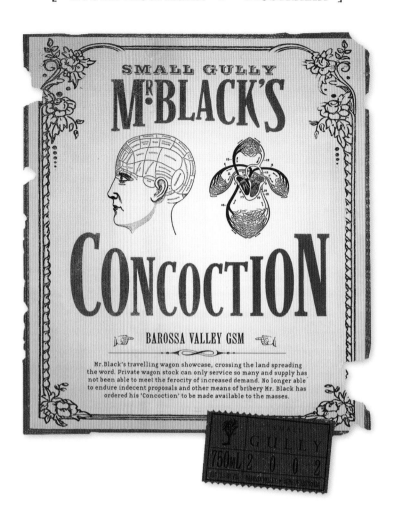

The road to Stephen Black's success in the wine industry was not one achieved overnight. In fact, it was over twenty years in the making, starting when he was just a young man finishing high school and entering university. Despite his father's desire for him to study geology, Stephen gravitated towards becoming a chemist in the wine industry. He says that he was good at math, chemistry, and physics and not quite certain why he was bitten by the wine bug at that time. Wanting to ensure that he was well prepared for the industry upon graduation, Stephen wrote to some of the most well-known wineries in Australia to determine what courses he should be enrolling in. Their response: chemical engineering and applied chemistry was the way to go. Five years later, degree in hand, an eager Stephen Black wrote to the very wineries that had influenced his schooling to announce his academic success and eagerness to begin his new career. Unfortunately at that time, an enthusiastic response was not as forthcoming as it had previously been. He was informed that the industry had taken a downward turn and was halting hiring.

Coincidently, at the same time, Stephen received a phone call from one of his lecturers informing him of a job with F. H. Faulding, an Australian pharmaceuticals company. While it wasn't what he had originally intended, he took the offer as a developmental chemist and engineer. For seventeen years, Stephen worked on developing three very successful antibiotic medications and eventually worked his way (as Stephen puts it) "from back to boffan" to being in charge of Faulding's manufacturing division and later,

SMALL GULLY	
Appellation:	**Barossa Valley**
State:	**South Australia**
Country of Origin:	**Australia**
Type of Wine:	**Grenache, Shiraz, and Mourvèdre Blend**
Web Site:	**www.smallgullywines.com.au**
Design:	**Mash**
Designer's Web Site:	**www.mashdesign.com.au**

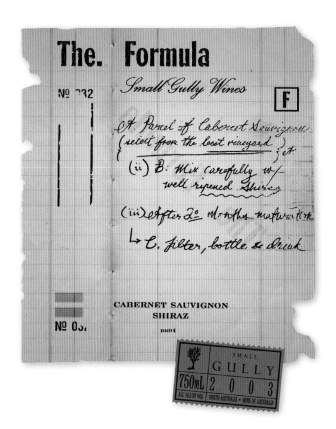
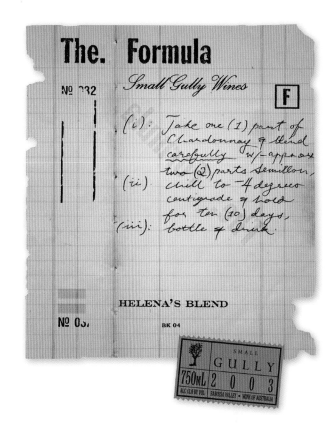

SMALL GULLY

Appellation:	**Clare Valley/Barossa Valley**
State:	**South Australia**
Country of Origin:	**Australia**
Type of Wine:	**Cabernet Sauvignon and Shiraz Blend**
Web Site:	**www.smallgullywines.com.au**
Design:	**Mash**
Designer's Web Site:	**www.mashdesign.com.au**

SMALL GULLY

Appellation:	**Barossa Valley**
State:	**South Australia**
Country of Origin:	**Australia**
Type of Wine:	**Sémillon and Chardonnay Blend**
Web Site:	**www.smallgullywines.com.au**
Design:	**Mash**
Designer's Web Site:	**www.mashdesign.com.au**

was promoted to Scientific Affairs manager.

Despite this change in career direction, Stephen didn't throw wine completely to the wayside. Instead, he indulged his curiosities with tasting courses and by reading about a variety of wine-related topics, including the process of making wine. In 1992, when Faulding and Stephen decided to part ways, he looked up that old list of wineries instead of continuing his career in pharmaceuticals. Despite being told by many that, at forty-two, he was too old to make a start in wine, his persistence paid off—proof that forty is the new thirty!

In 2000, with eight vintages under his belt and a postgraduate certificate from the University of Adelaide on his wall, Stephen began making wine under the Small Gully label with two partners, Robert Brader and Darren Zimmermann. The labels give a connection between Stephen's two professional lives, both of which provide a remedy of sorts. The wines were once to be called "Prescription" and "Mr. Black's Remedy," but Stephen was told politely by the powers that be that the only people that could make a connection between wine and health was the U.S. government—which they routinely did with a Surgeon General's Warning on the back label! A label resembling a doctor's notepad with a drug store and snake oil medicinal mixture were kept, but the names changed to Formula and Mr. Black's Concoction. The remedy that is provided inside the bottle works no matter what they're called or what they are called on to remedy!

> **Just as we form opinions of people on the whim of a first impression, so we often judge what's on the inside by what's on the outside. Manipulating this first impression is what good packaging is all about.**
>
> —Dom Roberts
> Creative Director, Mash

When friends Michael Cobb and Jeff Munsey made their first wine together, they hadn't really thought of actually naming it. Stuck, a scene from one of their mutually favorite movies, *Made*, came to mind. The scene was one that had incited much laughter and referred to the Cardiff Giant—a fabulous name, but neither had any idea what this giant was all about.

As it turns out, the friends had happened upon one of the greatest hoaxes in American history. The "giant" was a 10-foot-tall petrified man, who was "unearthed" on October 16, 1869, in Cardiff, New York, by well diggers working behind the barn of one William Newell. Upon the "discovery" of this mummified and monstrous man, Newell and his cousin, George Hull, set up a tent and exhibited his giant for twenty-five cents a viewing. Capitalizing on the immediate interest, Newell increased admission to fifty cents two days later. People came from far and wide to see the mysterious phenomenon. Despite the fact that some archaeological academics denounced the legitimacy of the artifact, George Hull was an entrepreneur and eventually sold his "share" of the sideshow to an interested syndicate for the whopping amount of $37,500. The syndicate, headed by David Hannum, then took the exhibition to Syracuse, New York.

Of course, Hull was the instigator of this entire hoax, which had stemmed from a disagreement between himself (an atheist) and a fundamentalist minister named Mr. Turk, regarding a passage in Genesis 6:4, suggesting that giants once inhabited the earth. Perhaps owing to various claims of petrified people at that time, Hull took it upon himself to hire a German stonecutter, whom he swore to secrecy, to shape a 10-foot block of gypsum into the form of a man. This fraudulent dummy was then buried in his cousin's backyard for a year, at which point Hull then hired two men to dig a well and "inadvertently" unearth the "giant."

In the end, the entire hoax blew up when P. T. Barnum offered to lease the giant from the syndicate for three months at an exorbitant amount of money and was flatly turned down. Outraged, he commissioned a secret duplicate to be made for him to display in New York, forging the original giant. In turn, the syndicate sued Barnum for calling their giant a fake and eventually both petrified imposters were deemed shams in court.

So what does all this have to do with two friends making wine together? The Cardiff Giant is not only a testament to a shared sense of humor, but also a symbol of two small winemakers alone in this massive, serious wine industry, just trying to make a go at it. At times, it all feels like one big joke believing they will be able to survive doing what they love, but with an authentic passion to make great wines for a new generation of wine drinkers and the ability to have fun along the way, the only giant hoax will be the one from Cardiff.

SORT THIS OUT CELLARS	
Appellation:	**Non-Designated Appellation**
State:	**California**
Country of Origin:	**United States**
Type of Wine:	**Sangiovese and Cabernet Sauvignon Blend**
Web Site:	**www.sortthisoutcellars.com**
Design:	**Internal**

SOUTHBROOK VINEYARDS

[ONTARIO ✥ CANADA]

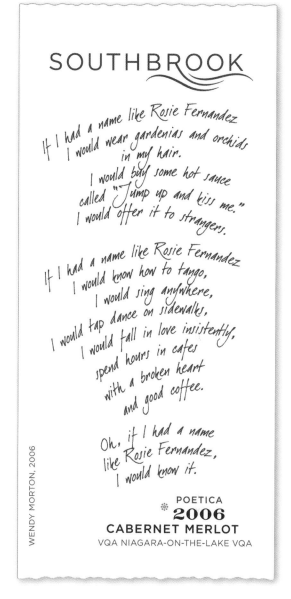

SOUTHBROOK

If I had a name like Rosie Fernandez
I would wear gardenias and orchids
in my hair.
I would buy some hot sauce
called "Jump up and kiss me."
I would offer it to strangers.

If I had a name like Rosie Fernandez
I would know how to tango,
I would sing anywhere,
I would tap dance on sidewalks,
I would fall in love insistently,
spend hours in cafes
with a broken heart
and good coffee.

Oh, if I had a name
like Rosie Fernandez,
I would know it.

WENDY MORTON, 2006

❋ POETICA
2006
CABERNET MERLOT
VQA NIAGARA-ON-THE-LAKE VQA

By definition, poetry (though traditionally written verse) can also represent any composition that (though not in verse) is characterized by great beauty of expression and an intensely imaginative interpretation that exudes poetic qualities, however manifested, of a subject matter. Poetic qualities are rhythmical compositions inciting pleasure through a written art form using beautiful and imaginative thoughts. Winemaking, a creative composition using natural elements in place of written verse, can be considered an example of poetry of the earth.

Southbrook Vineyards is the love story dreamt of and realized by Bill and Marilyn Redelmeier. According to their mantra, their primary values include "a deep connection to the earth—and to the senses." The poetic likenesses found between crafting written prose (with a scrupulous selection of artful words) and meticulous winemaking (using careful respect for the vine and the earth) result in a liquid art with a most sensuous character.

Conducting an extensive study of Canadian poetry with themes of modern love, connectedness to the earth, and speaking to the sublime, graphic designer Laura Willis chose a selection that "spoke" to her about Southbrook's core values and felt right as part of the overall experience in sharing a bottle of delectable wine. The response from the poets themselves was overwhelmingly enthusiastic, and the end result is the Southbrook Vineyards Poetica series of limited edition wines that showcase the parallels between the art of words and the art of wine together as a combined experience of the senses.

It's a complicated language that a wine label must speak. It exists within a rich world of history, family, geography, marketing, and art. The creator of the label must learn this language, too, to know where to begin. But in the end, the creator must also be a good listener, for the wine label must be given the opportunity to speak and express its own personality. —LAURA WILLS
Founder and Creative Director,
Messenger

SOUTHBROOK VINEYARDS

Appellation:	**Niagara-on-the-Lake**
Province:	**Ontario**
Country of Origin:	**Canada**
Type of Wine:	**Cabernet Sauvignon and Merlot Blend**
Web Site:	**www.southbrook.com**
Design:	**Messenger**
Designer's Web Site:	**www.mssngr.com**

SOUTH COAST WINERY

[CALIFORNIA ❧ UNITED STATES]

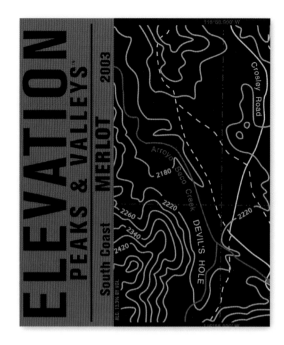

The South Coast Winery Elevation series highlights the diversity of geographic and geologic areas where the winery's grapes have been sourced. Using illustrative topographic maps, the bottle art graphically indicates the unique microclimates that influence the vineyards—which range from 1,200 feet in the Temecula Valley vineyards to 2,400 feet at the highest point of the Wild Horse Peak Mountain vineyards—the wines are truly from a higher plane.

But life wasn't always a walk in the clouds for South Coast Winery's owner, Jim Carter, who has definitely seen his own peaks and valleys of life over the years. Carter is a self-made developer, entrepreneur, and now, vintner. He came from humble beginnings in Ohio where he was taught the value of a quarter when he began work at the tender age of twelve. Working for his father at the time, the young Carter's goals were set high, with a promise of a raise of a quarter each time he should meet them. With ambition and an innate work ethic on his side, Carter consistently met his targets and approached his father for the cumulative $1 raise he had earned. His father, in turn, suggested that young Jim seek employment elsewhere in order to continue building his achievements, which he did.

By the age of sixteen, Jim had earned himself the reputation of a solid builder. Opportunity arose through the invitation of his father to work in California with the intention of spending six months in California and six months back home. But when the warm climate of California offered the opportunity to build 365 days a year, Jim decided to stay and open his own company.

Within a year, he had successfully built 2,500 homes. As years passed, Carter prospered and continued to invest in new ventures, building more developments and reinvesting into apartment complexes, shopping centers, a bank, a 260-acre tree farm, and a 400-acre piece of land. Then, in a turn of events, life as he knew it changed drastically for the worse with the savings and loan disaster of the 1990s. This devastating event would cause Jim to struggle to make ends meet and just scrape by to keep a roof over his family's head. Compounding all of his financial and asset losses, Jim also lost his beloved first wife tragically and unexpectedly.

Many people at this point would have packed it in and called it quits, but the ever-tenacious Jim Carter chose instead to be a survivor and keep fighting. It was when he least expected any luck was on his side that simply watching the movie *A Walk in the Clouds* triggered an epiphany that would drastically alter the course of Carter's life from then onwards.

According to Jim, he had an instant association with the movie's storyline about a thriving vineyard set in a gorgeous mountain valley. This backdrop distinctly resembled the only thing that he had not lost during the tumultuous financial times: his 400-acre parcel of land, which sits in the cradle of the Santa Rosa Plateau's Palomar Mountain. Using all of his determination, and every ounce of soul he had left coursing through his veins, he focused on turning this land into a vineyard. That was in 1995. Now, back on the high plane of life, South Coast Winery is thriving. The Elevation wine labels are a true testament that in order to get to life's elevated peaks, sometimes you have to make it through the lower valleys first.

SOUTH COAST WINERY

Appellation:	**South Coast**
State:	**California**
Country of Origin:	**United States**
Type of Wine:	**Merlot**
Web Site:	**www.wineresort.com**
Design:	**Chuck Williams (Electro Arts) and Jon McPherson**

THE SPANISH QUARTER
[SPAIN]

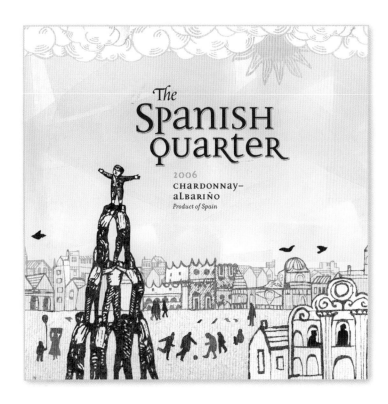

From cosmopolitan cities to sleepy villages, the world over has built itself around a central square. The squares vary in size, architecture, and style; some are dotted with residences, gardens, restaurants, and cafés; and some play host to open-air markets, while others conduct weekly religious ceremonies. No matter what the features, the main objective is the same—squares are public arenas for gathering. Every square has its own history, personality, and attributes that make it unique to the neighborhood, the town, the city, and the country.

Spain is known to have some of the most beautiful town squares in the world. They are always bustling with energy and provide a true sense of Spanish culture. People young and old gather regularly for moments big and small as part of Spanish tradition. Whether it's to share a ubiquitous *café con leche* with a friend while catching up on local gossip, or enjoying tapas and a glass of Albariño after a long day, or just enjoying a *siesta* in the sun while the world goes by, the Spanish plaza is the place to do it.

No matter what, where, or when, gathering in the square is certainly a part of Spanish life. Visitors are able to get a sense of true Spanish culture, including being mesmerized in Barcelona's Plaza St. Jaume where people can not only by awed by the fourteenth-century city hall, Catalonia's capitol building, and the statue of St. Jaume, the conqueror of Mallorca, but where during *festa*, the famous *castellers* build human towers up to nine stories tall. Or, in Plaza del Portal de la Pau, where climbing to the top of the Columbus Monument (built in 1888) at the end of La Rambla will give you a panoramic view of the city before promenading the most famous boulevard in Barcelona.

Of course, if you can't make it physically to these famous squares, The Spanish Quarter labels produced by Grupo Codorníu offer a glimpse without delay. For now, anywhere you are, the time-honored traditions of the vibrant Spanish plaza can be celebrated with free flowing wine, plentiful food, and endless music and laughter, but most importantly, where anything serious can always wait until *mañana* . . . just like in any Spanish quarter.

THE SPANISH QUARTER (GRUPO CODORNIU)	
Appellation:	**Non-Designated Appellation**
Country of Origin:	**Spain**
Type of Wine:	**Chardonnay and Albariño Blend**
Web Site:	**www.thespanishquarter.com**
Design:	**Voicebox Creative**
Designer's Web Site:	**www.voiceboxcreative.com**

Spring Valley Vineyard

[Washington ❧ United States]

Though the first vines at Spring Valley Vineyard were planted in 1993, the story of the land on which they are farmed traces back to the mid-1800s when owner Shari Corkrum Derby's grandfather, Uriah Corkrum, began farming wheat.

Uriah's son with wife Catherine, Frederick, was quite a catch and as such, this farmer, who eventually took the helm (or hitch in those days) of the family farm, attracted Nina Lee, a gorgeous vaudeville performer who worked at the Liberty Theater in town. Scheduled to begin touring on the performance circuit, Nina's friend and partner, Elva, took ill and passed away precisely at the time Nina and Frederick met. Nina, surprisingly to everyone who knew her, gave up her aspirations as a performer. The two married and ran the farm together with their thirty-two hitch of mules.

In those days, work began at three in the morning when Frederick would rise and feed the thirty-two mules that accompanied him to work in the field for the day. At five o'clock, breakfast was served and, afterwards, an hour was spent hitching the thirty-two mules. The brawny Frederick would take charge with his four sets of reins and tend to the wheat crops. Together, Frederick and Nina built a flourishing wheat farm while raising a family. Though it was said that Nina Lee would never make a good farmer's wife, when her husband passed away in 1957, Nina continued to run the farm herself for an additional twenty years.

SPRING VALLEY VINEYARD

Appellation:	**Walla Walla Valley**
State:	**Washington**
Country of Origin:	**United States**
Type of Wine:	**Syrah**
Web Site:	**www.springvalleyvineyard.com**
Art:	**Vintage Photograph**

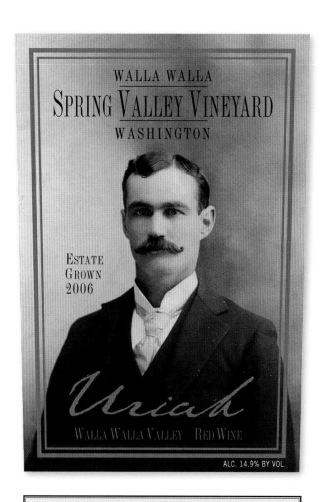

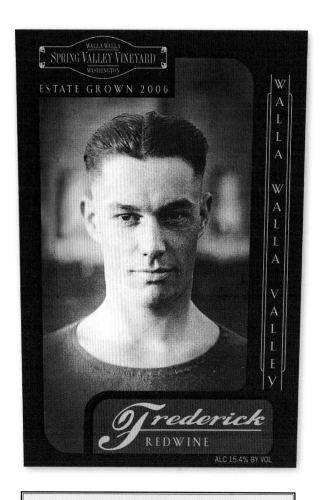

SPRING VALLEY VINEYARD

Appellation:	**Walla Walla Valley**
State:	**Washington**
Country of Origin:	**United States**
Type of Wine:	**Red Blend**
Web Site:	**www.springvalleyvineyard.com**
Art:	**Vintage Photograph**

SPRING VALLEY VINEYARD

Appellation:	**Walla Walla Valley**
State:	**Washington**
Country of Origin:	**United States**
Type of Wine:	**Red Blend**
Web Site:	**www.springvalleyvineyard.com**
Art:	**Vintage Photograph**

Following in her fancy footsteps was daughter Shari Corkrum, who eventually married her elementary school sweetheart, Dean Derby. The two met in 1945, and three years later, Dean would come to work on the farm for Frederick. Bonding over their love of football, which Dean eventually played at the university and professional level, Frederick was pleased when his daughter accepted Dean's marriage proposal at the end of their freshman year in 1954, just shy of a ten-year courtship.

Together, they followed the family's tradition of farming wheat until the price caused them to diversify and plant their first 2 acres of Merlot. These grapes proved to be sought after by area winemakers, and so more of the wheat fields were converted to vineyards. Though the family still farms wheat, they have found their calling in the grapevine. Despite this change, they remember the roots of family and farm with every Spring Valley Vineyard label, paying tribute to those who, along with thirty-two mules and vaudevillian wife, trod the land before them to leave a fertile legacy behind.

STAGE LEFT CELLARS

[CALIFORNIA ✺ UNITED STATES]

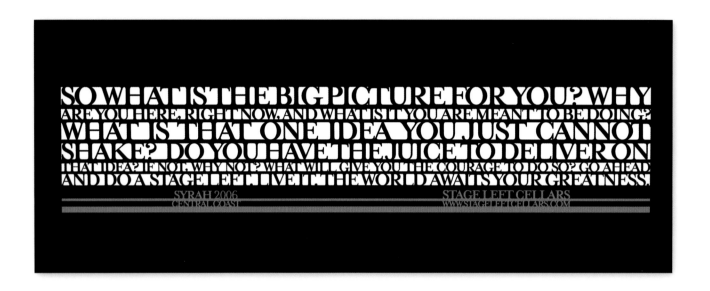

SO WHAT IS THE BIG PICTURE FOR YOU? WHY ARE YOU HERE, RIGHT NOW, AND WHAT IS IT YOU ARE MEANT TO BE DOING? WHAT IS THAT ONE IDEA YOU JUST CANNOT SHAKE? DO YOU HAVE THE JUICE TO DELIVER ON THAT IDEA? IF NOT, WHY NOT? WHAT WILL GIVE YOU THE COURAGE TO DO SO? GO AHEAD AND DO A STAGE LEFT. LIVE IT. THE WORLD AWAITS YOUR GREATNESS!

SYRAH 2006
CENTRAL COAST

STAGE LEFT CELLARS
WWW.STAGELEFTCELLARS.COM

Melinda Doty and Rich Williams were first introduced by a mutual friend on the basis that Rich collected wines and Melinda certainly liked to drink them—a perfect match made by this very insightful friend. The couple found themselves continually gravitating to wine- and food-related holidays and developed their palates together. Melinda and Rich say that these shared experiences opened doors to fresh cultures, new friends, and unfading memories, while also providing an escape from the mundane realities of everyday business life. Often during these juicy gastronomic adventures, the age-old discussion surfaced about what they would do if they weren't bound to their respective, corporate "golden handcuffs." The couple says, "The more we drank, the better starting a winery sounded." Ah, the power of grape juice.

When the couple was honeymooning in New Zealand, they again fed their passion for wine, food, and imagining life without the rat race. This voyage became a true catalyst for change, as the newlyweds became certain that this mutual passion needed to progress beyond the garage. They knew that there would never be a great time or a best time, which led them to the conclusion that the only way would be to dive right in. And dive they did.

Every weekend for three years, the couple made the laborious commute together to pursue this common passion. During the week, they worked their full-time jobs, though loosening the restraints of the corporate clutch little by little until, finally, it was time to bid farewell to their office lives for good. Stage Left Cellars was born.

Many describe wine labels as the finishing touch, the icing on the cake. That's nice, but no matter what, the cake better be damn good!
—MELINDA DOTY
Co-Owner, Stage Left Cellars

Stage Left Cellars is proof that pursuing what really drives you is well worth it. The name, inspired by the catchphrase of the 1970s Hanna-Barbera cartoon character Snagglepuss (who remarked, "Exit, stage left"), is testimony that every backup plan is possible. You just need to let yourself have one and then take the leap.

STAGE LEFT CELLARS

Appellation:	**Central Coast**
State:	**California**
Country of Origin:	**United States**
Type of Wine:	**Syrah**
Web Site:	**www.stageleftcellars.com**
Design:	**Brandever**
Designer's Web Site:	**www.brandever.com**

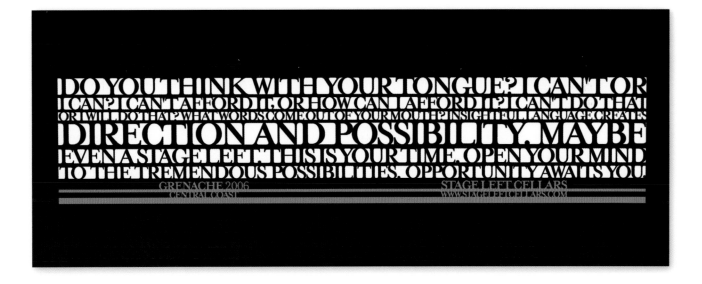

LIFE IS ALL ABOUT BALANCE. TIME FOR FAMILY, FRIENDS, CAREER, AND YOU. IT SOUNDS SIMPLE ENOUGH. HAVE YOU FOUND YOUR BALANCE? ARE THERE TOO MANY BALLS IN THE AIR? WHAT DO YOU NEED TO STOP DOING? WHAT DO YOU NEED TO START DOING? TWO SIMPLE QUESTIONS WITH POWERFUL RESULTS POSSIBLE. IN FACT, ESSENTIAL. GO ON. DO AS STAGE LEFT, FIND THE BALANCE YOU DESERVE.

THE BREADWINNER 2006
CENTRAL COAST

STAGE LEFT CELLARS
WWW.STAGELEFTCELLARS.COM

DO YOU THINK WITH YOUR TONGUE? I CAN, OR I CAN? I CAN'T AFFORD IT, OR HOW CAN I AFFORD IT? I CAN'T DO THAT OR I WILL DO THAT? WHAT WORDS COME OUT OF YOUR MOUTH? INSIGHTFUL LANGUAGE CREATES DIRECTION AND POSSIBILITY. MAYBE EVEN A STAGE LEFT. THIS IS YOUR TIME. OPEN YOUR MIND TO THE TREMENDOUS POSSIBILITIES. OPPORTUNITY AWAITS YOU.

GRENACHE 2006
CENTRAL COAST

STAGE LEFT CELLARS
WWW.STAGELEFTCELLARS.COM

STAGE LEFT CELLARS	
Appellation:	**Central Coast**
State:	**California**
Country of Origin:	**United States**
Type of Wine:	**Red Blend**
Web Site:	**www.stageleftcellars.com**
Design:	**Brandever**
Designer's Web Site:	**www.brandever.com**

STAGE LEFT CELLARS	
Appellation:	**Central Coast**
State:	**California**
Country of Origin:	**United States**
Type of Wine:	**Grenache**
Web Site:	**www.stageleftcellars.com**
Design:	**Brandever**
Designer's Web Site:	**www.brandever.com**

STOLPMAN VINEYARDS
[CALIFORNIA ❧ UNITED STATES]

Roussanne gets limited "airtime" in California, with less than 200 acres planted across the U.S.'s wine capital. Despite being a very unique and complex grape, people don't seem to be as familiar with this big white wine whose robust flavor improves with the length of the growing season.

When planning their vineyard site, the Stolpmans knew that it would be the Rhône varietals that would optimally thrive in their vineyard plots, which witnessed intense temperature fluctuations between exceptionally cool nights to intense heat for a few hours during the day. Knowing that the reds needed to be planted atop their three steep vineyard hills, they decided to optimize the acreage sitting at the bottom between the peaks and plant the Roussanne there, in the narrow strip of land. Due to the unconventional plot space, they opted to plant fifteen long rows instead of a hundred short rows to facilitate harvesting.

Looking down from the red varietal vineyards atop the hills, the plantings of the white Rhône counterparts are eye-catching and distinctly resemble an airplane landing strip. Coincidentally, when the Stolpmans were visiting with a local rancher, Anker Johnson, he just happened to mention that this land, once upon a time, had been just that.

Up until the late 1940s, this particular 4.3-acre parcel had actually been used by the Santa Ynez Flying Club, of which Anker Johnson was an original member. The building of the Santa Ynez Airport, the lack of need for the landing strip, and subsequent development of the land for farming forced the airstrip into retirement.

L'Avion and the retro-style image of the landing strip on the label represents the uniqueness that is Roussanne with its extended growing season and its long and lean vineyard home.

STOLPMAN VINEYARDS	
Appellation:	**Santa Ynez Valley**
State:	**California**
Country of Origin:	**United States**
Type of Wine:	**Rousanne and Viogner Blend**
Web Site:	**www.stolpmanvineyards.com**
Design:	**Heroist**
Designer's Web Site:	**www.heroist.com**

THE STORY WINES

[VICTORIA ❧ AUSTRALIA]

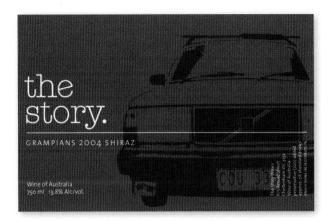

Winemaker Rory Lane had no idea what he was going to call his winemaking project. He had brainstormed a few ideas, but didn't have anything scream out at him. He knew that he needed something that captured the vintage year's story, and that he, like many other winemakers of his generation, did not want to name his wine after a creek, canyon, river, plain, valley, hill, or anything else similar in nature. To do this would be uncharacteristic of what his wines were all about. After all, as Rory says, "The wine is made in a light-industrial area of suburban Melbourne—not exactly the stuff of poetry." However, poetry or not, there was no lack of effort, journey, or story of the wines made year to year. And the difference between the 2004 and 2005 vintage experiences couldn't have been more dissimilar for Rory.

Like a new parent, his firstborn wine was coddled and had the utmost attention paid to it. Not having its own winery yet, this inaugural wine was forced to move around quite frequently, and as a doting parent, so did Rory. He drove thousands of miles: to the vineyard to check the grapes' ripeness; to the winery to craft the wine, manage fermentation, and top up barrels; to two different storage facilities; and then finally to another winery for bottling—all of which were at different locations within Victoria. (And Victoria is a big state.) The image of the car on the label is the story of this voyage of commitment and love of a winemaker's first vintage that will likely be inimitable.

As with anything, the second time around seems like a breeze. Of course, it helps a winemaker when he gets his own winery and no longer has to commute to watch every step of the progress. So, having the confidence of a seasoned parent, Rory set off to Europe for four months immediately after harvest, leaving his baby behind to ferment or perhaps, lament over his desertion. Though he had arranged a "sitter" in order to ensure that the wine was still breathing, he still felt the parental guilt of neglect, though the wine was never far from his mind. This label tells the story of The Orphan and how, perhaps by leaving, he actually made a stronger, more independent (yet still slightly vulnerable) wine.

From Rory's perspective, "the stories that come from making wine each year—be they climactic, be they an accident or coincidence, be they related to the winemaker and what he decides to do differently, or just a feeling for vintage—deserve their own label to tell their story."

And there he had his name: The Story Wines. To be continued.

THE STORY WINES

Appellation:	**Grampians**
State:	**Victoria**
Country of Origin:	**Australia**
Type of Wine:	**Shiraz**
Web Site:	**www.thestorywines.blogspot.com**
Design:	**Madeleine Hoy**

THE STORY WINES

Appellation:	**Grampians**
State:	**Victoria**
Country of Origin:	**Australia**
Type of Wine:	**Shiraz**
Web Site:	**www.thestorywines.blogspot.com**
Design:	**Madeleine Hoy**

StraightJacket Wines

[Western Australia ✖ Australia]

A nnual harvest is an extremely lively time at any vineyard. While it's a fun time, it's also a demanding, exhausting, and physically taxing time. Time is a ticking clock that requires a balance of precision and hard work in conjunction with nature to ensure that the grapes are picked at their prime condition and that the intricacies of the fermentation process are well managed. The only problem is, nature doesn't sleep during harvest. Consequently, it is a time when sleep is rare, sanity is even rarer, emotions are volatile, and people are pushed to the limits. No two harvests are ever the same, though there does seem to be one consistency: things at vintage can get a little crazy.

It is these mad harvest times that the Burch Family Wines StraightJacket label honors. It is a reflection of three long years of neurotic planning and truly psychotic work to make a wine with an objective to taste like pure genius. And we all know that there is a fine line between genius and, well, the loony bin.

StraightJacket Wines recognizes the positive aspects of being "a little out there" with ideas. After all, some of the most creative and important people in history have straddled this fine line and come out a little (or a lot, but who's judging?) left of center. They have been pioneers, innovators, visionaries, and people of extreme passion, knowledge, talent, and skills. They've had the integrity and courage to stand outside the world of mediocrity to follow a particular pursuit. Groundbreakers. Image-makers. Earth-shakers. Those whose inner voice is louder than the judgment received from the outside world.

What man experiences is not reality, but rather his dynamic interaction with it. The goal of an effective label is to override impressions, to captivate, and to draw one in to get a taste of what is inside.

—David W. Burch
Sales and Marketing,
Burch Family Estates

StraightJacket Wines salutes those who have rejected the confines of conformity in the wine world, especially in Western Australia, and anyone who seeks and supports change, growth, new perspectives, and new partnerships, and is essentially open for taking a wild ride to make the world a better place. The StraightJacket wine labels may be a little crazy, but what they represent doesn't really seem like such an insane idea after all.

**STRAIGHTJACKET WINES
(BURCH FAMILY ESTATES)**

Appellation:	**Great Southern/Blackwood Valley/Margaret River**
State:	**Western Australia**
Country of Origin:	**Australia**
Type of Wine:	**Shiraz**
Web Site:	**www.straitjacketwines.com.au**
Design:	**David Burch and Public Creative**
Designer's Web Site:	**www.publiccreative.com.au**

ST. SUPÉRY VINEYARDS & WINERY
[CALIFORNIA ❧ UNITED STATES]

In 1994, St. Supéry Vineyards and Winery unveiled the first vintage of its version of a blend of noble Bordeaux varietals. The grapes were hand-selected vigilantly; so cautiously, in fact, that those designated for the wine were likened as being the winners of an election—the best chosen amongst all the lots of grapes. These most expressive grapes were then artfully crafted into a sum greater than all its parts.

In 2000, this regal blend was crowned Élu, a French word for exactly what the wines were: "elected." Needing a majestic match in a white wine, its counterpart, Virtú (Italian for "virtuous") was introduced. To celebrate the pedigree of this perfect pair, at each vintage a new, saintly illustration is commissioned that interprets the innocently alluring layers of the blends. Limitless creative freedom is given to the artists and the saintly faces produced are, like the wines, highly stylized and always a little sinful, as even the purest of wines should be.

ST. SUPÉRY VINEYARDS & WINERY

Appellation:	**Napa Valley**
State:	**California**
Country of Origin:	**United States**
Type of Wine:	**Red Blend**
Web Site:	**www.stsupery.com**
Art:	**Jody Hewgill**
Artist's Web Site:	**www.jodyhewgill.com**

ST. SUPÉRY VINEYARDS & WINERY

Appellation:	**Napa Valley**
State:	**California**
Country of Origin:	**United States**
Type of Wine:	**Cabernet Sauvignon, Merlot, and Petit Verdot Blend**
Web Site:	**www.stsupery.com**
Art:	**Scott McKowen**

ST. SUPÉRY VINEYARDS & WINERY

Appellation:	**Napa Valley**
State:	**California**
Country of Origin:	**United States**
Type of Wine:	**Sauvignon Blanc and Sémillon Blend**
Web Site:	**www.stsupery.com**
Art:	**Daniel Chang**
Artist's Web Site:	**www.danielchang.net**

STUART WINES COMPANY
[VICTORIA ❦ AUSTRALIA]

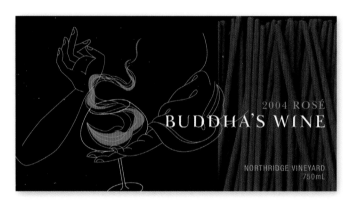

Growing up in a Buddhist family, Stuart Wines Company managing director Hendra Widjaja was exposed to the guiding principals of charity, compassion, and moderation at an early age. As an adult, upon hearing his own young child conversing with a beloved stuffed animal about living in a single-parent home, a deep sympathy arose within him for orphans lacking any family whatsoever.

Admiring the teachings of Buddha prompted his own questioning of how he could help displaced children in his own small way. Recognizing that all children, despite their circumstances, deserve hope and opportunity, Mr. Widjaja and his team created Buddha's Wines and Buddha's Wine Global Children's Fund. The fund recognizes and assists the needs of homeless and otherwise unfortunate children within the global community. Buddha's Wines, though dressed with gorgeous labels infused with images that bring to mind Eastern religion and culture, are more than just gorgeous labels—the driving force of the wines and their label design is actually a compassionate cause.

STUART WINES COMPANY	
Appellation:	**Yarra Valley**
State:	**Victoria**
Country of Origin:	**Australia**
Type of Wine:	**Sauvignon Blanc**
Web Site:	**www.buddhaswine.com.au**
Design:	**Smart Works**
Designer's Web Site:	**www.smartworks.com.au**

STUART WINES COMPANY	
Appellation:	**Yarra Valley**
State:	**Victoria**
Country of Origin:	**Australia**
Type of Wine:	**Rosé**
Web Site:	**www.buddhaswine.com.au**
Design:	**Smart Works**
Designer's Web Site:	**www.smartworks.com.au**

The backyard is known to be the quintessential embodiment of Australian family tradition. Being Australian means playing French cricket, "kicking a footy," children swinging from the "Hill's Hoist," having a "tinnie" with mates and "relies in the arvo," and of course, tossing chops and sausages on the barbie. Today's shrinking properties are causing backyards to be sacrificed to expand the living space of bigger houses. The Australian outdoor and backyard culture is so ingrained that, no doubt, those Aussies will always find a way to it no matter how small it may be. After all, an Aussie would be the first to tell you that a small yard is better than a poke in the eye with a sharp stick.

The Swings and Roundabouts Backyard series pays tribute to this important part of Aussie culture with its labels. Though looking quite traditional, it is evident upon closer inspection that aspects of this Australian backyard experience are entwined in the artwork.

And if the backyard isn't big enough for all the fun, the Laneways wine labels take the backyard culture one step further—leaping over the back fence, into the laneways for that little extra Aussie fun.

SWINGS & ROUNDABOUTS	
Appellation:	**Margaret River**
State:	**Western Australia**
Country of Origin:	**Australia**
Type of Wine:	**Nebbiolo and Sangiovese Blend**
Web Site:	**www.swings.com.au**
Design:	**Braincells**
Designer's Web Site:	**www.braincells.com.au**

SWINGS & ROUNDABOUTS	
Appellation:	**Margaret River**
State:	**Western Australia**
Country of Origin:	**Australia**
Type of Wine:	**Sangiovese**
Web Site:	**www.swings.com.au**
Design:	**Braincells**
Designer's Web Site:	**www.braincells.com.au**

TANYA WINERY

[JUDEA AND SAMARIA AREA ❧ ISRAEL]

They say that a picture is worth a thousand words, but in the case of the labels on Tanya Winery wines, what they tell goes well beyond. Perhaps more so than words, they signify years that exceed any word count.

Tanya Winery winemaker and owner Yoram Cohen is a retired professional-photographer-turned-passionate-winemaker. It therefore makes complete sense for him to showcase beautiful imagery on his labels, binding two very important aspects of his creative life together. Despite his ample time spent behind a lens, the images on the labels are not of his own creation. Instead, antique photographs have been chosen to visually integrate this young winery in a context that marries contemporary aspects with those of the past.

Historically, wine has long played an important role in Israel. Numerous Biblical passages mention the planting and farming of vineyards in the Holy Land. Further, there is evidence of ancient wine presses in the Ofra region, where Tanya Winery is located, indicating that winemaking was part of ancient civilizations dating back some three thousand years ago. While the centrality of winemaking in ancient times is undisputable, the modern Israeli wine industry is quite young, and has weathered historical hardships and change of rule that has strongly influenced the industry and wine consumption.

Like the place where Tanya Winery wines come from, the wines themselves are complex time capsules and have their own chronicles to tell. Resembling an onion, the layered photographic labels reveal the personality of the wines, each with something new and novel as they age and fresh layers appear, while others waft away with time. Just like moments caught in photographs, no two are ever the same. These are the stories that Yoram Cohen tells with his fruit, creativity, and passion, through wines that cross boundaries between ancient and modern, always changing and ever in flux.

When I wanted to devise a label for my wine, I contacted an artistic designer. As I walked into her studio, I saw creations that stunned me, creations that were layered with different themes and designs, with different eras and people—a veritably astounding mosaic unifying the worlds of old and new. It was immediately clear to me that I wanted these creations on my labels.
—YORAM COHEN
Founder, Owner, and Wine Master,
Tanya Winery

TANYA WINERY

Appellation:	**Judea Hills**
District:	**Judea and Samaria Area**
Country of Origin:	**Israel**
Type of Wine:	**Cabernet Franc**
Web Site:	**www.tanyawinery.co.il**
Design:	**Meirav Uriah**

VQA OKANAGAN VALLEY VQA
GEWÜRZTRAMINER 2007

MERLOT 2007

Escape. Remedies. Tonics. Vices.

Stress-relievers—we all have one, whether it is a rowdy night out, a serene and meditative yoga class, trips to explore far-off places, the pursuit of a retail remedy, or even a shrink that listens to your every woe.

For the owners of Therapy Vineyards, the perfect prescription for breaking free from the big city was escaping to the calm and unperturbed ambiance of Canada's Naramata Bench in British Columbia. Eventually, intermittent escapism turned into routine therapy and a more permanent move was made to the Penticton region with the purchase of property and a vineyard.

As part of an ongoing remedial theme of the winery, Therapy Vineyards wine labels have been designed with the immediately recognizable inkblot test imagery developed by Swiss psychiatrist Hermann Rorschach, which was part of his individual personality and psychodiagnostic assessments. Unlike other tests that could be administered in a group fashion, the Rorschach technique focused on the individual, each being diagnosed through their own unique thinking.

Much like individual interpretation of Rorschach's inkblots, Therapy wines are a unique style of bottled therapy. Each is administrable as part as regular treatment in a group or individual setting as a delightful discharge from the hustle and bustle of everyday life.

THERAPY VINEYARDS	
Appellation:	**Okanagan Valley**
Province:	**British Columbia**
Country of Origin:	**Canada**
Type of Wine:	**Gewürztraminer**
Web Site:	**www.therapyvineyards.com**
Design:	**Brandever**
Designer's Web Site:	**www.brandever.com**

THERAPY VINEYARDS	
Appellation:	**Okanagan Valley**
Province:	**British Columbia**
Country of Origin:	**Canada**
Type of Wine:	**Merlot**
Web Site:	**www.therapyvineyards.com**
Design:	**Brandever**
Designer's Web Site:	**www.brandever.com**

THREE FAMILIES WINERY

[CALIFORNIA ❦ UNITED STATES]

They say that behind every great man, stands a great woman. The same, in the case of Three Families Winery, can be said about great wines. Three Families Winery is comprised of just that: three families. These three families came together through three best friends and their mutual loves of theater as a hobby and communications as a career. After introducing their respective husbands, they soon realized that they all shared a common love for wine and philosophy, and that there is no wrong or right with it—it's all based on what you like: individual palates, specific moods, and changing foods. Each different set of variables and circumstances always creates a unique wine experience.

Of the three husbands, it was Doug Hackett who spearheaded the winemaking with the premise that the only thing better than sharing a great bottle of wine with friends might be making a great bottle of wine with them, too. Dogwood Cellar, the first of the ventures between the gents, became the threesome's premium single varietal wine endeavor.

Wanting to make something a bit more fun, interesting, and reflective of the *staggering* times spent together as three families, they decided to make a party wine that still had quality juice from overproduced fruit, with an underpriced tag. Of course, the name had to be Three Families. The concept of the label is equally as fun as what's in each of the wines. Envisioned while enjoying an evening together with another mutual friend, artist Kathrine Lemke Waste, the idea was born to create a suite of ongoing stories for each wine's vintage. These stories feature a variety of different characters, each with individual personalities, just like the varied personalities found amongst the three families.

THREE FAMILIES WINERY

Appellation:	**Mendocino**
State:	**California**
Country of Origin:	**United States**
Type of Wine:	**Merlot**
Web Site:	**www.threefamilieswinery.com**
Art:	**Eric Royal**
Artist's Web Site:	**www.royallyeric.com**

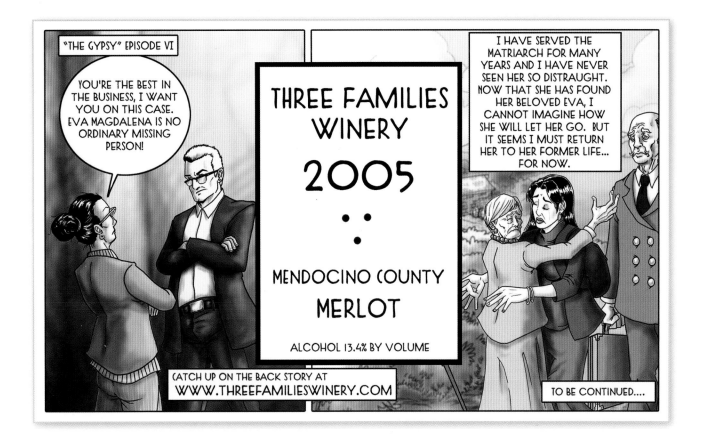

THREE FAMILIES WINERY

Appellation:	**Mendocino**
State:	**California**
Country of Origin:	**United States**
Type of Wine:	**Merlot**
Web Site:	**www.threefamilieswinery.com**
Art:	**Eric Royal**
Artist's Web Site:	**www.royallyeric.com**

THREE FAMILIES WINERY

Appellation:	**Mendocino**
State:	**California**
Country of Origin:	**United States**
Type of Wine:	**Merlot**
Web Site:	**www.threefamilieswinery.com**
Art:	**Eric Royal**
Artist's Web Site:	**www.royallyeric.com**

THREE FAMILIES WINERY

Appellation:	**Mendocino**
State:	**California**
Country of Origin:	**United States**
Type of Wine:	**Merlot**
Web Site:	**www.threefamilieswinery.com**
Art:	**Eric Royal**
Artist's Web Site:	**www.royallyeric.com**

THREE THIEVES

[CALIFORNIA ❦ UNITED STATES]

Three Thieves—partners Roger Scommegna, Joel Gott, and Charles Bieler—takes its cues from the Wild West when it comes to challenging the convention of the wine industry.

It all started with the rebels' "stealing" of surplus wines from "rich" vineyards and bringing affordable, but quality and convenient, wines to the masses. Being true wranglers in all their blazing glory, the Three Thieves, as they call themselves and their beacon product, brought the iconic 1970s wine jug back and gave it a place in the hearts of fun-loving wine drinkers everywhere. Then, they went on to turn things completely upside-down, taking a lead from their European paisans by boxing their wines in Bandit Tetra Paks.

When it came to headlining their next great steal, the Three Thieves agreed on one thing and one thing only: This wine was a true treasure and was going to cause a stir. Aside from this, each of the thieves had their own ideas about the wine. Joel Gott (Thief 1) thought the wine was a sure "show-stopper" and good for any occasion. Charles Bieler (Thief 2) thought the wine was a "best in show" and displayed absolutely everything that was right about crafting wine. Roger Scommengna (Thief 3) thought the wine was a "showpiece" for all those industry varmints who treated Three Thieves and its wines like B-list gunslingers. Three thieves, three different ideas. It was a showdown of sorts. And ultimately, a truce was made possible by one word they all shared in common for this one great wine: The Show.

In its best form, a label expresses the terroir of a winemaker or brand owner's psyche.   —CHARLES BIELER
Thief 2, Three Thieves

Appropriately, Three Thieves turned to an American icon, Nashville's Hatch Show Print, for inspiration. The print and design shop has been a true piece of Americana for over 125 years, having created the essence of show business with highly distinctive posters. Most notably, Hatch posters promoted some of the biggest names in country music such as Johnny Cash and Patsy Cline, amongst other great performers including Louis Armstrong and Elvis Presley.

Hatch Show Print is an American design icon that employs the dying art of letterpress printing. In fact, committed in every way to the authenticity of the historic artistry, both from the design style right down to the equipment used to achieve their retro style, the newest machine in the studio dates to 1967. When it comes to wanting to imprint a legacy, Three Thieves couldn't have picked a better place to start. Now part of the Country Music Foundation, not one of the carved blocks used for the designs has been thrown away or auctioned off. Instead, they continue to form a wall of fame ensuring that their chronicles continue, which now extends to Three Thieves' best in show, show–stopper, and showpiece known affectionately as The Show.

THREE THIEVES	
Regions:	**Central Coast/North Coast**
State:	**California**
Country of Origin:	**United States**
Type of Wine:	**Cabernet Sauvignon**
Web Site:	**www.threethieves.com**
Design:	**Brad Vetter (Hatch Show Print)**
Designer's Web Site:	**http://bradvetterdesign.carbonmade.com and www.hatchshowprint.com**

THE TRADITIONS COLLECTION
[CALIFORNIA ✤ UNITED STATES]

The Traditions Collection was developed by husband and wife P. J. and Nic Ferrante, tattoo artists and owners of Energy Tattoo in Santa Barbara, California. This unconventional extension of their art started when an unanticipated next-door nuisance came a-knockin' in the form of winemaker Christian Garvin. After mistakenly cutting their phone lines, imposing the screeching uproar of a circular saw, and acquainting the couple with the wafting of extremely odd fumes, the three became quick friends. Out of this unlikely partnership evolved what the trio affectionately call "the love child between Ozzy Osbourne and Julia Child!"

Centered on each side's longtime respect of the creative artistry found within both the wine and the tattoo industries, as well as as a response to recent commercial exploitation of traditional tattoo art, they took matters into their own hands. By creating a novel wine label, they have attempted to protect the integrity of their craft. Their wines provide tattoo art enthusiasts with great wines and original commissioned art without the long-term commitment of a personal and permanent embellishment. It's definitely an alternative medium for art that most often is kept under wraps.

THE TRADITIONS COLLECTION	
Appellation:	**Non-Designated Appellation**
State:	**California**
Country of Origin:	**United States**
Type of Wine:	**Merlot**
Web Site:	**www.thetraditionscollection.com**
Art:	**Philip Jack**

THE TRADITIONS COLLECTION	
Appellation:	**Non-Designated Appellation**
State:	**California**
Country of Origin:	**United States**
Type of Wine:	**Merlot**
Web Site:	**www.thetraditionscollection.com**
Art:	**Philip Jack**

Truffle Pig Wine

[Ontario ❧ Canada]

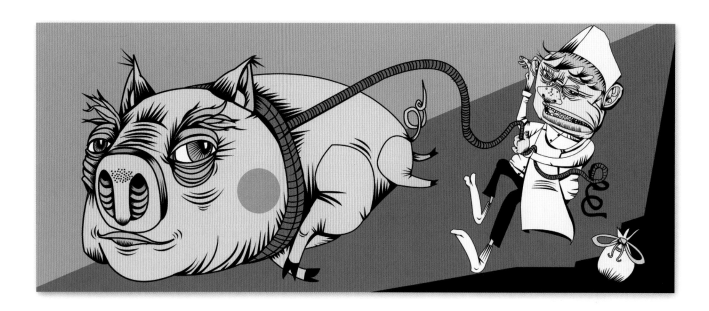

Many people dream of a simpler life, but not everyone can put their finger on exactly what that life would be defined as.

Not for Nathan Arnold. His had been a consistent vision for such a long time that he had it all mapped out: a one- or two-year stint of romantic living in a cozy cottage in the south of France. His only responsibilities would be to make his way into the village each day to pick up some warm bread and succulent French wine for dinner. Of course, the neighbors would own a truffle-hunting pig that he would volunteer to take for long walks in search of those buried black diamonds of French cuisine. Basking in the relaxed lifestyle of Provence and celebrating slower living, where taking time to make connections with people over glorious food, mouthwatering drink, and captivating conversation is commonplace. Now, who could say no to that?

The Truffle Pig wine label acts as an *aide-mémoire* for this Torontonian winemaker. Yes, that's right—he's a winemaker living in Canada's booming metropolis of downtown Toronto. Having friends in the wine industry in California and Ontario's grape growing belts, though, he set out to learn some tricks of his own. And though he may not physically be in France just yet, he is certainly well on his way to living the charmed southern France lifestyle. When he gets there, he'll have to make no assimilation, as he's been practicing in the heart of the city for now . . . with his own truffle pig (of sorts) and all.

> **To me, the great romance of wine goes beyond the product itself; it goes to the passion of the people involved in making it, and the place that they choose to do it. And a great wine label goes a long way towards telling that story.**
>
> —Nathan Arnold
> Owner and Winemaker, Truffle Pig Wine

TRUFFLE PIG WINE

Appellation:	**Niagara-on-the-Lake**
Province:	**Ontario**
Country of Origin:	**Canada**
Type:	**Icewine**
Web Site:	**www.trufflepigwine.com**
Art:	**Ferris Plock**
Artist's Web Site:	**www.ferrisplock.com**

TWISTED OAK WINERY

[CALIFORNIA ❧ UNITED STATES]

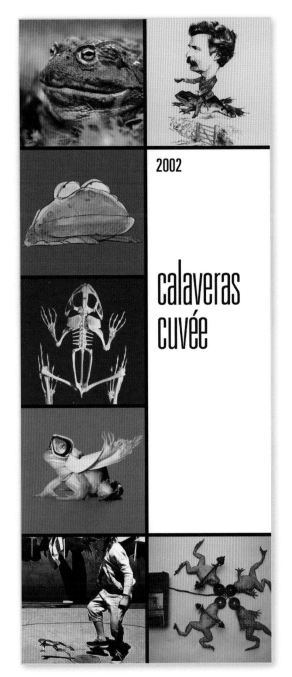

2002

calaveras cuvée

Most people would agree that wine and frogs don't naturally go hand in hand, but in Calaveras County, they certainly do. Well, they do at least once a year, and when it comes around, you might think you're at the Kentucky Derby.

Calaveras County's long-standing tradition dates back from 1928 when the first Jumping Frog Jubilee was held in honor of Mark Twain's famous short story, "The Celebrated Jumping Frog of Calaveras County." The nineteenth-century classic is a story of an insurmountable frog named Dan'l Webster, who could out-jump any other frog, and a curious gambler named Jim Smiley, who would bet on anything. The short story captured a worldwide audience and put Mark Twain on the map as an author. It also put Calaveras County there with him, as the jumping frogs became one of the first things that people associated with the county.

This wine label pays tribute to the delightful, though a bit peculiar, heritage by use of an equally distinctive and quirky label. Of the images included, one is an illustration representing Mr. Twain and his fabulous jumping frog. Another is an actual historic image of the famed frog jump. And given the county's namesake—*calaveras,* which means "skulls" when translated from Spanish—the inclusion of a frog's skeleton seems quite appropriate.

The jubilee draws an estimated attendance of 35,000 visitors over the event's weekend each year, and the current world record jump was set in 1986 by Rosie the Ribeter, whose little green legs managed to jump a whopping 21.75". And that's certainly a record to jump for joy at and toast with a good glass of red.

TWISTED OAK WINERY

Appellation:	**Sierra Foothills**
State:	**California**
Country of Origin:	**United States**
Type of Wine:	**Red Blend**
Web Site:	**www.twistedoak.com**
Design:	**Troy Monroe Stacey**
Designer's Web Site:	**www.defyg.com**

TWISTED OAK WINERY

[CALIFORNIA ❧ UNITED STATES]

Upon first glance of this wine label, you likely wouldn't have an inkling as to the story behind it. You might think that maybe Twisted Oak Winery has a lovely three-hundred-year-old California Blue Oak that graces their vineyard. True. And perhaps you'd venture that the name "The Spaniard" is a tributary epithet to one of the Twisted crew's prospecting ancestors—after all, the name "Calaveras County" certainly didn't come from an Englishman. Good guess, but this is not so true.

The fact of the matter is, you'd have to be a very, very big movie aficionado to put the pieces of this puzzle together, just from the words "the spaniard" on the front of the label. Being a Spanish Tempranillo, the name does make sense. But coupled with a few clues—the back ramblings of "winemakers of unusual size," being a blend as big as Fezzik himself, and requiring six fingers to hold the glass—you might suspect a bit more. The gentle recommendation to "share it with your Buttercup, a gentle giant, or the entire kingdom . . . as you wish," would be a sure sign that the magical muse for this label is, in fact, the movie *The Princess Bride*. A favorite amongst the twisted crew of Twisted Oak Winery, male and female alike, this wine label pays tribute to the spirit of the movie ever so quietly, as they wish.

TWISTED OAK WINERY	
Appellation:	**Sierra Foothills**
State:	**California**
Country of Origin:	**United States**
Type of Wine:	**Tempranillo, Grenache, and Graciano Blend**
Web Site:	**www.twistedoak.com**
Design:	**Bethany Lund (Action Photo Works)**
Designer's Web Site:	**www.actionphotoworks.com**

TWO HANDS WINES

[SOUTH AUSTRALIA ⁓ AUSTRALIA]

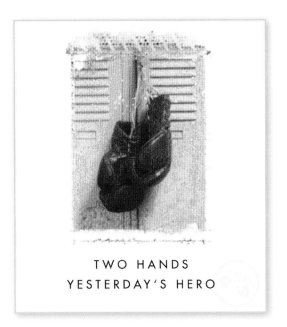

TWO HANDS
YESTERDAY'S HERO

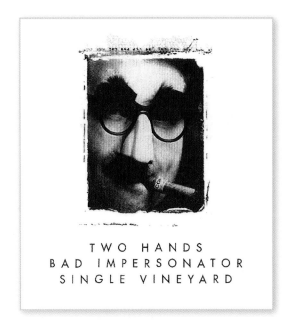

TWO HANDS
BAD IMPERSONATOR
SINGLE VINEYARD

Each of the Two Hands Picture Series wines uses an unexpected photographic image to visually depict deeper thoughts about what's inside the bottle.

For example, the Two Hands wine named Bad Impersonator has a label adorned with a visual of Michael Twelftree (one half of Two Hands) incognito. How on earth does this correspond to the Shiraz it represents? Well, people who love Shiraz love it because it is traditionally a wine packed full of big flavor, deep in crimson color, and rich in bold plum and peppery flavors. But when the folks at Two Hands tasted their Barossa Valley Shiraz, they knew that they weren't dealing with a typical Shiraz. As they interviewed current winemaker Matt Wenk, they had him take a taste. His response: "I didn't know you guys made Pinot." Not wanting to mislead the consumer and have them expect a big, bold red, Michael decided that this Shiraz should be coined Bad Impersonator. And, following suit, he put a photo of himself on the label doing his bad impersonation of Groucho Marx.

The Yesterday's Hero wine label tells the story of the underdog grape Grenache, which has rarely seen any of the spotlight in recent years. These days, Shiraz seems to get all the glory. About a hundred years ago, however, this wasn't the case. These were considered the quintessential grapes for Australian winemaking because the biggest wine market was a mere 10,000 miles away—by *boat*. This meant a very long journey for the wine, which meant plenty of time for oxidation to set in. To circumvent spoilage, winemakers would fortify the wine, stick it in barrels, and put it on the ships where it would arrive well received in England. The great thing about Grenache was that the grapes could be picked late and then less spirits had to be added, meaning a huge cost savings. So, Grenache was a hero, rather than a second-class citizen like today, as it holds onto its nostalgic glory much like a retired prize-fighting boxer.

Thus, as in Yesterday's Hero and Bad Impersonator, each label in the Two Hands Picture Series links its wine very appropriately, though often inconspicuously, by means of creative photography.

TWO HANDS WINES	
Appellation:	**Barossa Valley**
State:	**South Australia**
Country of Origin:	**Australia**
Type of Wine:	**Grenache**
Web Site:	**www.twohandswines.com**
Design:	**Mash**
Designer's Web Site:	**www.mashdesign.com.au**

TWO HANDS WINES	
Appellation:	**Barossa Valley**
State:	**South Australia**
Country of Origin:	**Australia**
Type of Wine:	**Shiraz**
Web Site:	**www.twohandswines.com**
Design:	**Mash**
Designer's Web Site:	**www.mashdesign.com.au**

TWO MILE WINES
[CALIFORNIA ✇ UNITED STATES]

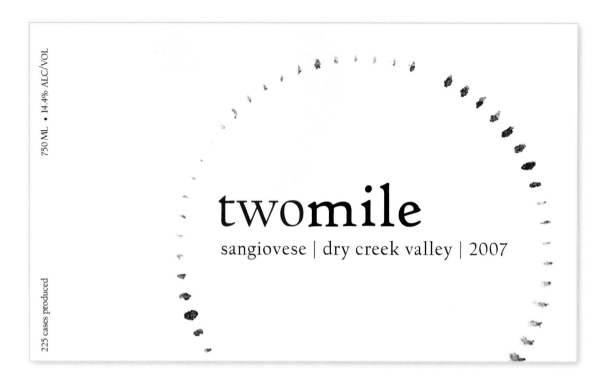

750 ML • 14.4% ALC/VOL

225 cases produced

twomile
sangiovese | dry creek valley | 2007

Two Mile Wines began in Berkeley, California, as a cooperative of friends from all walks of life brought together by a love of wine. Thirteen different personalities, thirteen different professions, but thirteen people who had one goal: to make good wine while enjoying their social circle of friends. Their second vintage, which saw a harvest of between 100 lbs. and 200 lbs. of grapes, saw some people come and some people go, all while the winemaking experimentation continued. Originally called Thomas Knight Wines, in 2005, the group—which had whittled itself down to the closest friends—decided it was time to get serious and take its wines to the next level: directly to the people.

Needing a new name for the commercial venture, the group looked to its old stomping grounds for inspiration and decided to pay homage to the community and local history of Berkeley.

In 1873, California legislators, appalled at seeing students stumbling inebriated across the UC Berkeley campus, instituted a 2-mile circumference around the campus where the consumption of alcohol was prohibited. After the West Berkeley community raised a fuss, the radius was reduced to 1 mile in 1876, where it remained steadfast until post-Prohibition, only repealing the legislation in 1978. It is this radius that has provided Two Mile Wines their epithet.

Ideally in the everyday celebration of wine, food, and friends, a label is inspiration for another conversation. —ADAM NELSON
Co-Founder, Two Mile Wines

While Two Mile Wines doesn't necessarily condone the well-known UC Berkeley booze-infested riots of 1937 that had rioting Cal football revelers overturning cars in downtown Berkeley, or the 1956 mass panty raid of Berkeley sorority houses and female dormitories (which are both indeed a piece of Berkeley's inebriated history), it does stand for the coming together of friends over wine, good food, and merrymaking. Of course, evenings like these can get messy—literally and figuratively. One look at the tablecloth from a previous night of festivities says it all. And that's exactly what Two Mile Wines labels represent: dirty, messy evenings, making memories over wine with friends old and new.

TWO MILE WINES
Appellation: **Dry Creek Valley**
State: **California**
Country of Origin: **United States**
Type of Wine: **Sangiovese**
Web Site: **www.twomilewines.com**
Design: **Stolen Plate Press**
Designer's Web Site: **www.stolenplatepress.com**

TWO TUN WINE

[WESTERN CAPE ꙮ SOUTH AFRICA]

With a little liquid lubrication to the imagination, the lips become a bit looser, the conversation is fierce, imagination is running wild, and anything seems possible. Ever have one of those "night out ideas"—those brilliant plans that are inspired while under the influence of too much of the good stuff? The ideas that are so often left abandoned on the pub floor at the end of the night, never to see the light of day?

Such wasn't the case for Guy Smith and Richard Addison, two aggrieved wine traders who found themselves missing what they got into the wine industry for in the first place. It all began with an evening at the pub and a bit of quipping over a few pints in Wimbledon. By pint number two, one of them had the brilliant idea of buying a couple tons of grapes and making their own wine. The other thought that, at least if they couldn't sell the stuff, they could relish drinking it over a year or two—what's a couple tons of grapes worth of wine? By pint number three, they were back to the footie scores.

Though it seemed like a passing conversation without any legs, they actually didn't leave the idea there on the pub floor to be mopped away. Instead, they pursued finding the grapes through an industry friend in South Africa who pointed them to Valley Vineyards, and bought six barrels. With a little help from their friends, they began making the wine they wanted to—without having to appease anyone but themselves.

Of course, you can't have a wine without a label, so they called up their friend, abstract artist Emyr Wyn Williams, and simply asked him to draw something up. Being one to think a bit more conceptually, Emyr actually hung his design on "tun," rather than "ton," which although related from an industry perspective, mean two totally separate things. Still used today, a "tun" is an old English word for a brewer's fermenting vat. Serendipitously, the term also means "a large beer," which is where the two mates started out in the first place. Two Tun Wine is a true 6-pint-to-1,800-bottle dream realized, which now includes Smith's own vineyards planted in the United Kingdom. Luckily on that eve way back when it all started, they weren't enjoying cigars, or things might have turned out more smoke and mirrors, rather than their two tuns.

TWO TUN WINE	
Appellation:	**Riebeek Valley**
Province:	**Western Cape**
Country of Origin:	**South Africa**
Type of Wine:	**Shiraz**
Web Site:	**www.twotun.blogspot.com**
Art:	**Emyr Wyn Williams**
Artist's Web Site:	**www.emyrww.com**

TYRRELL'S WINES
[NEW SOUTH WALES ❧ AUSTRALIA]

From the first vintage in 1864, the Tyrell's tradition has been built on a deep passion for its winemaking craft, from the cultivation of grape varieties it believed would thrive in Hunter Valley in New South Wales, to remaining devoted to its convictions that nothing great ever comes out of conformity.

Murray Tyrell, a third-generation cattleman-turned-winemaker, was certain that Hunter Valley had the ability to produce world-class white wines. So convinced of the region's white wine potential, he has been quoted as saying, "If you can't make a good Sémillon from the Hunter Valley, you shouldn't be making wine at all." Murray, however, wanted to push the possibilities of region further than the Sémillon status quo. Having a strong affinity for the wines of Burgundy, he felt that Chardonnay was an obvious choice for the region. The only problems were that Chardonnay was virtually unknown in Australia in the 1960s and the Tyrells didn't have Chardonnay amongst the varietals planted in their vineyards. Knowing that he had picked Chardonnay grapes to eat as a child from the neighboring Penfolds vineyard, he approached the Penfolds manager to state his cause and appeal for some cuttings during their pruning season. The response: absolutely not.

As the Tyrell's way went, Murray was not about to abandon this great confidence in the region's capability with Chardonnay on the dictate of someone else, so he devised a plan to "free" a selection of Chardonnay cuttings on his own accord. His mission over the barbed wire fence under the midnight sky was successful and in 1967, the cuttings were planted. The first Chardonnay was made in 1969 and in 1971, Tyrell's Wines released the first commercial Chardonnay release in Australia.

Now, not everyone was poised to be an early adopter of this virgin white in Australia. In fact, when Tyrell entered his 1973 Chardonnay into the Brisbane Wine Show, the judges reportedly spat it out and scored it 6 out of 20. But Murray was adamant that he had something special in Chardonnay and remained committed to the varietal. Within the year, the same Chardonnay was awarded winning distinctions around the country.

In 1983, Murray lawfully purchased Penfold's HVD vineyard—the same vineyard that he first tasted Chardonnay grapes from so long ago. Midnight Leap celebrates the resolute ways Murray Tyrell demonstrated through his leap of faith and leap over the barbed-wire fence, in turn pioneering the Chardonnay grape in Australia.

> The important thing with a designer is to make sure they know you and you know them before the design process starts. The designer has got to understand where the winemaker is coming from and where they want to go. —BRUCE TYRRELL
> Owner and Winemaker, Tyrell's Wines

TYRRELL'S WINES

Appellation:	**Hunter Valley**
State:	**New South Wales**
Country of Origin:	**Australia**
Type of Wine:	**White Blend**
Web Site:	**www.tyrrells.com.au**
Design:	**Hoyne Design**
Designer's Web Site:	**www.hoyne.com.au**

VAN DUZER VINEYARDS
[OREGON ✤ UNITED STATES]

Throughout the ages, many cultures and religions have embraced goddesses of the elements as part of their belief systems. The essence of the mystical figures is similar, yet each is interpreted uniquely in each tale. The goddess is ubiquitous, present here on earth where she reigns and manifests herself not only in the distant heavens.

Respecting the intricate and powerful influence that the westerly winds of the Pacific have on its vineyards, Van Duzer looked to mythological tales for inspiration to represent its true respect for nature on its labels. The company found it in the mythical Greek Zephyr, the spirit of the west wind. Known to be the gentlest of the mythological Greek wind figures, the delicate female portrayal of Zephyr (or, as Van Duzer calls her, Zephra) is praised for her capacity to fructify lands with the breeze of her fresh breath. Through her, the spirit of the vineyard is embodied, the unique tastes of the wines revealed.

Artist John Martinez was commissioned to bring the Van Duzer Vineyards Zephyra to life on the wine labels, ensuring that she was depicted as energetic, generous, wise, and knowing; an engaging, but petulant goddess who gently nurtures the grapes. Through Van Duzer's feminine and romantic rendition, the magic of the goddess's spirit is shared with everyone that captures this little piece of Greek mythology.

VAN DUZER VINEYARDS

Appellation:	**Willamette Valley**
State:	**Oregon**
Country of Origin:	**United States**
Type of Wine:	**Pinot Noir**
Web Site:	**www.vanduzer.com**
Design:	**Flint Design Co.**
Designer's Web Site:	**www.flintdesignco.com**
Art:	**John Martinez**

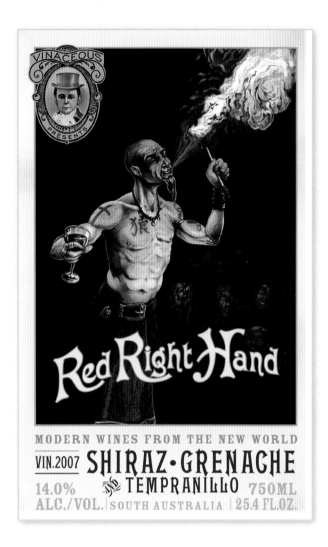

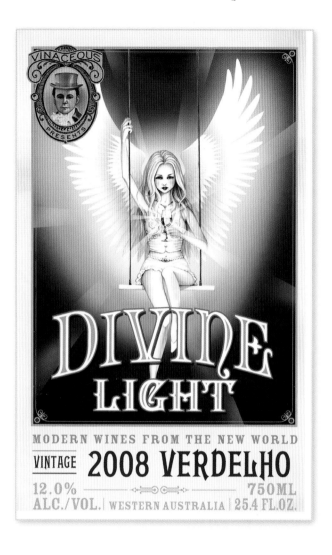

B y definition, Nick Stacy is a true *bon vivant*—someone who has refined tastes, especially when it comes to superb food and drink. From a young age (too young in most countries), Nick began a love affair with wine after tasting his first sip of a Western Australian Cabernet Sauvignon that led to the advent of his underage cellar at the age of seventeen. A few years later, on a whim, he registered the name "Vinaceous," not knowing where it would go, but realizing that the word embodied a sense of delicious and tempting vibrancy that is 100% true of wine and grape.

Over fifteen years later, Nick's alter ego Vinaceous was finally ready to step onto the stage and dazzle those seeking a new experience in wines. Together with partners Michael Kerrigan and Gavin Berry, the three winemakers have endeavored to make show-stopping wines that would charm the world over.

With an alluring cast of characters of vaudeville variety, Vinaceous Presents . . . ! sets the stage with

VINACEOUS PRESENTS . . . !

Appellation:	**Non-Designated Appellation**
State:	**South Australia**
Country of Origin:	**Australia**
Type of Wine:	**Shiraz, Grenache, and Tempranillo Blend**
Web Site:	**www.vinaceous.com.au**
Design:	**Public Creative**
Designer's Web Site:	**www.publiccreative.com.au**

VINACEOUS PRESENTS . . . !

Appellation:	**Non-Designated Appellation**
State:	**Western Australia**
Country of Origin:	**Australia**
Type of Wine:	**Verdelho**
Web Site:	**www.vinaceous.com.au**
Design:	**Public Creative**
Designer's Web Site:	**www.publiccreative.com.au**

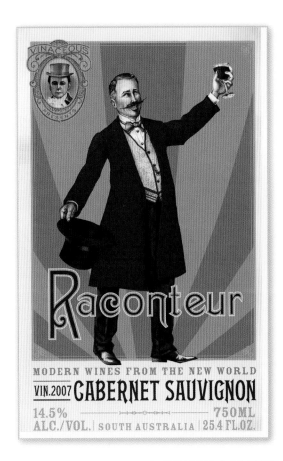

MODERN WINES FROM THE NEW WORLD

VIN.2007 **CABERNET SAUVIGNON**

14.5% —————— 750ML
ALC./VOL. | SOUTH AUSTRALIA | 25.4 FL.OZ.

VINACEOUS PRESENTS . . . !

Appellation:	**Non-Designated Appellation**
State:	**South Australia**
Country of Origin:	**Australia**
Type of Wine:	**Cabernet Sauvignon**
Web Site:	**www.vinaceous.com.au**
Design:	**Public Creative**
Designer's Web Site:	**www.publiccreative.com.au**

MODERN WINES FROM THE NEW WORLD

VINTAGE **2009 PINOT GRIGIO**

12.0% —————— 750ML
ALC./VOL. | SOUTH AUSTRALIA | 25.4 FL.OZ.

VINACEOUS PRESENTS . . . !

Appellation:	**Non-Designated Appellation**
State:	**South Australia**
Country of Origin:	**Australia**
Type of Wine:	**Pinot Grigio**
Web Site:	**www.vinaceous.com.au**
Design:	**Public Creative**
Designer's Web Site:	**www.publiccreative.com.au**

unknown and exotic elixirs prescribed to "educate, edify, amaze, and uplift." The Vinaceous Presents . . . ! wine labels provide a designate cast of characters true to their respective wines, which open up to unveil more and more each time one looks at them.

The Red Right Hand will tempt you with a complex and intriguing flavor story with multiple layers, told only as a spicy, fire-eating fallen angel could. Conversely, the Vinaceous Divine Light cherub, though not as pure as an angel, will indulge you to take an innocent risk with her and her crystal-clear and crisp glass. The Raconteur will captivate and keep you engaged for hours, while telling a story of regal tannins, full of ripe berries and classic cassis without ever losing his austerity. After all, this is how he conquered the world to become the noblest of reds.

A great label design—like an exquisite framed picture—can speak a thousand words. The imagery can engage with the potential buyer, and connect (and reconnect) long after the liquid has been savored.
—NICK STACY
Partner, Vinaceous Presents . . . !

Vinaceous *(not pictured)*, the "vintner extraordinaire," is said to have a discerning eye for ways in which to stupefy. Using his trained nose to uncover rare and beautiful wines, and his skilled taste buds to lure beauteous women, he always has tricks up his sleeve to transport even the most unassuming on an exciting adventure of the palate. Beware the seduction of the Snake Charmer *(not pictured)* and her sidekick, the sultry Sirenya—they have been known to emprison people in their hedonistic lairs, something that, being a *bon vivant*, Nick Stacy would likely highly recommend.

Viña Cobos
[Mendoza ❧ Argentina]

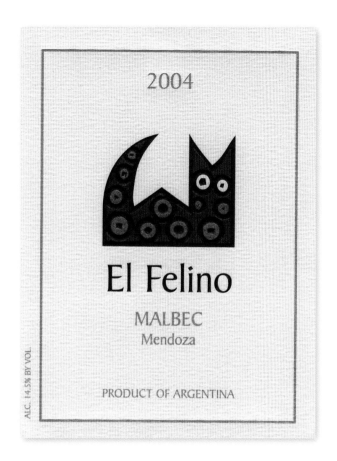

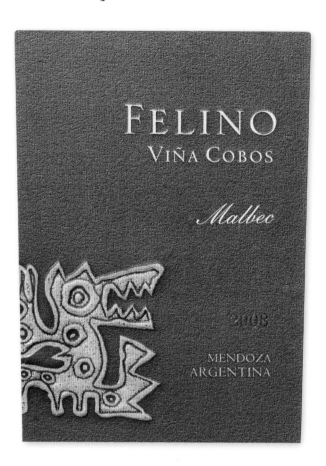

In 2000, designer Chuck House traveled to Argentina to be submerged in and learn firsthand about the lifestyle and culture that was very much part of Viña Cobos. While there, he feasted on empanadas, enjoyed *dulce de leche*, explored native artwork in Mendoza, and came to know the regional Indian culture of the Huarpes, which is influenced by the Incas.

When it came time to design the label for the Viña Cobos Felino wine label, House brought together the mythical creature and Argentine faunal icon of the puma—or, as another national treasure, the Argentina national rugby team, calls them, *los pumas*—in an artwork style influenced by the regional indigenous culture.

The puma, native of the Andes Mountains, was revered by the Incas as a mighty and magical animal, known for its grace and power. Given Malbec is Argentina's emblematic varietal that expresses a distinctive flavor characteristic, it was only fitting for Viña Cobos to give it a distinctive name and identity while marking respect for two features that are very much Argentine, the puma and the historical Incan influence.

VIÑA COBOS	
Appellation:	**Mendoza**
Province:	**Mendoza**
Country of Origin:	**Argentina**
Type of Wine:	**Malbec**
Web Site:	**www.vinacobos.com**
Design:	**Chuck House**
	(Icon Design Group)
Designer's Web Site:	**www.icondesigngroup.net**

VIÑA COBOS	
Appellation:	**Mendoza**
Province:	**Mendoza**
Country of Origin:	**Argentina**
Type of Wine:	**Malbec**
Web Site:	**www.vinacobos.com**
Design:	**Guillo Milia**
Designer's Web Site:	**www.guillomilia.blogspot.com**

One of Argentina's greatest exports the world over is the tango. Known internationally, the dance has represented Argentina's culture and people since this local lyrical tradition was born in the back-streets of Buenos Aires during the 1880s. Even today, it can be seen being danced passionately in parks, plazas, and dancehalls everywhere. Because of the tango's Argentine trademark, the tango *firulete* has been chosen as a visual translation that embodies the typicity of each Tempus Alba Preludio wine variety, which corresponds best with characteristic features or different forms of the national dance.

The name of the Biondolillo family's wines, Preludio, is a perfect fit, as each specially selected tango *firulete* movement elegantly foretells or provides a prelude to what's inside the bottle. The wines are said to be elegant and harmonious, but at the same time demonstrate a great strength, complexity, and passionate seduction that is also intrinsically linked to the character of the tango. For example, the Preludio Malbec, with round tannins and a long finish, is elegant but cannot deny its moments of temperament, much like the intensity of the tango's *malevo*. The Preludio Syrah, known as a lively and even perhaps openly exhibitionist wine as the night wears on, is befitting to the tempestuous and unstructured *milonga* dance from the slums of Argentina.

Each expressive movement that can be seen performed with symmetry, balance, and style in the tango dancehall is also expressed through the perfect harmony and fusion that exists to create the Tempus Alba wines. Despite the consistency of styles, each individual tango is danced with a new expression of feelings, relationship with partner, and response to music. Likewise, each representative *firulete* depicts a cross between slow and rhythmical graphic movements, followed by quick and closed virtual spins, that allow for a different dance to not only be imagined as it would be performed on the dance floor, but in the glass and on the palate each time as well.

VIÑEDOS Y BODEGA TEMPUS ALBA	
Appellation:	**Maipú**
Province:	**Mendoza**
Country of Origin:	**Argentina**
Type of Wine:	**Malbec**
Web Site:	**www.tempusalba.com**
Design:	**Latin Brand Lovers**
Designer's Web Site:	**www.latinbrandlovers.com**

VIÑEDOS Y BODEGA TEMPUS ALBA	
Appellation:	**Luján de Cuyo**
Province:	**Mendoza**
Country of Origin:	**Argentina**
Type of Wine:	**Syrah**
Web Site:	**www.tempusalba.com**
Design:	**Latin Brand Lovers**
Designer's Web Site:	**www.latinbrandlovers.com**

WANTED MAN VINEYARD
[VICTORIA ❧ AUSTRALIA]

SINGLE VINEYARD WINE • HEATHCOTE

Across countries and cultures, outlaws bearing different names have found a place in history as mythologized and romanticized folk heroes. In Australia, Ned Kelly and his famed Kelly Gang have been iconicized as the most eminent colonial bushrangers, or highwaymen. Indeed, Ned Kelly has transcended his vocation as an outlaw to become transformed into almost a rebellious aspect of Australian identity and, in turn, immortalized by painters, writers, musicians, and filmmakers across every possible media.

Ned Kelly was born in Beveridge, Victoria, in 1855, the son of Edward "Red" Kelly, an Irish Catholic ex-con sent to Australia for the theft of two pigs, and Ellen Quinn, a bounty migrant from what would later become known as Tasmania. The two would settle in Victoria where Red would supplement his income as a rural worker by stealing horses. A young Ned Kelly grew up hearing tales of bushrangers under the influence of his father, and at the young age of fourteen, he announced that he would follow in his father's footsteps.

Though Ned had run into some minor trials with the law, it wasn't until his mother was wrongly arrested and sentenced to three years in gaol for the attempted murder of a constable that Ned began partaking in more serious criminal activities. Ned and his gang took to hiding out in the Wombat Ranges to escape from the Felons' Apprehension Act, which lawfully allowed the instant shooting of criminals, rather than their preliminary apprehension. In 1880, the Kelly Gang had their last stand in Glenrowan, Victoria, where they took sixty hostages at the Glenrowan Inn. Though they wore protective suits of armor weighing 90 lbs. each, the police shot and killed Kelly Gang members Joe Byrne, Steve Hart, and Ned's brother, Dan.

Ned was shot and retreated to the bush with injuries to arm and thumb. Despite injuries, a relenting Kelly eventually approached police peacefully, but was shot in both unprotected legs, captured, and convicted of the murder of a constable. While in custody, Kelly advocated against the discrimination of poor Irish settlers. The sentence prevailed and Ned Kelly was hanged at the age of twenty-five on November 11, 1880, at Melbourne Gaol. His final words were, "Such is life."

Ned Kelly was seen as a flawed hero who sought justice for the poor and liberty for the innocent. While he led the criminal life of an outlaw, he was a hero to the common man as he demonstrated the courage and defiance that is characteristically Australian. The most enduring image of this part-villain, part-hero is of Ned and his armor. Wanted Man Vineyard from Victoria, where he thrived and perished, pays tribute to the national Australian icon through its wine labels.

WANTED MAN VINEYARD
Appellation: **Heathcote**
State: **Victoria**
Country of Origin: **Australia**
Type of Wine: **Merlot**
Web Site: **www.wantedman.com.au**
Design: **Clyde Terry**
Art: **Mark Knight**

WARRUMBUNGLE WINES

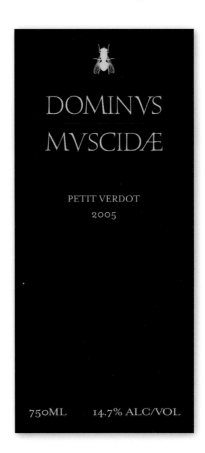

Gareth Trickey's wine moniker wasn't immediately spotted, although it was almost staring him straight in the face, bug-eyed. While it was quite easy to envision what he didn't want to be—another bloody butterfly label on Australian shelves amidst a sea of the other twenty thousand—it wasn't easy to catch hold of what he did want. He knew that the name would have to be "bold"—the family vineyard was small, but that didn't mean insignificant. So if he didn't want to be a butterfly, why not just be the polar opposite?

The blowfly is an Australian icon—so grotesque that Gareth thought it verged on being a turn-off. At the end of the day, though, those who got it, got it, and those who didn't, *he* would just blow off and not be bothered by. As off the wall as it was, "Blow Fly" was actually the perfect name, Gareth just didn't know it yet. He then extended his species to Green Bottle for his white blend, Blue Bottle for his red blend, and Dominus Muscidae, or The Lord of the Flies, for his reserve wine, and boldly emblazoned them on his bottles.

It wasn't until all was said and done that it dawned on Gareth that what he had racked his head over was actually staring at him, eye-to-buggy-eye. There, ingrained already in the land, in the name of their family farm was *burloo*, Aboriginal for "place of many flies."

WARRUMBUNGLE WINES	
Appellation:	**Coonabarabran** **(Non-Designated Appellation)**
State:	**New South Wales**
Country of Origin:	**Australia**
Type of Wine:	**Petit Verdot**
Web Site:	**www.blowflywines.com**
Design:	**Rhodes Wingrove**
Designer's Web Site:	**www.rhodeswingrove.com.au**

WARRUMBUNGLE WINES	
Appellation:	**Coonabarabran** **(Non-Designated Appellation)**
State:	**New South Wales**
Country of Origin:	**Australia**
Type of Wine:	**Petit Verdot**
Web Site:	**www.blowflywines.com**
Design:	**Rhodes Wingrove**
Designer's Web Site:	**www.rhodeswingrove.com.au**

WEINGUT ANDREAS TSCHEPPE

[SÜDSTEIERMARK ❧ AUSTRIA]

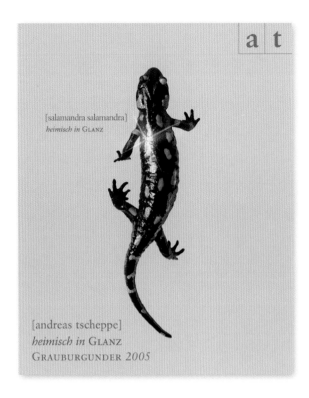

With societal changes constantly impacting our planet, the threat of extinction has become a universal problem unfortunately witnessed across almost every corner of the earth. While there are numerous factors that negatively affect our earth (and the plant, insect, fish, bird, and animal species who call it home), one of the largest contributors happens to be those that cohabitate with nature—humans. Austria, too, is not isolated from having a list of endangered species. Some of these include the Danube salmon, the Slender-billed curlew, Freya's damselfly, and the Dusky Large Blue butterfly.

Many people aren't aware of the little things inadvertently done that take a toll on the earth and our earthmates, or might think that small changes don't really have any positive impact in the grand scheme of saving our plant. Austrian winemaker Andreas Tscheppe certainly isn't one of them. Tscheppe is farmer and winemaker in the small Austrian village of Glanz, and is absolutely aware of the impact he has on the planet. By choosing organic vinicultural methods, insects and reptiles native to Austria that are endangered elsewhere in the country have been able to survive, and even thrive, in Glanz due to Tscheppe's personal decisions in the manner in which he farms.

The Andreas Tscheppe wine labels feature three of these species—the Stag beetle, the dragonfly, and the Fire salamander—that can rest assured in calling Glanz home. The labels feature a high gloss over the reptile and insects as a double-entendre. The name of the village also means "gloss," "sparkle," or "splendor" in German—very fitting for the splendid contribution that Tscheppe is making in his own right to his ecosystem and the planet at large.

WEINGUT ANDREAS TSCHEPPE	
Appellation:	**Glanz**
	(Non-Designated Appellation)
State:	**Südsteiermark**
Country of Origin:	**Austria**
Type of Wine:	**Sauvignon Blanc**
Web Site:	**www.at-weine.at**
Design:	**Demner, Merlicek & Bergmann**
Designer's Web Site:	**www.dmb.at**

WEINGUT ANDREAS TSCHEPPE	
Appellation:	**Glanz**
	(Non-Designated Appellation)
State:	**Südsteiermark**
Country of Origin:	**Austria**
Type of Wine:	**Grauburgunder**
Web Site:	**www.at-weine.at**
Design:	**Demner, Merlicek & Bergmann**
Designer's Web Site:	**www.dmb.at**

Weingut Dr. Loosen

[Rhineland-Palatinate ᧞ Germany]

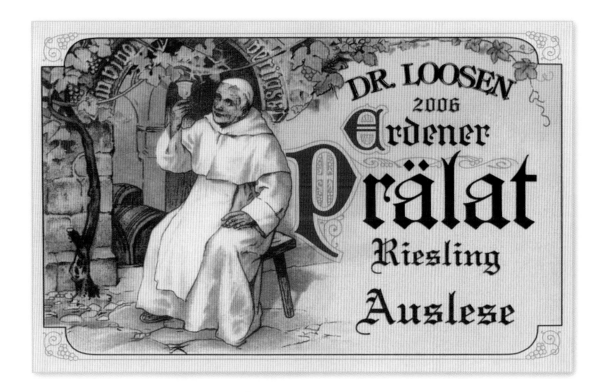

The Electorate of Trier was a religious principality of the Holy Roman Empire from the late ninth century until the early nineteenth century. It was a region under the rule of the archbishop who functioned as prince-elector of the empire under rule by the German king. In early modern times, the capital of the electorate was Trier, which encompassed territory along the Mosel River between Trier, in close proximity to the French border, and Koblenz on the Rhine.

During this period, castles of barons dotted the river and the top of the steep cliffs, and it was customary for them to command tolls from travelers that passed through the region. One of the castles in the area came up with what they thought would be an even better way to make some money. It was decided that the empire's bishop would be kidnapped for ransom, as they thought that surely they'd be paid a great sum for his return. Unbeknownst to his captors, however, the imprisoned bishop wasn't heavily favored by his constituents and nobody was sent or volunteered to pay his toll. Annoyed by the unsuccessful monetization of their captive, legend has it that the bishop was thrown off the cliffs and into the steep, rocky vineyards below, where he undoubtedly perished. The deceased Bishop Kuno held his prestigious post for less than a year in 1066.

The site where Kuno is said to have plunged to his death today is a prime Weingut Dr. Loosen vineyard—a small 4-acre vineyard built on 100% rocky slope. The previous owners of the vineyard named it Erdener Prälat, paying homage to the fallen ecclesiastical prelate.

Upon purchase of the property and vineyards, Dr. Ernst Loosen discovered a label dating back to 1931 that depicts an idealized image of the late bishop— the same label which graces the top-tier Dr. Loosen wine from the Erdener Prälat vineyard today, described by Dr. Loosen himself as "bloody good wines."

WEINGUT DR. LOOSEN	
Appellation:	**Mosel (Non-Designated Appellation)**
State:	**Rhineland-Palatinate**
Country of Origin:	**Germany**
Type of Wine:	**Riesling**
Web Site:	**www.drloosen.com**
Design:	**Thomas Lutz**

WEINGUT JOSEF LEITZ
[HESSE ❧ GERMANY]

To provide the consumer with a stronger connection to the Leitz wine from their Drachenstein vineyard, owner Johannes Leitz decided to translate the vineyard's name from German to English, which literally means "dragon stone." Of course, many people might think that this name has nothing actually to do with the land itself and perhaps more to do with famous dragons of Germanic mythology, the most famous being the one slain by Sigurd in the medieval epic poem, *Nibelungenlied*. The reality is that the name has a real relationship with the soils of the vineyard.

The fruit for Leitz's Rüdesheimer Drachenstein Riesling comes from a single vineyard that is characterized not only by its higher elevation on the 50th latitude, but by the influence of the heavy quartzite—perhaps the "stone" part of dragonstone. However, the name of the vineyard reputedly comes from the sighting of a "dragon in a stone" in the form of fossilized dinosaur prints found in the region. In fact, the natural history museum in Mainz, which opened its doors in 1910, boasts one of the largest collections of prehistoric dinosaur tracks in the world. They hold over 25,000 specimens, which are said to have lived in the region 500,000 years ago. Perhaps the sustenance of these creatures all that time ago was grapes?

WEINGUT JOSEF LEITZ	
Appellation:	**Rheingau**
State:	**Hesse**
Country of Origin:	**Germany**
Type of Wine:	**Riesling**
Web Site:	**www.leitz-wein.de**
Design:	**Helga Schmidthuber**

Weingut Max Ferd. Richter

[Rhineland-Palatinate ❧ Germany]

Germany has made many famous contributions to society in terms of the arts, sciences, fashion, and engineering. Think Ludwig van Beethoven, Johann Sebastian Bach, Johann Wolfgang von Goethe, Albert Einstein, Konrad Zuse, Levi Strauss, and even Claudia Schiffer! The list is long.

For winemaker Dr. Dirk Max Richter, however, there was one celebrated German invention at the beginning of the twentieth century that has become synonymous with Riesling produced by Max Ferd. Richter at its Mulheimer Sonnenlay vineyard in the region of Mosel.

In 1890, long before Dr. Richter's days, a retired German officer from the state of Württemberg, Count Ferdinand von Zeppelin, had an interest in the use of aircraft for military purposes that led to his development of the first Zeppelin rigid airship. The year 1909 saw the start of the first passenger-service airship company in history. By 1914 and until World War I broke out, the airships were carrying paying passengers throughout Germany. Count von Zeppelin died in 1917 and when Germany surrendered in 1918, with a crushed economy, the promise of the Zeppelin passenger ship was put on hold until 1928. From then onwards, Zeppelin's legacy was lived out by his successor, Dr. Hugo Eckener, who was successful in raising the finances and raising a new Zeppelin back up in the air. This time, however, the airship became the epitome of luxury and was unlike any vessel ever seen.

In accordance with everything grandiose about what became known as *Graf Zeppelin* (775 feet from nose to tail, and a girth of 3.7 million cubic feet—equating to a height that was ten stories high and more than two city blocks long), the service was first-class, the views were exquisite and the food and drink, only the finest. It was then that the winegrowers of Mülheimer were able to boast that their Rieslings from Max Ferd. Richter's own Mülheimer Sonnenlay vineyard was the wine most often poured during the flights of the Zeppelin during the 1920s and 1930s. Hand-selected to be served to aristocrats on board the *Graf* as it crossed the ocean and eventually circumvented the globe, a label was commissioned for the wines by famed painter and member of the Weimar and Dessau Bauhauses, Hans Schlosser. While those at Mülheimer Sonnenlay were thrilled, those in neighboring vineyards were not happy at all. At the time, the late relatives of Dr. Richter had previously been laughed at for making light wines; however, in the end, it was they who had the last laugh with the privilege of having their wines served on board the famed *Graf* and consequently, the wine became known as "Zeppelinwein."

After World War II, the label was essentially withdrawn from Max Ferd. Richter's wine label range until it was uncovered in the winery office during the 1970s. It was then that the Max Ferd. Richter Zeppelinlabel was reintroduced, in its very original form, as a symbol of the wine's historical and geographical identity.

WEINGUT MAX FERD. RICHTER

Appellation:	**Mosel (Non-Designated Appellation)**
State:	**Rhineland-Palatinate**
Country of Origin:	**Germany**
Type of Wine:	**Riesling**
Web Site:	**www.maxferdrichter.com**
Art:	**Hans Schlosser**

WILLIAM DOWNIE PINOT NOIR

[VICTORIA ❧ AUSTRALIA]

Wine found William Downie long before he found wine. Growing up, and long before Downie had any inkling that one day he would become a crafter of his own fine wines, a young William got his first glimpse of wine through art. His father's closest friend was an avid wine enthusiast and, accordingly, was friendly with one of the local wine merchants. This particular wine merchant owned a barrel of fortified wine from which he would use a little to blend each year. Sadly, the wine merchant took ill and offered his barrel to William's father's friend, which he in turn purchased to continue the annual tradition. When his first blend was born, wanting to honor the original owner of the wine who had since passed, he commissioned friend of the family and renowned contemporary artist Arthur Boyd to create an illustration for the label. William was seven years old at the time, and remembers thinking that they label was so absolutely beautiful, but never thought that the astounding beauty of the artwork would continue to influence him or affect him many years later. However, when William made his own first wines professionally, the memory of this great image rushed back to him.

Wanting to use imagery of an artist who was influential to his generation in the manner Arthur Boyd was to his father's, he looked to the dynamic and characteristic artist Reg Mombassa. When he approached Mombassa's rep, William was told that Mombassa didn't produce any commissioned commercial work, but that the message would be passed on regardless. Much to his surprise, soon afterwards, he received a call saying that Mombassa was in fact interested in the project and that William could choose whatever artwork he liked for the label. Enjoying some of Mombassa's cheeky canine art, Downie suggested that perhaps one of those pieces would work, to which Mombassa's response was less than enthusiastic, as he didn't think that it fit with the wine. Instead, William was invited to review more of Mombassa's work in person with the artist, and he jumped at the opportunity.

On the day they met, Downie admired an abundance of provocative artwork, but was still undecided until he opened the last portfolio book to a page that immediately spoke to him. The art reminded him immediately of an image of Yarra Valley—the home of Downie's wine. When he asked Mombassa about that particular piece, Mombassa replied sentimentally that he had painted that very image on the front verandah of Arthur Boyd's house. Some may call it coincidence and others may call it a fluke, but the universe speaks in such quiet but profound ways at times. Immediately, Downie knew he had his label that spoke volumes to him and the providence of his wine.

WILLIAM DOWNIE PINOT NOIR

Appellation:	**Yarra Valley**
State:	**Victoria**
Country of Origin:	**Australia**
Type of Wine:	**Pinot Noir**
Web Site:	**www.williamdownie.com.au**
Art:	**Reg Mombassa**
Artist's Web Site:	**www.regmombassa.com**

One look at this label, and you know that someone behind the scenes probably has a penchant for comics and quite possibly has the name Brad!

Having always enjoyed the iconic pop art of Roy Lichtenstein, a retro cartoon wine label was always in the back of Brad Wehr's mind. The fact that Lichtenstein often referred to his male characters as—you guessed it—Brad made the style resonate even more. Wehr had such a vision that he even conceptualized the initial wine label artwork himself. Although he didn't set out to name his wine after himself, when asked what the name of his wine in the works would be called, it was just called "the wine by Brad." People liked it and it stuck.

Seeing this type of pop art on a label isn't common in the wine industry and one not easily forgotten. It's so memorable, in fact, that *Rolling Stone* magazine even gave them a plug. Now that certainly doesn't happen to just anyone. As the famous Lichenstein print says: "Oh, Brad."

Our label says a lot about who we are: fun, irreverent, and unpretentious. It's certainly designed for striking visual appeal, however the single most important component of our brand is the quality of the wine in the bottle. We take that bit very seriously—we're not just a pretty face! —BRAD WEHR
Chief Executive, Wine by Brad

WINE BY BRAD

Appellation:	**Margaret River**
State:	**Western Australia**
Country of Origin:	**Australia**
Type of Wine:	**Cabernet Sauvignon and Merlot Blend**
Web Site:	**www.winebybrad.com.au**
Design:	**Brad Wehr**

WINE BY BRAD

Appellation:	**Margaret River**
State:	**Western Australia**
Country of Origin:	**Australia**
Type of Wine:	**Sémillon and Sauvignon Blanc Blend**
Web Site:	**www.winebybrad.com.au**
Design:	**Brad Wehr**

WINE BY SOME YOUNG PUNKS

[SOUTH AUSTRALIA ✤ AUSTRALIA]

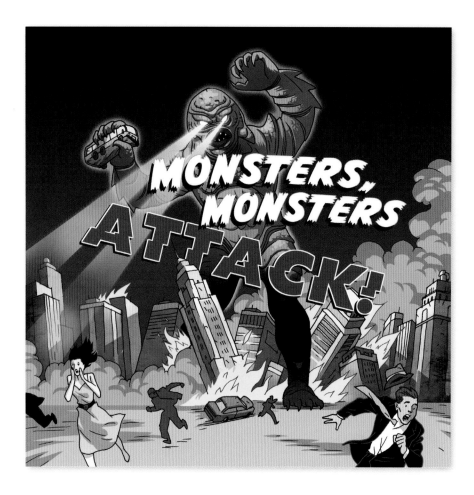

Wine by Some Young Punks is made up of three relatively new, young, passionate winemakers. Jen Gardner, Col McBryde, and Nic Bourke "blame the booze" for their consuming need to make more. The friends, who have known each other for many years, share a passion for making exceptionally tasty and sexy wines with small-estate character. They say that this shared mania is a monster bigger than the three of them combined and has often led them to "soapboxing, grandstanding, and sometimes passing out on the couch."

The threesome's charismatic wines have equally captivating labels inspired by Nic's expansive collection of sultry, sexy pulp fiction novels with alluring imagery—attention-grabbers, just like their wine. Based on original pulp novels, names like Passion Has Red Lips, Naked on Rollerskates, and Quickie are more than certain to get the juices flowing.

The Tessa 'n Trixie Love series has that overpowering monster attacking both in and on the bottle. The Squid's Fist was originally conceived during a blending session where the three joked about a label that might celebrate the age-old tales of man's rivalry against gigantic mythical monsters. At the time, they never thought they'd carry the concept of the battle against the beasts to their bottles, but upon enlisting artist Asaf Hanuka to do the illustrative honors, they've obviously proven themselves wrong.

Pulp fiction novels got their name from the cheap, wood-pulp paper they were printed on and were published widely from the 1920s through the 1950s. While inspired by cheap pulp, there is nothing but cheek to these wines.

WINE BY SOME YOUNG PUNKS
Appellation:	**Clare Valley**
State:	**South Australia**
Country of Origin:	**Australia**
Type of Wine:	**Riesling**
Web Site:	**www.someyoungpunks.com.au**
Art:	**Asaf Hanuka**
Artists's Web Site:	**www.asafhanuka.com**

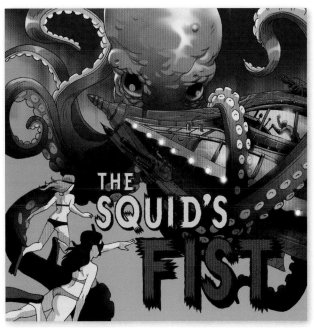

WINE BY SOME YOUNG PUNKS

Appellation:	**Adelaide Hills/Clare Valley**
State:	**South Australia**
Country of Origin:	**Australia**
Type of Wine:	**Trempranillo and Shiraz Blend**
Web Site:	**www.someyoungpunks.com.au**
Art:	**Asaf Hanuka**
Artists's Web Site:	**www.asafhanuka.com**

WINE BY SOME YOUNG PUNKS

Regions:	**Barossa Valley/Clare Valley**
State:	**South Australia**
Country of Origin:	**Australia**
Type of Wine:	**Sangiovese and Shiraz Blend**
Web Site:	**www.someyoungpunks.com.au**
Art:	**Asaf Hanuka**
Artists's Web Site:	**www.asafhanuka.com**

WINERY ARTS

[NAVARRE ❧ SPAIN]

Numbernine
•
WINERY ARTS

Squared Three
•
WINERY ARTS

Numbers are inescapable all around us, every day. From culture to culture and person to person, numbers have different meanings, usages, and even skepticisms. For some, a particular number might mean the providence of enormous fortune, while that very same number for another might mean a cesspool of misfortune. For most, however, the number 10 seems to have a positive connotation. It is symbolic of completion or the end of an important cycle and is often considered the number of perfection.

It is widely believed that perfection on earth is truly impossible and, therefore, as Winery Arts suggests, many cultures regard the number 9 as "the figure of supreme knowledge, the figure that induces totality of existence of the 10." The number 9 is also considered representative of change and growth sprung forth from incredible inspiration, as well as a triple synthesis of the body, intellect, and soul.

Winemaker Ricardo Arambarri envisioned a wine project centered around limitless possibility, innovation, creative freedom, and the merging of both the New and Old World winemaking philosophies. The Vintae project Winery Arts, born in Ribera del Queiles, Spain, allowed for such exploration to occur. The chosen theme for this spirited collection of wines was one that embraced the conceptual thinking surrounding the number 9. Being part of nature, wine is in constant natural flux and ultimately journeys through the winemaking process towards a state of full essence and flavors. In order to achieve its fullest potential, the wine must traverse through another two states of permutated possibility.

First, wine passes through material elements measurable by the objective physical world. It is here, according to Winery Arts, that the blend of soil, water, and wind, coupled with experimental science, achieves "nine in the making" and is symbolized through 3^2 on the wine bottle. Next, Reverse Six *(not pictured)* represents the intellectual world on the bottle, which through ideation, imagination, and creativity allows an alternate route towards the ultimate achievement, the exercise of transformation to the number 9.

Finally, to complete the trilogy, Numbernine represents the spiritual or transcendental world. It is here that the essence of the number 9 is truly achieved as the grapes achieve plenitude and balance.

The Numbernine wines allow for the exploration of possibility through various levels of experimentation—from pragmatic to esoteric—viewed through growing practices, the selection of new varieties, and winemaking innovation, ultimately in pursuit of the provocative, surprising, original and, at the same time, irresistible wines.

WINERY ARTS (VINTAE)	
Appellation:	**Navarra**
Community:	**Navarre**
Province:	**Zaragoza**
Country of Origin:	**Spain**
Type of Wine:	**Tempranillo, Cabernet Sauvignon, and Merlot Blend**
Web Site:	**www.vintae.com**
Design:	**Moruba**
Designer's Web Site:	**www.moruba.es**

WINERY ARTS (VINTAE)	
Appellation:	**Navarra**
Community:	**Navarre**
Province:	**Zaragoza**
Country of Origin:	**Spain**
Type of Wine:	**Merlot, Tempranillo, and Cabernet Sauvignon Blend**
Web Site:	**www.vintae.com**
Design:	**Moruba**
Designer's Web Site:	**www.moruba.es**

WINE THAT LOVES

[TRENTINO-ALTO ADIGE ❧ ITALY]

There are some things that are just meant to be together: fish and chips; peanut butter and jelly; ham and eggs; peaches and cream; wine and cheese.

And when it comes to wine and cheese, most people have heard that when paired properly, the combination can be magic in the mouth. But most people can't be certain because they've never experienced how good it is when paired properly—because they don't have the slightest idea how to match a myriad of cheeses with the countless types and brands of wines. Nor does the average person have the time to research what and how to put them together, and even if they did, who's to say their research is going to lead them down the right trail?

This conundrum was the initial beginning of the inspiration behind Wines That Love. Knowing that if matched properly, the right food with the right wine could create a symphony of the senses, one of the founders asked a sommelier to pair wines with each course of his meals while on vacation. While this wasn't a new request at mealtime, in this instance, the pairings were simply matches made in heaven.

As the saying goes, "Once you taste the milk from the cow, you're always thirsty," and upon return home from vacation, this sense-sational pleasure experience was attempted to be recreated with different chefs, different foods, and different wines. However, nothing quite matched the perfect pairing that had previously been experienced. The question then became, if some of the most highly trained professionals were hit-and-miss with being able to heighten the food consumption experience with professionally se-lected wines, how hard would it be for the average person to experience the joy of food and wine working together at their peak? And further, how on earth could the average person enjoy these creature comforts right in the serenity of their own homes? More likely than not, it wasn't going to happen.

The Amazing Food Wine Company was formed by bringing together a team of talented, world-class gastronomical experts, some of the best winemakers in the world, top chefs, and experienced foodies to de-velop a suite of wines that love the food served in the home and on the tables for an everyday basis in a foolproof manner. Wines That Love enables great food to taste even better by providing the average person accessibility to wines that, when paired together with simple food recommenda-tions, bring out the best dining experience each and every night. Effortlessly. Just look for the food match on the bottle—it's that easy to make magic.

WINE THAT LOVES
(THE AMAZING FOOD WINE COMPANY)

Appellation:	**Trento**
Region:	**Trentino-Alto Adige**
Country of Origin:	**Italy**
Type of Wine:	**Red**
Web Site:	**www.winethatloves.com**
Design:	**Lipincott Brand Strategy & Consulting**
Designer's Web Site:	**www.lippincott.com**

Every person leaves a legacy when they retire from their earthly life. What is left is a direct reflection on the size of spirit, strength of character, and a certain *joie de vivre* embraced in the smallest aspects of everyday life, and is certainly not indicative of one's financial wealth (or lack thereof).

The RGT range of wines is an honorary tribute to the late, great Gregory Trott, who lived fully and purposefully every day, in all his quirkiness. He is fondly remembered for his big ideas and colorful imagination for which each of the RGT wine labels commemorate. The illustrated stories on the labels are all true, including the one representing Trott's vision of building a medieval trebuchet to catapult neighboring wineries with bottles of wine in the hope that they would in turn reciprocate. Called an "Olympic hiding champion" by the team at Wirra Wirra, many of Trott's ideas were born while he was out wandering—a trip to the shops often evolved into an interstate luncheon with nary a phone call. Failing to wear a watch since the day he lost the one gifted to him by his father in 1947, time seemed to elude Trott. Claiming to tell the time by the sun, he was notoriously hours, or even days late for almost every commitment, but always seemed to charm his way out of it by way of his endearing personality.

Those who knew the late winemaking pioneer of McLaren Vale would agree that, despite him no longer being physically present, his larger-than-life spirit prevails each and every day at Trott's beloved Wirra Wirra. Trott once said, "Never give misery an even break, nor a bad wine a second sip. You must be serious about quality, dedicated to your tasks in life, especially winemaking, but this should all be fun." This philosophy is definitely one lived by those at Wirra Wirra through the legacy left behind by Trott, who has inspired those following in his footsteps both on the inside of the colossal post-and-rail fence called Woodhenge, bordering Wirra Wirra and those well beyond.

WIRRA WIRRA	
Appellation:	**McLaren Vale**
State:	**South Australia**
Country of Origin:	**Australia**
Type of Wine:	**Shiraz and Viognier Blend**
Web Site:	**www.wirra.com.au**
Design:	**Tucker Creative**
Designer's Web Site:	**www.tuckercreative.com.au**

HIDING CHAMPION

Adelaide Hills

SAUVIGNON BLANC

13.5% VOL   WINE OF AUSTRALIA   750ML

WOODHENGE

McLaren Vale

SHIRAZ

14.5% VOL   WINE OF AUSTRALIA   750ML

WIRRA WIRRA	
Appellation:	**Adelaide Hills**
State:	**South Australia**
Country of Origin:	**Australia**
Type of Wine:	**Sauvignon Blanc**
Web Site:	**www.wirra.com.au**
Design:	**Tucker Creative**
Designer's Web Site:	**www.tuckercreative.com.au**

WIRRA WIRRA	
Appellation:	**McLaren Vale**
State:	**South Australia**
Country of Origin:	**Australia**
Type of Wine:	**Shiraz**
Web Site:	**www.wirra.com.au**
Design:	**Tucker Creative**
Designer's Web Site:	**www.tuckercreative.com.au**

YALUMBA

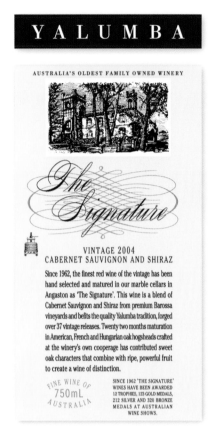

Yalumba, Australia's oldest family-owned winery (founded in 1849), recognizes that the blending of Cabernet Sauvignon and Shiraz, though non-traditional in some countries, is a distinct, esteemed, and signature style of winemaking in the Land Down Under.

Since 1962, Yalumba has produced The Signature wine, which reflects the winery's steadfast dedication to the blend, utilizing the very best fruit of the vintage and by endeavoring to blend the very best wine that it is capable of. This premium wine also salutes the admirable skills, service, and contribution of the dedicated employees of Yalumba who are the heart, soul, and culture of the company. Each year a signatory, the highest distinction that can be bestowed on an individual by Yalumba, is named for the wine. Those that have held the honor have stretched far and wide, including Samuel Smith (founder and inaugural Signatory) and winery friend Colin Hayes (1978 Signatory), one of Australia's most talented racehorse trainers. Hayes was responsible for forming a syndication to purchase Lindsay Park, and included Wyndham's family as part owner. This collaborative purchase gave the Smith family partial ownership of the very place Samuel Smith had initially worked as a gardener, paying his salary and allowing him to establish the first 14 acres of Yalumba vines in 1849.

Yalumba's standards are set to the highest degree for The Signature wine, and some vintages fail to produce fruit that achieves the caliber required, while others might produce more than one signatory due to a harvest producing a high standard of fruit. To date, the list of signatories is forty-seven deep, each honored on The Signature label, and each having monumentally contributed to the longevity and shape of Yalumba today.

In keeping with its dedication to the traditional Australian blend of Cabernet Sauvignon and Shiraz, The Scribbler honors the benchmark that Yalumba has set for this national treasure. As the more youthful version of The Signature, The Scribbler label pays tribute to its elders and provides an accessible and approachable wine to be enjoyed widely, while remaining inspired by what Yalumba does best.

	YALUMBA
Appellation:	**Barossa Valley**
State:	**South Australia**
Country of Origin:	**Australia**
Type of Wine:	**Cabernet Sauvignon and Shiraz Blend**
Web Site:	**www.yalumba.com**
Design:	**Harcus Design**
Designer's Web Site:	**www.harcus.com.au**

	YALUMBA
Appellation:	**Barossa Valley**
State:	**South Australia**
Country of Origin:	**Australia**
Type of Wine:	**Cabernet Sauvignon and Shiraz Blend**
Web Site:	**www.yalumba.com**
Design:	**Harcus Design**
Designer's Web Site:	**www.harcus.com.au**

YALUMBA

[SOUTH AUSTRALIA ✤ AUSTRALIA]

> ### YALUMBA
>
> *In 1974, Yalumba created an outstanding Cabernet & Shiraz blend known simply as FDR1A. The wine soon became a legend in winemaking circles, appreciated both for its fruit expression and restrained power. Vintage 2004 Fine Dry Red 1A is a continuing example of Yalumba's commitment to, and mastery of, the quintessential Australian red wine that is Cabernet and Shiraz. Aged in American Oak barrels hand-made in our own cooperage FDR1A is a testament to winemaking craftsmanship.*

In 1974, Yalumba crafted one of the finest examples of the traditional Australian Cabernet-Shiraz blend that it felt it had ever created. In winemaking circles, it gained notoriety as a legendary wine. It was known only as FDR1A, the indicator written in chalk on the barrels and label, stating the lot coding "1A" of a "fine dry wine".

The 2000 vintage saw a wine blended to the equivalent caliber as an acclaimed predecessor of 1974. Twenty-six years later, this became the second vintage of FDR1A. While the label may have evolved to a more modern version, the name is still testimony of the proudly committed craftsmanship of the traditional Australian red blend that is the Yalumba Cabernet-Shiraz.

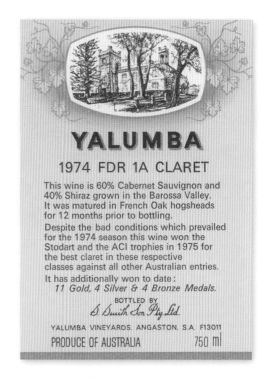

YALUMBA
1974 FDR 1A CLARET

This wine is 60% Cabernet Sauvignon and 40% Shiraz grown in the Barossa Valley. It was matured in French Oak hogsheads for 12 months prior to bottling.
Despite the bad conditions which prevailed for the 1974 season this wine won the Stodart and the ACI trophies in 1975 for the best claret in these respective classes against all other Australian entries. It has additionally won to date :
11 Gold, 4 Silver & 4 Bronze Medals.
BOTTLED BY
S. Smith Son Pty Ltd.
YALUMBA VINEYARDS, ANGASTON, S.A. F13011
PRODUCE OF AUSTRALIA   750 ml

YALUMBA

Appellation:	**Barossa Valley**
State:	**South Australia**
Country of Origin:	**Australia**
Type of Wine:	**Cabernet Sauvignon and Shiraz Blend**
Web Site:	**www.yalumba.com**
Design:	**Harcus Design**
Designer's Web Site:	**www.harcus.com.au**

YALUMBA

Appellation:	**Barossa Valley**
State:	**South Australia**
Country of Origin:	**Australia**
Type of Wine:	**Cabernet Sauvignon and Shiraz Blend**
Web Site:	**www.yalumba.com**
Design:	**Harcus Design**
Designer's Web Site:	**www.harcus.com.au**

Acknowledgments

As with any substantial accomplishment, success is never achieved in a vacuum. There are countless people that have enabled this backyard reverie to evolve into a dream come true. First and foremost, the most sincere thanks must be given to all of the wineries that have so graciously allowed me to include them in my project. Without them, there would be no book. I am not a sommelier, nor am I an international design superstar. I am just a girl who had an idea. These wineries took my calls, answered my e-mails, and were generous with their time in teaching me more than I ever imagined possible about wine, farming, terroir and, of course, humanity and humility. These are their stories and I am but the curator of this wonderful collection.

Likewise, heartfelt thanks and the most admirable praises to all of the designers and design studios whose art is featured in this book. Without their immense talent, insight, and creative ingenuity, nobody would be reading these acknowledgments. I must also extend a huge amount of praise to both Alex and Jen from Oxygen Design Agency in Toronto, who both taught me so much about the appreciation of design in all its various forms. They are two of the most talented people I know and I owe them many thanks for inspiring me to find my own creative pursuits while also learning and being inspired by others.

I am not sure how to possibly thank Jeffrey Goldman, my esteemed publisher at Santa Monica Press, for taking a chance on a girl with an idea. Not only has he made this book possible, but he provided me with the confidence in myself to believe further in my idea. His collaboration, expertise, and guidance have clearly been the reason that I have been able to achieve this massive feat. Of course, a huge amount of gratitude must be given to Breanna Murphy for her amazing attention to detail and shrewd editing. If anyone knows the work that has been put into this book it is Breanna as she has lived the minute details along with me—thank you so much for all your help (or perhaps blood, sweat, and tears is more appropriate). And to Amy Inouye, graphic designer extraordinaire, thank you for your creativity and for making my mass of words look so beautiful on the page—you have turned the dream of my book into a tangible reality. Merci!

To Michael Mondavi, who so generously has written the foreword of this book—thank you so very much for believing in this project and believing in me. I am speechless and honored to be able to include my name on the same page, or cover, as yours.

To Mandy at Creative Niche in Toronto for being flexible and supportive, and providing me with the one resource I never would have had enough of to fulfill my dream without you: time. Thank you. And to the Creative Niche team who were always there to pick up my slack when I was off investigating and writing my heart out. Though I am no longer there, you will always be my team. Of course, a huge thank you especially to Jenny Gilbert, photographer extraordinaire, for not only shooting my portrait, but for making it relaxed, fun, and oh-so glamorous. It was your talent and your ability to manipulate magic from your camera that made me look like I do, that's for certain.

On a personal level, I must thank all of my girls for being my best friends and for being understanding, remaining steadfast in their support during both good and bad, for teaching me the value of friendship and laughter, and generally accepting me for who I am: your friend, the dreamer. You know who you are: Bano, C. A., Carmani, Er, Finner, Guzzo, Meggie, Murph, and Weave.

To my "Well Reds," thank you sharing so adventures in books and in life over the nearly eleven years we've been drinking wine and reading fabulous (and not-so fabulous) books together: Alison, Dianna, Er, H. B., Krystyna, Lisa, Marts, Nance, Noreen, and Zemins. Let us always be together in wine, words, and friendship.

To Erin S. for always keeping my glass half full even when, in reality, it may have been empty. I adore you.

To my fabulous family in Oz for being a huge support of all of my endeavors, especially this one, and for loving me like I was a true Aussie: Mama, Rob, Jenny, Matt, Lea, Nick, Emily, Amy, James, Alice, Henry, Caroline, and Ross.

To my brothers and sister for being family, always there no matter what: Andrew, Keith, and Laura. And to my younger brother Brady: We are more alike than you think. This book is a testament that anything is possible if you make it possible. Keep writing and follow your dreams.

To my parents, Cathy and Morley, for always being my biggest fan club (if sometimes my only fan club) and being supportive and encouraging me to give everything my all. Morley, thank you being the man in my mom's life and also in mine when I needed one and didn't have one to call my own. And to my mom, for being my rock and teaching me to follow my dreams, to be tenacious, to stay on the right path, and stay true to my own person—even when it's been hard. I owe you my life. You are the reason I am the woman I am today and, like you, have such an enormous creative spirit. The saying "like mother, like daughter" couldn't be more true. I am *your* daughter and words really cannot convey the admiration and thanks I have for you.

Zemins, you have been absolutely pivotal in this project—and all of my other far-out ideas. I could not have done this without you. This is as much my project as it is yours.

And to you, Greg, my dearest friend and husband. You have changed my life in ways that I never thought possible. Thank you for loving the Raj absolutely, in all my eccentricities, and for truly letting me follow my personal dreams. There is so much more for us to conquer together. And we will.

Thank you to Barclay and Tallulah for their unconditional love every single day and for being such amazing canine citizens of the world.

Inevitably, there are so many other people that I would like to say thanks to, but since this is a book on telling other peoples' stories and not my own, all I can say is: Those of you who have supported and inspired me every day know who you are—thank you for everything you bring to my life.

TANYA SCHOLES